To Dr. Martin Ritchie, for being such a great model of personal integrity and professional excellence

Mark S. Gerig is Chair of the Division of Graduate Counseling at Indiana Wesleyan University in Marion and Indianapolis, Indiana. He is a Licensed Mental Health Counselor and Licensed Psychologist and has over 28 years of experience in professional counseling and counselor education. He previously served as the Manager of Crisis and Elderly Services at Hiawatha Behavioral Health, Sault Sainte Marie, Michigan, and as an adjunct professor of psychology at Algoma University, Sault Sainte Marie, Ontario, Canada.

Dr. Gerig has been a leader in state and national professional organizations. He has served as President and Chair of Professional Development of the Indiana Mental Health Counselors Association and as a member of the Professional Issues Committee of the American Mental Health Counselors Association. In recognition of Dr. Gerig's professional service, he was named the recipient of the 2005 American Mental Health Counselors Association Counselor Educator of the Year award and was also the recipient of the Mental Health Counselor of the Year award by the Indiana Counseling Association (2003).

Dr. Gerig resides near Marion, Indiana, with his wife, Michelle, and daughter, Laurán. His son, Brandon, is a fish biologist for the state of Utah. In addition to his professional activities, Mark enjoys hiking, biking, fishing, gardening, and ice hockey.

Foundations for Clinical Mental Health Counseling

An Introduction to the Profession

Second Edition

Mark S. Gerig

Indiana Wesleyan University

PEARSON

Boston   Columbus   Indianapolis   New York   San Francisco   Upper Saddle River
Amsterdam   Cape Town   Dubai   London   Madrid   Milan   Munich   Paris   Montreal   Toronto
Delhi   Mexico City   São Paulo   Sydney   Hong Kong   Seoul   Singapore   Taipei   Tokyo

Vice President and Editorial Director: Jeffery W. Johnston
Senior Acquisitions Editor: Meredith Fossel
Editorial Assistant: Krista Slavicek
Vice President, Director of Marketing: Margaret Waples
Senior Marketing Manager: Christopher Barry
Senior Managing Editor: Pamela D. Bennett
Production Manager: Susan EW Hannahs
Senior Art Director: Jayne Conte
Cover Designer: Karen Salzbach
Cover Photo: Anyka/Fotolia
Full-Service Project Management: Niraj Bhatt/Aptara®, Inc.
Composition: Aptara®, Inc.
Text and Cover Printer/Bindery: Courier/Westford
TextFont: ITC Berkeley Oldstyle Std

Credits and acknowledgments for material borrowed from other sources and reproduced, with permission, in this textbook appear on the appropriate page within the text.

Every effort has been made to provide accurate and current Internet information in this book. However, the Internet and information posted on it are constantly changing, so it is inevitable that some of the Internet addresses listed in this textbook will change.

Page 115, Figure 5.3 (CACREP note): The parts of the CACREP Standards reproduced in this work represent only selected parts of the 2009 CACREP Standards. Inclusion of the CACREP Standards in this work is in no way intended to imply CACREP endorsement or approval of this work, and use of this work as a teaching tool does not establish or connote compliance with CACERP Standards for purposes of determining CACERP accreditation of any education program.

The first edition of this text was published under the title *Foundations for Mental Health and Community Counseling: An Introduction to the Profession.*

Library of Congress Cataloging-in-Publication Data

Gerig, Mark S.
 Foundations for clinical mental health counseling : an introduction to the profession/Mark S. Gerig.—2nd ed.
  p. ; cm.
 Rev. ed. of: Foundations for mental health and community counseling/Mark S. Gerig. c2007.
 Includes bibliographical references and index.
 ISBN-13: 978-0-13-293097-0
 ISBN-10: 0-13-293097-8
 I. Gerig, Mark S. Foundations for mental health and community counseling. II. Title.
 [DNLM: 1. Counseling. 2. Community Mental Health Services. WM 55]
 362.2'04256—dc23
                                                    2012037267

10 9 8 7 6 5 4 3 2 1

PEARSON

ISBN 10:   0-13-293097-8
ISBN 13: 978-0-13-293097-0

The clinical mental health counseling profession is recognized as the new kid on the block of allied mental health professions. It is embedded in an economic, political, cultural, and sociohistorical context that is ever changing. Just as their clients operate in and are best understood from the point of view of their unique position within an ecological context, clinical mental health counselors best understand who they are and what they do when viewed within the ecological context in which the profession is embedded.

My primary purpose for writing *Foundations for Clinical Mental Health Counseling: An Introduction to the Profession* is to provide a text that paints an accurate picture of the mental health counseling profession in its contemporary environment. Its content is flavored by my years of experience as a counselor educator; as a practitioner, supervisor, and manager in agency and behavioral health settings; and as a leader in professional associations. The reader will discover a fresh perspective that reflects a professional view from the trenches that is academically informed. I am passionate about this profession and hope that readers will capture the vision of what it truly means to be a clinical mental health counselor.

Current and future mental health practitioners must be cognizant of the contemporary context if they are to be perceived as relevant service providers who deliver effective treatment. I have attempted to present up-to-date foundations for understanding the current professional identity and scope of practice of clinical mental health counselors. However, mental health counselors enact who they are and what they know within a unique ecological context. Thus, a second goal in writing this text is to present a well-informed description of relevant settings, public policies, and trends. Readers should discover within the pages that follow how to be most beneficial to their clients, marketable to potential employers, and relevant voices when sitting at the table of stakeholders or public policymakers and given the opportunity to advocate for consumers and the profession. Thus, readers will learn about TRICARE and Medicare provider status, controversies surrounding the construction of the fifth edition of the American Psychiatric Association's *Diagnostic and Statistical Manual of Mental Disorders* (*DSM-V*), recovery philosophy and its impact on the provision of services to persons with severe and persistent mental illness, the implications of health care reform, and integrated behavioral health in primary care settings. Professional identity and scopes of practice take on increased meaning when viewed as interacting within this ecological context.

NEW TO THIS EDITION

The content of this text has been thoroughly updated as indicated by the citation of more than 50% new references. While most of the chapter titles and headings are similar to those found in the first edition, the information contained is quite current and reflects the current expanse of professional literature. The following provides a partial list of the new content in this edition:

- The *20/20* definition of professional counseling, and its implications, and application in professional practice and increasing licensure portability.
- A consideration of historical forces entering into the 21st-century shaping of the mental health professions, such as the increased application of technology in counseling, counselor education, and counselor supervision; the influence of the wellness orientation and positive psychology; and the impact of human-made and natural disasters.
- New research that provides additional validation and rationale for the clinical mental health counseling paradigm, with special attention given to understanding mental health in terms of two separate, but interacting, dimensions that operate in client-specific ecological contexts.
- Discussion of newer, evidenced-based treatment approaches, such as dialectic behavior therapy; acceptance and commitment therapy; emotionally focused therapy; the transtheoretical model; motivational interviewing; integrated dual-diagnosed treatment; equine therapy; home-based therapy; critical incident stress debriefing; and psychological first aid.
- Infusion of the 2009 Council for Accreditation of Counseling and Related Educational Programs Standards; the 2010 American Mental Health Counselor Association (AMHCA) Code of Ethics; the 2005 American Counseling Association Code of Ethics; and the 2011 AMHCA Standards of Professional Practice.
- Innovations in the provision of services in community mental health contexts, such as emergency management and disaster preparedness; approaches related to mental health concerns within correctional settings (jail diversion, reentry programs, and legal processes like not guilty by reason of insanity and guilty but mentally ill, mental incompetence, mental health courts); implications of health care reform (e.g., the pooling of financial streams of Medicaid and Medicare, the merging of medical and mental health treatment, and integrated behavioral health in primary care settings).
- Detailed discussion of recovery philosophy, its relationship to the clinical mental health counseling paradigm, and the integration of consumer-delivered services and programs within the context of community mental health.

I sincerely believe the contents of this text provides readers with the necessary foundations to become highly marketable as effective and efficient service providers in the contemporary mental health care marketplace.

ORGANIZATION OF THE TEXT

The text consists of three parts: Part 1: Theoretical and Historical Foundations; Part 2: The Credentialing and Practice of Clinical Mental Health Counseling; and Part 3: Contemporary Issues and Trends. Chapter 1 answers the foundational question "What is a licensed mental health or professional counselor?" It presents current definitions of clinical mental health counseling and connects it to the relevant professional organizations, other counseling specializations, and the allied mental health professions. Chapter 2 views clinical mental health counseling from within its developmental context with the idea that any understanding of the current configuration of the profession is enhanced when its development is placed in the historical context in which other mental health professions were also developing. Chapter 3 describes the theoretical foundations of clinical mental health counseling and presents a clinical mental health paradigm that organizes these theoretical foundations along three dimensions: levels of wellness and pathology that interact within a multilayered ecological context. Chapter 4 presents a set of classic and contemporary theories of counseling that are applied in assessment and treatment.

In Part 2, the focus shifts to the credentialing and practice of clinical mental health counselors. Chapter 5 surveys the training, licensure, and certification of mental health counselors. Chapter 6 examines current codes of ethics and legal issues critical in providing professional service with integrity. Chapter 7 examines what mental health counselors do and the settings in which they work. Information gathered from practicing mental health counselors helps readers grasp how the knowledge and skill sets of the profession are applied to effectively work with a variety of clients in diverse work environments. Approaches to the appraisal of and research into clients, their ecological contexts, and program evaluation are presented in Chapter 8. Chapter 9 describes contemporary practice in multicultural contexts. Special attention is given to concepts, principles, and ethical practices that generalize across the persons and systems served.

Part 3 begins with Chapter 10 and the exploration of managed care and its profound impact on the profession. Special attention is given to understanding the logic that underlies managed care, factors that contribute to the actual cost of mental health services, and approaches used for cost containment. Chapter 11 explores the rapidly changing world of community mental health. Readers learn about contemporary trends affecting the delivery of mental health services. They also discover particular roles, opportunities, and services rendered to homeless populations, dual-diagnosed clients, persons incarcerated in local jails and state correctional facilities, and victims of trauma and disaster. The final chapter, Chapter 12, explores the future of clinical mental health counseling. This discussion concludes by suggesting specific ways clinical mental health counselors can live out who they are in the contemporary context and become instrumental in the shaping of public policy and the profession's direction.

ACKNOWLEDGMENTS

Numerous persons have made direct and indirect contributions to the content and production of this text. Several counselor educators have played an important role in shaping my own professional development. I am deeply grateful to Martin Ritchie, who influenced me while I was a graduate student at the University of Toledo and continues to do so through modeling professional integrity, leadership, and humility. Nick Piazza, Robert Wendt, and Gary R. Collins played key roles in introducing me to the profession. Special thanks go to Bill King and Kimble Richardson, who cleared the path for me to assume leadership roles in the Indiana Mental Health Counseling Association. I am also indebted to Mark Hamilton, CEO, and Beth Powell, of AMHCA, who fueled my passion for the mental health counseling profession. Lisa Simpson and Terrie Valentine gave me firsthand accounts of providing home-based and equine therapy, respectively, which helped bring to life content presented in Chapter 7. Finally, I must acknowledge Sam Harma, Lisa Hinkson, and the staff and consumers of Hiawatha Behavioral Health, Sault Sainte Marie, Michigan. My professional orientation has been shaped by my in-the-trenches experiences at HBH more than words can express.

Several persons played key roles in the production of this text. My graduate assistants, Kelsie Hampshire and Kate Denlinger, proofed the initial drafts and provided valuable feedback on the book's readability. And a special thank you goes to the editorial and production staff at Pearson Education. Meredith Fossel, Senior Acquisitions Editor at Pearson, helped me to shape the focus of this second edition. Carol Bleistine, Developmental Editor, provided valuable editorial assistance and guided me throughout the writing process. In addition, I greatly appreciate the constructive comments of the following reviewers, whose comments enabled me to bring certain topics into better focus: Judith A. Burnett, Stetson University; Chris Erickson, George Washington University; and Gwendolyn K. Newsome, North Carolina Central University.

Finally, this second edition is truly made possible through the support of my wife, Michelle. Her constant support and encouragement enabled me to stay focused on this project, especially at those times when she knew I would rather have been fishing.

BRIEF CONTENTS

CONTENTS

Part 1

Theoretical and Historical Foundations

1

What Is a Mental Health or Professional Counselor?

OUTLINE

I was a young counselor freshly groomed and searching for my first professional position. With a Master of Arts degree in counseling in hand, I began to wade through the classified ads in several newspapers, seeking to find a job where I could engage in the professional practice. (Yes, this was a pre-Internet search.) First, I looked under Administration and Professional and, then, under the Medical and Dental section. Finally, I looked over the General Help Wanted category.

To my chagrin, I did not find any advertisements using the professional title of clinical mental health counselor. In fact, the term *counselor* did not appear in any mental health–related advertisement. What I did find surprised me greatly! One entry was titled, "Counselor Needed," but went on to describe an opening for a person to work behind a cosmetics counter at a local department store and provide counsel to its customers regarding the relative benefits of the store's products. In another advertisement, a mortgage company sought experienced loan officers to provide credit counseling. A large grocery store was looking to hire a counselor to work in the fresh meats department and assist customers in selecting the proper cut of meat. Since I didn't have meat-cutting experience, I didn't qualify!

Yes, I did find classified ads that related to the mental health profession. However, they were seeking therapists, psychologists, psychiatric nurses, and social workers. Most of these positions required at least two years of experience and an appropriate license. Discouraged, I persisted in sending out resumes to a variety of human service organizations and mental health centers.

This true story does have a happy ending. I did find a position! Interestingly, the position I accepted was in response to an advertisement that had not even mentioned the term *counselor*. Rather, the small, private not-for-profit agency had a job opening for an individual, group, and family therapist. The official job description noted that an MSW (Master's in Social Work) was required and an ACSW (Academy of Certified Social Workers) was preferred. I had neither! But I did have entry-level knowledge and skills in doing individual, group, and family counseling. The director of the agency, who held the ACSW credential, was unfamiliar with the training model of graduate programs in counseling and was impressed with the broad-based, skill-oriented approach to training. Once she understood the training model of the counseling profession, she became very open to hiring other appropriately trained counselors for positions that had formerly been reserved for persons who had graduated from master's-level programs in social work or psychology.

Clinical mental health counseling is still the "new kid" setting up residence on the block where the other mental health professions have lived. We have many things in common with our neighbors. Yet, our profession possesses a unique identity that sets us apart from those professions. The identity of mental health counselors is rooted in a unique historical and philosophical tradition. In addition, clinical mental health counseling draws from a specific training model where specialization builds on a common core of curricular experiences that links us with closely related counseling professions. Certainly, the profession has come a long way since the days of my first job search.

This text is written to serve as an introduction to the profession of clinical mental health counseling, one of the most exciting and upcoming professions in the field of mental health. Licensed Mental Health Counselors (LMHCs), who are also referred to as Licensed Professional Counselors (LPCs), currently number 105,000 and are recognized as licensed practitioners in all 50 states and the District of Columbia (American Mental Health Counselors Association, 2011a; Department of Labor, 2011). Persons entering into this profession receive their academic training from graduate programs in counseling or counselor education. Such programs typically offer specializations in clinical mental health counseling and are designed to prepare students to fulfill licensure requirements for licensure as an LMHC or LPC.

This text is titled *Foundations for Clinical Mental Health Counseling: An Introduction to the Profession* and reflects recent changes in the training model of clinical mental health counselors and the contexts in which they practice. My goal in writing this text is to explore the foundations of the clinical mental health counseling specialization, as identified in the 2009 standards for accreditation of counselor education programs put forth by the Council for Accreditation of Counseling and Related Educational Programs (CACREP, 2009a). Historically, two unique specializations were accredited under previous CACREP standards (CACREP, 2001): mental health counseling and community counseling. Students who graduated from programs designed according to the standards of one or the other often competed for the same positions and sought to meet requirements for the same license types (e.g., Licensed Professional Counselor, Licensed Professional Clinical Counselor, or Licensed Mental Health Counselor). However, the realities of the contemporary mental health delivery system clearly demonstrated that persons graduating from these respective specializations and holding counseling-related licenses work in similar settings and provide similar services. They direct their services to individuals, groups, families, and organizations that seek to enhance their levels of mental health, often through the treatment of mental illness. The 2009 CACREP standards bring increased unity to the profession by bringing the training of mental health counselors under one umbrella.

Throughout this text, I will refer to licensed professionals as *licensed mental health and/or professional counselors*. In addition, recognizing that licensed mental health and professional counselors provide a similar range of services, I will use the term clinical mental health counseling when referring to their general professional identity. A unifying model for the profession, which I have titled the *Clinical Mental Health Counseling Paradigm,* is presented in Chapter 3. I hope that the chapters that follow provide a voice of unity, clarity, and inspiration to those seeking to join a profession that has been increasingly viewed as a major player in the mental health delivery system (Hinkle, 1999; Ivey, 1989).

WHAT IS A COUNSELOR? ENTER A LAND OF CONFUSION!

The words *counselor* and *counseling* are commonly used but often misunderstood terms. Seiler (1990) notes that the term *counseling* is used by business and government to describe occupations ranging from retail sales counselors to the tax counselors of the Internal Revenue Service. These words are used in so many ways that it becomes difficult to understand their specific meanings apart from the context in which the words appear. Even then, confusion can reign.

There are several reasons for this confusion and ambiguity. First, to *counsel* commonly refers to activities such as deliberating, consulting, guiding, or advising. Numerous professions engage in activities that fall under the rubric of counseling when the word is used in this general way. Attorneys, car salespersons, and, yes, even meat cutters can be described as being counselors to their respective clientele. Thus, the word *counsel* can refer to a very broad range of helping processes in which one person provides assistance to others in a particular manner.

Second, mental health and licensed professional counselors are not the only mental health–related professionals who counsel. Professional counseling is a basic role that is part of a wide range of mental health professions (Hanna & Bemak, 1997; Mellin, Hunt, & Nichols, 2011). Psychiatrists, psychologists, social workers, marriage and family therapists, psychiatric nurses, and pastors rightfully describe their professional roles as counselors. In addition, these mental health professions sometimes utilize theories and techniques of counseling. These are not the property of any given profession but are processes of facilitating change that may be used by each of the professions. Furthermore, a number of professional organizations and accrediting bodies use the term *counseling* as well (e.g., American Counseling Association [ACA], Division 17 of the American Psychological Association [APA], or the American Association of Pastoral Counselors [AAPC]).

Third, the counseling profession itself unintentionally contributes to the confusion. The term *counselor* is used as a generic title that follows the areas of specialty within the profession. Thus, *addiction, school, career, marriage and family, clinical mental health,* and *student affairs and college* are all qualifying terms that specify counseling specialties. While persons in these specialties correctly view themselves as being professional counselors, the title *licensed professional counselor* relates to a statutory credential used to regulate a specific mental health profession.

Confused? If so, you are in the company of many persons who, in the process of applying for admission into graduate programs in the counseling-related disciplines, experience uncertainty regarding which specific discipline and program to choose. I have directed graduate programs in counseling and have found that the most frequently asked question prospective students pose to me is "What is the difference between being a mental health counselor and a social worker or marriage and family therapist?" The uncertainty experienced by such inquirers in part reflects the identity confusion that plagues the mental health professions. The remainder of this chapter provides a response to such questions and dispels confusion by clarifying what it means to call oneself a licensed mental health or professional counselor. In addition, the professional organizations that represent counselor interests are identified and described briefly. Finally, similarities and differences among the mental health counseling profession, other counseling specializations, and related professions are discussed.

WHAT IT MEANS TO BE A CLINICAL MENTAL HEALTH OR PROFESSIONAL COUNSELOR: SOME HELPFUL DEFINITIONS

The definition of *counseling* has evolved in response to forces both from within the profession and from the contemporary mental health care environment (Nugent, 2000). Several past noteworthy attempts to define counseling, generally, and mental health counseling, specifically, may be found in the professional literature. For example, the ACA defined professional counseling as follows: "the application of mental health, psychological, or human development principles, through cognitive, affective, behavioral, or systemic intervention strategies that address wellness, personal growth, or career development, as well as pathology" (ACA Governing Council, 1997, p. 8). The definition developed by the ACA (1997) related very closely to an earlier and more detailed definition of mental health counseling put forth by the American Mental Health Counselors Association (AMHCA) in 1987:

> Mental Health Counseling is the provision of professional counseling services, involving the application of principles of psychotherapy, human development, learning theory, group dynamics, and the etiology of mental illness and dysfunctional behavior to individuals, couples, families, and groups, for the purposes of treating psychopathology and promoting optimal mental health.
>
> The practice of Mental Health Counseling includes, but is not limited to diagnosis and treatment of mental and emotional disorders, psychoeducational techniques aimed at the prevention of such disorders, consultation to individuals, couples, families, groups, organizations, and communities and clinical research into more effective psychotherapeutic treatment modalities. (AMHCA, 1987, p. 6).

Lewis, Lewis, Daniels, and D'Andrea (2003) provided additional clarification by defining community counseling as "a comprehensive helping framework of intervention strategies and services that promotes the personal development and well-being of all individuals and communities" (p. 5). Their model contains four categories of service components provided by community counselors: (a) direct client services, (b) indirect client services, (c) direct community services, and (d) indirect community services.

While each of these definitions provides insight into the essence of the counseling profession and the specialization of mental health counseling, they also presented counseling as a very diverse collection of specialties lacking cohesiveness at its core. It was like describing the splendor of a forest by defining it in terms of its resident types of trees. Could it be that the abundance of definitions contributed to, rather than reduced, the confusing landscape of mental health professions?

Enter on the scene a major ACA initiative known as *20/20: A Vision for the Future of Counseling*. A group of leaders, who met at the 2005 ACA Annual Convention at Atlanta, recognized the disunity in the profession, the troubling consequences of significant variations in licensure laws across states, and the resulting inability to establish a workable process of license portability (Kaplan, & Gladding, 2011). The broad and ambitious goal of *20/20* was to address the issues of disparate licensure titles, scopes of practice, and develop "a strategic plan for optimal positioning of the counseling profession in the year 2020" (p. 367).

An important outcome of the *20/20* process has been a consensus definition of *counseling*. Representatives from 30 counseling organizations came together as a group, presenting and exploring the diverse definitions and themes that represented the contemporary understanding of counseling, from both within and outside the profession (Rollins, 2010). Using the Delphi method, they identified, refined, and synthesized recurring key themes and words into a 21-word definition. In a long, focused, and research-based process, multiple articulations, insights, and passions yielded a single definition.

On October 28, 2010, the ACA Governing Council approved a definition of the profession of counseling as "a professional relationship that empowers diverse individuals, families, and groups to accomplish mental health, wellness, education, and career goals" (ACA, 2010). This definition covers the major components of professional counselor identity, yet allows for further articulation of specific emphases that are embraced by various specialty areas within the profession (Rollins, 2010). *Clinical mental health counseling* can be understood as the specialization of counseling that applies wellness and remedial approaches to the assessment and treatment of individuals and their related systems within relevant ecological contexts (Gerig, 2011).

Several major themes emerge from these definitions that help us to understand better what it means to be a licensed mental health or professional counselor. First, LMHCs and LPCs possess knowledge and skills for the promotion of wellness. Indeed, the assessment and treatment of pathology are understood from a *mental health and wellness* perspective. Being trained from this perspective is foundational as clinical mental health counselors work with client systems in their quest to move toward optimal human functioning as well as away from emotional distress, dysfunction, and mental illness (Bloom et al., 1990). As Hill (1991) noted, "Such terms as *personal empowerment, competencies,* and *positive health* (wellness) may be new to psychology, but they are integral to the very heritage of our profession" (p. 47).

Second, wellness and pathology are understood within the framework of normal human development. This points to the application of human development principles, psychoeducation, and strengths-based interventions in addition to the traditional techniques of psychotherapy as primary tools of intervention for the LMHC and LPC. Van Hesteren and Ivey (1990) note that counseling and human development go hand in hand. From this positive developmental orientation, mental health counselors find a theoretical base from which to view presenting issues related to mental health promotion as well as remediation of psychopathology (Ivey & Rigazio-DiGilio, 1991). Clients are understood as having the capacity to learn and apply skills taught rather than being seen as patients (Dinkmeyer, 1991). Furthermore, it has been established that psychoeducation can accelerate and add depth to the counseling process (Guerney, 1977).

Third, an ecological model (Bronfenbrenner, 1979) provides the theoretical foundation for guiding both the assessment and intervention strategies implemented by mental health counselors. All persons develop within an ecological context. Thus, case conceptualization, when conducted by mental health counselors, considers the multiple levels of the client's environment. Individuals are not assessed or treated as if they are isolated or autonomous from the larger social system. Services provided may address presenting issues by using direct or indirect approaches and may be directed to multiple levels of the client system (Lewis et al., 2003). In this way, interventions capitalize on the strengths and resources that are available within the social milieu of the client. In addition, this framework enables mental health counselors to respond to the needs of individuals, couples, families, groups, and organizations in ways that are culturally sensitive.

Fourth, the preceding definitions clearly communicate the multidisciplinary nature of the profession (Pistole & Roberts, 2002). Weikel and Palmo (1989) note that the profession of mental health counseling was born as a hybrid, with psychology and education as the uneasy bed partners. Much of the theoretical foundation on which the profession stands originated elsewhere. The disciplines of education, psychology, cognitive science, philosophy, and the medical sciences have made important contributions to our knowledge base. In addition, LMHCs and LPCs frequently work as members of a multidisciplinary treatment team (Coyne & Cook, 2004). It is logical and even essential that training should, therefore, include the best of scientific information from the other mental health professions (Pistole, 2001; Seiler & Messina, 1979). The professional benefit from such collaboration is that counselors are able to provide more comprehensive interventions and treatment services for their clients. Furthermore, treatment teams benefit from the unique perspective of prevention, wellness, and personal growth provided by mental health counselors.

RELEVANT PROFESSIONAL ORGANIZATIONS

Four organizations are very important in understanding the professional identities of licensed mental health and professional counselors. These include the American Counseling Association (ACA), American Mental Health Counselors Association (AMHCA), National Board of Certified Counselors (NBCC), and Council for the Accreditation of Counseling and Related Educational Programs (CACREP).

The ACA is the organization that represents the interests of professional counselors in general. The ACA was founded in 1952, and nearly 45,000 members call the it their professional home (ACA, 2011a). The organization was originally known as the American Personnel and Guidance Association (APGA) and was formed through the alliance of four smaller groups: the National Vocational Guidance Association, American College Personnel Association, National Association of Guidance Supervisors, and Student Personnel Association for Teacher Education (Myers, 1995). These smaller groups, representing the specializations of career counseling, student development, counselor education and supervision, and teacher education, formed the original four divisions of the association. This historical tradition continues, with the ACA presently serving as the home for 19 divisions. These divisions are identified and described briefly in Table 1.1.

TABLE 1.1

Divisions
of the
American
Counseling
Association

American College Counseling Association (ACCA)
Promotes student development in colleges, universities, and community colleges.

American Mental Health Counselors Association (AMHCA)
Promotes advocating for client access to quality services within the health care industry.

American Rehabilitation Counseling Association (ARCA)
Promotes the enhancement of people with disabilities as well as excellence within the rehabilitation counseling profession in practice, research, consultation, and professional development.

American School Counselor Association (ASCA)
Promotes school counseling professionals and interest in activities that affect the personal, educational, and career development of students. ASCA members also work collaboratively with parents, educators, and community members to provide a positive learning environment.

Association for Adult Development and Aging (AADA)
Promotes information sharing, professional development, and advocacy related to adult development and aging issues as well as addressing counseling concerns across the lifespan.

Association for Assessment in Counseling and Education (AACE)
Promotes the effective use of assessment within the counseling profession.

Association for Counselor Education and Supervision (ACES)
Emphasizes the need for quality education and supervision of counselors for all work settings.

Association for Counselors and Educators in Government (ACEG)
Promotes counseling clients and their families in local, state, and federal government or in military-related agencies.

Association for Creativity in Counseling (ACC)
Promotes awareness, advocacy, and understanding of the diverse and creative approaches to counseling.

Association for Gay, Lesbian and Bisexual Issues in Counseling (AGLBIC)
Promotes awareness of the unique needs of client identity development and provides a nonthreatening counseling environment by aiding in the reduction of stereotypical thinking and homoprejudice.

The Association for Humanistic Counseling (AHC)
Provides a forum for the exchange of information about humanistically oriented counseling practices and promotes changes that reflect the growing body of knowledge about humanistic principles applied to human development and potential.

Association for Multicultural Counseling and Development (AMCD)
Promotes cultural, ethnic, and racial empathy and understanding through programs that advance and sustain personal growth.

Association for Specialists in Group Work (ASGW)
Promotes professional leadership in the field of group work, establishes standards for professional training, and supports research and the dissemination of knowledge.

TABLE 1.1	**Association for Spiritual, Ethical, and Religious Values in Counseling (ASERVIC)**
(Continued)	Promotes spiritual, ethical, religious, and other human values that are essential to the full development of the person as well as the discipline of counseling.
	Counselors for Social Justice (CSJ)
	Promotes equity and ending oppression and injustice affecting clients, students, counselors, families, communities, schools, workplaces, governments, and other social and institutional systems.
	International Association of Addiction and Offender Counselors (IAAOC)
	Promotes the development of effective counseling and rehabilitation programs for people with substance abuse problems or other addictions, and for adult and/or juvenile public offenders.
	International Association of Marriage and Family Counselors (IAMFC)
	Promotes the development of healthy family systems through prevention, education, and therapy.
	National Career Development Association (NCDA)
	Promotes career development for all people across the lifespan through public information, member services, conferences, and publications.
	National Employment Counseling Association (NECA)
	Provides professional leadership to people who counsel in employment and/or career development settings.

The American Mental Health Counselors Association (AMHCA) is the premier professional organization representing the interests and serving the needs of mental health counselors in the United States and elsewhere (Colangelo, 2009). The organization was founded in 1976 as a professional association representing the interests of professional counselors having the following characteristics in common: They (a) were academically prepared at either the master's or doctoral level; (b) were working in community mental health, private practice, or agency settings; (c) were delivering a wide range of mental health services similar to those offered by more established mental health care professions; and, up to 1976, (d) had no professional home due to their uniqueness (Smith & Robinson, 1996). In 1978, the AMHCA became a division of the APGA. Its membership grew quickly, and it soon became the largest division of the umbrella association. The relationship of AMHCA and ACA has frequently been "stormy and fraught with miscommunication and misinformation" (Smith & Robinson, 1996, p. 159). Currently, while still a division of the ACA, AMHCA operates in an autonomous manner. Its finances are separate from the ACA's and its members can join AMHCA independently of the ACA. The AMHCA offers a variety of member benefits, such as liability and group health insurance, annual conferences, newsletters, and journals that supplement those benefits provided by the ACA. In addition, its relationship to the ACA is better described as collaborative than affiliative (Pistole & Roberts, 2002). The primary agenda of AMHCA includes professional credentialing and recognition, right to practice, legislative activity, and third-party reimbursement.

Both the ACA and AMHCA have chapters at the state level. State chapters provide numerous services for the profession. These include the development of continuing education opportunities presented through state conventions and regional workshops. State chapters also serve as advocates for the consumers of mental health services in their respective states. In addition, licensure of the profession involves a statutory process that is specific to each state. State associations work closely with state licensure boards through consultation and advocacy for the development and implementation of licensure laws. Finally, issues concerning reimbursement for services typically have regional dimensions. While ACA and AMHCA advocate for the profession at the national level, state chapters are called on to respond to policy and practice concerns that affect mental health counselors in their respective states. Examples include Medicaid reimbursement, professional recognition and panel membership, and right-to-practice and scope-of-practice issues. Therefore, many professionals become members of both national and state professional organizations.

The National Board of Certified Counselors (NBCC) is an independent corporation whose purpose is to certify professionals who meet standards to qualify as certified counselors or specialists. Since its establishment in 1981, the NBCC has certified more than 44,000 counselors who have demonstrated knowledge and skills at a minimum competency level in specific areas of study deemed foundational for all professional counselors regardless of specialization (NBCC, 2011). Upon certification as a National Certified Counselor (NCC), professionals can qualify for specialty certification in three areas: mental health counseling, school counseling, or addictions counseling. The following titles are granted:

- Certified Clinical Mental Health Counselor (CCMHC)
- National Certified School Counselor (NCSC)
- Master Addictions Counselor (MAC)

National certification is a voluntary, nonstatutory credential that verifies that the professional has met certain professional standards. The certifications most frequently sought by LMHCs and LPCs are the NCC and CCMHC.

The Council for the Accreditation of Counseling and Related Educational Programs (CACREP) was also established in 1981 and is an independent accrediting body recognized by the Council for Higher Education Accreditation (CACREP, 2009). It was created by the ACA and its divisions to "develop, implement, and maintain standards of preparation for the counseling profession's graduate-level programs" (CACREP, 2001, p. 15). CACREP accomplishes this mission by developing academic training standards for the counseling professions, encouraging excellence in program development, and granting accreditation of professional preparation programs. The standards identify specific objectives for the following areas within an academic program (CACREP, 2009):

- The Learning Environment: Structure and Evaluation
- Professional Identity
- Professional Practice
- Program Area Standards

Master's- and doctoral-level programs in counseling that demonstrate that they meet or exceed these standards are granted accreditation. The following master's-level program areas may be accredited by CACREP:

- Addiction Counseling
- Career Counseling
- Clinical Mental Health Counseling
- Marriage, Couple, and Family Counseling
- School Counseling
- Student Affairs and College Counseling

CACREP also grants accreditation to doctoral programs in counselor education and supervision.

Thus, CACREP sets the national standard by which the quality of all counselor education programs can be assessed. Most LMHCs and LPCs graduate from counselor education programs either that are accredited by CACREP or whose objectives mirror the standards set for the specializations of clinical mental health counseling. In addition, the educational requirements specified in most state licensure laws have integrated CACREP standards. Graduates from CACREP-approved programs, therefore, are at an advantage when applying for professional licensure. A more detailed discussion of the training model for clinical mental health counselors along with their relationship to certification and licensure is provided in Chapter 5.

OTHER SPECIALTIES WITHIN THE COUNSELING PROFESSION

According to the 2011 ACA Policies and Procedures Manual (ACA, 2011), specialties are recognized when specialty accreditation or certification processes are established by CACREP, NBCC, the Council on Rehabilitation Education (CORE), or the Commission on Rehabilitation Counselor Certification (CRCC). Based on these criteria, recognized specialties in addition to mental health counseling include addictions counseling, career counseling, college counseling, gerontological counseling, couple and family counseling, counselor education, rehabilitation counseling, and school counseling. Each of these is discussed briefly next.

ADDICTION COUNSELING

Addiction counselors assist persons who have problems with alcohol, narcotics, and other harmful or addictive substances; gambling; or eating disorders. They find employment in chemical abuse treatment facilities, chemical abuse/dependence programs housed within community mental health centers, outpatient clinics, or employee assistance programs.

The National Association of Alcohol and Drug Abuse Counselors (NAADAC) has developed a three-tier certification system based, in part, on academic degree requirements. Criteria for National Certified Addiction Counselor I and II do not require the master's degree. The highest level of certification granted is the Master Addictions Counselor (MAC).

Addiction counselors possess skills in a variety of intervention strategies and can use individual, group, and family modalities of treatment. Increasingly, clients present with substance abuse/dependence disorders and co-occurring mental illness. To provide optimal care for such clients, addiction counselors become integral parts of a multidisciplinary approach to treatment.

CAREER COUNSELING

Career counselors work primarily with persons who seek help in the processes of career planning and decision making. Such issues have lifespan implications and occur in an ecological context. Thus, in addition to helping persons match personal characteristics to specific job requirements, career counselors frequently address personal, family, and social factors that influence or are influenced by career-related decisions and stressors. Social roles, discrimination, stress, sexual harassment, bias, stereotyping, pay inequities, and tokenism can be aspects of the presenting problem (Engels, Minor, Sampson, & Splete, 1995).

COLLEGE COUNSELING

College and university students benefit from an environment that fosters positive growth. Professional college counselors work in a variety of settings within higher education, such as residence life, student activities, career counseling, multicultural affairs, admissions, academic advising, financial aid, and mentoring. They may provide direct service to students, engage in program development and implementation activities, and assume leadership roles toward the goals of facilitating personal growth and wellness in student populations. In addition, college counselors are called upon to prevent disruptive events and experiences in the students' lives that can inhibit their development. College counselors often provide comprehensive counseling and referral services that help students achieve educational goals, strengthen problem-solving skills, develop healthy relationships, and reach full potential for continued growth after graduation.

GERONTOLOGICAL COUNSELING

As the aging of the U.S. population continues, counselors are called on to provide specialized services for older persons. Gerontological counselors possess general competencies to empower older persons and facilitate wellness. They possess a working knowledge of specific conditions, such as Alzheimer's disease, chronic and terminal illness, substance abuse and complications due to polypharmacy, and life transitions that affect the quality of life of older persons. They must keep abreast of new state and federal legislation as well as other organizational policies that influence the daily lives of their clientele. In addition to traditional techniques of counseling, gerontological counselors have skills in the use of life review, resocialization therapies, bereavement counseling, community assessment and intervention, advocacy, and consultation.

COUPLE AND FAMILY COUNSELING

Marriage and family counselors work in private practice and agency settings and possess skills in family systems assessment and treatment. The family unit, often viewed as a three-generational system, is recognized as the most basic emotional entity and becomes the focus of treatment. In contrast to marriage and family therapists, marriage and family counselors receive training in the core areas of counseling as specified by CACREP and complete a set of courses that relate to the treatment of family dysfunction and promotion of family wellness. Thus, couples, premarital, marriage, family, and divorce counseling are all important skills that marriage and family counselors use to enhance the quality of life in families as they progress through the family life cycle.

REHABILITATION COUNSELING

Rehabilitation counselors are prepared to assist persons with disabilities in adapting to environments as well as assist environments in adapting to the specific needs of the disabled person. They work in an ever-expanding number of traditional and nontraditional employment settings. These include public and private rehabilitation centers, employee assistance programs, disability management programs, school-based transition programs, university programs for students with disabilities, and hospitals (Leahy & Szymanski, 1995). General counseling skills are essential for adequate performance in these settings. In addition, rehabilitation counselors must be knowledgeable in current rehabilitation-related legislation, federally funded programs, and the organizational structures and processes of the rehabilitation service system. Vocational evaluation, assessment, and work adjustment techniques are used by rehabilitation counselors to help clients reach their full potential of productivity.

SCHOOL COUNSELING

School counselors are employed in elementary, middle/junior high, senior high, and postsecondary school settings. They work with the full range of students, including at-risk and special needs populations. Overall, the primary goal of school counselors is to facilitate the whole-person development of all students.

A variety of approaches are used, including individual and small- and large-group counseling, as well as advocacy and consultation. Individual and small-group counseling are used to help students develop and implement effective strategies for coping with and resolving a variety of personal problems and developmental concerns. Career and social development guidance is also offered to larger groups with the use of psychoeducational techniques. Frequently, school counselors consult with educational specialists, including school psychologists, administrators, and medical professionals, to facilitate the development and implementation of individualized educational plans. In such roles, they may serve as a type of case manager who oversees the networking of services to ensure that the specific needs of the students are being met. Clearly, school counselors must possess a working knowledge of human development principles in order to develop and implement preventive and remedial programs that meet the needs of a culturally diverse student population.

CLINICAL MENTAL HEALTH COUNSELING AND THE ALLIED MENTAL HEALTH PROFESSIONS

As noted earlier, the profession of mental health counseling is multidisciplinary at its foundation and in practice. This contributes to some of the identity confusion that exists within the profession as well as among consumers. In order to clarify the place of LMHCs and LPCs among other contemporary mental health providers, it is useful to describe other professions that license and certify practitioners who also deliver mental health care to individuals, groups, couples, and families. These are psychiatrists, psychologists, social workers, and marriage and family therapists. A list of the professional organizations that represent these various mental health professions is presented in Appendix A.

Psychiatrists are physicians, typically holding doctorates in medicine (MDs), who specialize in the diagnosis, treatment, and prevention of mental illness. They must graduate from medical school and then complete up to 4 years of residency training in psychiatry. Frequently, additional training is acquired so that the practitioner can specialize in such areas as child or geriatric psychiatry, psychopharmacology, or a specific mode of therapy. Given their extensive medical training, psychiatrists are qualified to understand the complex relationship between psychological disorders and physical illness. They are the mental health professionals who can prescribe medications. In addition, authorization by psychiatrists is often required for involuntary admission of patients for inpatient hospitalization. The American Psychiatric Association is the professional organization that represents and supports the interests, practice, and research of psychiatrists.

Psychologists are doctorally trained professionals who assess, diagnose, and treat mental illness and emotional distress. Clinical psychology is the subdiscipline that is primarily focused on the study, assessment, treatment, and prevention of abnormal behavior (Carson & Butcher, 1992). In contrast, counseling psychologists have focused traditionally on the presenting problems of relatively normal populations. However, this distinction has become less pronounced in recent years. Typically, state licensure laws for psychologists utilize the generic title of "psychologist" and rarely make any distinctions among the specializations within the discipline. Psychologists have the statutory right to diagnose and treat mental illness. In addition, psychologists are highly trained in the administration, scoring, and interpretation of psychological tests. Recently, psychologists are seeking and have achieved mixed success in attaining drug prescription privileges in several states, particularly with neuroleptic or psychotropic medications (Cummings, 1990; "Prescription Failure," May 2010). The American Psychological Association represents the professional interests of psychologists.

Social work has a long and distinguished history among the allied mental health professions. It can be defined as "the professional activity of helping individuals, groups, or communities to enhance or restore their capacity for social functioning and creating societal conditions favorable to this goal" (Barker, 1987, p. 154). Social workers provide important services to individuals, groups, and families by doing one or more of the following: assisting in linking people to tangible services, providing counseling, helping communities to provide and improve health and social services, and advocating for the inclusion of social work principles and values in relevant legislative processes.

The profession and practice of clinical social work are regulated by licensure laws in all 50 states. In addition, the Academy of Certified Social Workers (ACSW) grants certification to social workers who hold regular membership in the National Association of Social Workers (NASW), the national organization that represents the professional interests of social workers. In order to apply for certification, social workers must hold a master's degree (i.e., the MSW) from a graduate school of social work, must have accumulated 2 years or 3,000 hours of postgraduate degree experience in an agency setting under qualified supervision, and must pass the ACSW written exam.

Marriage and family therapy can be viewed as both a professional orientation and a specific vocation within the mental health professions. As a professional orientation, marriage and family therapy is a theoretical lens and set of techniques used by trained mental health professionals in the treatment of emotional disorders and relational problems. The presenting issues are viewed from a family systems perspective (Commission on Accreditation for Marriage and Family Therapy Education, 1997). This systems orientation is applicable to the treatment of individuals, couples, and family disorders or problems. In contrast, *marriage and family therapists* are members of a distinct profession who diagnose and treat a wide range of human conditions, including individual psychopathology, parent-child problems, and marital distress and conflict, within the context of marriage and family systems (American Association of Marriage and Family Therapy [AAMFT], 2005). In a systems orientation, the family is viewed as the most basic emotional unit and therefore becomes the target of assessment and intervention. In order to be licensed as a marriage and family therapist, the practitioner must have earned either a master's or doctoral degree in marriage and family therapy and have at least 2 years of clinical experience conducted under qualified supervision (e.g., an AAMFT Clinically Approved Supervisor). The AAMFT is the professional organization that represents the professional interests of marriage and family therapists.

CONCLUSION: THE PROCESS OF CONSOLIDATING PROFESSIONAL IDENTITY

It is useful to view the process of consolidating a professional identity in mental health counseling as a developmental process. Students entering counseling programs as well as recent graduates often wrestle with their own set of "who am I?" questions. They may not see clear distinctions between who they are relative to the other mental health professions. Or they may continue to feel uncomfortable performing in their professional roles despite adequate levels of skill and training. A "self as identity" emerges as one's personal attributes, professional training, and experiences are tested through receiving feedback from clients, supervisors, and the professional community (Gibson, Dollarhide, & Moss, 2010).

Be patient. In many ways, the process of attaining a stable professional identity can be likened to the adolescent process of attaining *identity achievement* (Marcia, 1966, 1980). Explore alternatives and ask questions that enable you to see the "lay of the land" more clearly. Proceed down the path with trusted peers and a knowledgeable mentor to walk alongside. Fully invest yourself in your training experience.

Friedman and Kaslow (1986) postulated a six-stage developmental model for counseling professionals that starts with an anticipatory stage, in which new counselors learn they will be meeting with clients. This stage ends when counselors start to meet with their clinical supervisors. Stage 2, the dependency stage, is where novice counselors rely heavily on supervisors for answers. In stage 3, counselors continue to rely on their supervisors but are beginning to move toward independent activity. At stage 4, counselors experience the excitement that comes with initiating autonomous counseling interventions and seeing clients' positive responses. Counselors develop a sense of identity and autonomy in stage 5. In the final stage, counselors have settled in to their profession and exhibit calmness and collegiality. Kral and Hines (1999) found that it takes from 5 to 6 years before new counseling professionals gain a stable sense of identity and competence.

In addition, establishing a sense of professional identity involves integrating the sense of belonging to the mental health counseling profession and comfort with the professional roles performed into one's overall sense of self. This is a dynamic process that occurs within an ecological context. The counselor is a person who takes on a particular set of roles that involves specific intra- and interpersonal processes regulated by the profession. The unique shape of these factors and how they integrate into a coherent professional identity depend on forces external to both the person and the profession. Thus, the development of professional identity is a function of a person-environment interaction. Figure 1.1 illustrates this developmental process.

FIGURE 1.1 Developing Professional Identity: A Person-Environment Interaction

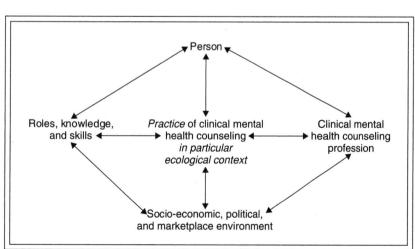

Within this ecological context, counselors-in-training perform three transformational tasks that lead to professional identity development (Gibson et al., 2010). The first task, definition of counseling, takes place as trainees move from definitions that reflect external input to internalized definitions. Responsibility for professional growth is the second task and involves moving from a reliance on an external scaffold that encourages training experiences to assuming personal responsibility for one's professional development. In the final task, transformation to a systemic identity, counselors-in-training move from the predominance of license types and job titles to understanding one's professional identity within the larger context of professional communities and associations. Thus, professional identity moves from an externally-based to an internally-based working model.

Achieving a coherent professional identity as a professional mental health counselor has much to do with who you are as a person and your personal developmental context and history. The shape that your professional identity takes is influenced by your ongoing interaction with a number of sociocultural forces. These include the economic system; societal and cultural values, mores, and beliefs; governmental policies and funding; the nature of public and private institutions; related mental health professions; and trends and forces of the marketplace.

This chapter has provided you with foundational information to help you see more clearly what it means to be a clinical mental health counselor. As your professional identity consolidates, you will experience a sense of well-being and congruity as you move through time as well as the comfort and security of knowing where you are going. It is only by possessing a clear view of who you are and where you are going that you can be a helpful facilitator, guide, or anchor for those you serve. Ultimately, your personal satisfaction and survival in the profession depend on it.

DISCUSSION QUESTIONS

1. On page 17, a six-stage developmental model for counseling professionals is described briefly. What specific personal characteristics or experiences might facilitate one's positive professional development? What specific personal characteristics or experiences might hinder one's professional development?

2. Given that the establishment of a professional identity is a developmental process, suppose you are in your first year of professional practice and a client challenges your competency. What would be your internal experience in such a situation? How would you respond?

3. From a consumer point of view, is it possible to clearly differentiate the specific roles or strengths of the various mental health professions? What specific recommendations would you make to increase the visibility and accurate perception of the mental health counseling profession?

4. To what extent do you see the various counseling specializations as constituting a common profession? Identify potential strengths and resources that arise by having *unity* in the midst of this *diversity*. Does the *20/20* definition of counseling

(ACA, 2010) contribute to unity? Can you see any potential weaknesses or potential conflicts of interest? Be specific.

5. To what extent do you believe the definitions, professional associations, and training model of clinical mental health counselors have clearly differentiated the profession from the allied mental health professions?

SUGGESTED ACTIVITIES

1. Review classified ads from a variety of sources (e.g., local newspapers and Web sites of mental health organizations) and identify how employers differentiate between or among the mental health professions in the postings. Discuss your findings.
2. Explore the Web sites of the professional associations representing the interests of clinical mental health counselors. Investigate and report on the types of information and varieties of services provided by them.
3. You might want to learn more about the similarities and differences among mental health counselors and the allied mental health professions. What similarities do you detect as you compare the Web sites of these organizations? What distinct emphases do you detect through the materials found on their Web sites?
4. Suppose you have a friend who is experiencing emotional distress and would like to receive some professional services. Why, specifically, might you refer your friend to a mental health counselor instead of a comparable member of the allied mental health professions. In other words, what distinctions do mental health counselors bring to the table that you would mention in responding to your friend? Practice your response by doing role-plays with members of your class.
5. In this chapter, the common practice of working as part of a multidisciplinary team was discussed briefly. Design your ideal multidisciplinary team whose goal is to provide an effective and efficient wraparound mental health service to persons with chronic mental illness living in the community.
6. Conduct a survey among members of your state counseling association or a sample of licensed counselors. Explore the extent to which their professional identities align with the definitions of the profession. (You may obtain results worthy of publication or presentation).

REFERENCES

American Association of Marriage and Family Therapy. (2005). *Commission on accreditation for marriage and family therapy education: Accreditation standards* (version 11.0). Alexandria, VA: Author.

American Counseling Association Governing Council. (1997). *Definition of professional counseling.* Alexandria, VA: Author.

American Counseling Association. (2010). Definition of counseling. Retrieved from http://www. counseling.org/Resources

American Mental Health Counselors Association. (1987, June). Mental health counseling training standards. *AMHCA News*, p. 6.

Barker, R. L. (1987). *The social work dictionary*. Silver Springs, MD: National Association of Social Workers.

Bloom, J., Gerstein, L., Tarvydas, V., Conaster, J., Davis, E., Kater, D., et al. (1990). Model legislation for licensed professional counselors. *Journal of Counseling and Development, 68,* 511–523.

Bronfenbrenner, U. (1979). *The ecology of human development: Experiments by nature and design.* Cambridge, MA: Harvard University Press.

Carson, R. C., & Butcher, J. N. (1992). *Abnormal psychology and modern life* (9th ed.). New York, NY: Harper Collins.

Colangelo, J. J. (2009). The American Mental Health Counselors Association: Reflection on 30 historic years. *Journal of Counseling and Development, 87,* 234–240.

Commission on Accreditation for Marriage and Family Therapy Education. (1997). *Manual on accreditation.* Washington, DC: COAMFTE.

Council for Accreditation of Counseling and Related Educational Programs. (2001). *CACREP accreditation manual: 2001 standards.* Alexandria, VA: Author.

Coyne, R. K., & Cook, E. P. (2004). Understanding persons within environments: An introduction to ecological counseling. In R. K. Coyne & E. P. Cook (Eds.), *Ecological counseling: An innovative approach to conceptualizing person-environment interaction.* Alexandria, VA: American Counseling Association.

Cummings, N. A. (1990). The credentialing of professional psychologists and its implication for the other mental health disciplines. *Journal of Counseling and Development, 68,* 485–490.

Department of Labor, Occupational Employment Statistics. (2011). Occupational employment and wages, May 2010: 21-1014 mental health counselors. Retrieved from http://www/bls.gov/oes/current/oes211014.htm

Dinkmeyer, D. (1991). Mental health counseling: A psychoeducational approach. *Journal of Mental Health Counseling, 13,* 37–42.

Engles, D. W., Minor, C. W., Sampson, J. P., & Splete, H. H. (1995). Career counseling specialty: History, development, and prospect. *Journal of Counseling and Development, 74,* 134–138.

Friedman, D., & Kaslow, N. (1986). The development of professional identity in psychotherapists: Six stages in the supervision process. In E. W. Kaslow (Ed.), *Supervision and training models, dilemmas and challenges* (pp. 29–50). New York, NY: Haworth Press.

Gerig, M. S. (2011). *Being a Mental Health Counselor: A Paradigm for Professional Practice and Counselor Education.* Workshop presented at 2011 Indiana Counseling Association Annual Conference.

Gibson, D. M., Dollarhide, C. T., & Moss, J. M. (2010). Professional identity development: A grounded theory of transformational tasks of new counselors. *Counselor Education and Supervision, 50,* 21–38.

Guerney, B. G., Jr. (1977). *Relationship enhancement: Skill-training programs for therapy, problem prevention, and enrichment.* San Francisco, CA: Jossey-Bass.

Hanna, F. J., & Bemak, F. (1997). The quest for identity in the counseling profession. *Counselor Education and Supervision, 36,* 194–207.

Hill, L. K. (1991). Microstrategies: Creating paradigm versus paradigm thinking. *Journal of Mental Health Counseling, 13,* 43–50.

Hinkle, J. S. (1999). Promoting optimum mental health through counseling: An overview. In J. S. Hinkle (Ed.), *Promoting optimum mental health through counseling.* Greensboro, NC: ERIC/CASS.

Ivey, A. E. (1989). Mental health counseling: A developmental process and profession. *Journal of Mental Health Counseling, 11,* 26–35.

Ivey, A. E., & Rigazio-DiGilio, S. A. (1991). Toward a developmental practice of mental health counseling: Strategies for training, practice, and political unity. *Journal of Mental Health Counseling, 13,* 21–36.

Kaplan, D. M., & Gladding, S. T. (2011). A vision for the future of counseling: The 20/20 principles for unifying and strengthening the profession. *Journal of Counseling and Development, 89,* 367–372.

Kral, R., & Hines, M. (1999). A survey study on the developmental stages in achieving a competent sense of self as a family therapist. *Family Journal, 7,* 102–112.

Leahy, M. J., & Szymanski, E. M. (1995). Rehabilitation counseling: Evolution and current status. *Journal of Counseling and Development, 74,* 163–166.

Lewis, J. A., Lewis, M. D., Daniels, J. A., & D'Andrea, M. J. (2003). *Community counseling: Empowerment strategies for a diverse society* (3rd ed.). Pacific Grove, CA: Brooks/Cole.

Marcia, J. E. (1966). Development and validation of ego identity status. *Journal of Personality and Social Psychology, 3,* 551–558.

Marcia, J. E. (1980). Identity in adolescence. In J. Adelson (Ed.), *Handbook of adolescent psychology* (pp. 159–187). New York, NY: Wiley.

Mellin, E. A., Hunt, B., & Nichols, L. M. (2011). Counselor professional identity: Findings and implications for counseling and interprofessional collaboration. *Journal of Counseling and Development, 89,* 140–147.

National Board for Certified Counselors. (2011). About NBCC. Retrieved from http://www.nbcc.org/About

Nugent, F. A. (2000). *Introduction to the profession of counseling* (3rd ed.). Upper Saddle River, NJ: Prentice Hall.

Pistole, C. (2001). Mental health counseling: Identity and distinctiveness. Retrieved from ERIC database. (ED462672)

Pistole, C. M., & Roberts, A. (2002). Mental health counseling: Toward resolving identity confusions. *Journal of Mental Health Counseling, 24,* 1–9.

Prescription failure in Oregon frustrates psychologists. (2010, May). *Psychotherapy Finances,* p. 1.

Rollins, J. (2010, June). Making definitive progress: 20/20 delegates reach consensus on definition of counseling. *Counseling Today.* Retrieved from http://ct.counseling.org/2010/06/making-definitive-progress/

Seiler, G. (1990). Shaping the destiny of the new profession: Recollections and reflections on the evolution of mental health counseling (p. 85). In G. Seiler (Ed.), *The mental health counselor's sourcebook* New York, NY: Human Sciences Press.

Seiler, G., & Messina, J. J. (1979). Toward professional identity: The dimensions of mental health counseling in perspective. *American Mental Health Counselors Journal, 1,* 3–8.

Smith, H. B., & Robinson, G. P. (1996). Mental health counseling: Past, present, and future (pp. 38–50). In W. J. Weikel, & A. J. Palmo (Eds.), *Foundations of mental health counseling* (2nd ed.). Springfield, IL: Thomas.

Van Hesteren, F., & Ivey, A. E. (1990). Counseling and development: Toward a new identity for a profession in transition. *Journal of Counseling and Development, 68,* 524–528.

Weikel, W. J., & Palmo, A. J. (1989). The evolution and practice of mental health counseling. *Journal of Mental Health Counseling, 11,* 7–25.

2

The Counseling Professions in Historical Perspective

OUTLINE

When gathering information about clients in initial sessions, I find it useful to utilize genograms. These are structural diagrams that describe a family's three- or four-generational relationship system (Sherman & Fredman, 1986). As I gather verbal information regarding clients' families of origin, I diagram not only the connectedness among blood relatives, but also key events, roles, and communication patterns existing within the family over three or more generations. This technique provides a tool for efficient documentation of individual and family history, and it also helps clients better understand who they are by placing them within the context of those from whom they came.

In this chapter, you will learn more about the professional identity of Licensed Mental Health Counselors (LMHCs) and Licensed Professional Counselors (LPCs) in a developmental and ecological context. For the purpose of establishing a relatively secure professional identity, history is necessary and relevant. With regard to the discipline of psychology, Leahey (1980) notes,

> The events of today are influenced by the historical past and will influence the historical future. To understand what we are doing and why we are doing it, we need to understand what psychologists did before us as well as the nature of historical change. To ignore the past is to cut off a source of self-understanding. (p. 14)

Our professional identity, which sometimes appears overly confusing when viewed in the isolation of the here and now, takes on a distinct appearance when viewed in its historical context. In the pages that follow, you will see how each of the various mental health professions emerged. As a profession evolves, new or existing professions step in to provide unique services that either complement the services of existing professions or fill gaps by meeting identified yet unfulfilled needs of certain populations.

In reading this chapter, you will gain a more complete understanding of the clinical mental health counseling profession. But beyond that, you might be able to capture a glimpse of the passion and vision that was part of the founding of the profession. This understanding of the profession will contribute to your sense of professional pride, which is helpful in developing professional identity and integrity.

EARLY VIEWS AND TREATMENT OF MENTAL HEALTH AND ILLNESS

Archaeological discoveries yield clues to the earliest views of humanity regarding health and mental illness. The discovery of human skulls that date back to 8000 B.C. in which crude holes appear to have been created by chipping away bony material leads to the hypothesis that ancient people recognized the source of abnormal behavior as being within the person's head. These holes, were made to provide an exit for the source of the symptoms (Halgin & Whitbourne, 2010). In addition, ancient papyri have been discovered that indicate belief that the brain was the site of mental functions. These papyri also show that early humans relied on magic and incantations for the cure of disease (Carson, Butcher, & Mineka, 2002).

Incised bones discovered in archaeological excavations tell us little about earliest perspectives on the nature of persons, views of wellness and mental disorder, and treatment. Useful sources of information are the study of myth, comparative religion, and the writings of early philosophers. For example, the Old Testament of the Christian Bible contains references to madness and confusion of the mind. King David feigns madness as he allows a flow of saliva to run down his beard. In the biblical context, madness is distinguished from folly, which seems to be contrasted with wisdom. Madness was seen as the consequence of evil spirits or an angry God, whereas folly or foolish behavior stemmed from a lack of wisdom. Thus, we see that early distinctions were made between behavioral conditions that were essentially beyond human control and those related to poor judgment and faulty decision making.

Early Greek philosophy provides additional insight into early views of mental health illness and its treatment. Hippocrates (460–377 B.C.), who is referred to as the father of medicine, related general behavioral tendencies and temperament to the relative balance of four bodily fluids: blood, black bile, yellow bile, and phlegm. Significant imbalances caused aberrations in behavior. For example, an excess of black bile was considered the underlying cause of melancholia. To treat melancholia, Hippocrates recommended a tranquil lifestyle, sobriety, abstinence from all excesses, vegetable diets, strenuous exercise (but not to the point of fatigue), and bloodletting (Viney & King, 2003). Plato (428–348 B.C.) contended that aberrant behaviors resulting from madness were a societal issue that required a community response (Plato, n.d.).

Promotion of happiness and wellness also found expression in the philosophies of early Greeks and Romans. Epicurus (341–270 B.C.) advocated hedonism but recognized that such an approach to life carried with it a risk of pain if the pleasures were withdrawn. Epictetus (A.D. 50–138) advocated peace of mind. He believed that people were disturbed not by things, but by the view they took of those things. The treatment recommendations of Galen (A.D. 130–200) included massage and drinking chilled wines while reclining in a warm bath (Carson et al., 2002).

The Middle Ages were marked by both cruel and humane treatments of persons who displayed deviant behaviors. Those behaviors that could not be explained readily were attributed to supernatural causes. Humans were thought to be the site where the ultimate battle between good and evil took place. Thus, "water tests" were used to determine whether or not a person was in league with the devil. In contrast, centers for the humane treatment of the mentally disturbed arose in Baghdad and Damascus in the ninth and tenth centuries (Polvan, 1969). Beginning in the 1300s, the Colony of Gheel, located in Belgium, became a center of care for the mentally ill that was characterized by love and kindness (Korchin, 1976).

However, by the 16th century, a system of hospitals known as asylums was developed in Europe to provide shelter for persons unable to care for themselves. Conditions in many of these institutions were deplorable, with residents frequently kept in restraints and left to lie in their own waste (Halgin & Whitbourne, 2010). By the late

1700s, voices of reform were being heard from advocates such as Phillipe Pinél, William Tuke, and Benjamin Rush (Carson et al., 2002). The result was a more humane approach, referred to as *moral treatment* (Linhorst, 2006). The primary goal of moral treatment was to provide respite both for the mentally ill and for society. The regimen of treatment included organized schedules of productive labor, spiritual and cultural improvement, socializing, entertainment, education, nutrition, and exercise (Fancher, 1995).

In summary, we can see that throughout recorded history people have distinguished between healthy and unhealthy forms of behavior. Furthermore, some of the unhealthy forms of behavior were believed to be under conscious control, whereas other forms of behavior were not. As will be seen in the sections that follow, this basic framework remained relatively intact as the various mental health professions emerged and sought either to treat pathology or to enhance human functioning. As Fancher (1995) notes, "Professional care for mental health has evolved from giving 'moral treatment' to the clearly deranged to claiming to offer, in the name of scientific advance, access to life reasonably free from emotional distress" (p. 53).

THE EMERGENCE OF PSYCHIATRY

The application of moral treatment was far removed from the application of medical science. However, members of the medical profession served as supervisors for this treatment. These medical professionals, seeking to apply humanitarian ideals to the condition of the mentally ill, became the foundation of psychiatry.

In 1844, 13 asylum supervisors gathered to form the Association of Medical Superintendents of American Institutions for the Insane (AMSAII) (McGovern, 1985). Predating the formation of the American Medical Association by 2 years, the AMSAII became the first organized medical specialty society in America (Fancher, 1995). Thus, it became a primary force in the treatment of the insane. Advocating moral treatment, which did not require significant medical knowledge, the AMSAII upheld its standards while keeping such well-known advocates as Dorothea Dix from becoming members of the organization.

However, science advanced and new approaches to the treatment of mental illness were being discovered. A second generation of medical specialists emerged—neurologists—who had more interest in science and its application to the mentally ill. In contrast to the asylum superintendents, neurologists were more scientifically minded and were eager to apply their specialization to the treatment of persons with nervous conditions. These doctors were not welcome in the AMSAII. However, they were successful in exerting pressure on the AMSAII to endorse a policy that did not challenge the authority of the superintendents but called for all future superintendents to be competent scientists. In 1892, the organization changed its name to the American Medico-Psychological Association, which in 1927 became the American Psychiatric Association (Fancher, 1995).

Several milestones came out of this tradition. First, the physiological cause for paresis (syphilis of the brain) was discovered (Davidson, Neale, Blankstein, & Flett, 2005). Paresis was one of the most serious forms of mental illness of the day. Now, for the first time, brain pathology was demonstrated to be the cause of a form of mental illness. In 1917, a cure was found, which led to an expectation that many other forms of mental illness had biological roots that could be treated successfully. Thus, the medical model was applied to the treatment of mental disorders.

Second, a neurologist by the name of Sigmund Freud began to treat a range of nervous conditions, referred to as *neuroses,* using hypnosis and talking therapies. He soon discovered that hypnosis was unnecessary as his patients, who were females, improved through a talking-out and working-through process (Halgin & Whitbourne, 2010). Believing that neuroses were deeply rooted in the person's psyche, Freud developed a theory of mental and emotional functioning that captured the attention of young psychiatrists and neurologists. Rather than train psychoanalysts in universities, Freud established the Institute of Psychoanalysis in Vienna. In his model, psychoanalysts were trained in rigorous residencies at centers apart from colleges and universities.

Third, a German psychiatrist named Emil Kraepelin (1856–1926) developed the first major classification system of all mental illnesses. He based his system on thousands of case studies. His work made an important contribution to the medical model and laid the foundation for the modern-day American Psychiatric Association's *Diagnostic and Statistical Manual of Mental Disorders,* which is now in its revised fourth edition (*DSM-IV-TR*) (Davidson et al., 2005).

ROOTS OF THE COUNSELING-RELATED PROFESSIONS

The historical antecedents of psychology lie in philosophy (Cangemi & Kowalski, 1993; Resnick, 1997). As noted earlier in this chapter, Hippocrates, Plato, and other Greek philosophers speculated on the functional relationship between the mind and the body. The origin of psychology dates back to 1879, when Wilhelm Wundt established the first psychological laboratory at the University of Leipzig in Germany. He was a philosopher and physiologist who defined *psychology* as the study of immediate experience. His goal was to create a science of the mind and behavior. Thus, the discipline of psychology arose as an academic field that applies the methods of science to the investigation of the mind and behavior. Most of those who were significant in its formation as a discipline never considered themselves psychologists because they studied sensation, perception, and other intrapsychic phenomena (Resnick, 1997).

In 1892, the American Psychological Association (APA) was formed by a group of philosophers, educators, and physicians (Resnick, 1997). A defining event took place in 1898 when the organization chose not to incorporate a division of philosophical psychology. As a result, the American Philosophical Association was formed in 1901. Psychology chose a direction that moved it away from its philosophical heritage and toward psychophysics, animal behavior, and human assessment. This interest in assessment was noted as early as 1896, when the APA formed the Committee on Physical and Mental Tests. Its goal was to develop standards for the practice of human mental and behavioral assessment (Sokal, 1992). In 1906, the APA formed another committee, the Committee on the Standardization of Procedures in Experimental Tests, which was given the task of identifying standardized instruments for individuals and groups. Both of these committees had difficulty defining agendas and were disbanded by 1919.

Leightner Witmer established the first psychological clinic at the University of Pennsylvania in 1896. He wrote an article in *Pediatrics* that same year in which he defined *practical psychology* as the examination of physical and mental conditions of schoolchildren and the study of defective children (Witmer, 1896). In a published case study, Witmer (1896) described the treatment of a "feebleminded" child who experienced "mental defects as the result of severe convulsions while teething" (p. 466). His treatment consisted of 3-hour sessions each day, 5 days a week, for 4 years. He coined the term *clinical psychology,* borrowing the word *clinical* from medicine because he saw it as best describing the method he deemed necessary for this type of work.

In 1908, William Healy, a Freudian psychoanalyst, established the Juvenile Psychopathic Institute. The clinic, which was located in Chicago, is historically significant for several reasons. First, it was the first psychiatric clinic to be set in a community (Laughlin & Worley, 1991; Nugent, 2000). Second, it appears to have been the first institution to apply psychological skills and training to the treatment of social problems (Laughlin & Worley, 1991). Until this time, the practical application of psychology had focused almost exclusively on mental testing. Third, the clinic used a multidisciplinary approach to treatment (Nugent, 2000). The psychiatrist was the professional who did therapy, a psychologist conducted the testing and assessment, and a social worker dealt with the home problems. Healy's approach to the treatment of troubled youth fit well within the psychoanalytic tradition (Rogers, 1961).

Professional social work was the result of the merger of the Charity Organization Society (COS) and settlement house movements (Haynes & White, 1999). The goal of the COS movement was to help others help themselves and to encourage personal responsibility. The mechanism to accomplish this goal was termed *friendly visiting* (Haynes & White, 1999, p. 385). The settlement house movement emphasized the principle of social responsibility as well (Axinn & Levin, 1997). Settlement house workers sought to develop programs to create a just society through effective social action. These workers demonstrated a strong concern for the welfare of children, adolescents, and families who were disenfranchised and forgotten by the larger society. By the end of the 19th century, social workers had established the expertise of their profession in studying urban conditions, conducting home visits, and helping people to improve their circumstances (Fancher, 1995).

At about this same time, Frank Parsons was concerned with problems of youth. With the rapid urbanization of America that took place around the turn of the 20th century, youth unemployment quickly became a major concern in the normal developmental process of adolescents. The experience of unemployment was bewildering, especially for youth, who were accustomed to the steady work and family income afforded by the family farm (Whiteley, 1984). Parsons recognized the significance of this transition and, in 1908, founded the Boston Vocational Bureau. The goal of this organization was to match the interests and aptitudes of young persons with appropriate occupational choices (Brooks & Weikel, 1996).

Parsons created the role of vocational counselor and, in doing so, initiated an approach of interaction and facilitation that was a forerunner of the contemporary counseling process (Dawis, 1992). In *Choosing a Vocation* (Parsons, 1909), Parsons outlined this counseling process as being characterized by listening to and gathering information from the client regarding his or her personal interests and goals. To facilitate this process of self-exploration, Parsons developed a lengthy self-administered questionnaire that probed a wide range of variables believed to be relevant to identifying a good match between personal characteristics and vocational placement. The instrument consisted of straightforward questions but was quite lengthy. Its interpretation was complex and time consuming (Nugent, 2000).

Parsons played a key role in the development of professional counseling for several reasons. First, his approach was clearly directed to relatively normal youth who were facing a developmental transition. Second, the method of vocational counseling had prevention as a foundational goal. It may have been the first truly upstream approach (Egan & Cowan, 1979), catching a vulnerable population before more significant clinical or social problems emerged. Third, Parsons's questionnaire could be self-administered and included input from family, friends, and teachers. The ecological perspective is evident in his method. Thus, in the work of Parsons we can find many of the unique theoretical emphases and processes of clinical mental health counseling in its rudimentary form.

Finally, a former patient of mental hospitals named Clifford Beers wrote a book titled *A Mind That Found Itself* (Beers, 1908). In it, he detailed the deplorable conditions of these institutions and advocated for reforms. The book was quite popular and, with the heightened awareness of the plight of the mentally ill, Beers founded the National Committee for Mental Hygiene (1909). This group was a forerunner of the National Mental Health Association (Brooks & Weikel, 1996).

MOVEMENT TOWARD THE PROFESSIONALIZATION OF COUNSELING

By the 1920s and 1930s, the primary forces supporting movement toward creation of a counseling profession were in place. This period of time was marked by a quiet expansion of approaches and the development of new applications. Among these developments were the emergence of the private practice of psychology, the child guidance clinic movement, nondirective counseling, marriage and family counseling, rapid expansion of psychological assessment, and increased sophistication of vocational counseling.

THE PRIVATE PRACTICE OF PSYCHOLOGY

Psychiatry continued to be the preeminent profession addressing the needs of the mentally ill. However, the private practice of psychology was beginning to take hold. Casselberry (1935) wrote an article in which he described the nature of services provided by these private practitioners. They included "diagnosis using tests and questionnaires; a modified psychoanalytic procedure; re-conditioning and training; suggestion; relaxation; and instruction in diet, proper breathing, posture and voice placement and control" (p. 232). These approaches addressed "warped and inferior personalities, social maladjustment, cases of nervousness, timidity, and bashfulness; fears, phobias, and complexes, marriage maladjustment, vocational maladjustment, juvenile delinquency, and child training; hysteria, neurasthenia, and psychasthenia" (p. 58). Crane (1925) commented that the attitude of the medical profession toward practicing psychologists was "one of tolerant condescension" (p. 228).

THE CHILD GUIDANCE MOVEMENT

The 1920s and 1930s were marked by an increased interest in the mental health of children. In 1921, several child guidance demonstration clinics were established in key cities around the United States. Growth in this movement led to the establishment of many new clinics, and the team approach, first used by Healy, continued to evolve (Nichols, 2010). Multidisciplinary staffs were under the leadership of psychiatrists, who were responsible for most of the treatment decisions and therapy. Psychologists were involved primarily in psychological assessment and the provision of educational and remedial therapy. Social workers conducted intake and social history interviews, did casework with parents, and acted as liaisons to enhance the social environment of the child. This basic organization continued in the years following World War II (Korchin, 1976).

CARL ROGERS AND NONDIRECTIVE COUNSELING

One young professional, Carl Rogers, became disillusioned with the predominant form of treatment conducted at the child guidance clinics. He concluded that Healy might be wrong in his attribution of juvenile delinquency to sexual conflict. Rather, he came to believe that it was the client who best knew "what hurts, what directions to go, what problems are crucial, what experiences have been deeply buried" (Rogers, 1961, p. 12). He struggled, initially, with his own professional identity. And the university where he worked clearly indicated that he was not doing psychology. He began to teach courses on how to understand problem children, and the university wanted to house the courses in the department of education. His ideas were further refined as he taught treatment and counseling to graduate students at Ohio State.

Out of these experiences, a new approach to therapy developed, known first as nondirective counseling, later as client-centered therapy, and finally as the person-centered approach (Corey, 2009). Rogers (1961) summarized the essential hypothesis of this approach in one sentence: "If I can provide a certain type of relationship, the other person will discover within himself the capacity to use that relationship for growth, and change and personal development will occur" (p. 33). He firmly believed that the quality of the therapeutic relationship, which relied on the goodness and natural developmental tendencies toward personal growth of the client, provided a more effective orientation for therapy. These ideas, found in his early book *Counseling and Psychotherapy* (Rogers, 1942), were the start of a revolution in how clients were viewed and treated. These became important foundations for the profession and practice of counseling.

MARRIAGE AND FAMILY COUNSELING

People had discussed marital and family issues with clergy and doctors for years, but psychiatry and psychology, while recognizing the relevance and involvement of the family, focused primarily on the treatment of individuals. In the late 1920s, marriage centers began to emerge (Nichols, 2010). Abraham and Hannah Stone opened the first marriage clinic in New York City. Soon after, Paul Popenoe, a biologist, developed the American Institute of Family Relations in Los Angeles. The long-running series of articles he wrote in the *Ladies' Home Journal*, "Can This Marriage Be Saved?" did much to popularize marriage counseling. At about this same time, a small group of psychoanalysts broke from the Freudian tradition, which prohibited contact with the families of patients, by proposing that some couples had interlocking neuroses and required conjoint treatment (Fenell, 2012).

RAPID EXPANSION OF ASSESSMENT AND INCREASED SOPHISTICATION OF VOCATIONAL COUNSELING

During this period, the study and assessment of individual differences expanded greatly. Whereas the early intelligence tests measured mental abilities and potential, the post–World War I era marked the blossoming of personality and vocational testing (Dawis, 1992). The earliest personality tests were developed to screen military recruits. The Woodworth Personal Data Sheet, which attempted to present the psychiatric interview in a standardized form, was published immediately following the war. The construction of projective tests soon followed. Interest in the Rorschach inkblot test, first published in 1921, grew slowly. Its popularity increased, though, when Sam Beck wrote a doctoral dissertation in 1932 (Kaplan & Saccuzzo, 2009). In it, Beck investigated the scientific properties of the Rorschach. In 1935, Henry Murray and Christina Morgan developed the Thematic Apperception Test (TAT), a projective test that was based on Murray's personality theory of needs. Although none of these instruments had a direct or immediate impact on the profession of counseling, they did reflect distinct lines of inquiry that would prove relevant in the move toward increased specialization in the mental health professions.

Other advances in assessment, though, were linked directly to guidance and vocational counseling. In 1928, Clark L. Hull and Lewis M Terman published *Aptitude*

Testing. In this book, they advocated the use of aptitude-test batteries and matching human traits with specific job requirements (Hull, 1928). Hull promoted the idea of predicting job satisfaction and success based on standardized tests. Hull's text came on the heels of the publication of *The Strong Vocational Interest Blank* by Edward K. Strong Jr. in 1927. This measure provided career counselors with a standardized tool linking the personal interests of examinees to the interests of persons in specific professional groups (Anastasi & Urbina, 1997). This instrument gave counselors a valuable tool with which to facilitate vocational decision making.

The vocational testing movement prepared the way for E. G. Williamson Jr. to put forth the first true theory of counseling (Williamson, 1939). In 1939, Williamson published *How to Counsel Students: A Manual of Techniques for Clinical Counselors*. This text can be viewed as an extension of Parsons's formulations (Zunker, 1998). However, Williamson described a straightforward approach to counseling that came to be known as *directive counseling*. His approach consisted of six sequential steps: analysis, synthesis, diagnosis, prognosis, counseling, and follow-up. The term *clinical counseling* reflected an empirically based, scientific method that sought to eliminate nonproductive thinking and facilitate effective decision making (Lynch & Maki, 1981).

POST–WORLD WAR II AND THE VETERANS ADMINISTRATION

Psychologists, counselors, and social workers, relatively few with doctoral degrees and many with minimal clinical experience, found themselves working in the front lines with psychiatrists in military psychiatric units during World War II. There was also a strong need for the selection and training of specialists for the military and industry (Anastasi & Urbina, 1997). Counselors and psychologists had the necessary knowledge and skills to fulfill this important role. In addition, thousands of soldiers were emotionally impaired as a result of their combat experiences and were entitled to professional counseling services provided by the Veterans Administration (VA) upon discharge. In 1945, the VA obtained funding to support the training of mental health professionals. Numerous internship opportunities were made available at VA hospitals.

During this time, the APA developed a training philosophy and model of clinical training (APA Committee on Training in Clinical Psychology, 1947). In 1949, attendees of a conference held in Boulder, Colorado, endorsed this model, which has become known as the Boulder model. It stated that the newly defined clinical psychologist should be first and foremost a scientist-practitioner, a professional trained in a PhD program who would be equally adept as a clinician, a researcher, and a scholar. In response to this model, university programs, helped by the funding of the newly formed National Institute for Mental Health (NIMH), moved quickly to offer doctoral degrees in both counseling and clinical psychology (Cummings, 1990). Clinical psychologists were trained to diagnose and treat individuals with chronic disorders, whereas counseling psychologists dealt with issues presented by persons who displayed relatively high levels of mental health. In 1953, the APA responded to this new category of psychologists by changing the name of Division 17 from the Division of

Counseling and Guidance to the Division of Counseling Psychology (Dawis, 1992; Woody, Hansen, & Rossberg, 1989).

The impact of these changes on the counseling profession cannot be understated. First, a clear boundary between psychologists and counselors was created. The professional was required to complete a four-year program of study leading to a doctoral degree in psychology or a closely related discipline in order to be considered a psychologist (Morgan, 1947). Morgan articulates the rationale for requiring the doctorate in the following quotation:

> The well-earned prestige of the medical degree has affected the attitudes of physicians and laymen alike, and neither group is desirous of having clinical responsibility given to men not called "doctor." To delegate to psychologists without doctoral degrees the full duties of the profession in the V.A. would be to put them under a handicap, for these attitudes would prevent them from having adequate scope to exercise all of their skills. (p. 29)

Second, with the VA funding doctoral-level internships only, master's-level counselors were ineligible for many of the available training programs (Bronfenbrenner, 1947). Third, counseling psychologists began to move away from their historical link with vocational guidance and counseling. Fourth, mental health professionals with less than a doctoral-level education were now without a professional home. They were no longer eligible for full membership in the APA.

THE INFLUENCE OF PROFESSIONAL ORGANIZATIONS

By the early 1950s, the demarcation of the various counseling professions was well under way. The development of the professional identity of the various mental health professions was facilitated by the formation of professional organizations that served to represent the unique interests of those professions. As noted previously, the APA and the restructuring of Division 17 played a key role in setting psychologists apart from counselors. The formation of other professional organizations helped to define and accentuate distinctions among other counseling-related professions.

The American Association of Marriage and Family Counselors (AAMFC), founded in 1942, had already set a precedent by providing members of this fledgling profession a forum in which to share ideas, establish professional standards, and foster research (Nichols, 2010). By the mid-1950s, the AAMFC, which was later renamed as the American Association of Marriage and Family Therapists (AAMFT), was already establishing academic and training standards for programs specializing in marriage counseling.

The restructuring of Division 17 of the APA provided doctoral-level counseling psychologists with a professional organization that represented their interests. This move was instrumental in the formation of the American Personnel and Guidance Association (APGA) (George & Cristiani, 1986). Founded in 1952, the APGA came into being through the merger of several existing professional organizations (Kaplan, 2002). The National Vocational Guidance Association (NVGA) was the oldest of the founding groups. Established in 1913, it prepared youth for the work world. It therefore had a direct tie to the pioneering work of Parsons and provided an organizational link to the historical root of the counseling profession. A second group, the American College Personnel Association (ACPA), was founded in 1924. Members of this group assisted college students with admissions procedures, course selection, financial aid, student employment, academic performance, and mental health. A third group, the Student Personnel Association for Teacher Education (SPATE), was established in 1931. Finally, the National Association of Guidance Supervisors and Counselor Trainers (NAGSCT) was established in 1940, so it is youngest of the founding organizations. Now known as the Association for Counselor Education and Supervision, this organization brought a tradition of training and research to the APGA.

Super (1955) notes that the APGA initially functioned more as an interest group than as a bona fide professional organization, because it did not formulate standards for membership. Rather, it provided a canopy under which the original organizations were able to retain their separate identities while facilitating cooperative efforts (Brooks & Weikel, 1996). The primary reason for the coming together of these organizations was, first, to pool their resources in order to hold a national conference and, second, to share administrative staff in order to save money. Thus, from the start, the APGA (now ACA, the American Counseling Association) served as an umbrella organization for widely diverse professional groups.

The APGA provided the organizational structure necessary for the development of a true profession. With the establishment of the Council for Accreditation of Counseling and Related Educational Programs (CACREP, 2009a), the profession could demonstrate that it possessed a clearly defined training model that defined core as well as specialty competencies. Second, by creating NBCC (National Board of Certified Counselors), counselors could publicly demonstrate their competency by attaining professional certification. Third, the professional association as well as specific divisions developed codes of ethics, which provided the profession with a set of standards by which it could regulate the conduct of the profession.

THE PROFESSIONALIZATION AND EXPANSION OF MENTAL HEALTH COUNSELING

Although the profession of counseling did not rapidly expand during the 1950s and early 1960s, a number of circumstances paved the way for future expansion of the profession. They included overpopulated mental institutions, the increased effectiveness of pharmacological treatment of mental illness, limited community access to counseling services, and passage of the Community Mental Health Centers Act of 1963.

PROBLEMS IN THE MENTAL HEALTH SYSTEM

By the 1950s, public attention was again drawn to the inhumane care received by patients in mental health hospitals. These institutions were accused of being no more than places of detainment offering an inadequate solution to the social problem of mental illness. Deutsch (1948) stated that mental hospitals had become an American disgrace. Adding fuel to the argument that patients were not benefiting from long-term inpatient treatment, Hans Eysenck (1952) concluded in an important article that studies up to that time had failed to demonstrate the effectiveness of psychotherapy with neurotic clients: "Roughly two-thirds of a group of neurotic patients will recover or improve to a marked extent within about two years of the onset of their illness, whether they are treated by means of psychotherapy or not" (p. 322). Eysenck wrote this comment when the nation's population of patients in mental hospitals was at its highest level (Cutler, 1992).

INCREASED EFFECTIVENESS OF PSYCHOPHARMACOLOGICAL INTERVENTIONS

The modern era of psychopharmacology began in 1952 with the introduction of Chlorpromazine (thorazine), an antipsychotic medication that soon became the medication of choice in the treatment of schizophrenia (Preston, O'Neal, & Talago, 2010). By the late 1950s, two classes of antidepressants—tricyclics and monoamine oxidase (MAO) inhibitors—had demonstrated clinical effectiveness and were being prescribed by psychiatrists. Clinical tests were being conducted to determine the effectiveness of lithium to treat manic depression (i.e., bipolar disorder). With the introduction of chlordiazepoxide (Librium) in 1960, a new era of pharmacological treatment for anxiety disorders began (Pirodsky & Cohn, 1992).

The introduction of psychopharmacological interventions in the treatment of mental illness and emotional distress had significant consequences for the consumers of mental health services. These medications were providing successful treatment for a variety of mental conditions that, up to this point, had required inpatient care. In addition, it gave impetus to the development of innovative counseling theories and techniques that could be applied in outpatient settings. Furthermore, because of the poor track record of institutionalized care and the financial burden it placed on patients and taxpayers, the idea of community-based treatment for mental illness and emotional disorders gained traction among politicians and the service delivery community.

INNOVATIONS IN COUNSELING THEORIES AND TECHNIQUES

The publication of "The Effects of Psychotherapy: An Evaluation" by Eysenck (1952) challenged clinicians and researchers to demonstrate that psychotherapy was, in fact, effective. A number of counselors and psychotherapists had become quite disenchanted with the traditional theories and techniques of counseling and began to experiment with alternative approaches. The new breed of theorists and clinicians included Albert Ellis (1962), Aaron Beck (1967), and Joseph Wolpe (1958). These were scientist-practitioners who combined focused treatment of specific symptoms with the precision of empirically based outcome studies. They demonstrated the effectiveness of counseling and psychotherapy in the treatment of depressive and anxiety-based disorders. Murray Bowen (1960) and Nathan Ackerman (Ackerman & Sobel, 1950) pointed the treatment of mental illness in new directions by seeing the family system as the most basic unit of treatment.

The work of these pioneers in counseling theory paved the way for counselors and psychologists to work alongside psychiatrists in the treatment of mental illness and emotional disorder. Each discipline could make unique contributions to the successful treatment of a variety of diagnosed conditions in settings that were less restrictive than mental hospitals.

LIMITED AVAILABILITY OF AND ACCESS TO COMMUNITY-BASED SERVICES

By the mid-1950s, flaws in the existing mental health service delivery system were being exposed. Furthermore, clinically effective and time-efficient pharmacological treatments were being developed that could be readily applied in outpatient settings. However, the number of community-based clinics was few, and access to available services was limited.

It became clear that something needed to be done about making adequate treatment available to the mentally ill living in communities. Although the VA sought to train psychologists for service delivery to the public sector, more and more professionally trained psychologists entered into private practice. Enticed by the shortage of psychiatrists and attracted to the increased autonomy and income, many psychologists left public service to hang out their shingle (Cummings, 1990). In a study sponsored by the Joint Commission on Mental Illness and Health, Albee (1959) assessed the need for mental health professionals and concluded that only a significant increase in the recruitment and training of mental health workers would result in a sufficient number of professional personnel to eliminate the glaring deficiencies in our care of mental patients.

THE COMMUNITY MENTAL HEALTH CENTERS ACT OF 1963

Given the situation just described, the U.S. Congress passed the Mental Health Study Act of 1958. Its purpose was to provide "an objective, thorough, and nationwide analysis and reevaluation of the human and economic problems of mental illness" (Joint Commission on Mental Illness and Health, 1961, p. 301). The final report of this commission became part of the impetus for the proposal of a new National Mental Health Program. President John F. Kennedy believed that the implementation of this program could lead to the eventual phasing out of state mental hospitals, which would be replaced by high-quality treatment centers located in the patient's community (Cutler, 1992).

On October 31, 1963, President Kennedy signed into law the Community Mental Health Centers Act. This act set into motion the establishment of a large number of mental health centers around the country, which were mandated to provide five basic services: inpatient treatment for short-term care, outpatient treatment, partial hospitalization, crisis intervention, and consultation and education services. In addition, their designation as comprehensive centers required them to offer diagnostic, rehabilitation, precare and aftercare, training, and research and evaluation services. In 1968, the act was amended to support the creation of alcohol and drug abuse services (Cutler, 1992). The act was again modified in 1970 to require mental health services for children.

Staffing needs greatly increased with the development of this national network of community mental health centers (Hershenson & Berger, 2001). A decline in the number of school counseling positions, combined with an abundance of recent graduates from counselor education program, created a pool of trained employees for these centers (Brooks & Weikel, 1996). Other community-based agencies were inaugurated, and by the late 1960s, many counselors were employed in youth services, drug and alcohol treatment centers, and crisis and runaway shelters. Counselors were generally trained in academic programs that were not clinically oriented, so they were often hired initially as paraprofessionals. However, they were soon recognized as being among the primary providers of care in community mental health and other human service organizations (Brooks & Gerstein, 1990).

EMERGENCE OF MENTAL HEALTH COUNSELING

Recognizing this trend in work settings, counselor education programs began to develop courses and training models that would equip graduates for work in community settings. A variety of community counseling programs emerged after 1970, and interest was expressed in the development of specific training standards for community counseling programs. In 1981, CACREP was established and began to accredit master's programs in community and other agency settings (CCOAS) (Hershenson & Berger, 2001). Standards for the accreditation of programs in mental health counseling were established in 1988 (Smith & Robinson, 1996).

However, the APGA had no division that specifically served the interests and needs of community and agency counselors. Although many of the counselors working in community and private practice settings were members of APGA, a large number of them believed that they had unique professional concerns that the existing professional organizations were not addressing (Colangelo, 2009). They were not working in school settings or dealing with vocational and guidance issues. As Seiler (1990) notes, mental health counselors "did not work exclusively with mental illness; we did not work solely through the social service system; nor was our clinical work mainly with marriages or families in trouble" (p. 7). Yet the foundations of normal human development, prevention, and mental health education served counselors well in community settings.

Calls for the formation of a division within the APGA for mental health and community-based counselors began around 1975 (Brooks & Weikel, 1996). In discussing their concern about the lack of a professional organization for community counselors, James Messina and Mancy Spisso prompted a letter written by Edward Anderson and others to the *APGA Guidepost*, which called for greater representation and recognition of nonschool counselors within the organization. Messina contacted APGA president Thelma

Daley, who sent information regarding the establishment of new divisions. In May 1976, the American Mental Health Counselors Association was born (Weikel, 1996).

The first AMHCA conference took place in March 1977 and was scheduled concurrently with the annual APGA convention. AMHCA grew rapidly from 50 original members to almost 500 by the end of the first conference. One year later, the membership of AMHCA had increased to around 1,500. In July 1978, the APGA approved the AMHCA proposal for affiliation, allowing it to become the 13th division. Within a few years, the membership of AMHCA had ballooned to 12,000 (Weikel, 1996).

The new division quickly went about the work of establishing a solid foundation for the profession (Weikel, 1996). A special ad hoc committee created a "Blueprint for the Mental Health Counseling Profession," which proposed the founding of the National Academy of Certified Clinical Mental Health Counselors (NACCMHC). The academy, which eventually affiliated with the NBCC and the Association for Counselor Education and Supervision (ACES), established criteria for professional certification of MHCs (i.e., the CCMHC). Publications were developed by early 1979 to communicate professional news (i.e., *AMHCA News*) and support the accumulation of scholarly literature for the profession (i.e., *The American Mental Health Counselors Association Journal*).

LICENSURE OF MENTAL HEALTH AND PROFESSIONAL COUNSELORS

With increased numbers of mental health professionals working in private practice and agency settings, it became apparent among these practitioners that their legitimacy in the eyes of the public would occur only through regulation of their professions via state licensure. In 1950, professional psychology was the first mental health discipline to legislate state licensure laws (Cummings, 1990). Clinical social work followed the path blazed by psychology but stayed behind the pace of psychologists by about 10 years.

In 1974, the APGA adopted a position paper titled "Licensure in the Helping Professions" and appointed a special committee on counselor licensure (Bloom et al., 1990). These actions helped to secure passage of the first counselor licensure law through the Virginia legislature in 1976.

THE CONSOLIDATION OF THE MENTAL HEALTH COUNSELING PROFESSION

As mental health counseling moved into the 1980s, it had clearly established itself as a distinct profession. VanZandt (1990) identifies distinct professions as characterized by "role statements, codes of ethics, accreditation guidelines, competency standards, licensure, certification and other standards of excellence" (p. 243). APGA and AMHCA, along with affiliated organizations such as CACREP and NBCC, had secured a place for mental health counselors among other allied mental health professions.

However, recognition of the new kid on the block did not come easily. In 1982, the American Psychiatric Association, the National Association of Social Workers, the American Nursing Association, and the American Psychological Association initiated the Joint Commission on Interprofessional Affairs in an attempt to unite their efforts to raise funding for mental health (Cummings, 1990). This group saw the respective professions as the major mental health professions and acted to keep other emerging mental health professions from entering into the dialogue. Thus, although they possessed all of the properties of a profession, licensed mental health counselors were not permitted to sit at the same table with the "elite four." This state of affairs blocked the young profession from procuring its "piece of the pie," such as federal funding for programming, state licensure status, recognition as a service provider for government employees and members of the armed forces, and reimbursement for professional services from Medicare and Medicaid.

Furthermore, the nation, under the influence of Reaganomics, saw significant cutbacks in federal funding of mental health programs, research, and initiatives. This shift in federal policy coincided with the rise in managed mental health care. Marked shrinkage occurred in the number of private practices as cost containment measures cut deeply into profits. Community mental health centers no longer could support extensive outpatient programs because the practice of managed care placed limits on the number of sessions.

The counseling profession evolved with these changing times. First, it became clear that the name of the professional association did not reflect the type of work done by its members. It responded by changing its name, in 1983 to the American Association of Counseling and Development, and in 1993 to the American Counseling Association (its current name). Second, to support mental health counselors' efforts at achieving consistent reimbursement of services from third parties, a comprehensive set of national standards for mental health counselors was adopted. Third, to meet the needs of a changing American society, the professional association moved to promote multicultural competencies among its practitioners. Fourth, the AMHCA moved out from under the ACA umbrella. While remaining as a division within the organization, AMHCA took steps that enabled it to function in a more collaborative and less affiliative relationship with the ACA.

CHANGING ROLES, TOOLS, AND CONTEXTS: THE MENTAL HEALTH PROFESSIONS MOVE INTO THE 21ST CENTURY

The mental health professions continued to adapt to changing times as they entered the 21st century. Several important trends exerted influence on the roles, tools, contexts, and training of mental health counselors and allied practitioners. These trends include

- applications of technology in basic research, mental health services, and counselor education and supervision;
- influence of positive psychology and increased research into wellness; and
- responses to natural and human-made disasters.

Each of these trends has had far-reaching effects. These will be discussed briefly in this section. More detailed considerations of these trends are found in the chapters that follow.

APPLICATION OF TECHNOLOGY

In the early 1980s, I typed my master's thesis on an electronic typewriter and calculated many of the statistical tests using a handheld calculator. Page by page, I leafed through psychological abstracts in search of articles for my review of the literature. Soon afterward, I found employment as a licensed professional counselor in Ohio, where I communicated my progress notes to the secretary via a dictaphone. She would then listen to my mutterings on the cassette tape and type each entry onto the appropriate form. By 1991, I was able to write my doctoral dissertation on my desktop computer, and I used SPSS on the university-based computer for the statistical analysis. I kept the U.S. Postal Service in business by regularly using overnight delivery to relay the most recent drafts to my committee chairperson. Today, I have access to SPSS on my desktop computer, carry around a laptop when I am "writing on the run," search for the pertinent professional literature by conducting detailed searches of databases in mere minutes without leaving the confines of my office, and distribute drafts of this text to readers and editors as attachments to e-mail messages.

In recent years, computers and the ability to transfer information electronically have revolutionized our profession. The applications of such technology are too numerous to mention. But clearly, the mental health counseling profession has fully entered the era of electronic information transmission. For example, Riemer-Reiss (2000) notes the usefulness of e-mail systems for the delivery of mental health counseling services. Telecounseling can assist in connecting underserved clients with needed or desired services. For example, Warren (2012) reports the enhancement of rational emotive behavior therapy with the use of mobile mind-mapping tools. Distance individual and group counseling can take place in Internet-based chat rooms and are potentially conducive to openness and honesty in a less threatening environment than traditional service settings (Ancis, 1998). Consumers have increased access to a wide array of online mental health–related resources (Kreutzer, West, Sherron, Wehman, & Fry, 1992), and counselors play a critical role in directing clients to credible sources of information. Employee assistance and psychoeducational programming on topics such as stress management, eating disorders, depression, or parenting skill training can be delivered to persons who might not otherwise take advantage of traditional services. Video conferencing is being used to conduct supervision of practicum and internship students across international borders (Panos, Panos, Cox, Roby, & Matheson, 2002).

The application of technology in neuroscience and cognitive psychology has also advanced our understanding of the involvement of the neurological mechanisms that underlie addictions, mental illness, recovery, and wellness. The nature-nurture chasm has been bridged. Increasingly, the bidirectional, reciprocal connection between biology and psychology informs the practice of clinical assessment and intervention. Insight into plasticity of the brain illuminates the person-environment interactions underlying counseling-related processes of change (Oss, 2011). The mental health professions are quickly moving toward the linking of neuroscience and prevention work as our understanding of the brain's ability to produce new cells is harnessed. Furthermore, use of scanning technologies to test for presence of addiction, schizophrenia, or bipolar disorder looms on the horizon.

Distance education, counseling, and supervision have become common with the innovative application of technology. Increasingly, counselor education is going online. Counselors deliver services across state and international boundaries in virtual therapy rooms. Software applications, such as Skype © and Adobe Connect ©, enable expert consultation and supervision to be delivered to remote areas. Training models have been revised to accommodate the changing knowledge base and skills required of mental health professionals (e.g., CACREP, 2009). Standards for ethical and best practice of technology have been integrated into the 2005 ACA and 2010 AMHCA codes of ethics (ACA, 2005; AMHCA, 2010).

INFLUENCE OF POSITIVE PSYCHOLOGY AND RESEARCH INTO WELLNESS

The mental health professions have been influenced by recent research into positive psychology and the distinction between mental health and mental illness. M.E.P. Seligman (2002, 2011) has been a pioneer in the expansion of basic psychological research into the nature of positive emotional experience and behavior. Likewise, Fredrickson (2009) has demonstrated that a 3:1 ratio of positivity to negativity is critical if persons are to experience increased levels of wellness and resiliency. Research by Keyes (2005, 2007) and others has demonstrated the separate but related dimensions of mental health and mental illness. Persons without mental illness may still languish in the experience of daily living. Furthermore, persons diagnosed with moderate and severe mental illness can recover from their condition through the application of wellness-based interventions (Ralph & Corrigan, 2005).

The influence of this trend on the mental health professions has been profound. Principles of wellness and positive psychology are clearly integrated in *Transforming Mental Health Care in America: The Federal Action Agenda* (Substance Abuse and Mental Health Services Administration, 2005), which puts forth an agenda for changing the existing national mental-health-service-delivery system and proposes a system "driven by consumer and family needs that focuses on building resilience and facilitating recovery" (p. 3). Furthermore, mental health counselors, practicing from a wellness perspective, encourage clients to implement strength-based, solution-focused patterns of living that enable them to live their life rather than their diagnosis.

RESPONSE TO NATURAL AND HUMAN-MADE DISASTERS

Recent times have been marked by natural and human-made tragedies. Major earthquakes, tsunamis, and hurricanes have wrought destruction across parts of the world. In addition, mindless acts of terrorism, suicide bombings, and shooting rampages have destroyed the lives of many individuals and wreaked havoc and a culture of fear on survivors. The experiences of first responders and the low to moderate levels of felt risk brought on by the constant barrage of media presentations of these happenings contribute to a widespread epidemic of secondary trauma.

The vital importance of having available a nucleus of well-trained early-mental-health first responders is quite evident (Rogers, 2007). Clinical mental health counselors, given their historic emphasis on prevention, facilitation of wellness, and the ecological context, are uniquely positioned to provide emergency services to individuals, families, and communities. Increased service opportunities are emerging in community health, disaster preparedness programs, and emergency response/delivery systems. Counselor training has adapted to the need for a skilled mental health workforce. A variety of field manuals and protocols have been developed to guide mental health providers (e.g., DeWolfe, 2000). In addition, the 2009 CACREP standards set criteria for counselor education programs in training counselors in disaster and emergency preparedness, response, and service delivery (CACREP, 2009).

CONCLUSION

This chapter has provided a brief overview of the predominant historical views of mental health and mental illness. In addition, the roots and development of the allied mental health professions have been identified and are summarized in Figure 2.1. I hope the figure will give you a better understanding of who mental health and community counselors are and what their historical position is relative to the other professions. Clearly, the mental health counseling profession has distinct historical roots that give rise to a unique philosophical perspective on the nature of the human condition and how best to facilitate mental health among individuals, families, and communities.

The profession is well positioned to meet the needs and demands of our contemporary society, and it is increasingly recognized as a primary mental health care provider. As we have noted, psychology and social work have been recognized as service providers for over a century. As a result, they have greater political power and are therefore known by the public and potential consumers. Clinical mental health counselors are the new kids on the block, and their effectiveness is

FIGURE 2.1 Development of the Mental Health Professions

	Mid-1800s	1890s	1900–1920	1920–1940	1940–1960	1960–1980	1980–2000	2000–present
Psychiatry	AMSMII (1844); emergence of neurologists	American Medico-Psychological Association (1892); Kraepelin's diagnostic system	Cure for paresis (1917); Freud; Jung; Adler	APsychiA (1927) – American Psychiatric Association; development of counseling theories	WWII; beginnings of psychopharmacology; publication of *DSM-I* (1952)	Medicalization of mental illness	Decreased pole as provider of counseling-related interventions; publication of *DSM-III* (1980); *DSM-IV* (1994))	Development of *DSM-V*
Psychology	Wundt (1879) establishes first psychology lab	Witmer (1896) establishes first psychological clinic; coins term *clinical psychology*	Healy (1908) Juvenile Psychopathic Clinic; intelligence testing	Child guidance clinics; development of projective tests	Proliferation of psychological tests; increased role as providers in WWII; VA training program for PhDs only; APA Division 17	Development of counseling theories and techniques; licensure movement (late 1960s)	Managed care; role in direct service in agency settings decreases	Seeking prescription rights; evidence-based treatment (EBT); positive psychology
Social Work	Dorothea Dix	Charity Organization Society; settlement houses	"Friendly visiting" in home-based service; social justice and advocacy foundations		WWII; National Association of Social Work (1955)	Certification and licensure; establishes case management model in community mental health	Managed care	Evidence-based treatment
Clinical Mental Health Counseling			Frank Parsons (1908) Vocational Bureau in Boston; Clifford Beers and mental hygiene movement	Child guidance; vocational counseling; college counseling centers	WWII; American Personnel and Guidance Association (1952); Carl Rogers and nondirective therapy	Community Mental Health Centers Act (1963); AMHCA (1976); licensure movement begins (1976)	Managed care; increased roles in community and private practices; emphasis on wellness and prevention	Licensure in all 50 states; TRICARE provider status; 20/20 definition of counseling; wellness; EBT
Marriage and Family Therapy				Paul Popenoe; marriage and family counseling	WWII; AAMFC established (1945; now AAMFT)	Development of classic family systems theories –Bowen, Minuchin, Haley	Licensure movement; internal family systems theory	Emotion-focused therapy; evidence-based treatment

becoming recognized by legislators, policymakers, third-party reimbursers, and allied professions). Yet the need for professional advocacy remains (Myers & Sweeney, 2004).

The chapters that follow will provide you with additional understanding of the mental health counseling profession as they explore its underlying theoretical foundations and selected approaches to working with individuals, groups, families, and communities. This information will help you to develop your personal professional identity.

DISCUSSION QUESTIONS

1. Compare and contrast the views of early Greek philosophers with current views of mental health and wellness.
2. To what extent does our current understanding reflect advances resulting from the scientific study of behavior? Is the view that "what goes around comes around" justifiable?
3. Is it appropriate to view the early treatments of abnormal behavior (in, e.g., the Greek era and Middle Ages) as primitive and inferior? Or is it reasonable to view such treatments through a cross-cultural lens and see degrees of relevance and validity in these approaches?
4. In what ways did the material discussed in this chapter help you to better understand the nature of mental health counseling?

SUGGESTED ACTIVITIES

1. Do further research on the historical roots of the mental health professions. Then draw a genogram of the mental health counseling profession that communicates its connections to a philosophical heritage and the allied professions.
2. Explore in more detail the life of one of the founders of the mental health professions. Consider the extent to which that person's heritage and life experiences were reflected in his or her professional legacy.
3. Identify a specific category of mental illness and investigate how the understanding of it has evolved over time. For example, you might explore the historical development of the understanding of autism, attention deficit hyperactivity disorder, dissociative identity disorder, or personality disorder.
4. Investigate in more depth the interaction between sociocultural trends and the development of the counseling profession. To what extent have these forces shaped the contours of the mental health counseling profession over the past century?

REFERENCES

Ackerman, N., & Sobel, R. (1950). Family diagnosis: An approach to the preschool child. *American Journal of Orthopsychiatry, 20,* 744–753.

Albee, G. W. (1959). *Mental health manpower trends.* New York, NY: Basic Books.

American Counseling Association. (2005). *ACA code of ethics.* Alexandria, VA: Author.

American Mental Health Counselors Association. (2010). *Code of ethics of the American Mental Health Counselors Association–2010 revision.* Alexandria, VA: Author.

American Psychological Association, Committee on Training in Clinical Psychology. (1947). Recommended graduate training programs in clinical psychology. *American Psychologist, 2,* 539–558.

Anastasi, A., & Urbina, S. (1997). *Psychological testing* (7th ed.). Upper Saddle River, NJ: Prentice Hall.

Ancis, J. R. (1998). Cultural competency training at a distance: Challenges and strategies. *Journal of Counseling and Development, 76,* 134–142.

Axinn, J., & Levin, H. (1997). *Social welfare: A history of the American response to need* (4th ed.). New York, NY: Dodd-Mead.

Beck, A. T. (1967). *Depression: Clinical, experimental, and theoretical aspects.* New York, NY: Harper & Row.

Beers. C. W. (1908). *A mind that found itself.* Garden City, NY: Longman Green.

Bloom, J., Gerstein, L., Tarvydas, V., Conaster, J., Davis, E., Kater, D., et al. (1990). Model legislation for licensed professional counselors. *Journal of Counseling and Development, 68,* 511–523.

Bowen, M. (1960). A family concept of schizophrenia. In D. D. Jackson (Ed.), *The etiology of schizophrenia.* New York, NY: Basic Books.

Bronfenbrenner, U. (1947). Research planning in neuropsychiatry and clinical psychology in the veterans administration. *Journal of Clinical Psychology, 3,* 33–38.

Brooks, D. K., & Gerstein, L. H. (1990). Counselor credentialing and interprofessional collaboration. *Journal of Counseling and Development, 68,* 477–484.

Brooks, D. K., & Weikel, W. J. (1996). Mental health counseling: The first twenty years. In W. J. Weikel & A. J. Palmo (Eds.), *Foundations in mental health counseling* (2nd ed.) (pp. 5–29). Springfield, IL: Thomas.

Cangemi, J. P., & Kowalski, C. J. (1993). Does a hierarchy of significance exist in psychology and the mental health disciplines? *Education, 113,* 489–497.

Carson, R. C., Butcher, J. N., & Mineka, S. (2002). *Fundamentals of psychology and modern life.* Boston, MA: Allyn & Bacon.

Casselberry, W. S. (1935). The psychologist in private practice. *Psychological Exchange, 4,* 57–58.

Colangelo, J. J. (2009). The American Mental Health Counselors Association: Reflection on 30 historic years. *Journal of Counseling and Development, 87,* 234–240.

Corey, G. (2009). *Theory and practice of counseling and psychotherapy* (8th ed.). Pacific Grove, CA: Brooks/Cole.

Crane, L. (1925). A plea for the training of psychologists. *Journal of Abnormal and Social Psychology, 20,* 228–233.

Cummings, N. A. (1990). The credentialing of professional psychologists and its implication for the other mental health disciplines. *Journal of Counseling and Development, 68,* 485–490.

Cutler, D. L. (1992). A historical overview of community mental health centers in the United States (pp. 1–22). In S. Cooper & T. H. Lentner (Eds.), *Innovations in community mental health.* Sarasota, FL: Professional Resource Press.

Davidson, G. C., Neale, J. N., Blankstein, K. R., & Flett, G. L. (2005). *Abnormal psychology* (2nd Canadian ed.). Mississauga, ON: Wiley Canada.

Dawis, R. V. (1992). The individual differences tradition in counseling psychology. *Journal of Counseling Psychology, 39,* 7–19.

Deutsch, A. (1948). *The shame of the states.* New York, NY: Harcourt, Brace.

DeWolfe, D. J. (2000). *Field manual for mental health and human service workers in major disasters.* (DHHS Publication No. ADM 90-537). Washington , DC: Substance Abuse and Mental Health Services Administration: Department of Health and Human Services.

Egan, G., & Cowan, M. A. (1979). *People in systems: A model for development in the human-service professions and education.* Monterey, CA: Brooks/Cole.

Ellis, A. (1962). *Reason and emotion in psychotherapy.* New York, NY: Lyle Stuart.

Eysenck, H. (1952). The effects of psychotherapy: An evaluation. *Journal of Consulting Psychology, 16,* 319–324.

Fancher, R. T. (1995). *Cultures of healing: Correcting the image of American mental health care.* New York, NY: W. H. Freeman.

Fenell, D. L. (2012). *Counseling families: An introduction to marriage, couple, and family therapy.* Denver, CO: Love.

Fredrickson, B. L. (2009). *Positivity.* New York, NY: Three Rivers Press.

George, R. L., & Cristiani, T. S. (1986). *Counseling theory and practice* (2nd ed.). Upper Saddle River, NJ: Prentice Hall.

Halgin, R. P. & Whitbourne, S. K. (2010). *Abnormal psychology: Clinical perspectives on psychological disorders* (6th ed.). Boston, MA: McGraw-Hill.

Haynes, D. T., & White, B. W. (1999). Will the "real" social work please stand up? A call to stand for professional unity. *Social Work, 44,* 385–392.

Hershenson, D. B., & Berger, G. P. (2001). The state of community counseling: A survey of directors of CACREP-accredited programs. *Journal of Counseling and Development, 79,* 188–193.

Hull, C. L. (1928). *Aptitude testing.* Yonkers, NY: World Books.

Jaffee v. Redmond, 518 U.S. 1. (1996). Joint Commission on Mental Illness and Health. (1961). *Action for mental health.* New York, NY: Basic Books.

Kaplan, D. M. (2002). Celebrating 50 years of excellence! *Journal of Counseling and Development, 80,* 261–263.

Kaplan, R. M., & Saccuzzo, D. P. (2009). *Psychological testing: Principles, applications, and issues* (7th ed.). Belmont, CA: Wadsworth.

Keyes, C. L. M. (2005). Mental illness and/or mental health? Investigating axioms of the complete state model of health. *Journal of Consulting and Clinical Psychology, 73,* 539–548.

Keyes, C. L. M. (2007). Promoting and protecting mental health as flourishing: A complementary strategy for improving national mental health. *American Psychologist, 62,* 95–108.

Korchin, S. J. (1976). *Modern clinical psychology: Principles of intervention in the clinic and community.* New York, NY: Basic Books.

Kreutzer, J. S., West, M., Sherron, P., Wehman, P., & Fry, R. (1992). Computer technology in vocational rehabilitation for persons with traumatic brain injury. *Journal of Head Trauma Rehabilitation, 7,* 70–80.

Laughlin, P. R., & Worley, J. L. (1991). Roles of the American Psychological Association in the development of internships in psychology. *American Psychologist, 46,* 430–436.

Leahey, T. H. (1980). *A history of psychology: Main Currents in psychological thought.* Englewood Cliffs, NJ: Prentice Hall.

Linhorst, D. M. (2006). *Empowering people with severe mental illness: A practical guide.* New York, NY: Oxford University Press.

Lynch, R. K., & Maki, D. (1981). Searching for structure: A trait-factor approach to vocational rehabilitation. *Vocational Guidance Quarterly, 30,* 61–68.

McGovern, C. M. (1985). *Masters of madness: The social origins of the American psychiatric profession.* Hanover, NH: University Press of New England.

Morgan, J. (1947). Training clinical psychologists in the veterans administration. *Journal of Clinical Psychology, 3,* 28–33.

Myers, J. E., & Sweeney, T. J. (2004). Advocacy for the counseling profession: Results of a national survey. *Journal of Counseling and Development, 82,* 466–471.

Nichols, M. P. (2010). *Family therapy: Concepts and methods* (9th ed.). Boston, MA: Allyn & Bacon.

Nugent, F. A. (2000). *Introduction to the profession of counseling* (3rd ed.). Upper Saddle River, NJ: Prentice Hall.

Oss, M. E. (2011). Wellness and prevention: Key elements in the next generation of behavioral health service delivery systems. In N. A. Cummings & W. T. O'Donohue (Eds.), *Understanding the behavioral healthcare crisis: The promise of integrated care and diagnostic reform.* New York, NY: Routledge.

Panos, P. T., Panos, A., Cox, S. E., Roby, J. L., & Matheson, K. W. (2002). Ethical issues concerning the use of videoconferencing to supervise international social work field practicum students. *Journal of Social Work Education, 38,* 421–437.

Parsons, F. (1909). *Choosing a vocation.* Boston, MA: Houghton Mifflin.

Pirodsky, D. M., & Cohn, J. S. (1992). *Clinical primer of psychopharmacology: A practical guide* (2nd ed.). New York, NY: McGraw-Hill.

Plato, n.d. *The laws* (Vol. 5). (G. Burges, Trans.). London, England: George Bell & Sons.

Polvan, N. (1969). Historical aspects of mental ills in Middle East discussed. *Roche Reports, 6*(12), 3.

Preston, J. D., O'Neal, J. H., & Talaga, M. C. (2010). *Handbook of clinical psychopharmacology for therapists* (6th ed.). Oakland, CA: New Harbinger.

Ralph, R. O. & Corrigan, P. W. (2005). *Recovery in mental illness: Broadening our understanding of wellness.* Washington, DC: American Psychological Association.

Resnick, R. J. (1997). A brief history of practice—Expanded. *American Psychologist, 52,* 463–468.

Riemer-Reiss, M. L. (2000). Utilizing distance technology for mental health counseling. *Journal of Mental Health Counseling, 22,* 189–203.

Rogers, C. (1942). *Counseling and psychotherapy.* Boston: Houghton Mifflin.

Rogers, C. (1961). *On being a person.* Boston, MA: Houghton Mifflin.

Rogers, J. R. (2007). Disaster response and the mental health counselor. *Journal of Mental Health Counseling, 29,* 1–3.

Seiler, G. (1990). Shaping the destiny of the new profession: Recollections and reflections on the evolution of mental health counseling (p. 85). In G. Seiler (Ed.), *The mental health counselor's sourcebook.* New York, NY: Human Sciences Press.

Seligman, M. E. P. (2002). *Authentic happiness.* New York, NY: Free Press.

Seligman, M. E. P. (2011). *Flourish: A visionary new understanding of happiness and well-being.* New York, NY: Free Press.

Sherman, R., & Fredman, N. (1986). *Handbook of structured techniques in marriage and family therapy.* New York, NY: Brunner/Mazel.

Smith, H. B., & Robinson, G. P. (1996). Mental health counseling: Past, present, and future (pp. 38–50). In W. J. Weikel, & A. J. Palmo (Eds.), *Foundations of mental health counseling* (2nd ed.). Springfield, IL: Thomas.

Sokal, M. M. (1992). Origins and early years of the American Psychological Association, 1890–1906. *American Psychologist, 47,* 111–122.

Substance Abuse and Mental Health Services Administration. (2005). *Transforming mental health care in America. Federal Action Agenda: First steps.* DHHS Pub. No. SMA-05-4060. Rockville, MD: Author.

Super, D. E. (1955). Transition: From vocational guidance to counseling psychology. *Journal of Counseling Psychology, 2,* 3–9.

VanZandt, C. E. (1990). Professionalism: A matter of personal initiatives. *Journal of Counseling and Development, 68,* 243–245.

Viney, W., & King, D. B. (2003). *A history of psychology: Ideas and context* (3rd ed.). Boston, MA: Allyn & Bacon.

Warren, J. M. (2012). Mobile mind-mapping: Using mobile technology to enhance rational emotive behavior therapy. *Journal of Mental Health Counseling, 34,* 72–81.

Weikel, W. J. (1996). The mental health counselors association. In W. J. Weikel, & A. J. Palmo (Eds.), *Foundations of mental health counseling* (2nd ed.). Springfield, IL: Thomas.

Whiteley, J. M. (1984). A historical perspective on the development of counseling psychology as a profession (pp. 3–55). In S. Brown & R. Lent (Eds.). *Handbook of counseling psychology.* New York, NY: Wiley.

Williamson, E. G. (1939). *How to counsel students: A manual of techniques for clinical counselors.* New York, NY: McGraw-Hill.

Witmer, L. (1896). Practical work in psychology. *Pediatrics, 2,* 462–471.

Wolpe, J. (1958). *Psychotherapy by reciprocal inhibition.* Stanford, CA: Stanford University Press.

Woody, R. H., Hansen, J. C., & Rossberg, R. H. (1989). *Counseling psychology: Strategies and services.* Pacific Grove, CA: Brooks/Cole.

Zunker, V. G. (1998). *Career counseling: Applied concepts of life planning* (5th ed.). Pacific Grove, CA: Brooks/Cole.

Theoretical Foundations for Clinical Mental Health Counselors

OUTLINE

Joe has a history of skipping work to go to the bar. He works third shift (12:00 to 8:00 a.m.) at a local factory. On most evenings, he wakes up at around 9:30 p.m. and begins to think about going to work on the assembly line. He does not find much personal satisfaction in the work. Furthermore, Joe complains about the ongoing conflict he has with supervisor and about not getting along with others on the job. As he reflects on his work situation, he begins to think about his favorite bar, which he passes on his way to work. Several friends are there throughout the evening hours.

Joe has become stuck in a pattern in which he tells his wife that he is going in to work early but instead goes to the bar. Joe tells himself that he will only have a beer or two in order to help him cope with his work problems. As he continues to contemplate the tension at work, he concludes that he really needs a few drinks in order to survive. The more he thinks about it, the stronger his urge is to get over to the bar. Joe can hardly wait! He can almost taste the beer by just thinking about it!

However, increasingly (two or three nights a week), Joe never makes it to work. His wife learns about his absences at work when she looks at the automatic bank deposit reports. His take-home pay has decreased significantly and is now a major source of marital conflict and economic hardship. But Joe feels very angry when his wife confronts him. He concludes that she doesn't understand how bad it is for him at work and that he is trying to cope the best he can.

Place yourself in the role of counselor. What is going on with Joe? What do you see as the basic problem, and what factors have contributed to its development? At its root, is Joe struggling with a conflict within himself? Is this problem an indicator of moral weakness or a spiritual problem? Is Joe dealing primarily with an intrapsychic or interpersonal conflict? Or does he have a disease that has no cure and is, perhaps, fatal unless he gets help? As Joe's counselor, what are you going to do about it?

Although you may have felt that a lack of detailed information placed you at a disadvantage, you probably came up with answers to the questions listed. And you may have accomplished this feat without the aid of formalized training! Each of you has personal theories that helped you to make sense of Joe's presenting problem in specific ways. If you take the time to discuss the vignette with classmates, you will find that Joe's presenting problem could be conceptualized in a number of ways.

In a sense, everyone is a theorist of sorts. The term *implicit personality theory*, coined by Bruner and Tagiuri (1954), refers to how people develop ideas regarding the way other people's personal traits and behavioral tendencies fit together. Years of living in close proximity to other people have allowed all of us to develop theories regarding partners, relatives, friends, and specific situations. Understanding a person's characteristics from past observations, we make predictions regarding how that person will act in a specific situation. We then apply our theory to guide our behaviors in relation to that person in this situation.

For example, the telephone rings and I pick up the receiver. I am not familiar with the pleasant-sounding voice that casually but confidently says, "Good afternoon, Mr. Gerj." After a quick assessment, I come to some conclusions: I do not recognize this person's voice; he used *Mr.* instead of my first name or *Dr.,* and he mispronounced my last name; therefore, he must be a telemarketer. My conclusion, then, guides how I listen and respond to what this person has to say. A set of internalized rules, concepts, and assumptions that I hold to be valid enables me to make sense of this situation and respond accordingly.

Returning to Joe, how do your conceptualization and recommendations for Joe differ from those of a mental health or community counselor? In this chapter and the next, you will learn about the types of theories used by mental health practitioners. This chapter explores theories that provide a foundation for mental health and community counseling. In Chapter 4, theories used in counseling and psychotherapy are examined. As you will discover, theory provides lenses through which counselors assign meaning to the client's story and construct cognitive maps that guide every therapeutic move they make.

THEORY AND PERSONAL CHARACTERISTICS OF THE COUNSELOR

None of you entered into your graduate training program with an empty head. Ongoing experience interacts with inherited characteristics to make you the unique person you are—a whole physical, cognitive, social, and spiritual being. This interaction takes place within a specific ecological context and contributes to the development of a self-schema, a worldview, and an interpersonal style. These play a critical role in the formation of your motives for entering the mental health counseling profession. They also influence your functioning in the professional role—your conceptualization of cases, generation of clinical hypotheses, and selection and application of specific theories and techniques.

SELF-SCHEMA

Persons are not passive recipients and processors of information. Rather, as incoming stimuli are sensed, it is necessary to screen and organize new information and integrate it with preexisting knowledge. As we move through early life experiences, internal cognitive structures about ourselves develop that are referred to as *self-schemas* (or *self-schemata*) (Thompson, 1999). These are defined as "cognitive generalizations about the self, derived from past experience, that organize and guide the processing of self-related information contained in the individual's social experiences" (Markus, 1977, p. 64). They may also become generalizations constructed from repeated categorizations and evaluations of others with whom the person interacts with in some way (Cozolino, 2006; Newman & Newman, 2006). Self-schemas serve as templates through which we organize our world.

The processing of information gleaned from ongoing experience is affected by the operation of self-schemas. They exert powerful influences over how we perceive, remember, and evaluate ourselves and others. Markus and Wurf (1987) note several important consequences of their operation: (a) heightened sensitivity to self-relevant stimuli; (b) more efficient information processing of stimuli that are self-congruent;

(c) enhanced recall and recognition of information that is self-congruent; (d) more confident behavioral predictions, attributions, and inferences in areas relevant to one's self-schema; and (e) resistance to information that is incongruent with one's self-schema.

These consequences have important implications for counselors, especially since the operation of the self-schema is outside one's conscious awareness (Carlston, 2010). Information provided by the client is screened, sorted, and categorized through the operation of the counselor's self-schema. Counselors may experience delays in processing and categorizing data that are beyond their experience and do not readily fit with preexisting schemes. Furthermore, in more extreme cases, counselors may simply fail to pick up on data critical to understanding the perspective of the client, especially a client from a different cultural background. Picking up on aspects of the presenting problem that they, too, have experienced, counselors might inadvertently assume sameness and, as a result, respond in ways that are insensitive or disrespectful to the culturally diverse client.

Competent counselors are aware of what they bring to the counseling table. Specifically, they recognize how their self-schemas can interact with their implicit theories to bias their assessments and interventions. Developing a working knowledge of counseling theory helps counselors to understand and respond to the presenting situations of their clients in ways that are not overly tainted by their own personal bias.

WORLDVIEW

Our *worldview* can be defined as the sum total of our beliefs about the world. It is the big picture, a vision that we hold of our universe that shapes the way we make decisions and act in situations. Baruth and Manning (2012) define *worldview* as "one's individual experiences and social, moral, religious, educational, economic, or political inputs shared with other members of one's reference group, such as culture group, racial or ethnic group, family, state, or country" (p. 7). Through the socialization process, people develop this set of presuppositions and assumptions about the makeup of the world as well as about their place and future in it (Sarason, 1984).

All persons entering into counselor training programs have personal worldviews. These preconceived notions about the "way things really are" develop within the context of a sociocultural setting, are deeply ingrained, operate outside of personal awareness, and are often accepted without question. The contents of one's worldview includes basic assumptions about human nature, social relationships, how people relate to nature, time, human activity, the universe, ultimate reality, and the meaning of life (Mahalik, Worthington, & Crump, 1999).

Williams (2003) notes that various psychological processes, such as well-being, attributional style, and relationality, can be reliably predicted by one's worldview. For example, Oyserman, Coon, and Kemmelmeier (2002) found that persons who have worldviews emphasizing individualism tend to display conflict resolution styles characterized by goal orientation, direct communication, confrontation, and arbitration. In contrast, persons holding worldviews that emphasize collectivism prefer indirect high-context communication, accommodation, and negotiation (Oyserman et al., 2002).

Counseling is an interpersonal process where there is potential for the collision of conflicting worldviews. Indeed, a worldview is embedded in the predominant theories of counseling. Furthermore, the worldviews of many counselors are heavily flavored by Western culture and values, which place high value on individuality, personal autonomy, freedom, timeliness, and productivity. Lyddon and Adamson (1992) found that counselors' worldviews influence their preference for counseling approaches. It is vital, therefore, that clinical mental health counselors develop an awareness of their own worldviews (Mahalik et al., 1999). In addition, they must enter into and understand their clients' worldviews so as to facilitate interculturally sensitive communication and relationships, as well as effective counseling (Baruth & Manning, 2012).

INTERPERSONAL STYLE

Persons seeking admission into counseling programs often note the many experiences they have had in which friends and relatives have sought them out for informal counsel when faced with difficult life situations. They see such experiences as affirming their "natural disposition" toward the counseling professions.

Personality characteristics do play a role in our selection and application of counseling theories. For example, extroverts often choose an active role in counseling, gravitate to theories that are action oriented, and set a therapeutic tone of energy and expressiveness (Day, 2007). In contrast, introverts can make good use of time in session and not be overly alarmed by occurrences of silence. In addition, they can be very effective when in low-key, Columbo-type confrontations (Day, 2007). However, timing and sensitivity are critical to successful interventions, and a counselor's natural inclinations might, at times, override good clinical judgment and lead to less than positive outcomes. Thus, counselors do well to identify how interpersonal styles can be used to the benefit of their clients.

So what are some of the implications of one's personal characteristics for his or her application of counseling theory? It is important that counselors be virtuous (Cohen & Cohen, 1999). Counselors who are very knowledgeable in counseling theory and technique but lack virtue, or a fundamental moral goodness, can pose risks to clients by allowing their self-interests to interfere with their primary ethical responsibility of contributing to their clients' welfare. It is critical that counselors be able to set their self-interests aside in order to be fully mindful of the present moment of the clients' experience-in-session (Siegel, 2006).

Furthermore, mental health counselors need resilience to survive the day-to-day work of counseling. The ability to apply counseling theories is compromised if the helping professional cannot bounce back from a difficult session to be effective in the counseling hour that follows.

Mental health professionals who have an accurate awareness of their own personal characteristics are better equipped to effectively integrate client strengths into their intervention strategies (Smith, 2006). I concur with Corsini (1995), who states:

> I believe that if one is to go into the fields of counseling and psychotherapy, then the best theory and methodology to use have to be one's own. The reader will not be either successful or happy using a method not suited to his or her own personality. The really successful therapist adopts or develops a theory and methodology congruent with his or her own personality. (p. 14)

The initial step for counselors in training is to develop accurate self-awareness to guide themselves in choosing approaches that are a good personal fit. A theory is effective only to the extent that a counselor is comfortable using its principles and procedures.

Messer and Gurman (2011) noted that the "buffet table" of counseling theories contains hundreds of items from which to choose! Thus, difficulty in finding an adequate approach is not due to a lack of alternatives. Rather, the mind-boggling task is to find counseling theories that are good matches to the attributes and personal style of the counselor, that fit with the specific client and his or her story, and that, at the same time, provide useful conceptualizations and direction in specific cases.

CLIENT MOTIVATION AND THE PROCESS OF CHANGE: THE TRANSTHEORETICAL MODEL

Clients enter into counseling with different levels of motivation. Some have a great deal of insight into the dynamics of their presenting problems, whereas others have no such insight and really do not understand the necessity for or benefit of treatment. Mental health counselors facilitate change more efficiently when they recognize their client's readiness to change or lack of it. This recognition helps the counselor to work alongside and move with the client rather than engaging in an unproductive game of clinical cajoling.

Prochaska and DiClemente (1984) provide an integrative framework for understanding, assessing, and facilitating behavioral change. Referred to as the *transtheoretical model of behavioral change,* it posits that clients move through five stages in making successful changes in their lives. The five stages of change—precontemplation, contemplation, preparation, action, and maintenance—describe the processes of client change in most counseling theories. Clients can enter into counseling at any of these stages.

Clients in the precontemplation stage are unaware of their behavioral problem, unwilling to change, or discouraged about making helpful changes in their lives (Velasquez, Maurer, Crouch, & DiClemente, 2001). Because they do not see the personal costs or negative aspects of the problem, such clients are not highly motivated to change. These clients benefit from a cost/benefit analysis of their current situation to become more aware of its negative consequences.

The contemplation stage occurs as clients acknowledge the existence of a problem and begin to consider making changes to resolve it (Prochaska & DiClemente, 1984). However, they may not fully understand the nature of the problem, its causes, or its implications. In addition, contemplative clients may experience the ambivalence of desiring a better situation but not wanting to give up old and familiar patterns of behavior. Clients at this stage require encouragement, support, and gentle prodding so that the balance is tipped toward making behavioral change.

Clients in the preparation stage have made an initial commitment to changing and are on the verge of acting on that commitment (Velasquez et al., 2001). As many of us have discovered, the best intentions do not necessarily translate into effective action. So it is with clients in the preparation stage. They are now motivated to change, but they need a systematic plan and a firm commitment to its implementation. Counselors' critical role in this stage is to support the client through the construction of an action or treatment plan. This construction is a collaborative effort in the context of a strong therapeutic relationship.

The action stage is where clients implement the plan to modify their behavior (Prochaska & DiClemente, 1984). Two potential pitfalls must be avoided if clients are to move successfully through this stage. First, initial positive change may be confused with goal attainment. Clients may underestimate the energy and sustained motivation necessary to maintain the desired behavioral pattern over the long haul. Second, after making early strides toward the desired goal, clients may stumble, experience a relapse, or return to a preaction stage. Counselors become "voices of reality" by pointing out such potential traps, consistently encouraging clients, and facilitating relapse prevention planning.

The final stage, maintenance, consists of consolidation of gains made during the action stage and continued efforts to prevent relapse. Traditional counseling addresses termination issues as the intensity and frequency of ongoing treatment decreases. In contrast, the transtheoretical model views maintenance as an ongoing stage that may last up to a lifetime (Velasquez et al., 2001). Follow-up and booster sessions are often scheduled to give clients "check-in" points. Clients are encouraged to schedule additional appointments as desired. Finally, a maintenance plan may be developed that encourages clients to use naturally occurring support systems in their specific ecological setting.

Throughout this process, clinical mental health counselors can assess the client's readiness to change and calibrate dialogue and interventions to the specific stage of the client (Parsons, 2009). Furthermore, the transtheoretical model can be used to promote mental health as well as to treat mental illness.

THE ROLE OF THEORY IN COUNSELING

Formal theories of counseling can be defined as sets of interrelated principles that describe, explain, predict, and guide the counselor's actions in relevant situations. Without such a set of interrelated principles, counselors would be "vulnerable, directionless creatures bombarded with literally hundreds of impressions and pieces of information in a single session" (Prochaska & Norcross, 2010, p. 4). Can you imagine describing the situation of a client without an agreed-on set of constructs and related terminology? Adequate theory provides tools with which counselors systematically select which bits of information presented by the client are relevant to the description of his or her story. When the counselor looks at the information through a theoretical lens, the client's story becomes clear and coherent as the "figure" against the "ground" of the developmental and ecological context. As Millon (2003) notes, "Theory, when properly fashioned, ultimately provides more simplicity and clarity than unintegrated and scattered information" (p. 952).

A good theory also enables counselors to posit reasonable responses to the "why" questions regarding the client's current situation and level of functioning. Although no counseling theory can make truth statements regarding underlying causes, counseling theories do help counselors identify and organize the available data in ways that provide an etiological explanation. For example, psychodynamic theories call attention to the contribution of early childhood development, whereas behavioral theory points to environmental stimuli and consequences. Plausible explanations of the current condition can be derived from either perspective.

With a clear description of the client's condition and an explanation of how it developed, counselors are in a better position to make predictions of the developmental course or prognosis. Being able to identify the present location of the client (description) as well as where he or she has been (explanation), the counselor can generate reasonable hypotheses regarding where the client is likely to go in the near future.

Finally, good theory guides counselors as they work to facilitate change in clients' lives. Each theory suggests specific techniques for influencing clients' thoughts, emotions, and behaviors in directions predicted by that theory. For example, if I view a person's depression through the lens of cognitive theory, I may conclude that the client's condition is at least partly maintained by the subtle operation of cognitive distortions. Using such a theoretical analysis, I will look for cognitive restructuring techniques to lessen these distortions.

For every person you counsel, you develop a case conceptualization, that is, a theory that pulls together the data you have and organizes it in a way that helps explain your client's current, past, and future behavior (Day, 2007). Counseling theory provides the organization that will allow you to accomplish this task. Millon (2003) concludes, "What is elaborated and refined in theory is understanding—an ability to see relations more plainly, to conceptualize more accurately, and to create greater overall coherence in a subject, that is to integrate its elements in a more logical, consistent, and intelligible fashion" (p. 952). Theoretically based case conceptualizations have a natural flow that closely links observations to a coherent rationale for specific forms of intervention. Day (2007) encourages counselors to apply theory on two levels: first, to understand what makes people tick in general (the counseling theory), and second, to understand what makes this particular client tick (the theory of this client or case conceptualization).

Theories are integrated systems that drive the counseling process from start to finish. However, not all theories are created equal. Of the more than 400 counseling theories, some are better than others. On what basis are they evaluated? The following criteria are suggested by Sharf (2012, pp. 2–4) and Millon (2003):

1. *Precision and clarity.* Good theories are based on rules that are clear and use terms that are specific. In addition, they are parsimonious. They use only as many concepts and principles as are necessary to provide adequate descriptions and explanations.
2. *Comprehensiveness.* Good theories explain and predict wide ranges of human behaviors. For example, a comprehensive theory applies to persons of different cultures or in a variety of contexts. A theory that applies only to single males reared by ultraconservative parents is limited in its comprehensiveness.

3. *Testability.* There must be an empirical basis for the theory. If the ideas of a given theory cannot be tested, its validity or reliability cannot be determined. Anecdotal reports or reasoning is an inadequate support for the accuracy (i.e., validity) and consistency (i.e., reliability) of a theory.

4. *Utility.* A good theory proves to be useful to practitioners. It assists counselors in developing helpful descriptions, explanations, and predictions. In addition, a good theory suggests workable plans of interventions to facilitate behavioral change.

5. *Heuristic value.* Good theories promote novel conclusions that, in turn, lead to new experimentation and discoveries.

Although none of the counseling theories fully meet all of the criteria listed, evidence acquired through empirical investigations lends increased support for some theories more than others.

FOUNDATIONAL THEORIES FOR CLINICAL MENTAL HEALTH COUNSELORS

In this section, several sets of theories are described that are the bedrock on which clinical mental health counselors stand. Taken together, these theories provide an orientation for the profession that sets mental health and community counselors apart from the allied mental health professions.

THEORIES OF HUMAN DEVELOPMENT

The emergence of developmental psychology was an important antecedent in the development of mental health counseling (Brooks & Weikel, 1996) and is central to the identity of the profession (Mellin, Hunt, & Nichols, 2011). Indeed, the preamble to the code of ethics for the ACA (American Counseling Association) states that association members are "dedicated to the enhancement of human development throughout the lifespan" (ACA, 2005, p. 3). Beyond providing a theoretical platform for the profession, these theories are applied in the daily work of clinical mental health counselors as they seek to facilitate growth in those whom they treat.

Theories of lifespan development help us understand the unfolding story of persons from conception to death—from the beginning of life to its end as we know it. Several important principles underlie the lifespan perspective (Lefrancois, 1999; Santrock, 2010; Smith & Baltes, 1999):

- *Development is a continuous, lifelong process.* No specific age-related stage dominates the life cycle, and change is a dynamic process occurring throughout one's life. Skillful application of neuroimaging reveals that the brain transforms itself on the basis of daily experience from birth through late-late adulthood (Restak, 2003).
- *Development is relative and plastic.* The course of healthy development can follow a variety of paths and should not be viewed as a simple, straightforward linear

process. In most cases, human development has an ebb and flow much like the tide. For most people, the general direction is increased growth, although the movement may be two steps forward and one step back. Human development is therefore a dynamic process.

- *Human development takes place in a context.* It is common to talk about the ecology of human development. This principle is so basic that it will be discussed further later in this section. For now, we will simply note that lifting persons from their specific environmental context—social, historical, or cultural—leads to a distorted understanding of who they are and what they are experiencing. Individuals' development is influenced by multiple dimensions of a changing universe.
- *Human development is an interactional and bidirectional process.* The interaction between persons and their environment is ongoing and lifelong. The person influences his or her environment, which concurrently influences the person. For example, in the ongoing interactions of parent-child relationships, parents exert an important influence on the behavior of their children, and at the same time, the children are influencing the behavior of their parents.

Broderick and Blewitt (2010) identify three classes of developmental theories: stage models, incremental models, and multidimensional models. I will briefly examine stage and incremental models in this section. Multidimensional models relate, generally, to the ecological perspective and will be considered in a later section of this chapter.

Stage Models. Stage models describe persons as passing through a sequence of stages over the course of the lifespan. Each stage represents a level of functioning that is qualitatively different from the levels of preceding stages. Thus, human development is conceptualized as consisting of a series of steps and plateaus. Several of these theories are based on the epigenetic principle, which states that the various characteristics of organisms have specific times of ascendancy until all parts integrate to form a functioning whole (Erikson, 1968). Several prominent theories of development constructed according to the stage model include Freud's psychosexual theory, Erikson's psychosocial theory, Piaget's theory of cognitive development, Kohlberg's theory of moral development, and Atkinson, Morten, and Sue's theory of racial/cultural identity development. Stage models also serve as frameworks for understanding processes such as language development and social referencing.

Incremental Models. These models view human development as a gradual, cumulative process of change that takes place from conception to death. Whereas stage models emphasize developmental milestones, incremental models focus on smaller, often unnoticed changes that converge so that new skills can emerge. For example, little Beth's first step is a monumental event that enables her to get around with greater efficiency. However, between crawling and walking, a number of foundational physiological, neurological, cognitive, and social factors had to converge for the walking skill to be displayed at a particular time. Prominent theories of development whose tenets are configured according to the incremental model include Pavlov's theory of classical conditioning, Skinner's theory of operant conditioning, Bandura's theory of social learning, Vygotsky's sociocultural theory, Bowlby's attachment theory, and information-processing theory.

Implications for Clinical Mental Health Counselors.   It is beyond the scope of this text to engage in a detailed discussion of the various theories identified in this section. With so many relevant theories from which to choose, my selection of several specific theories may seem somewhat arbitrary and influenced by personal bias. The importance of a working knowledge of human development theories is made clear by the decision of CACREP (Council for Accreditation of Counseling and Related Educational Programs) to include human growth and development as one of its eight common core areas. Ginter (1996, p. 100) identifies the "developmental perspective" as one of the three pillars of mental health counseling.

The foundation of human development across the lifespan has numerous implications for mental health counselors. First, in mental health counseling human normality is the baseline used to understand the human condition. This stance contrasts starkly with that of other mental health professions, whose theories were derived from the study of emotionally distressed and psychologically disordered persons. Rather than generalizing from the abnormal to the normal, Van Hesteren and Ivey (1990, pp. 524–528) point out that mental health counselors conceptualize remedial, crisis, and psychopathological issues from a positive developmental orientation. Achieving wellness, as opposed to the mere absence of symptoms, is therefore the goal of mental health counseling.

Second, individuals are viewed holistically. Our clients are physical, cognitive, psychological, social, and spiritual beings whose component parts form a well-integrated whole. It is a therapeutic error to ignore the complex interrelationship of the component parts. In addition, an intervention focusing on one dimension necessarily influences the other dimensions.

Third, while the study of human development identifies characteristics shared by all persons, each individual is also viewed as a unique being—unlike any other person in the world. From this vantage point, mental health counselors can truly appreciate the unfathomable worth of each client with whom they interact.

Finally, developmental theories help mental health counselors understand normal and atypical life transitions. The quality of clients' adaptation through these transitions is greatly influenced by the unique combinations of strengths and deficits resulting from their developmental histories (Anderson, Goodman, & Schlossberg, 2012). It is critical for mental health counselors to assess clients and their environments in such a way that they are able to capitalize on existing strengths (Cook, 2012). In addition, clients benefit from skill-building approaches through which new strengths can develop.

ECOLOGICAL PERSPECTIVE

As noted in the previous section, persons are best understood when viewed within their unique developmental context. In addition to the foundation of human development, clinical mental health counselors are trained to view the human condition from an ecological perspective.

The ecological theory of Urie Bronfenbrenner (1979, 1989) is a multidimensional model that provides mental health professionals with a framework for viewing human functioning within a developmental and environmental context. Bronfenbrenner sees human development as consisting of a series of ongoing changes involving interactions between individuals and their immediate contexts. In addition, the immediate contexts of individuals also interact with the larger systemic contexts of the environment.

Bronfenbrenner (1979, 1989) identifies four different levels of environmental context in which development occurs. From most proximal to most distal, these are the microsystem, mesosystem, exosystem, and macrosystem. Figure 3.1 illustrates how each level relates to the others.

The microsystem is defined as "a pattern of activities, roles, and interpersonal relationships experienced by developing persons in a given face-to-face setting with particular physical and material features, and containing other persons with distinctive characteristics of temperament, personality, and systems of belief" (Bronfenbrenner, 1989, p. 227). At this level, persons develop within the context of primary face-to-face relationships at home,

FIGURE 3.1 The Ecological Context of Human Development

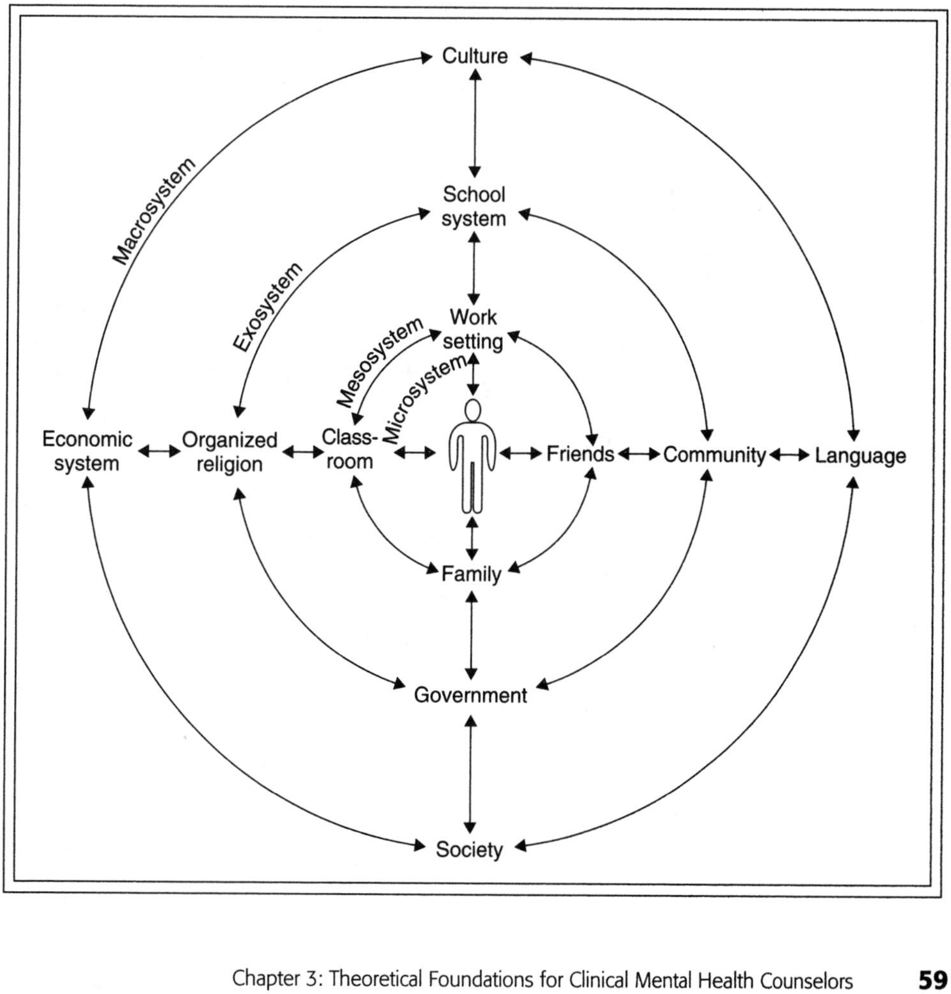

at school, on the playground, in the workplace, and so on. The person enacts specific behaviors in each context that instigate a response from persons in that environment. These responses, in turn, influence and shape the behavior of the developing person. Thus, the relationships within the microsystem are best described as reciprocal and interactive.

The mesosystem refers to "the linkages and processes taking place between two or more settings containing the developing person (e.g., the relations between home and school, school and work place, etc.)" (Bronfenbrenner, 1989, p. 227). The mesosystem, then, is the system of microsystems. The peer group, school, and parents interact with each other while simultaneously interacting with the developing person. For example, Sarah's parents recently had an argument with her schoolteacher. A week later, they are informed that Sarah has misbehaved in class and is receiving an in-school suspension. The parents' response to the misbehavior of their daughter may be tempered by their negative experience with the teacher.

Bronfenbrenner defines the exosystem as encompassing the linkages and processes occurring between two or more settings, at least one of which does not contain the developing person. Events influence the processes in the immediate settings containing the developing person (Bronfenbrenner, 1989). If we continue with the illustration from the previous paragraph, the reaction of Sarah's parents to her in-school suspension might be flavored by their own negative experiences in school, in addition to the experience of their daughter. They may discount Sarah's personal responsibility and see school administrators as being unfair.

The fourth level identified by Bronfenbrenner is the macrosystem. It is defined by all micro-, meso-, and exosystems that characterize a given culture or subculture (Bronfenbrenner, 1989). All of the interactive systems are embedded within a milieu that can be described according to predominant roles, values, expectations, lifestyles, or belief systems (Lefrancois, 1999). For example, the relationship of my adolescent child to his school is quite different from my relationship to my school in the late 1960s. His relationships with peers and teachers are greatly influenced by the time in which he lives.

Implications for Clinical Mental Health Counselors. The implications of ecological theory for mental health counselors are profound. Viewing personal development from the ecological perspective sheds additional light on how specific developmental principles and concepts play out in real-world contexts. Assessment necessarily takes into consideration a broader array of variables that function as separate but related levels of the client's environment. Personal behavior is viewed as a function of the interaction of the person with his or her particular environment (Cook, 2012). The physical and social environments are rarely tidy. The number of potential person-environment interactions make the process of developing case conceptualizations quite complex (Ungar, 2011). This same complexity, though, enables mental health counselors to creatively integrate a variety of personal and environmentally based resources into their treatment plans. Approaches to facilitating change can include both direct and indirect strategies of change.

Consider how the operation of person-environment interactions tempers the benefits of being raised by authoritative parents (Baumrind, 1967, 1991). In a longitudinal study, Steinberg, Lamborn, Darling, Mounts, and Dornbusch (1994) found, as hypothesized, that adolescents whose parents use an authoritative approach display increased academic competence even after ethnicity, socioeconomic status, and household composition are controlled for. However, further analysis (Steinberg, Darling, & Fletcher, in collaboration with Brown & Dornbusch, 1995) of the data revealed that African- and Asian-American high school students whose parents were authoritative did not perform better in school than those adolescents whose parents were not. The expected relationship did appear, though, when the parents of peers were authoritative.

These studies led to a focus on what is termed the *functional community* (Steinberg et al., 1995). In such neighborhoods and communities, nonrelated adults know one another (in, i.e., network closure), and a dominant set of values is accepted within that community (value consensus). Children raised in functional communities receive consistent messages about their behavior and obligations, and both family and nonfamily adults encourage them to behave according to those norms. Steinberg and colleagues (1995) concluded that the key to understanding the influence of parenting during adolescence must go beyond the boundaries of the home and consider the broader context in which the family lives.

The community counseling model (Lewis, Lewis, Daniels, & D'Andrea, 2003) provides an ecologically based framework through which mental health counselors can conceptualize assessment, treatment, program development, and research. Lewis et al. distinguish between services that are directed to clients and those directed to the community. In addition, these services may be delivered through direct and indirect approaches. The model identifies four distinct categories of service: direct client services, direct community services, indirect client services, and indirect community services.

As Lewis and colleagues (2003) note, a truly comprehensive program requires mental health counselors to provide services related to each of the four categories. Effective implementation of such a multifaceted array of services rests on counselors' ability to develop conceptualizations that consider the big picture of direct and indirect influences on their clients. In addition, techniques for intervention go beyond traditional individual, group, and family therapies to include consultation, advocacy, and various forms of psychoeducation.

THEORIES OF MENTAL HEALTH AND THE PREVENTION OF MENTAL ILLNESS

We noted in Chapter 1 that in theory, the emphasis on mental health sets clinical mental health counselors apart from allied mental health professions. Unfortunately, this philosophy does not find consistent expression in practice. Frequently, licensed mental health and professional counselors working in private practice and agency settings rely on—and are therefore, accountable to—third-party reimbursers. The guidelines for most managed care organizations and insurance companies can be stated succinctly: If it is not broken, it doesn't need fixing! So the promotion of mental health is not a billable service. Practitioners engaged in the promotion of mental health obtain funding for their services through grants, independent contracting, and direct billing to clients. Clinical mental health counselors are only beginning to envision and capitalize on opportunities to apply the promotion of mental health within integrated primary health care settings or to persons with severe and persistent mental illness who are working on their recovery.

Although the mental health emphasis seems straightforward, several critical issues loom beneath the surface. First, what is the relationship of mental health to mental illness? Is mental health defined, basically, as the absence of mental illness? If a professional engages in prevention work, has he or she promoted mental health? If mental health is more than mere absence of mental illness, then what is involved in the professional practice of mental health promotion? Indeed, is it possible to promote the mental health and recovery of persons diagnosed with severe and persistent mental illness (e.g., schizophrenia or bipolar disorder)? You will search the professional literature in vain to find any definitive answers to these questions. Theories and opinion abound as scholarly debate continues.

The traditional medical model maintains that mental illness and mental health are the poles on one continuum. This model is illustrated in Figure 3.2. According to this perspective, mental health is normally distributed among the general population, and most of us are within a standard deviation of the mean. However, in times of stress, any one of us is vulnerable to a breakdown in our line of defenses, which cause us emotional distress or diagnosable mental illness. The remediation of mental illness has the effect of promoting mental health. Acceptance of this model underlies the widely held view that controlling or remediating symptoms through medication, in itself, promotes mental health among persons with moderate and severe mental illness. Movement toward increased wellness simply involves progress toward the positive end of the continuum. Hansen (2003) sees the one-dimensional model as closely linked to the medical model and a primary source of professional identity confusion for mental health counselors.

Unfortunately, counseling professionals' unintentional acceptance of the implicit assumptions of this one-dimensional view has had negative consequences for the profession. Sometimes it is assumed that mental health counselors treat relatively normal populations, whereas the treatment of more severe and persistent syndromes is reserved for others in the allied mental health professions. It is as though a theoretical line has been drawn at a certain point along the single dimension dividing the population we serve from the population we do not serve. Such views place artificial boundaries on remedial, preventive, and wellness work, where remediation applies to those

FIGURE 3.2 Traditional Medical Model of Mental Illness/ Mental Health

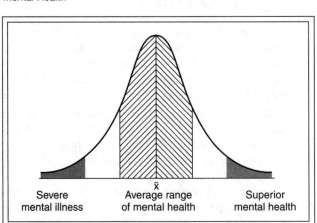

| Severe mental illness | Average range of mental health | Superior mental health |

who are *sick*, prevention to those who are *either sick or at-risk*, and wellness work to *relatively healthy populations*. This application of the single-dimension model, however, is valid only if normality and abnormality are viewed as lying at the poles of a single continuum. Adherence to the single-dimension model puts artificial limitations on our profession's scope of practice that simply do not fit the reality. Contemporary clinical mental health counselors serve the full range of clientele in a wide array of settings.

The implicit acceptance of the assumptions of the single-dimension perspective also implies a focus on the assessment and treatment of individuals. In this perspective, it is the individual who moves along the continuum and is the primary unit in the diathesis-stress model. The disregard of ecological context narrows the gathering of data for valid assessments, oversimplifies case conceptualizations, and sets artificial limits on the development of more creative, ecologically based interventions.

If the assumptions of the single-dimension model are accepted, it logically follows that decreases in mental illness represent increases in levels of mental health. But as Tudor (1996) notes, to define something by the absence of its opposite is simply a semantic sleight of hand that only further confuses our understanding of either condition. Finding a miraculous cure for or a complete eradication of mental illness will not ensure a mentally healthy population. Perry (1999) states that health is more than the prevention of premature death or the absence of disease. When I review the concepts and principles contained in the various definitions of mental health, I see a number of characteristics that seem to go well beyond what might be considered the mere absence of symptoms. In fact, some of these characteristics can be found in persons with mental illness. Viewed holistically, mental health is a dynamic state of physical, psychological, social, and spiritual well-being (Nutbeam, 1997; Perry & Jessor, 1985).

A clinical mental health counseling orientation suggests the validity of applying interventions that promote mental health and wellness in all persons, whether or not they are diagnosed with mental illness. Thus, a two-dimensional model presents a theoretical foundation on which mental health counselors can assess, conceptualize, and treat both the mentally healthy and the mentally ill. Such a conceptualization was suggested by the Canadian Ministry of National Health and Welfare (MNHW), which placed mental disorder and mental health on separate continua. Downie, Fyfe, and Tannahill (1990) linked well-being and ill health and represented their relationship by crossing the two axes. Figure 3.3 illustrates the two-dimensional model of mental health/wellness and mental illness.

Evidence is beginning to support the two-dimensional model. In a nationally representative sample of U.S. adults between the ages of 25 and 74, Keyes (2005) was able to distinguish a single dimension of mental health in which persons ranged from high levels of mental health (i.e., flourishing) to very low levels of mental health (i.e., languishing). As levels of flourishing decreased, Keyes found an increase in dysfunction characterized by work reduction, increased health limitations, and increased problematic psychosocial functioning. Pure languishing was found to be as dysfunctional, if not more so, than pure mental illness. And high levels of mental illness *and* languishing were markedly worse than pure mental illness alone, a finding suggesting the effect of an interaction of the two dimensions.

Keyes (2007) calls for a shift in the prevailing paradigm of mental health research and services based on the mounting evidence. First, the measurement of mental health and mental illness reveals two distinct but interacting dimensions. Second, the measurement of

FIGURE 3.3 A Two-Dimensional Model of Mental Health/Wellness and Mental Illness

	Level of mental health/wellness	
	Low	**High**
Low	Low degree of mental health and wellness; little or no diagnosable mental illness	High degree of mental health and wellness; little or no diagnosable mental illness
Mental illness/ pathology		
High	Low degree of mental health and wellness; severe mental illness	High degree of mental health and wellness; severe mental illness

disability, psychosocial functioning, and health care utilization indicates that anything less than flourishing is related to "increased impairment and burden to self and society" (Keyes, 2005, p. 95). Third, only a small percentage of those without mental illness can be described as flourishing. Keyes (2005) concludes, "Put simply, the absence of mental illness is not the presence of mental health; flourishing individuals function markedly better than all others, but barely one-fifth of the U.S. adult population is flourishing" (p. 95).

The two-dimensional model fits well with the underlying philosophy of clinical mental health counselors. First, mental health counselors recognize and are trained to diagnose and treat mental illness. Yet they conceptualize presenting problems from a mental health/wellness perspective. Second, mental health counselors believe all individuals, families, and groups can benefit from services that promote mental health in addition to those that remediate mental illness. Clinical mental health counselors work from a model that integrates these services, as opposed to the one-dimensional model, which creates a fuzzy boundary between interventions related to mental health enhancement, those related to prevention, and those related to mental illness remediation.

The two-dimensional model of mental health has several implications for the practice of clinical mental health counseling. First, it demonstrates that persons diagnosed with mental illness may have a good level of mental health/wellness (Tudor, 1996). For example, a client diagnosed with bipolar disorder may experience relatively high levels of mental health/well-being. Second, it is possible and desirable for mental health counselors to include in their interventions enhancements of the well-being/ mental health of persons diagnosed with mental disorders (Tudor, 1996). Third, a model of professional practice for mental health counselors is provided that integrates and synthesizes the roles of remediation, prevention, and mental health enhancement. It becomes truly possible, according to this model, for the mental health emphasis to inform the interventions of clinical mental health counselors, regardless of the specific nature of the presenting problem. The mental health emphasis applies equally well to working with the mentally well and working with the mentally disordered. As Remley (1991) notes, both populations "can benefit from a counseling philosophy that offers hope for a better tomorrow" (p. 2). Such an underlying theoretical model fits well with the application of recovery philosophy, where mental health counselors assist persons with severe and persistent illness to live out their *lives* rather than their diagnoses.

APPROACHES TO MENTAL HEALTH PROMOTION

In general, the fields of mental health promotion and positive psychology are still in their infancy. Myers (2000) notes that during most of psychology's first century, questions regarding personal happiness and wellness tended to be unasked as the discipline focused on illness. Myers (2000) conducted electronic searches of *Psychological Abstracts* since 1887 and found that the ratio of articles reporting on negative emotions to positive emotions was 14:1. Whereas his search turned up 8,072 articles on anger, 57,800 on anxiety, and 70,857 on depression, merely 851 articles focused on joy and 2,958 on happiness. Seligman and Csikszentmihalyi (2000) observe that we know much about surviving adverse conditions, but little about how to flourish in more normal life circumstances. Clearly, mental health has taken a backseat to mental illness in scholarly research and theory building.

The times are changing, though, and researchers and scholars are now very interested in mental health (Gibson & Mitchell, 2003). However, the terminology used tends to lack clarity and precision. Often, the terms *mental health, wellness, positive psychology, well-being, personal growth,* and *prevention* are used synonymously. Frequently in both theory, research, and practice, these terms are confused with *happiness*. In addition, the dimensions of mental health and wellness lack empirical validation. Donnelly, Eburne, and Kittleson (2001) surveyed the vast array of definitions and created a list of 10 characteristics that characterize mentally healthy individuals:

1. a positive outlook on life
2. a realistic set of expectations and approaches to life
3. effective management of emotions
4. the ability to function well with others
5. the ability to draw strength from others without being overly dependent upon them
6. reasonable appetites
7. a spiritual nature

8. effective coping skills
9. an honest self-regard and self-esteem
10. the ability to view the world honestly, accurately, and realistically (p. 24)

It is unreasonable to expect mentally healthy persons to display these characteristics at all times. However, such a pattern of behavior should be evident over given periods of time (Donnelly et al., 2001).

Fredrickson (2009), drawing conclusions from the findings of her research program that spans over 100 empirical investigations, concludes that persons who *flourish* are highly engaged with their family, work, and communities. They transcend self-interest which enables them to not only feel good, but *do* good by making contributions of value to the betterment of the world. According to Fredrickson, persons who flourish display ten forms of *positivity*: joy, gratitude, serenity, interest, hope, pride, amusement, inspiration, awe, and love. The opposite of positivity, *negativity*, is operationalized as the experience of anger, shame, contemptuousness, disgust, embarrassment, guilt, hate, sadness, scare, and stress. Persons who are flourishing in life, on the average, experience these forms of positivity over negativity at a ratio of three to one. She notes, "Just as zero degrees Celsius is a special number in thermodynamics, the 3-to-1 positivity ratio may well be a magic number in human psychology" (p. 121).

Several other models of wellness and mental health have been put forth. Zimpfer (1992) developed a model of wellness based on his treatment of cancer patients. Areas of treatment vital for the wellness of patients, according to his theory, include medical health, immune function, lifestyle management, spiritual beliefs and attitudes, psychodynamics, energy forces, and interpersonal relationships. Hettler (1986) identified six dimensions of wellness in his model: intellectual, emotional, physical, social, occupational, and spiritual wellness.

Based on theory and research from a variety of disciplines, the Wheel of Wellness (Witmer & Sweeney, 1992) is a model of treatment comprised of five life tasks vital for optimal health: spirituality, self-direction, work and leisure, friendship, and love. Hartwig and Myers (2003) see the Wheel of Wellness as a strength-based paradigm useful in the prevention and treatment of delinquency and concomitant mental illness. Myers and Sweeney (2008) found that statistical analysis of aggregated data from previous studies failed to support the circumplex model and the centrality of spirituality in the Wheel of Wellness. Applying structural equation modeling, a revised evidence-based model, The Indivisible Self, has emerged.

These models serve as springboards from which clinical mental health counselors develop, implement, and evaluate a variety of approaches for the enhancement of mental health. These include self-management; stress management; learned optimism and resourcefulness; resiliency and psychological hardiness; self-efficacy; diet, exercise and leisure; interpersonal competence; and spiritual practices and religious faith. By integrating such methods, counselors assist individuals, families, and communities to not simply get by, but to flourish.

PREVENTION IN THE CONTEXT OF PROMOTING MENTAL HEALTH

Efforts toward the prevention of mental illness are central to the mental health emphasis of clinical mental health counselors. Normal living provides numerous events that serve as opportunities for either growth or hazard. Although stress is a common denominator in every person's life, discouraging circumstances, timely and untimely transitions, conflicts, and emergencies can precipitate crises in which the demands placed on individuals overwhelm their coping responses. Prevention programs and interventions seek to limit the likelihood that vulnerable persons will experience undesirable consequences when facing difficult situations. Such programs target at-risk, disorder-prone, and infected members of our society.

Mental health counselors have adopted a model of prevention from the health professions. A number of approaches, referred to as primary, secondary, and tertiary prevention, have been developed to enhance growth, promote crisis resistance, and limit crisis reactions (Conyne, 2004).

Primary prevention often comes in the form of education, consultation, and crisis intervention. Its goal is to reduce the likelihood of persons contracting the disorder. Programs and interventions are directed toward persons identified as being at risk for experiencing adverse situations or negative reactions. Approaches to primary prevention include modifying the hazardous situation, reducing exposure to hazardous situations, and increasing coping abilities (Hoff, Hallisey, & Hoff, 2009). Examples include:

* the elimination of substandard housing for older populations and persons of lower socioeconomic status
* teen pregnancy prevention programs
* Drug Abuse Resistance Education (DARE) programs
* midnight basketball programs in urban areas
* 24-hour crisis hotlines

To be successful, adequate and accurate needs and risk assessment must be conducted. Furthermore, awareness and sensitivity to cultural values and existing support systems are essential. Organizational support for proposed programs must be strong. Finally, effective primary prevention programs integrate helpful resources already existing in the community.

Secondary prevention refers to programs and interventions that seek to limit the negative impact of disorders in persons already affected (Conyne, 2004). The goal is to shorten the duration of the condition. For example, many colleges and universities have implemented early detection programs known as "screening days." Students have the opportunity to receive information on specific emotional disorders, such as eating disorders, depression, and anxiety; complete self-administered questionnaires; and receive referral information if professional counseling is recommended. Other secondary prevention measures include accessible crisis intervention services, walk-in clinics, critical incident stress management interventions, and programs for the homeless mentally ill.

Tertiary prevention aims to reduce the long-term consequences for persons recovering from mental disorders (Conyne, 2004). For example, relapse prevention programs for recovering alcoholics provide skills that decrease the likelihood of falling back into the former dysfunctional pattern of thinking and drinking. Other tertiary prevention services include aftercare, assertive community treatment, and day treatment.

Clinical mental health counselor training provides an excellent foundation for doing prevention work. Knowledge of human development enables the mental health and community counselor to anticipate normal, age-related transitions and initiate primary prevention measures. In addition, it provides a knowledge base that assists counselors in differentiating normal from abnormal coping responses, which is critical in the timely implementation of secondary prevention interventions. In addition, by calling attention to the environmental context, the ecological perspective increases the sensitivity of mental health counselors to additional stressors and resources that may either help or hinder coping responses. Finally, the mental health emphasis encourages strength-based, problem-solving approaches to prevention that are essential for the creation of workable intervention plans.

CONCLUSION: THE CLINICAL MENTAL HEALTH COUNSELING PARADIGM

We have surveyed a number of theories that are fundamental to the profession of mental health counseling. These foundational areas are human development across the lifespan, ecological theory, mental health, and mental health promotion. Taken together, they form a unique base from which clinical mental health counselors practice.

It is possible to integrate each of these emphases and construct a comprehensive paradigm for clinical mental health counseling (see Figure 3.4). This paradigm is based upon three assumptions:

1. Mental health/wellness and mental illness/pathology lie on distinct, but interacting dimensions;
2. Persons must be viewed within their unique ecological context;
3. The dimensions of wellness and pathology interact and extend through the specific levels of ecological context.

This paradigm serves as the lens through which clinical mental health counselors assess, conceptualize, and treat their clients, who are viewed holistically as well-integrated physical, cognitive, social, and spiritual beings, embedded within unique ecological systems. It is in the consistent application of this paradigm that the profession can distinguish itself from the allied mental health professions.

The clinical mental health counseling paradigm has numerous implications for professional practice and research. For example, assessment is comprehensive, necessarily involving consideration of multiple levels of the environment. Mental health counselors assess for personal and ecological strengths and assets in addition to symptoms and deficits. Thus, our concepts of mental health and wellness relate not only to individuals, but to groups, families, organizations, communities, and subcultures. The target and focus of assessment and treatment encompasses this broader context. Second, factors that directly and indirectly influence the client system must be examined. These factors must not be assessed as though they operate in isolation. Rather, mental health counselors must keep in mind the complex, reciprocal interactions that characterize personal behavior in situations. Third, treatment and mental health enhancing interventions can be directed to all ecological levels. It is from the perspective of this model that consultation, advocacy, and prevention can be

FIGURE 3.4 The Clinical Mental Health Counseling Paradigm

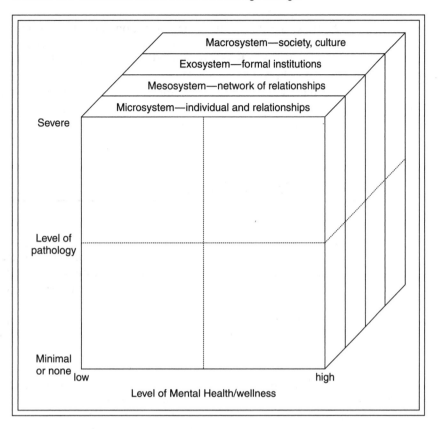

conceptualized tools of intervention that fall within the clinical mental health counselors' scopes of practice.

DISCUSSION QUESTIONS

1. Return to the brief case study found at the beginning of this chapter. Explore the operation of your implicit theories by answering the following questions:
   a. What is the etiology of Joe's condition? To what extent do you see his situation as reflecting a substance abuse/dependence problem, employee-supervisor conflict, or marital conflict? Although each of these is present, which is primary?
   b. To what extent would you feel comfortable in developing a clinical diagnosis for Joe? Discuss your position with others in the class.
   c. To what extent is Joe ready to engage in the change process? Consider the transtheoretical model in your response.
   d. What type of interventions do you see as being most helpful? What specific goals would you identify? Which of the following modalities would be your

primary approach—individual, marital, family, ecological (employee-spouse-supervisor)?

2. How, specifically, does the foundation of human development influence the work of mental health and community counselors? To what extent do you see such a foundation as being incompatible with traditional diagnosis and treatment of clients who are mentally ill?

3. Analyze the case of Joe by applying the comprehensive mental health counseling model. How specifically can this model guide your assessment and treatment planning in this particular case?

SUGGESTED ACTIVITIES

1. Interview two mental health counselors and explore the extent to which they hold to the theoretical foundations discussed in this chapter. Seek professionals who work in clinical and nonclinical settings. To what extent does their particular work setting influence the extent to which they apply these specific theoretical foundations in practice? Do they see the application of the comprehensive mental health counseling model as setting their professional practice apart from professionals of other disciplines (e.g., social workers, marriage and family counselors, or psychologists)?

2. Interview an LMHC or LPC working in a community mental health setting. Examine the ways in which his or her organization has programs and/or goals related to the prevention of emotional and psychological distress. What are some of these programs and what specific roles can be filled by mental health and community counselors?

3. Do a computer-assisted search of several community mental health centers in your area. Identify the extent to which the concepts of wellness, healthy human development, and human ecology are reflected in the centers' mission statements, programs, and specific goals/objectives.

4. To what extent do you see your personal characteristics and interpersonal style as being a good fit for the mental health counseling profession? Seek out the views of several persons who know you well. To what extent do they see your personal characteristics and interpersonal style as being a good fit?

REFERENCES

American Counseling Association. (2005). *ACA code of ethics*. Alexandria, VA: Author.

Anderson, M. L., Goodman, J., & Schlossberg, N. K. (2012). *Counseling adults in transition: Linking Schlossberg's theory with practice in a diverse world* (4th ed.). New York, NY: Springer.

Baruth, L. G., & Manning, M. L. (2012). *Multicultural counseling and psychotherapy: A lifespan approach* (5th ed.). Upper Saddle River, NJ: Pearson Education.

Baumrind, D. (1967). Child care practices anteceding three patterns of preschool behavior. *Genetic Psychology Monographs, 75,* 43–88.

Baumrind, D. (1991). Parenting styles and adolescent development. In J. Brooks, R. Lerner, & A. C. Petersen (Eds.)., *The encyclopedia of adolescence* (pp. 758–772). New York, NY: Garland Press.

Broderick, P. C., & Blewitt, P. (2010). *The lifespan: Human development for helping professionals.* Upper Saddle River, NJ: Pearson.

Bronfenbrenner, U. (1979). The ecology of human development: Experiments by nature and design. Cambridge, MA: Harvard University Press.

Bronfenbrenner, U. (1989). Ecological systems theory. *Annals of Child Development, 6,* 187–249.

Brooks, D. K., & Weikel, W. J. (1996). Mental health counseling: The first twenty years. In W. J. Weikel & A. J. Palmo (Eds.), *Foundations in mental health counseling* (2nd ed.) (pp. 5–29). Springfield, IL: Thomas.

Carlston, D. (2010). Models of implicit and explicit mental representation. In B. Gawronski & B. K. Payne (Eds.), *Handbook of implicit social cognition: Measurement, theory, and applications.* New York, NY: Guilford Press.

Cohen, E. D., & Cohen, G. S. (1999). *The virtuous therapist: Ethical practice in counseling and psychotherapy.* Belmont, CA: Brooks/Cole.

Conyne, R. K. (2004). *Preventive counseling: Helping people to become empowered in systems and settings.* New York, NY: Brunner-Routledge.

Cook, E. P. (2012). *Understanding people in context: The ecological perspective in counseling.* Alexandria, VA: American Counseling Association.

Corsini, R. J. (1995). Introduction. In R. J. Corsini & D. Wedding (Eds.), *Current psychotherapies* (5th ed.). Itasca, IL: Peacock.

Cozolino, L. (2006). *The neuroscience of human relationships: Attachment and the developing social brain.* New York, NY: Norton.

Day, S. X. (2007). *Theory and design in counseling and psychotherapy* (2nd ed.). Boston, MA: Houghton Mifflin.

Donnelly, J. W., Eburne, N., & Kittleson, M. (2001). *Mental health: Dimensions of self-esteem and emotional well-being.* Boston, MA: Allyn & Bacon.

Downie, R. S., Fyfe, C., & Tannahill, A. (1990). *Health promotion: Models and values.* Oxford, England: Oxford University Press.

Erikson, E. (1968). *Identity, youth, and crisis.* New York, NY: Norton.

Fredrickson, B. L. (2009). *Positivity.* New York, NY: Three Rivers Press.

Gibson, R. L., & Mitchell, M. H. (2003). *Introduction to counseling and guidance* (6th ed.). Upper Saddle River, NJ: Merrill Prentice Hall.

Ginter, E. J. (1996). Three pillars of mental health counseling—Watch in what you step. *Journal of Mental Health Counseling, 18,* 99–107.

Hansen, J. (2003). Including diagnostic training in counseling curricula: Implications for professional identity development. *Counselor Education and Supervision, 82,* 131–138.

Hartwig, H. J., & Myers, J. E. (2003). A different approach: Applying a wellness paradigm to adolescent female delinquents and offenders. *Journal of Mental Health Counseling, 25,* 57–75.

Hettler, B. (1986). Strategies for wellness and recreation program development. In F. Leafgren (Ed.), *Developing campus recreation and wellness programs.* San Francisco, CA: Jossey-Bass.

Hoff, L. A., Hallisey, B. J., & Hoff, M. (2011). *People in crisis: Clinical and diversity perspectives* (6th ed.). New York, NY: Routledge.

Keyes, C. L. M. (2005). Mental illness and/or mental health? Investigating axioms of the complete state model of health. *Journal of Consulting and Clinical Psychology, 73,* 539–548.

Keyes, C. L. M. (2007). Promoting and protecting mental health as flourishing: A complementary strategy for improving national mental health. *American Psychologist, 62,* 95–108.

Lefrancois, G. R. (1999). *The lifespan* (6th ed.). Belmont, CA: Wadsworth.

Lewis, J. A., Lewis, M. D., Daniels, J. A., & D'Andrea, M. J. (2003). *Community counseling: Empowerment strategies for a diverse society* (3rd ed.). Pacific Grove, CA: Brooks/Cole.

Lyddon, W. J., & Adamson, L. A. (1992). Worldview and counseling preference: An analogue study. *Journal of Counseling and Development, 71,* 41–47.

Mahalik, J. R., Worthington, R. L., & Crump, S. (1999). Influence of racial/ethnic membership and 'therapist culture' on therapists' worldview. *Journal of Multicultural Counseling and Development, 27,* 2–18.

Markus, H. (1977). Self-schemata and processing information about the self. *Journal of Personality and Social Psychology, 35,* 63–78.

Markus, H., & Wurf, E. (1987). The dynamic self-concept: A social psychological perspective. In M. R. Rosenzweig and L. W. Porter (Eds.), *Annual review of psychology.* Palo Alto, CA: Annual Reviews.

Mellin, E. A., Hunt, B., & Nichols, L. M. (2011). Counselor professional identity: Findings and implications for counseling and interprofessional collaboration. *Journal of Counseling and Development, 89,* 140-147.

Messer, S. B., & Gurman, A. S. (2011). Contemporary issues in psychotherapy theory, practice, and research: A framework for comparative study (pp. 3–29). In S. B. Messer & A. S. Gurman (Eds.), *Essential psychotherapies: Theory and practice* (3rd ed.). New York, NY: Guilford Press.

Millon, T. (2003). It's time to rework the blueprints: Building a science for clinical psychology. *American Psychologist, 58,* 949–961.

Myers, D. G. (2000). The funds, friends, and faith of happy people. *American Psychologist, 55,* 56–67.

Myers, J. E., & Sweeney, T. J. (2008). Wellness counseling: The evidence base for practice. *Journal of Counseling and Development, 86,* 482–493.

Newman, B. M., & Newman, P. R. (2006). *Development through life: A psychosocial approach* (9th ed.). Belmont, CA: Thomson Wadsworth.

Nutbeam, D. (1997). Promoting health and preventing disease: An international perspective on youth health promotion. *Journal of Adolescent Health, 20,* 396–402.

Oyserman, D., Coon, H. M., & Kemmelmeier, M. (2002). Rethinking individualism and collectivism: Evaluation of theoretical assumptions and meta-analyses. *Psychological Bulletin, 128,* 3–72.

Parsons, R. D. (2009). *Translating theory to practice: Thinking and acting like an expert counselor.* Upper Saddle River, NJ: Merrill.

Perry, C. L. (1999). *Creating health behavior change: How to develop community-wide programs for youth.* Thousand Oaks, CA: Sage.

Perry, C. L., & Jessor, R. (1985). The concept of health promotion and the prevention of adolescent drug abuse. *Health Education Quarterly, 12,* 169–184.

Prochaska, J. O., & DiClemente, C. C. (1984). *The transtheoretical approach: Crossing traditional boundaries of treatment.* Homewood, IL: Dow Jones-Irwin.

Prochaska, J. O., & Norcross, J. C. (2010). *Systems of psychotherapy: A transtheoretical analysis* (7th ed.). Pacific Grove, CA: Brooks/Cole.

Remley, T. P., Jr. (1991, August). On being different. *Guidepost,* p. 2.

Restak, R. (2003). *The new brain: How the modern age is rewiring your mind.* Emmaus, PA: Rodale.

Santrock, J. W. (2010). *The lifespan* (13th ed.). Columbus, OH: McGraw-Hill.

Sarason, S. B. (1984). If it can be studied or developed, shouldn't it be? *American Psychologist, 39,* 477–485.

Seligman, M. E. P., & Csikszentmihalyi, M. (2000). Positive psychology: An introduction. *American Psychologist, 55,* 5–14.

Sharf, R. S. (2012). *Theories of psychotherapy and counseling: Concepts and cases* (5th ed.). Belmont, CA: Brooks/Cole.

Siegel, D. (2006). An interpersonal neurobiology approach to psychotherapy: Awareness, mirror neurons, and neural plasticity in the development of well-being. *Psychiatric Annals, 36,* 248–256.

Smith, E. (2006). The strength-based counseling model. *Counseling Psychologist, 34,* 13–79.

Smith, J., & Baltes, P. B. (1999). Life-span perspectives on development (pp. 377–409). In M. H. Bornstein & M. E. Lamb (Eds.), *Developmental psychology: An advanced textbook* (4th ed.). Mahwah, NJ: Erlbaum.

Steinberg, L., Darling, N. E., & Fletcher, A. C., in collaboration with Brown, B. B., & Dornbusch, S. M. (1995). Authoritative parenting and adolescent adjustment: An ecological journey (pp. 423–466). In P. Moen, G. H. Elder, Jr., & K. Luscher (Eds.), *Examining lives in context: Perspectives on the ecology of human development*. Washington, DC: American Psychological Association.

Steinberg, L., Lamborn, S., Darling, N., Mounts, N. S., & Dornbusch, S. M. (1994). Over-time changes in adjustment and competencies among adolescents from authoritative, authoritarian, indulgent, and neglectful families. *Child Development, 65,* 754–770.

Thompson, R. A. (1999). The individual child: Temperament, emotion, self, and personality (pp. 377–409). In M. H. Bornstein & M. E. Lamb (Eds.), *Developmental psychology: An advanced textbook* (4th ed.). Mahwah, NJ: Erlbaum.

Tudor, K. (1996). *Mental health promotion: Paradigms and practice*. New York, NY: Routledge.

Ungar, M. (2011). *Counseling in challenging contexts: Working with individuals and families across clinical and community settings*. Belmont, CA: Brooks/Cole.

Van Hesteren, F., & Ivey, A. E. (1990). Counseling and development: Toward a new identity for a profession in transition. *Journal of Counseling and Development, 68,* 524–528.

Velasquez, M. M., Maurer, G. G., Crouch, C., & DiClemente, C. C. (2001). *Group treatment for substance abuse*. New York, NY: Guilford Press.

Williams, B. (2003). The worldview dimensions of individualism and collectivism: Implications for counseling. *Journal of Counseling and Development, 81,* 370–374.

Witmer, J. M., & Sweeney, T. J. (1992). A holistic model for wellness and prevention over the lifespan. *Journal of Counseling and Development, 71,* 140–148.

Zimpfer, D. G. (1992). Psychosocial treatment of life-threatening disease: A wellness model. *Journal of Counseling and Development, 71,* 203–209.

4

Traditional and Contemporary Theories of Counseling

OUTLINE

Traditional Theories of Counseling and Psychotherapy

Contemporary Trends in the Application of Counseling Theory

Conclusion

I am a mental health counselor. Providing individual, group, and family counseling is primary and central to my professional identity. In contrast to other mental health–related professionals who provide counseling services, we call ourselves counselors, as Gibson and Mitchell (2003) state, "not because we give tests, offer career planning information, or provide consultation, but because we counsel" (p. 135).

In this chapter, we will review a number of theories of counseling. These theories provide frameworks that help counselors organize data, make inferences, and develop intervention strategies from the numerous bits of information observed in and gathered from clients. If we are lucky, our clients provide a straightforward description of the following:

- Who they are
- The nature of their presenting problem(s)
- The background history that links past events to current issue(s)
- The environmental context of their development and current issue(s)
- Their motivations (why they think they do what they do)

With the client's information in mind, clinical mental health counselors use the theories described in this chapter as tools to conceptualize the client's current condition, explain its development and maintenance, predict what is likely to take place (i.e., the prognosis), and exert influence so that the client's problems can be resolved and her or his mental health enhanced.

Although counseling theories can guide us to valid conceptualizations of clients' situations, they are not foolproof means of developing clinical inferences. Stevens and Morris (1995) identify several inferential errors that can distort our assessment and subsequent selection/implementation of treatment strategies:

1. *Single-cause etiologies.* We select one cause for the client's problem while dismissing all other potential alternatives.
2. *Availability heuristics.* Sometimes a particular theory or a recent article stays in our consciousness and becomes the lens through which we interpret all newly gathered client information (Myers, 2010). For example, I may tend to interpret my clients' stories through the lens of the particular theory of counseling that I am teaching at that time in my Theories and Techniques class. Somehow, all clients seem to benefit from Gestalt therapy one week and cognitive-behavioral therapy the next. In actuality, I may risk using the model that is most available in my consciousness rather than the one that is most relevant.
3. *Fundamental attribution errors.* We tend to explain our behavior in terms of situational characteristics (Myers, 2010; Ross, 1977). In contrast, we tend to explain the behaviors of others in terms of their personal characteristics. I might attribute my client's inappropriate interpersonal behaviors to her deep-seated insecurity, while I attribute my similar behavior to uncertainty residing in the situation itself.
4. *Illusory correlations.* We frequently perceive two independent events occurring together in time as being related (Myers, 2010). For example, I may attribute my

client's anxiety to an anniversary reaction because her panic appears to have begun 2 years after the death of a loved one. Although this cause is plausible, numerous other explanations may be equally valid.

Mental health counselors do well to remember that they are human and vulnerable to making these inferential errors in their professional practice. They can also be too readily convinced of the accuracy of their after-the-fact analyses and erroneous diagnoses. Several cautions are in order:

- Be aware that a client's verbal agreement with something you say does not establish its *validity*.
- Recognize that each of the errors mentioned can lead you to be too confident while gathering information and making decisions.
- Guard against these tendencies by asking questions that can elicit client responses that will disconfirm your tentative conclusions.
- Consider opposing ideas and put them to the test.

With these cautions in mind, we will now turn to some of the traditional theories of counseling. Our focus is those theories that are well known and accepted. Later in this chapter, we will look at some recent trends and their influence on contemporary theory development.

TRADITIONAL THEORIES OF COUNSELING AND PSYCHOTHERAPY

PSYCHOANALYSIS

Key Theorist.   Psychoanalysis is an approach to counseling derived from the discoveries of Sigmund Freud (1856–1939). Trained as a neurologist, Freud developed a private practice in Vienna, where he specialized in the treatment of "nervous disorders." Many of his patients sought treatment for hysteria, a condition in which clients experience physical complaints with no apparent physical cause.

Freud's theory building was influenced by several cutting-edge treatment approaches of his day (Thorne & Henley, 2005). Around 1880, Heinrich Erb was exploring the therapeutic value of administering electrical shock to neurotic clients. At about the same time, Jean-Martin Charcot was using hypnotism to treat nervous conditions. He had discovered that symptoms of hysteria could be induced through hypnotic suggestion and believed that such symptoms could be removed by a similar process.

In collaboration with Josef Breuer, Freud began to use a "talking-out" approach: He encouraged his patients to talk freely about any of their thoughts and feelings regardless of their relationship to the presenting symptoms. Many patients experienced a reduction or removal of symptoms through this process. Conclusions that Freud derived from keen observations of his patients led to the development of psychoanalysis.

Essential Principles and Concepts. Freud saw no reason to believe that the energy that runs the human organism is any different from the energy that runs the universe. Furthermore, energy can take several forms—mechanical, thermal, or nuclear. Freud posited a psychic energy ("libido") that "powers" psychological work such as thinking, perceiving, and remembering. This energy, he believed, is used by the "life instincts" to satisfy needs for survival and reproduction (Corey, 2012). These instincts are mostly sexual and aggressive in nature and are expressed not only in overt actions, but also in dreams, feelings, fantasies, wishes, and thoughts (Hall, 1954).

The fulfillment of basic needs is essential for human survival. Thus, individuals continuously seek immediate gratification of their basic needs. But the demand for immediate gratification inevitably conflicts with social rules that require control over these urges. Furthermore, conditions in the specific situation limit the extent to which a basic need can be fulfilled at any given time. The core of Freud's theory is this conflict among impulses, societal rules, and the realities of a situation.

Two Basic Assumptions. Freud made two basic assumptions about human beings (Hall, 1954). First, he assumed that everything we do, think, or feel has meaning and purpose. Nothing is left to chance; everything relates in some way to our quest for need fulfillment. This assumption is termed *psychic determinism.* Second, most human behavior stems from urges that lie beyond our general awareness, or what is referred to as *unconscious motivation.* Of course, people explain why they do what they do, but such explanations lack insight. The actual source of all behavior is the attempt to resolve the conflict among urges, realities, and rules that reside in our unconscious. The nature of this unconscious conflict can be determined through a careful interpretation of the content of thoughts, feelings, self-defeating behaviors, and Freudian slips (e.g., saying "mom" when intending to say the name of one's wife).

Levels of Awareness. Freud saw humans as having various levels of awareness (Hall, 1954). The *conscious* is limited to those sensations, thoughts, feelings, and behaviors that a person is aware of at any given moment. The *preconscious* contains memories of past events, related facts, and associated thoughts and feelings that were not in the person's awareness at the given moment but can now be easily accessed. Finally, the *unconscious* is the reservoir of urges, wishes, and conflicts that threaten to overwhelm the person's conscious mind and are therefore pushed out of awareness.

Structure of Personality. Freud identified three basic structures of personality (Nystul, 2011). The *id* is the deep, inaccessible component of personality that holds all instinctual urges. Its goal is to obtain immediate fulfillment of basic needs. It operates according to the *pleasure principle,* which seeks to experience pleasure and avoid pain. Nothing else matters! The personality of the neonate and the infant are almost entirely id.

Developing children learn that they cannot always get what they want. So, soon after the first year, a second personality structure arises, the *ego.* It mediates between the environment that surrounds the child and his or her urges and instincts. The ego is the rational problem-solver component of the mind that finds realistic means to fulfill the demands of the id.

The *superego* forms around the time the child reaches the age of 4 to 6. This structure is a reflection of the values of society and culture as represented to the child through the words and actions of the parents. The primary task of the superego is to block unacceptable impulses of the id and guide the ego in the direction of moral action rather than merely to do what works.

As noted earlier, personality is driven by psychic energy. This flow of energy occurs within a closed system. There is only so much energy available, and when the libido energizes one structure of personality, less energy is available for the other structures (Corey, 2012). Thus, a highly charged id results in diminished energy for the ego and the superego. Persons with highly charged ids tend to be impulsive and to "act without thinking." Persons with highly energized superegos might be immobilized in decision-making situations, unable to determine the "right" decision or vacillating between personal desires and meeting the expectations of others. Mentally healthy persons, in contrast, are characterized by a relative balance of energy among the three structures, which leads to their cooperative and harmonious operation.

Anxiety.   The concept of anxiety is central to psychoanalytic theory (Hall, 1954). Anxiety is used by the ego as a signal of impending danger and thus becomes a call for action. *Reality anxiety* is experienced when an external threat is accurately perceived. The intensity of the anxiety is proportionate to the degree of threat. In contrast, *moral anxiety* is experienced as guilt or shame resulting from a perceived threat of disapproval or punishment. Finally, *neurotic anxiety* is the emotional response to the threat that an unconscious impulse will emerge into one's awareness.

Internal conflicts among the structures of personality are not easily controlled. The ego's job is to satisfy the demands of reality, the moral demands of the superego, and the id's demands for immediate gratification. Through the use of *ego defense mechanisms,* impulses emanating from the id are blocked from reaching consciousness or distorted in such a way that the superego is fooled (Hall, 1954).

All ego defense mechanisms have several things in common. First, the person does not consciously choose to use them. Second, they involve at least some degree of denial or distortion of reality. Third, we all use them (Freud, 1914). They become pathological only when they are used in excess or to the extreme. Table 4.1 lists and defines specific types of ego defense mechanisms.

Nature of Psychological Disturbance.   Emotional distress and behavioral problems are displayed in many ways. Yet, according to the psychoanalytic perspective, all are rooted in intrapsychic conflicts occurring at the unconscious level. Such a notion may seem far-fetched and speculative. In my early days as a counselor trainee, although intrigued by Freud's ideas, I wanted to believe that the clients I saw in my practice had more insight into the nature of their presenting problems. However, I soon learned this was not always the case.

One of my first clients was a female in her early 30s, married and a parent of three children. Her childhood had been marked by a strict upbringing, and she remained in a very close relationship with her parents. Her father was quite dominant and it was very important to her to please him. She described her presenting problem by saying,

TABLE 4.1

Examples of
Ego Defense
Mechanisms

Defense Mechanism	Example
Repression—the involuntary removal of material from one's conscious awareness.	A child who was sexually abused at age 7 but has no conscious recollection of the abuse.
Regression—reversion to forms of behavior characteristic of an earlier age when the person was more secure.	A 6-year-old child experiencing the divorce of parents and beginning nocturnal bed-wetting after 4 years of appropriate bladder control.
Projection—attribution of one's unacceptable desires, motives, or characteristics to others.	A husband accuses his spouse of not loving him when, in fact, it is he who does not love his spouse.
Displacement—discharging pent-up feelings or behaviors onto less threatening targets.	A father in unresolved conflict at work comes home and yells at his children for not cleaning their bedrooms.
Rationalization—contrived "reasons" that explain away or mask personal failures or questionable motives.	A person who is not hired for a position that she truly wanted states that she probably would have become bored with the job if it had been offered to her.
Reaction Formation—defense against unacceptable impulses or desires by expression of a seemingly opposite behavior.	A college student who wants to drop out of his program signs up for an overload of classes for the semester.
Denial—refusal to believe, accept, or face an unpleasant reality.	A parent whose child tragically dies in an automobile accident expresses disbelief at the funeral that the tragedy has actually happened.
Sublimation—redirecting sexual or aggressive energies into a more socially acceptable alternative activity.	A recently divorced person diverts her anger and sexual energy by enrolling in college and immersing herself in studies.

"I will be talking and suddenly, without warning, I lose my voice. I become mute." A complete medical exam failed to reveal an underlying physical cause.

As treatment proceeded, my client began to identify a pattern in which she often became mute when needing to assert herself, particularly with her father. For example, she might have plans to go out for an evening with her husband but would then receive an invitation to dine with her parents. In such situations, she would "lose her voice."

From the psychoanalytic perspective, my client was experiencing a conflict that was entirely out of her conscious awareness. She wanted to have a night out with her spouse yet felt guilty if not abiding by the wishes of her parents. Trapped in a conflict between mutually exclusive alternatives, her "loss of voice" provided her with a convenient way not to assert herself and at the same time not offending either her spouse or her father. This solution did not resolve the actual problem at hand, but it did protect her from the pain that would come with acting autonomously in relation to her parents.

Goals of Treatment. If symptoms arise from deep, hidden unconscious conflicts, only a treatment that penetrates the deepest recesses of the psyche can facilitate lasting change. According to Freud, the goal of counseling is to modify the structure of personality (Nystul, 2011). This modification is accomplished through a process that makes the unconscious material conscious, thereby increasing clients' awareness and enabling them to recognize unproductive, self-defeating patterns of behavior and to develop more effective alternatives.

Process and Techniques. Classical psychoanalysts attempt to be "blank slates" that facilitate the development of *transference* in the relationship (Corey, 2012). In transference, the patient experiences thoughts and feelings toward the counselor that do not fit the reality of the relationship. The thoughts and feelings actually apply to significant others from the client's past but are "transferred" to the counselor. Within the immediacy of the counseling sessions, these thoughts, feelings, and actions emerge as reflections of underlying conflicts between impulses and defenses that are at the core of the person's pathology. In counseling sessions, these patterns recur in the context of transference and become a major source of content for analysis.

To facilitate the production of unconscious material, clients engage in *free association* (Nystul, 2011). They are encouraged to say anything and everything that comes into their minds—dreams, memories, fantasies, wishes, thoughts. All of these are important.

Confrontation, clarification, and interpretation are primary tools for the analysis of unconscious contents. For example, in confrontation, the counselor's statement "You seem to be feeling angry at me" may help the client to become aware of what material is being analyzed. Counselors' interpretations of client responses, interpretations based primarily on psychoanalytic theory, allow clients to gain insight into their behavior. Such insights are *worked through* again and again as clients slowly move to a higher, more effective level of functioning. The result is increased self-awareness, which permits clients to base their behavior on present realities. Freudians see this evolution as representing structural changes in personality.

Object Relations. Although around 2% of practicing counselors embrace classical psychoanalytic theory (Prochaska & Norcross, 2010), a larger proportion practice modified versions such as *object relations,* or *self-psychology.* Object relations theory goes beyond Freud's analysis of personality structures by focusing on the relationship between the self and objects, which are mental representations of others (Corey, 2012). We tend to represent others mentally in ways that resemble our earliest relationships, typically how we related to our primary caregivers. Infants learn that primary caregivers have elements of "good" and "bad," and healthy development occurs as these elements gel to form a cohesive object. In a failure in object relations, the good and the bad do not synthesize, so that the bad parts "split off." As a result, the client cannot simultaneously keep in mind both the good and the bad when frustrated by another. In such situations, the person moves rapidly from perceiving the person as all good to seeing the person as all bad.

These objects stay with us, and much of our adult life involves a repetition of our early object relations in one form or another. Persons with poor object relations tend to be emotionally unstable and insecure, quickly moving from adulation to anger when a loved person makes them feel disappointed or abandoned.

The goal of object relations therapy is to revise impaired object representations (Corey, 2012). This process, too, involves a reconstruction of the personality, as in classical psychoanalysis. However, the focus is on the nature of the person's interactions with others and the extent to which these actions are based on unconscious images (object relations) from the past. The techniques used in object relations therapy are similar to those used in classical psychoanalysis. However, free association, transference, interpretation, and working through are used to increase the client's awareness of the influence of distorted objects. Clients can then work toward the development of more autonomous functioning, characterized by increased self-trust, acceptance of others, and less exaggerated emotional reactivity.

INDIVIDUAL PSYCHOLOGY (ADLERIAN THERAPY)

Key Theorist.   The system of counseling known as *individual psychology* was developed by Alfred Adler (1870–1937). Adler earned his MD in psychiatry from the University of Vienna and was initially a strong defender of the Freudian perspective. However, Adler began to criticize Freud's theory for its overemphasis on sexuality and its discounting of conscious processes. A sharp break in Adler and Freud's relationship resulted, and Adler quickly established individual psychology as an important alternative perspective (Corey, 2012).

Essential Principles and Concepts.   Six assumptions are the foundation of the Adlerian perspective. First, behavior is goal oriented, purposeful, and socially motivated (Corey, 2012; Nystul, 2011). Adler believed that, rather than being determined by unconscious conflicts or past determinants, behavior is determined by one's outlook on the future. In addition, he believed that behavior results from conscious choice and is motivated by stimuli present in the social situation.

The second assumption is that behavior is best understood from the vantage point of the client's subjective reality (Nystul, 2011). Personal behavior is influenced by the person's thoughts, beliefs, perceptions, and conclusions. To make sense of the client's behavior, the counselor is advised to see the world through the eyes of the client.

Third, personality is an organized whole that interacts within a specific and unique social system (Dinkmeyer & Sperry, 2000). Clearly, Adlerian theory focuses on interpersonal dynamics rather than intrapsychic structures. Each person is best understood as the central piece in a social jigsaw puzzle.

Fourth, the core motive for behavior is to *strive for superiority* (Corey, 2012). In other words, persons seek to rise above what they currently are. Each of us has self-identified deficits, or *inferiorities,* that we desire to overcome. This desire becomes the powerful force that drives behavior. Adler believed each person has some idealistic notion of who he or she would like to be, referred to as *fictional finalism,* which provides direction to each person's strivings.

Fifth, each person develops a type of cognitive map, referred to as a *lifestyle,* that lends consistency to his or her behavior in striving for chosen goals (Corey, 2012). This private logic provides the rationale for acting in specific ways. Thus, although one's behavior may not make sense to others, it might make perfect sense once the personal reasoning is revealed and understood. For example, a child might feel academically inferior to other children in his classroom. To compensate for this inferiority and the accompanying rejection by his peers, he may choose to gain acceptance through athletic achievements or being the class clown.

Finally, humans find personal fulfillment and well-being by acting for the general *social interest* (Dinkmeyer & Sperry, 2000). In choosing behaviors that will move us toward our fictional finalisms, our personal well-being is enhanced to the extent that our behavior does not conflict significantly with the goals of those who surround us. We must recognize that we are not self-sufficient and that merely looking out for number one brings us into inevitable conflict with others. Thus, being socially connected is critical to our emotional well-being.

Nature of Psychological Disturbance. Adlerians see psychological disturbance as rooted in discouragement and faulty conceptions and lifestyle beliefs (Dinkmeyer & Sperry, 2000). In families where competition, distrust, domination, neglect, or pampering predominate, children become discouraged from attaining superiority in socially accepted ways. In addition, being raised in such an environment results in a diminished social interest. Such persons do the best they can to try to get to the place in life they think they should be (fictional finalisms). Their lifestyles, then, are characterized by the *basic mistakes* of overgeneralizing about the nature of life from their small but very influential sample of experiences in their families.

Such lifestyle patterns can be set early in development. For example, a child who is overly pampered and shielded from the normal challenges of life may use attention getting as a primary means of enlisting others to take care of his personal needs. Other children may have been raised by very dominant parents. Feeling impotent and unable to accomplish anything of worth, these children may resort to bullying and rebelliousness to rise above others. Such power-seeking behaviors are viewed as compensating for underlying feelings of inadequacy. Or parents who consistently nag, cajole, scold, deride, and blame raise children who fear, yet expect, failure. Forever trying, but never judging personal efforts as good enough, these persons often move through life hesitantly and indecisively.

Goal of Treatment. The fundamental goal in Adlerian counseling and psychotherapy is to help clients live a more complete and perfect life in ways that contribute not only to personal well-being but also to the general well-being of others (Sharf, 2012). In other words, clients develop more effective lifestyles and healthy social interests that facilitate positive strivings for superiority. Clients come to see their current lifestyles as self-defeating patterns of behavior leading to destructive goals. As personal insights increase, clients are more able to choose new and more creative ways of attaining goals that are socially useful and self-enhancing (Prochaska & Norcross, 2010).

Process and Techniques.   The process of counseling involves an analysis of clients' lifestyles to help them become aware of how they are directing their lives toward destructive goals. Clients are then encouraged to put these insights into action. Typically, Adlerian therapy involves four phases: establish the relationship, explore the individual's dynamics, encourage insight, and promote reorientation (Dinkmeyer & Sperry, 2000).

Initially, a collaborative relationship is established on a foundation of mutual trust and respect. In this phase, counselors utilize active listening and responding with genuineness and understanding, demonstrating their faith in the client's ability to make desired changes (Nystul, 2011).

The goal of the second phase, exploring the individual's dynamics, is to gain an understanding of the client's lifestyle and how it is affecting the client's functioning in life's tasks (Dinkmeyer & Sperry, 2000). Frequently, the counselor conducts a *lifestyle assessment,* asking the client questions that explore family constellation (e.g., psychological position in the family of origin, birth order, and family interactional patterns), earliest recollections, dreams, and priorities (Corey, 2012). The counselor then presents a summary of each area and identifies false or impossible goals of security, misperceptions of life's demands, and faulty values that support the self-defeating lifestyle. The summary also identifies the client's assets and strengths that can be harnessed to make beneficial changes.

In the encouraging-insight phase, counselors use a combination of supportive and confrontive approaches to help clients gain insight into mistaken beliefs and goals and self-defeating behaviors (Dinkmeyer & Sperry, 2000). While self-understanding is an important step toward change, these insights must be translated into productive action. Interpretation, as practiced by Adlerians, involves relating specific thoughts, attitudes, and behaviors to their undesirable consequences. Counselors move back and forth from here-and-now situations to the basic mistakes and lifestyle patterns identified through the lifestyle analysis. This process enables clients to grasp how they contribute to their own current problems and how they might contribute to their solution. Interpretations are always presented tentatively as hypotheses, rather than as factual statements of cause and effect. The collaborative efforts of clients are welcomed.

In the final phase, reorientation, clients put insight into action and make new decisions, goals, and action plans (Nystul, 2011). A wide range of techniques is used to motivate clients toward effective lifestyles (Dinkmeyer & Sperry, 2000):

1. Acting as if—Suggesting a limited task in which clients act as they would wish to but feel incapable of.
2. Spitting in the client's soup—Reframing clients' behavior so as to make it less appealing or desirable.
3. Paradoxical intention—Increasing clients' awareness of their ineffective behavior by prescribing an increase in the display of the symptom.
4. The question—Asking clients, "What would be different if you were well?"
5. Catching oneself—Once aware of their goals, clients are asked to consciously monitor the behavioral displays that they want to change.

The influence of Adlerian theory extends well beyond the counseling room. The emphasis on personal growth and the teleological focus lend themselves to applications in a variety of educational programs. Furthermore, a number of important parental skill-training programs are based on Adlerian principles. Finally, the concepts apply readily to communications training, problem solving, and rehabilitation programs.

BEHAVIOR THERAPY

Key Theorists. Classic behavior therapy is an application of the behavioral learning theories of Ivan Pavlov and B. F. Skinner (Follette & Callaghan, 2011). Ivan Pavlov was a Russian physiologist who initially investigated the role of the salivatory response of dogs in the digestive process. Specifically, he was trying to determine exactly how the stimulus of food in the mouth elicited saliva. However, he encountered a fundamental problem. The dogs would salivate before the food reached their mouths. He soon reasoned that he had stumbled on a basic principle of learning, which is referred to as *classical conditioning,* the type of learning that takes place when specific stimuli elicit particular behavior.

B. F. Skinner earned an undergraduate degree in English and aspired to be an author. However, he gave up his dream and was awarded a PhD in psychology by Harvard University in 1931. He did not see behaviorism as a theory of personality or psychotherapy. Rather, he saw it as the underlying philosophy of psychology, which was defined as the scientific study of behavior. He rejected general theories of personality and therapy because they fell short of the ideals of science, which, he believed, require the ability to truly control and predict behavior. He believed that psychology could be a science only if it established lawful relationships between behavior and its consequences. Cognitive factors lack precise measurement, and their relationship to overt behavior can be assessed only by speculation. Therefore, Skinner focused his theory building on environmental stimuli and overt behavior, the relationship of which could be empirically verified (Corey, 2012). His theory is known as *operant conditioning,* which concerns how a person's behavior *operates* on the environment to elicit specific consequences.

Essential Concepts and Principles. This section first reviews classical conditioning and then operant conditioning.

In his classic studies, Pavlov noted, first, that an unlearned stimulus (i.e., food—the unconditioned stimulus) elicited an unlearned response (i.e., saliva—the unconditioned response) from the organism. He viewed this response as reflexive, not as the result of prior learning. Then, he presented a neutral stimulus (i.e., the sound of a bell) just before he presented the unconditioned stimulus. Finally, after several presentations, he found that the bell elicited the saliva without any presentation of food. Once this learned stimulus-response was displayed, the bell and saliva were referred to as the conditioned (i.e., learned) stimulus and conditioned (i.e., learned) response, respectively.

Figure 4.1 illustrates the basic principles and concepts of classical conditioning.

Several other concepts are related to classical conditioning (O'Donohue, 1998). *Acquisition* occurs when the new conditioned response is elicited on presentation of

FIGURE 4.1 Basic Paradigm of Classical Conditioning

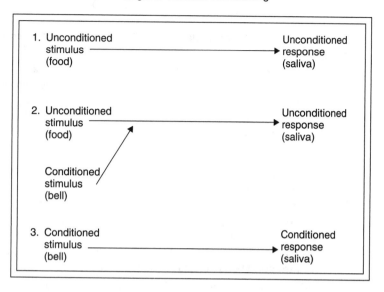

1. Unconditioned stimulus (food) ⟶ Unconditioned response (saliva)

2. Unconditioned stimulus (food) ⟶ Unconditioned response (saliva)

   Conditioned stimulus (bell)

3. Conditioned stimulus (bell) ⟶ Conditioned response (saliva)

a conditioned stimulus. *Extinction,* the "unlearning" of the conditioned response, takes place when the conditioned stimulus is no longer followed by presentation of the unconditioned stimulus, and eventually, the conditioned response stops occurring. In *stimulus generalization,* a neutral stimulus that approximates the conditioned stimulus is able to elicit the conditioned response. For example, a young child bitten by a dog may develop a strong fear not only of the specific dog but also of other dogs and four-legged household pets. Stimulus generalization occurs when the unconditioned response of fear to the specific dog is elicited when the child is presented with the stimulus of other similar creatures. Finally, one approach to preventing child sexual abuse involves teaching a child the difference between "good touch" and "bad touch." The ability to distinguish between the two types of touch illustrates *stimulus discrimination.*

Whereas classical conditioning concerns behavior elicited by antecedent conditions (i.e., environmental stimuli), operant conditioning focuses on the consequences of behavior (i.e., what happens after a behavior is emitted). Generally, behavior is followed by two types of consequences: reinforcers and punishers (O'Donohue, 1998). A *reinforcer* is defined as any event following a behavior that increases the likelihood that the specific behavior will recur. In contrast, a *punisher* refers to any event following a behavior that decreases the likelihood that the specific behavior will recur.

In addition, we can identify two types of reinforcers and punishers. A behavior is positively reinforced when a subsequent event increases the likelihood of recurrence of the behavior. In contrast, negative reinforcement removes something from the situation so as to increase the likelihood that the behavior will recur. Similarly, punishers can involve either the introduction or the removal of an event from the situation,

FIGURE 4.2 Basic Concepts of Operant Conditioning

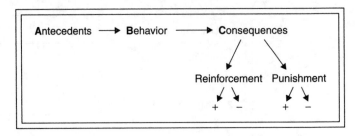

which decreases the likelihood that the behavior will recur. Figure 4.2 illustrates the basic concepts of operant conditioning.

Note that the determination of reinforcers and punishers does not lie in the qualities of the event per se. Whether or not an event serves as a reinforcer or a punisher depends solely on the effect of the event on the behavior. If the frequency of behavior increases, the event is a reinforcer, by definition. Thus, giving children candy bars to reward good behavior may or may not serve as a reinforcer. It all depends on the effect on the desired behavior. Similarly, parents who yell at their children do well to consider what effect their yelling is having on the child's specific behavior. It may bring an immediate cessation to the problem behavior, but does it decrease the likelihood that the behavior will recur? Sometimes, yelling has been found to serve as a reinforcer.

Goals of Behavior Therapy.   Behavior therapists view pathological behavior as being learned. It logically follows that the goals of counseling involve relearning (Nystul, 2011). If a behavior can be learned, it can also be unlearned and relearned!

Behavioral therapists see maladaptive behavior in itself as being the problem. Counseling is directed toward correcting problem behavior rather than focusing on underlying conflicts, personality structures, self-esteem, or faulty life decisions. The targets of counseling are typically formulated as belonging to one or several of the following categories:

1. Behavioral deficits
2. Behavioral excesses
3. Inappropriate environmental stimulus control
4. Inappropriate reinforcement contingencies

The principles of classical and operant conditioning are applied to facilitate the extinction of identified problem behaviors and the learning of more effective and functional alternatives.

Process and Techniques.   Behavior therapy is pragmatic. The validity of techniques cannot be assumed simply because they sound good or make logical sense. Rather, techniques are accepted and applied to the extent that they have demonstrated efficacy in relation to the specific problem. This empirical orientation applies to the therapeutic process itself. Scientific methods are used to identify problem behaviors, identify goals, and monitor therapeutic progress.

The process of behavior therapy begins with *functional behavioral analysis* (Follette & Callaghan, 2011). The counselor gathers detailed and specific information from the client or through direct observation of the client in problem-relevant situations. Specifically, counselors identify circumstances surrounding the development of the problem, the environmental factors associated with the maintenance of the problem, the changes in the problem over time, and the consequences related to the problem behavior. The statement of the problem is typically framed in terms of the ABCs (e.g., antecedents to the behavior, the problem **b**ehavior, and the **c**onsequences of the behavior).

A target behavior (e.g., goal statement) is identified and stated in terms that are specific, concise, and measurable. Initially, *baseline* data are gathered on the frequency of the target behavior. Approaches used to gather baseline data include client self-monitoring, behavioral rating scales, interviews, and direct observation. The counselor then selects and implements specific intervention strategies, based on empirical evidence of their efficacy, and monitors the client's response to treatment by gathering data on the occurrence of the target behavior after the intervention strategies have been implemented. Treatment goals are added or deleted as needed, and the overall treatment plan is revised according to the progress noted.

For our purposes, several specific techniques will illustrate the nature of behavioral therapy. Counterconditioning approaches are based on the classical conditioning paradigm and seek to alter clients' behavior by altering the antecedent conditions. *Systematic desensitization* is the treatment of choice for phobias involving nonhuman objects, animals, and anxieties (Wolpe, 1990). *Assertiveness training* is used to treat a variety of social anxieties (Wolpe, 1990). Clients learn to assert themselves in social situations that were previously anxiety provoking. In addition to counterconditioning, the assertive behavior is reinforced by the reduction of fear and increased success in social interactions.

Contingency management approaches are based on operant principles and seek to alter behavior by changing the link between the behavior and its consequences. For example, *self-management* techniques train clients to monitor and manipulate situational antecedents and consequences to change their own behavior (Logue, 1998). Making reinforcements contingent on desired behavior through the use of *token economies* is used in settings such as classrooms for troubled students, hospitals for chronic psychiatric clients, and skill training for the developmentally disabled (Ayllon & Azrin, 1968). *Behavioral exchange* is applied in marriage and family counseling to increase satisfaction with the relationship (Jacobson & Margolin, 1979).

COGNITIVE APPROACHES

A number of counseling approaches that arose beginning in the mid-1960s have a common emphasis on cognitive factors. Some arose out of a response to criticisms of the traditional psychoanalytic approaches. Others represented revisions or extensions of behavior therapy. However, all have in common the idea that behavioral and emotional change is best accomplished through interventions that seek to alter the client's cognitive style. The research of Albert Bandura (1974, 1977, 1986) provided an empirical foundation for what has become known as the *second wave* of behavioral therapies, that is, the cognitive-behavioral revolution (Hayes, 2004).

Generally, cognitive therapies accept behavioral principles but take into account the covert behaviors, such as the client's thoughts, beliefs, and underlying attitudes, which are not readily observable. The most widely practiced cognitive approaches are Albert Ellis's rational emotive behavior therapy, Aaron Beck's cognitive therapy, and Donald Meichenbaum's cognitive-behavioral modification.

Key Theorists.   Two pioneers of the cognitive approaches, Albert Ellis and Aaron Beck, practiced psychoanalytic therapy in the 1950s but became disillusioned by the approach (Corey, 2012). In addition, each was impressed by the role faulty cognitive processes played in the psychological distress of their clients. Ellis was especially impressed by the irrational thoughts contained in the internal dialogue of his clients. In rational emotive behavior therapy (REBT), clients are made aware of what they are saying to themselves and how such self-statements relate to the emotional pain they experience (Ellis, 1962). Clients become aware of the occurrence of such thoughts and learn to replace them with more rational alternatives. Beck was also impressed with how a person's *automatic thoughts* stemmed from the operation of cognitive distortions (Beck, 1976). Cognitive therapy (CT) seeks to alter these distortions and leads to the construction of thoughts that more accurately reflect the reality of situations.

In contrast to Ellis and Beck, Donald Meichenbaum came out of the behavioral camp. He was impressed by the research and theories of Bandura and Vygotsky, both of whom demonstrated the roles of social process and observational learning in the acquisition of new behavior. Meichenbaum's cognitive-behavioral modification (CBM) incorporates modeling, learning through observation, and verbal mediation to facilitate behavioral change (Meichenbaum, 1977).

Essential Principles and Concepts.   In each of these three approaches, cognition is the target of many of the interventions. However, we must note that the human thought process takes place at several different levels. An understanding of the distinction among these levels will clarify the differences among REBT, CT, and CBM.

At the deepest level, cognition takes the form of *cognitive structures.* Also referred to as *self-schemas,* these cognitive structures consist of the basic underlying assumptions individuals make about themselves and the world (Young, Klosko, & Weishaar, 2003). Past experiences establish these deeply ingrained and relatively enduring characteristics. Schemas play a critical role in the cognitive therapies because they can introduce bias and distortion into the processing of ongoing experience and influence the recall of past events. For example, Beck (1967) identifies a "cognitive triad" that consists of the following underlying assumptions: I am worthless and inadequate; the world (or the specific event) is an awful place; and the future is bleak. The cognitive triad provides the structure that supports the cognitive processing and products characteristic of emotional disorders.

The second level, cognitive processes, consists of the underlying reasoning styles we use in our actual processing of ongoing events. Emotionally healthy persons process events in such a way that they assign the events an accurate, realistic meaning. The consequent self-talk and emotional experience are appropriate, both in quality and in intensity. In contrast, the processing of specific events by emotionally distressed persons is often characterized by the use of cognitive distortions (Burns, 1980). These distortions lead to the misinterpretation of events because of the inaccuracy of the meanings assigned to the events (Beck, Rush, Shaw, & Emery, 1979). Examples of cognitive distortions identified by Beck include:

1. *Arbitrary inference.* Drawing conclusions without accurate supporting evidence or even despite contradictory evidence. For example, after receiving a C– on a research proposal, I conclude, "I might as well drop out of my doctoral program now, since I will never be able to write a doctoral dissertation."
2. *Selective abstraction.* Focusing on one aspect while ignoring or discounting other relevant features of the situation. As David Burns (1999) notes, it is like placing a drop of black ink in a beaker of clear water. The whole container of water is darkened by the small amount of ink. I engage in selective abstraction if I allow one negative comment made by a colleague to color my entire day.
3. *Overgeneralization.* Developing a general rule on the basis of only a few isolated events or facts. For example, my son's coming in late one evening leads me to conclude, "He never comes home on time!"
4. *Magnification or minimization.* Severely exaggerating or underestimating the significance of an event. As a result, the meaning assigned to the event is grossly distorted. For example, I might stutter over a word in giving a lecture and conclude, "Those students think I'm a bumbling idiot because of my speech deficit."
5. *Personalization.* Relating external events to yourself when there is no objective reason for doing so. The dean passes me in the hall and fails to say, "Hi." I say to myself, "The dean intentionally snubbed me."
6. *Dichotomous thinking.* Events are placed in one of two opposing, mutually exclusive categories. One's performance must be perfect or it was totally awful.

The third level of cognition, *cognitive products,* is most apparent to us. These are the statements we say to ourselves. This internal dialogue can be likened to the radio's play-by-play sports announcer, who sees, interprets, and verbally communicates what is happening on the playing field. These statements become the subjective reality on which our emotional and behavioral responses rest. In his book *Reason and Emotion in Psychotherapy* (1962), Ellis presented a list of 11 irrational beliefs that lead to emotional distress and psychological disorder. For example, "It is essential that a person be loved or approved by virtually everyone in the community" is an irrational statement because it is very possible to live a productive life without being loved by almost everyone.

Goals of Cognitive Therapies. The primary goal of all cognitive therapies is the removal of or relief from the presenting symptoms. But ultimately, cognitive therapies seek to correct the flawed cognitive structures, processes, and products that give rise to emotional distress. Thus, progress in counseling is noted as clients are able to catch onto styles of thinking that are associated with their presenting condition and substitute more reasonable and accurate alternative thoughts. For example, one of my previous clients displayed a very strong fear of flying and would report self-statements such as "I don't think I will make it through this flight." After eight sessions, the client stepped onto an airplane for the first time in 2 years and reported the following self-statement: "I may experience some turbulence during the flight, which will cause discomfort. But I can handle it. The presence of turbulence does not signal impending doom."

Process and Techniques.   In general, treatment progresses through several phases. First, a congenial, collaborative relationship is established with the client. Then, clients become aware of what they are thinking and doing and how these relate to the presenting problems. Third, clients learn to identify which specific thoughts represent distortions and are in need of revision or replacement. In addition, they identify behaviors that might interrupt the dysfunctional pattern. Finally, clients substitute the more productive style of thinking and behaving and gather evidence to determine the extent to which the alternative thoughts and behaviors are facilitating more effective functioning.

In REBT, clients are taught that emotional disturbances are explained by a simple ABC formula, where A = activating events; B = irrational beliefs; and C = the emotional and behavioral consequences. The counselor actively works with the client to modify the faulty beliefs into more rational alternatives. By learning to *dispute* (D) the irrational thoughts and replace them with rational alternatives, clients experience the positive *effect* (E).

Beck's CT makes extensive use of Socratic questioning and personal experiments to assist clients in changing thoughts and behaviors. This process is referred to as *guided discovery* (Freeman, Pretzer, Fleming, & Simon, 1990). Clients are taught to monitor the relationship of thoughts to emotional and behavioral consequences by keeping journals. A variety of cognitive and behavioral techniques are used to alter cognitive processes and promote more effective behaviors. Cognitive techniques include cognitive appraisal, cognitive restructuring, covert rehearsal, and imagery. Behavioral techniques include abdominal breathing, progressive muscle relaxation, systematic desensitization, activity scheduling, and assertiveness training.

Cognitive-behavioral modification (Meichenbaum, 1977) also makes use of the cognitive and behavioral techniques listed previously. In addition, CBM makes extensive use of self-instruction, self-reinforcement, graduated in vivo exposure, and personal narrative repair.

Third Wave of Cognitive-Behavioral Therapies: Mindfulness and Acceptance-Based Therapies.   Contemporary approaches to cognitive behavioral therapies have gone in different directions and do not fit as easily into the forms just described. These recent developments expand on the behavioral foundations and take into the account mindfulness and being present-in-the-moment, acceptance, distress tolerance, commitment, spirituality, and values. Two important contemporary approaches include acceptance and commitment therapy (ACT) and dialectic behavior therapy (DBT).

Acceptance and Commitment Therapy (ACT). ACT is described as a contextual cognitive-behavioral therapy that is designed to increase personal flexibility by helping clients to more fully experience and embrace their present emotional experience, while assisting them to move in self-selected, personally valued directions (Luoma, Hayes, & Walser, 2007). Important principles of ACT include:

- Psychological pain is normal, it is important, and everyone has it.
- You cannot deliberately get rid of your psychological pain, although you can take steps to avoid increasing it artificially.
- Pain and suffering are two different states of being.

- You do not have to identify with your suffering.
- Accepting your pain is a step toward ridding yourself of your suffering.
- You can live a life you value, beginning right now, but to do that you will have to learn how to get out of your mind and into your life. (Hayes & Smith, 2005)

In ACT, cognition is accepted, rather than challenged or disputed. Clients learn to recognize the operation of their *contextualized self* and put it aside, so they can give their *real self* full expression. This process involves taking a more objective stance by embracing and laying aside all of the thoughts and emotions that are related to persons' context so that they might make mindful decisions about what they truly value in life. Clients then engage in behavioral activities and homework to help them live by their values. The primary question posed to clients is

> Given the distinction between you as a conscious being and the private experiences you've been struggling with, are you willing to experience those private experiences now, fully and without defense, as they are, not as they say they are, and actually do what takes you in the direction of your chosen values at this time and in this situation? (Hayes & Smith, 2005, p. 177)

The number of empirical studies investigating ACT has exploded. Currently, there is a body of controlled outcome studies that support the effectiveness of ACT in addressing anxiety, stress, obsessive-compulsive disorder, depression, smoking cessation, substance abuse, stigma and prejudice, chronic pain, coping with psychosis, diabetes management, and coping with cancer and epilepsy. The approach appears to be well suited to practice within the clinical mental health counseling paradigm.

Dialectic Behavior Therapy. DBT is a cognitive-behavioral therapy that was originally developed to treat females diagnosed with borderline personality disorder (BPD) and having a history of self-destructive behaviors (Swales, 2009). Leaning heavily on classical and operant conditioning principles, DBT sees biological vulnerabilities and early childhood experiences as leading to the development of heightened emotional response systems such that clients diagnosed with BPD respond to stimuli in the environment with greater speed and emotional intensity than other persons. This response leaves them vulnerable to emotional and behavioral dysregulation, displayed outwardly through increased engagement in risky, impulsive, and self-harming behaviors and unstable relationships (Feigenbaum, 2010).

As with ACT, a central notion is that therapeutic change is most likely to take place as clients accept, rather than resist, "what is." Quite frankly, accepting "what is" is in itself a *change* for most clients. DBT makes the following assumptions about BPD clients and therapy (Linehan, 1993, pp. 106–108):

- Clients are doing the best they can.
- Clients want to improve.
- Clients need to do better, try harder, and be more motivated to change.
- Clients may not have caused all of their own problems, but they have to solve them anyway.
- The lives of suicidal borderline individuals are unbearable as they are currently being lived.

- Clients must learn new behaviors in all relevant contexts.
- Clients cannot fail in therapy.
- Therapists of borderline clients need support.

DBT involves four stages for the treatment of BPD (Smith & Peck, 2004). First, mental health counselors assist clients to increase their capability in three areas: decreasing life-threatening behaviors; decreasing therapy-interfering behaviors; and decreasing behaviors that interfere with the client's quality of life. These goals are accomplished by increasing client's mindfulness, interpersonal effectiveness, emotional regulation, distress tolerance, and self-management (Smith & Peck, 2004, pp. 31–32). The second stage focuses on the reduction of posttraumatic stress. This is accomplished as clients apply those skills attained in the first stage. In the third stage, mental health counselors work to increase the client's self-respect and attainment of individual goals. In the fourth stage, therapeutic work focuses on generalizing behaviors and skills so as to experience increased joy and self-acceptance as one who has had a past, lives in the present, and *has* a future (Linehan, 1993).

HUMANISTIC THERAPIES AND EXISTENTIAL THEORY

Key Theorist.   Carl Rogers (1902–1987) is the founder of person-centered therapy and has been recognized as one of the preeminent leaders in the humanistic movement. Raised in rural Wisconsin, Rogers initially went to college to prepare for a career in the Christian ministry at Union Theological Seminary (Bohart & Watson, 2011). After a period of searching and questioning, he left the seminary and received a PhD in psychology from Columbia University in 1931. He rejected his psychoanalytic training and developed an approach to counseling based on the "goodness of humanity." He believed in the inherent worth and growth potential of individuals. His approach downplays the importance of techniques while highlighting the vital significance of the therapeutic relationship and atmosphere.

Essential Concepts and Principles.   Rogers's approach advocates understanding clients as *persons* and developing case formulations from that vantage point rather that invoking a theory to understand *clients*. Thus, his approach is truly person centered and not theory centered (Day, 2007).

Elements of existential theory run through Rogers's approach (Corey, 2012). The concept of *self* is central and includes an awareness of one's total being, the way one relates to or is in touch with the immediate environment, and one's existence in the here-and-now. Person-centered therapy has a phenomenological orientation and underscores the significance of personal meaning and subjective reality. Other important themes include personal autonomy, freedom, responsibility, connectedness, and isolation.

Rogers believed all people have an inherent tendency to develop all of their capacities in ways that serve to maintain and enhance the person (the *actualizing tendency*). In addition, we possess a *valuing system* that places positive value on those experiences that are growth enhancing and negative value on those experiences that limit personal growth. Thus, we possess inherent tendencies that motivate us toward growth and direct us toward growth-enhancing experiences. Finally, as our awareness of self emerges, we develop a strong need for positive self-regard. This is a universal need to be valued and loved.

However, significant others tend to make their love contingent on what we do and not on who we are. According to Rogers, a positive correlation exists between the conditional love of our parents and one's level of pathology, because developing persons learn to regard themselves as they are regarded by others. As a result, they begin to forsake their own self-actualizing tendency and valuing system and substitute the values of those by whom they want to be accepted, causing in themselves a state of incongruence. Incongruence between aspects of self-concept and experience, then, is at the core of all emotional disorders (Bohart & Watson, 2011).

Goals of Person-Centered Therapy. People enter counseling for a variety of reasons. Whether one is seeking relief from severe stress, emotional breakdown, lack of meaningfulness, or social alienation, the goal of treatment is to increase the degree of congruence between oneself and one's experience. In other words, mentally healthy persons are more in touch with their immediate experience, more trusting and accepting of themselves, and more capable of self-validation.

Process and Techniques. As noted earlier, Rogers did not adhere to a specific set of therapeutic strategies. He believed the necessary and sufficient ingredients for successful treatment were contained in the counseling relationship (Rogers, 1961). This relationship requires six specific characteristics for constructive change:

1. Psychological closeness develops within the context of a meaningful relationship.
2. The client experiences vulnerability and is in a state of incongruency. This motivates the client to stay in the relationship.
3. The counselor is congruent and genuine within the relationship.
4. The counselor has unconditional positive regard for the client.
5. The counselor has an accurate empathic understanding of the client.
6. The client perceives the unconditional positive regard and empathic understanding of the counselor.

In such a counseling relationship, the client is more able and willing to be who he or she really is. The counselor actively attends to the client through listening, posture, and eye contact. He or she seeks clarification through a skillful use of questions. Often, such questions help clients clarify in their minds what they are truly thinking and feeling. Finally, the counselor's use of words to reflect accurately the client's subjective experience becomes a mirror in which clients see more clearly who they really are. As counseling proceeds, the self–experience discrepancy and tension that accompany incongruency decrease, and the outcome is a more autonomous, fulfilling life.

NARRATIVE THERAPIES

Given the multidisciplinary nature of clinical mental health counseling, many of the recent theoretical developments in this field are being shaped by the postmodern paradigm. This is perhaps most clearly seen in the rise of narrative therapy (White & Epston, 1990).

Key Theorists.   Narrative therapies have resulted from the work of many theorists (Corey, 2012). Some of the key figures are Insoo Kim Berg, Steve De Shazer, Michael White, and David Epstein.

Essential Concepts and Principles.   Counselors who practice narrative therapy note that clients come into sessions with personal stories that they tell in the present but that have also shaped their past. In other words, the events experienced are not nearly so important to the client's current level of functioning as is the subjective rendition of those events that become woven into their personal narrative. The client's story is the client's reality. In assessment, narrative therapists identify the subjective meanings, themes, and metaphorical objects and processes that run through their clients' stories.

Goals of Narrative Therapy.   The goal of counseling becomes personal narrative repair or reconstruction. The target is the story itself, not the client or the family system. For example, one of my female clients reported the following history: Her mother died on the client's twelfth birthday; her father, who was a heavy drinker, gave her, as the oldest child, excessive parental responsibility for her younger siblings; her father abused her verbally and physically; and she married a workaholic who was distant yet controlling. She concluded that she was a victim and characterized her life as a personal tragedy.

The goal for this client was to see herself not as the victim of a sad and repressive past but as a responsible person who was strong, competent, persistent, and resilient. The process of counseling was directed toward disconnecting old, hurtful themes from her story and weaving alternative meanings of empowerment into the fabric of the narrative.

Process and Techniques.   The primary techniques used by narrative therapists involve telling the story and examining it to identify alternative ways of reconceptualizing and retelling it. Essentially, the major tasks of treatment are the deconstruction and reconstruction or reauthoring of the client's story (Sharf, 2012). In the process, counselors help their clients beat the problem rather than hold onto their stories of the problem (Becvar & Becvar, 1999).

FEMINIST THERAPY

Key Theorists.   Many scholar-practitioners have contributed to the development of feminist therapy. These include Jean Baker Miller, Carolyn Zerbe Enns, and Oliva Espin (Corey, 2012).

Essential Concepts and Principles.   Feminist therapy is rooted in pluralism and the women's movement philosophy of the 1960s. It recognizes the social, political, and cultural forces that influence a person's identity and behavior. Sexism, racism, classism, and monoculturalism are harmful to personal well-being (Brown, 1994). Feminist therapists work to validate and empower clients while also advocating societal change. Women learn to value their female characteristics and female-centered values, such as empathy, cooperation, intuition, interdependence, and connectedness (Sturdivant, 1980).

Goals of Feminist Therapy.   The goals of feminist therapy include not only personal change, but also institutional change (Enns, 1997). After reviewing various theorists, Sharf (2012) identified the following goals as central to the feminist perspective: symptom removal, enhancement of self-esteem, increased quality of personal relationships, internal locus of acceptance of body and sexuality, increased valuing of diversity, and increased political awareness and social action. Feminist therapy assumes that the female point of view should be accepted, that equality should characterize personal relationships, and that the social processes of diverse societies may be discriminatory.

Process and Techniques.   In counseling, clients learn the repressive influences of gender roles and their negative impact on self-concept. Feminist therapy assists clients in developing a cognitive framework that supports the skills necessary for developing and maintaining positive self-evaluations (Russell, 1984). In addition, counselors in feminist therapy use assertiveness training to empower their clients. Sands (1998) found feminist therapy to be an effective approach to treating adolescent depression. Feminist therapy is frequently applied in consciousness-raising groups and has been integrated with other approaches in the treatment of men and children (Sharf, 2012).

FAMILY THERAPY

Essential Concepts and Principles.   Just as there are a number of individual approaches to counseling, family therapy also consists of a wide array of theories and techniques. Many of these approaches have unique theoretical foundations. Generally, though, family systems approaches focus on the interactions that occur among individuals in a three-generational family system. The entire system becomes the unit for analysis in assessment and therapeutic intervention.

Several general assumptions and related concepts guide family systems theory:

1. The family functions as a system (i.e., a complex unit consisting of interacting elements and relationships that organize them).
2. Circular causality provides more accurate explanations of personal behavior and emotional responses.
3. An accurate understanding of individuals can be attained only when persons are viewed within the context of their family system.
4. Understanding the nature of families involves more than simply summing its components. In other words, the whole is more than the sum of its parts.
5. Individual disorders are viewed as family disorders.
6. Pathology serves a family function.
7. *Boundaries* are largely emotional barriers that protect the integrity of individuals, subsystems, and nuclear families within the larger ecological system. *Enmeshment* occurs when individuals and subsystems lose autonomy due to a blurring of boundaries. In contrast, overly rigid boundaries around individuals and subsystems lead to *disengagement*.
8. *Triangles* are three-person subsystems that are the smallest stable emotional unit. When under stress, dyads become unstable and seek the support of a third person.

Generally speaking, assessment, diagnosis, and treatment in family therapy focus on the interpersonal rather than the intrapsychic. In addition, family therapists zero in on the transactions and interactions taking place within the system rather than on the specific contents of the presenting problem. Finally, whereas individual-oriented counselors tend to narrow their focus when stuck (reductionism), family therapists often enlarge the focus of treatment by inviting extended family into the sessions.

Goals, Processes, and Techniques. As noted previously, family therapy is a diverse field that encompasses a wide variety of orientations and techniques. Therefore, instead of attempting to impose an artificial set of conclusions regarding general goals, processes, and techniques, we discuss three *classic* approaches here: Bowenian family therapy, Minuchin's structural family therapy, and Haley's strategic family therapy. A fourth approach, emotionally focused therapy, is a recent development and is also discussed.

Bowenian Family Therapy. Bowenian family therapy sees personal, emotional, and behavioral problems as being due to difficulties the individual experiences in differentiating the self from the family of origin. In some cases, *fusion* blurs the psychological boundaries between the individual and other family members and contaminates the emotional and behavioral functioning of persons within the family. The result is the formation of an *undifferentiated ego mass.* In other family systems, individuals may be extremely *disengaged* because the boundaries between family members are so rigid that few or no emotional transactions take place. Sometimes *emotional cutoff* occurs, in which the person flees (physically) from an unresolved emotional attachment.

The goal of Bowenian family therapy is to develop a healthy differentiation of self from one's family of origin by separating one's intellectual from emotional functions. As a result, in stressful situations, one is able to respond more reasonably and autonomously than to react emotionally.

Primary techniques used by Bowenian counselors include teaching clients basic family system concepts to promote self-awareness, and conceptualizing the presenting problem in a systemic perspective. Counselors work with clients to strengthen their intellectual functioning while decreasing their emotional reactivity. When clients become able to act more reasonably, autonomously, the counselor coaches them as they return to their families of origin. The counselor supports clients' efforts to maintain an appropriate balance between personal autonomy and connectedness in the midst of the highly enmeshed or disengaged family system.

Minuchin's Structural Family Therapy. Minuchin sees families as governed by their *structure,* a set of covert rules that regulate family transactions. These rules are revealed as the counselor picks up on the consistent, repetitive, and predictable patterns of family behavior. Emotional boundaries, coalitions, and alliances are revealed by these patterns, and subsystems emerge that influence how individuals and these subsystems relate to one another within the family. Furthermore, the distribution of power and authority within the family reveals a power *hierarchy* that greatly influences the existing structure.

The goal of structural family therapy is to establish an effective hierarchical structure within the family. The parents must function as an executive coalition capable of providing mutual support and accommodation as well as presenting a loving but firm united front to their children. If the family is disengaged, the goal includes increasing interactions and easing boundaries between its members. The goal for enmeshed families is to facilitate differentiation and autonomy within the family.

Initially, counselors join with and accommodate to the interactional style of the family. They then work with the interactions and develop a systemic diagnosis. Techniques are used to accentuate and modify interactional patterns and boundaries.

Haley's Strategic Family Therapy. This approach is sometimes referred to as *brief problem-solving therapy* because it is method oriented and problem focused. It takes a very cognitive approach to the assessment of presenting problems but often makes little or no attempt to promote family insight into the nature of family problems. Rather, strategic family therapists direct family members to act in specific ways to disrupt patterns of behavior that maintain the presenting problems.

The goal of strategic family therapy is to solve the presenting problem. The counselor analyzes the behavioral sequences among family members in situations where the presenting problem occurs. Commonsense solutions have been attempted and have not succeeded in reducing symptoms, so strategic family therapists often resort to indirect and paradoxical techniques. Counselors may assign symptoms to bring about symptom control by the client. Or clients may be directed *not* to attempt to resolve the problem (i.e., the counselor restrains the client), an approach that may lead (paradoxically) to increased client effort. In addition, predicting relapses might be used paradoxically to prevent relapse. Finally, a variety of metaphorical tasks may be used that present clients with analogues that, when resolved, facilitate resolution of the presenting problems.

Emotionally Focused Therapy (EFT). A more recent approach to family therapy, EFT integrates features of attachment theory, systems theory, and humanistic experiential theories' emphasis on emotion in session to promote therapeutic change (Efron & Bradley, 2007). EFT counselors see most couples and family conflicts as related to the developmental attachment histories of the members, where interactions between family members activate underlying emotional schemes of inaccessibility and unresponsiveness (L. S. Greenberg, 2004). Persons become most overwhelmed by feelings of aloneness-in-relationships with those they most need. Repeated family interactions that activate such schemes produce self-reinforcing patterns of attack-withdraw, poor problem solving, and poor communication (Efron & Bradley, 2007).

The primary task for EFT counselors is to understand the presenting dysfunctional pattern of interaction in terms of attachment and to help family members to reconnect with each other in ways that lead to secure attachment bonds (Efron & Bradley, 2007). From this perspective, communication skill-building exercises will be successful *only if* more fundamental attachment themes are first addressed. As conflicts and related emotions are enacted within session, EFT counselors move from the initial conflict issue ("You did not get home from work on time as you promised") to the relationship ("I cannot depend on you") and then to the deeper schemes of attachment ("I feel anxious and insecure when I'm alone and you are nowhere to be found"). Such enactments are used by EFT counselors to increase clients' ability to approach, tolerate, regulate, and accept their emotional experience. Increased emotional self-regulation among family members becomes the foundation for building relational styles that are more responsive and security enhancing. Counselors are active and, sometimes, directive throughout the therapeutic process.

CONTEMPORARY TRENDS IN THE APPLICATION OF COUNSELING THEORY

The application of counseling theories occurs not in a vacuum but in a specific, dynamic, and ever-changing context. Thus, effective clinical mental health counseling is responsive to current characteristics and trends in the contemporary treatment environment. These trends influence the application of traditional theories and the development of new approaches. In this section, the following trends will be discussed briefly: spirituality (Young, Cashwell, Wiggins-Frame, & Belaire, 2002), the biologicalization of psychopathology and human behavior (Williams, 2001), and the contemporary economic context (Staton, 2000).

SPIRITUALITY IN COUNSELING

I was serving as cotherapist in an internship setting. My supervisors were sitting behind the one-way mirror doing live supervision. I was gathering information in an intake session with a family that was presenting with an adolescent boy described as being "out of control." The mother had just commented on how God and her church had been important sources of support for her when the telephone rang. At the other end was the familiar voice of my supervisor saying, "Get your client off the God thing … he is much too big for our counseling room." Religion, counseling, and psychology had been at odds for many years.

Recently, though, spirituality and religion in counseling have made a significant comeback. Take a glance through the local bookstore and you will discover numerous titles relating spiritual concepts and practices to the enhancement of personal well-being. This relationship is expressed in several ways in the professional literature.

First, the counseling profession recognizes spirituality as an integral aspect of the whole person. In fact, the Wheel of Wellness has viewed spirituality as "the core characteristic of healthy people" and "the source for all other dimensions of wellness" (Myers, Sweeney, & Witmer, 2000, p. 253). Thus, spirituality is central to our understanding of the mentally healthy person. Furthermore, the spiritual and religious dimensions can have either beneficial or negative repercussions in one's life (Kelly, 1995). Clinical mental health counselors must be sensitive to the developmental issues raised by spiritual and religious content/processes in the lives of clients.

Second, counselors' increased appreciation of social and cultural diversity includes a sensitivity to the religious and spiritual practices of their clients. Counselors must also be aware of the religious and spiritually related beliefs, values, and biases that they themselves bring to the table. For example, some counselors have had rather toxic personal experiences with religion. These counselors risk engaging in projection, displacement, or countertransference that can distort or disrupt the therapeutic relationship. In contrast, some religiously oriented counselors err by assuming like values, beliefs, and practices when working with clients with a similar faith tradition.

It is therefore essential that counselors be sensitive to the great diversity within specific religious groups. For example, persons practicing Christianity, Judaism, or Islam vary greatly in matters of faith and practice. Consider Christianity. Distinctions can be made on the basis of the following dimensions: Catholic versus Protestant; denominational affiliation; frequency of attendance; or religious orientation. In applying theory and techniques, mental health counselors must be careful not to take a one-size-fits-all approach. Numerous approaches have been developed recently to help counselors assess how their clients express spirituality and religiosity (Sherman & Simonton, 2001).

Third, many counselors are integrating spiritual and religious concepts and techniques into their counseling interventions. For example, a review of the counseling literature reveals numerous efforts to integrate religious beliefs with traditional counseling theory. For example, Polanski (2002) has found that Christian and Buddhist spiritual beliefs can be readily integrated into an Adlerian approach. Applicable Adlerian concepts include inferiority, striving for superiority, social interest, and lifestyle. Nielsen (1994) discusses how religious doctrine and biblical scripture can actually enhance and accelerate the impact of rational emotive behavior therapy in work with Christian clients. Gendlin's focusing procedure (Gendlin, 1981) can be used to help clients integrate their spiritual experiences into counseling (Hinterkopf, 1994). In addition, counselors are integrating religious beliefs with the treatment of substance abuse (Hanna, 1992) and in helping clients cope with chronic illness (Gordon et al., 2002).

BIOLOGICALIZATION OF PSYCHOPATHOLOGY AND HUMAN BEHAVIOR

With recent advances in research technologies, we are gaining greater insight into the physical and neurological foundations of normal and abnormal behavior. All aspects of human behavior, including motives, preferences, emotions, cognitions, and spirituality, are now being explained in biological terms (Newberg, D'Aquili, & Rause, 2001; Williams, 2001). While supporting the mind-body connection, this trend sometimes seems to trivialize the potency of counseling interventions as it overemphasizes medical interventions to treat emotional and psychological problems. Increasingly, the fast action of psychopharmacological interventions has become the benchmark in the selection of treatment alternatives. Somehow, taking a pill to find relief from emotional distress can appear more attractive than committing oneself to the difficult tasks that accompany working through issues in counseling. Interestingly, as much as 80% of psychotropic medications are prescribed by nonpsychiatric medical practitioners (Cummings, O'Donohue, & Cummings, 2011).

The mental health counseling profession has been influenced by the biologicalization of mental health in a number of ways. For example, many formal structures and processes that affect professional practice, such as agencies and managed care organizations, have increased their implicit support of the medical model and clinical diagnosis of presenting conditions. Therefore, clinical mental health counselors must have good handles on diagnostic and treatment planning processes, including the ability to write goals and objectives that meet the standards of agency and managed care policies. In addition, mental health counselors frequently consult with psychiatrists and nonpsychiatric family medicine practitioners regarding the appropriateness of psychopharmacological interventions. A working knowledge of psychopharmacological agents, indications/contraindications, and potential side effects is necessary to provide useful information to the psychiatrist as well as to monitor client response.

Finally, clinical mental health counselors are integrating their increased awareness of the mind-body connection into their professional practices. In doing so, the profession is well positioned to take its place as a provider of integrated health care. Mental health interventions may assist clients in coping with physical conditions. Furthermore, physically based interventions can be implemented as part of comprehensive treatment plans to treat emotional disorders or to enhance mental health. For example, Degges-White, Myers, Adelman, and Pastoor (2003) describe the application of cognitive-behavioral interventions in the management of migraine headaches. Other counselors, working from a wellness framework, have used physical exercise as a counseling intervention in working with self-esteem and locus-of-control issues (Okonski, 2003).

THE CONTEMPORARY ECONOMIC CONTEXT

One of the most significant trends in the development and application of theory concerns the economic context in which counseling services are delivered (Polkinghorne, 2001). Into the second half of the twentieth century, the delivery of counseling services was primarily one to one, office based, with no restrictions on the number of sessions. The severely disordered were treated in publicly funded institutions.

Since the 1970s, though, the costs of health care (and mental health care in particular) have increased dramatically. Staton (2000) notes that the aggregate cost of treating mental illness and substance abuse in the United States ranks third among disease categories, behind only heart disease and injury/trauma. Costs for mental health care are higher than many payers are able, or willing, to pay. Federal and state budget cutbacks have resulted in limited funding for mental health programs. At a time when mental health and community counselors are asserting their legitimate right to be service providers, they are experiencing increased competition for limited mental health funding with members of the allied mental health professions (Kelly, 1996).

For the field to remain viable as a profession, all mental health practitioners and the agencies they serve must answer questions such as:

- What theory and set of techniques works best and for whom?
- How many sessions are required to treat this specific condition?
- Is the specific client served well by the traditional 50-minute-hour session format?
- Could other formats be more effective and cost efficient?
- Can you demonstrate the necessity of each session?
- Are you using a form of treatment that has demonstrated efficacy for the specific presenting problem?

The contemporary economic environment demands increased validation and accountability from counseling theories and their application. These pressures have led to efforts to bring greater definition and control to the application of counseling theories through the creation of practice guidelines and treatment manuals (Erskine, 1998). Generally, such guidelines and protocols identify conditions for which a specific approach is the treatment of choice, and they go on to specify frequency, duration, objectives, and method of determining outcome. Hershenson (1992) recommends that the theory base for mental health counseling include empirically validated interventions, with an emphasis on existing theories that have established efficacy in helping clients cope with specifically defined problems of living.

Unfortunately, the use of treatment manuals limits the extent to which treatment plans can be derived through interactions in a collaborative counseling relationship. These limits are especially problematic for clinical mental health counselors because the reviews of the counseling literature consistently reveal that the counselor-counselee relationship is one of the most important factors in determining successful outcomes (Walborn, 1996). Thus, an important counseling skill in the current treatment environment is the ability to negotiate a workable treatment regimen in limited time frames, within the context of a warm, supportive, and collaborative counseling relationship.

CONCLUSION

As clinical mental health counselors, we have the privilege of helping our clients through difficult times to attain improved mental health and interpersonal relationships. Typically, they turn to us after having found their own efforts and the advice of others unhelpful. We look to our theories of counseling for guidance in how to proceed as we attempt to facilitate positive change in the lives of our clients.

You may now feel inundated and overwhelmed by the vast array of counseling theories presented in Chapters 3 and 4. On the one hand, you have so many theoretical options from which to choose. On the other hand, clients present with such diverse problems and backgrounds. How do counselors select a theoretical perspective that they call their own? How do counselors manage to relate theory to practice?

Prochaska and Norcross (2010) note that 23% of counselors do not hold to a single theoretical position but are eclectic in practice. The term *eclecticism* refers to the use of a wide variety of theories and techniques, sometimes in combination, so that treatment is tailored to best fit the specific needs of each client (Slife & Reber, 2001). Beginning counselors, though, need to proceed with caution before they jump onto this bandwagon. First, it is too easy for professionals to use the term *eclecticism* to mask what is more accurately described as being "jacks of all trades, masters of none." The worst case scenario is the misapplication of theory where clients are actually harmed. Second, without a firm grasp of specific theories, a quasi-eclectic counselor may blend a variety of concepts and principles in such a way that the result is fuzzy conceptualizations and incoherent treatment plans.

Your selection of a theoretical stance must consider not only the needs of the client but also your personality style and values. As noted in the previous chapter, you will impede your therapeutic effectiveness if you choose a stance that does not fit who you are as a person. Avoid yielding to the pressure of identifying a theoretical perspective prematurely. Give yourself time to try several on for size as you engage in your practicum and internship. You will initially gravitate toward those that fit well with your implicit theories. But also be aware of the goodness of fit between the theory and the ecological context (e.g., mission, policies, and culture of your agency; needs and cultural background of your client/system). Seek out the best supervision available. Finally, be open to new information and be willing to experiment.

It is likely that a particular theoretical orientation will rise to the surface. I suggest that you select that approach as a theoretical base of operations. Become very good at its application. Then begin to integrate one or two other approaches when their application is clinically justified. This method of proceeding will help to enlarge and enhance your theoretical foundation. Developing your personal theory takes time. Be patient with the process.

DISCUSSION QUESTIONS

1. In Chapter 3, the characteristics of good theories were listed. Discuss the extent to which the theories discussed in Chapter 4 actually meet these standards. For example, do the major traditional theories, such as psychoanalytic, Adlerian, or cognitive-behavioral theory, enable counselors to adequately describe, explain, predict, and facilitate change?
2. The theories described in this chapter vary in the extent to which they are precise, comprehensive, testable, and useful (see Chapter 3 for a discussion of these criteria). To what extent do the theories described in this chapter meet the criteria?
3. Identify several theories described in this chapter that fit best with your implicit theory of counseling. Discuss why you might gravitate to certain theories rather than to others. Consider your personal values and your worldview.
4. Do you believe it is important to consider and utilize issues of spirituality in mental health and community counseling? Cite several examples of how clients might benefit from such a focus. What cautions should the counselor be mindful of when integrating spirituality into the process of counseling?

SUGGESTED ACTIVITIES

1. Read the biographies or autobiographies of several theorists. Identify how their personal life experiences and values might have influenced the theories they developed.
2. Ask several mental health professionals to discuss how their practice has been influenced by the increased biologicalization of mental illness and its treatment. For example, has increased reliance on medication altered the role of traditional counseling interventions in treatment plans? Or have the roles of case managers, master's-level counselors, and psychologists changed?

3. Survey a sample of mental health and community counselors, social workers, and psychologists working in counseling settings. Determine which of the traditional and contemporary theories they find most useful in their professional practice. Are there significant differences in theory preference based on professional group or work setting? Do the practitioners see specific strengths and limitations in their application of traditional theories in contemporary treatment environments?

REFERENCES

Bandura, A. (1974). Behavior theory and the models of man. *American Psychologist, 29,* 859–869.

Bandura, A. (1977). *Social learning theory.* Englewood Cliffs, NJ: Prentice Hall.

Bandura, A. (1986). *Several foundations of thought and action: A social cognition theory.* Englewood Cliffs, NJ: Prentice Hall.

Beck, A. T. (1967). *Depression: Clinical, experimental, and theoretical aspects.* New York, NY: Harper & Row.

Beck, A. T. (1976). *Cognitive therapy and the emotional disorders.* New York, NY: International Universities Press.

Beck, A. T., Rush, A. J., Shaw, B. F., & Emery, G. (1979). *Cognitive therapy of depression.* New York, NY: Guilford Press.

Becvar, D. S., & Becvar, R. J. (1999). *Family therapy: A systemic integration* (4th ed.). Boston, MA: Allyn & Bacon.

Bohart, A. C., & Watson, J. C. (2011). Person-centered psychotherapy and related experiential approaches (pp. 223–260). In S. B. Messer & A. S. Gurman (Eds.), *Essential psychotherapies: Theory and Practice* (3rd ed.). New York, NY: Guilford Press.

Brown, L. (1994). *Subversive dialogues: Theory in feminist therapy.* New York, NY: Basic Books.

Burns, D. D. (1980). *Feeling good: The new mood therapy.* New York: Harper Collins.

Burns, D. D. (1999). *The feeling good handbook* (Rev. ed.). New York, NY: Plume Press.

Corey, G. (2012). *Theories and practice of counseling and psychotherapy* (9th ed.). Belmont, CA: Brooks/Cole.

Cummings, N. A., O'Donohue, W. T., & Cummings, J. L. (2011). The financial dimension of integrated behavioral/primary care. In N. A. Cummings & W. T. O'Donohue (Eds.), *Understanding the behavioral healthcare crisis: The promise of integrated care and diagnostic reform.* New York, NY: Routledge.

Day, S. X. (2007). *Theory and design in counseling and psychotherapy* (2nd ed.). Boston, MA: Houghton Mifflin.

Degges-White, S., Myers, J. E., Adelman, J. U., & Pastoor, H. (2003). Examining counseling needs of headache patients: An exploratory study of wellness and perceived stress. *Journal of Mental Health Counseling, 25,* 271–290.

Dinkmeyer, D., Jr., & Sperry, l. (2000). *Counseling and psychotherapy: An integrated, individual psychology approach.* Upper Saddle River, NJ: Prentice Hall.

Efron, D., & Bradley, B. (2007). Emotionally focused therapy (EFT) and emotionally focused family therapy (EFFT): A challenge/opportunity for systemic and post-systemic therapists. *Journal of Systematic Therapies, 26,* 1–4.

Ellis, A. (1962). *Reason and emotion in psychotherapy.* New York, NY: Lyle Stuart.

Enns, C. Z. (1997). *Feminist theories and feminist psychotherapies: Origins, themes, and variations.* New York, NY: Haworth Press.

Erskine, R. G. (1998). Psychotherapy in the USA: A manual of standardized techniques or a therapeutic relationship? *International Journal of Psychotherapy, 3,* 231–235.

Feigenbaum, J. (2010). Self-harm—The solution not the problem: The dialectical behavioural therapy model. *Psychoanalytic Psychotherapy, 24,* 115–134.

Follette, W. C., & Callaghan, G. M. (2011). Behavior therapy: Functional-contextual approaches. In S. B. Messer, & A. S. Gurman (Eds.), *Essential psychotherapies: Theory and practice* (3rd ed., pp. 184–220). New York, NY: Guilford Press.

Freeman, A., Pretzer, J., Fleming, B., & Simon, K. M. (1990). *Clinical applications of cognitive therapy.* New York, NY: Plenum Press.

Freud, S. (1914). *Psychopathology of everyday life* (A. A. Brill, Trans.). New York, NY: Macmillan.

Gendlin, E. (1981). *Focusing.* New York, NY: Bantam Books.

Gibson, D. M., Dollarhide, C. T., & Moss, J. M. (2010). Professional identity development: A grounded theory of transformational tasks of new counselors. *Counselor Education and Supervision, 50,* 21–38.

Gordon, P. A., Feldman, D., Crose, R., Schoen, E., Griffing, G., & Shankar, J. (2002). The role of religious beliefs in coping with chronic illness. *Counseling and Values, 46,* 162–174.

Greenberg, L. S. (2004). Emotion-focused therapy. *Clinical Psychology and Psychotherapy, 11,* 3–16.

Hall. C. S. (1954). *A primer of Freudian psychology.* New York, NY: World.

Hanna, F. (1992). Reframing spirituality: AA, the 12 steps, and the mental health counselor. *Journal of Mental Health Counseling, 14,* 166–179.

Hayes, S. C. (2004). Acceptance and commitment therapy, relational frame theory, and the third wave of behavioral and cognitive therapies. *Behavior Therapy, 35,* 639–665.

Hayes, S. C., & Smith S. (2005). *Get out of your mind and into your life: The new acceptance and commitment therapy.* Oakland, CA: New Harbinger.

Hershenson, D. B. (1992). The operation was a success, but the patient died: Theoretical orthodoxy versus empirical validation. *Journal of Mental Health Counseling, 14,* 180–186.

Hinterkopf, E. (1994). Integrating spiritual experiences in counseling. *Counseling and Values, 38,* 165–175.

Jacobson, N. S., & Margolin, G. (1979). *Marital therapy: Strategies based on social learning and behavior exchange principles.* New York, NY: Brunner/Mazel.

Kelly, E. W. (1995). *Spirituality and religion in counseling and psychotherapy.* Alexandria, VA: American Counseling Association.

Kelly, K. R. (1996). Looking to the future: Professional identity, accountability, and change. *Journal of Mental Health Counseling, 18,* 195–199.

Linehan, M. M. (1993). *Cognitive-behavioral treatment of borderline personality disorder.* New York, NY: Guilford Press.

Logue, A. W. (1998). Self-control (pp. 253–273). In W. O'Donohue (Ed.), *Learning and behavior therapy.* Boston, MA: Allyn & Bacon.

Luoma, J. B., Hayes, S. C., & Walser, R. D. (2007). *Learning ACT: An acceptance and commitment therapy skills-training manual for therapists.* Oakland, CA: New Harbinger.

Meichenbaum, D. (1977). *Cognitive-behavior modification.* New York: Plenum Press.

Myers, D. G. (2000). The funds, friends, and faith of happy people. *American Psychologist, 55,* 56–67.

Myers, J. E., Sweeney, T. J., & Witmer, J. M. (2000). The wheel of wellness counseling for wellness: A holistic model for treatment planning. *Journal of Counseling and Development, 78,* 251–266.

Newberg, A., D'Aquili, E., & Rause, V. (2001). *Why God won't go away: Brain science and the biology of belief.* New York, NY: Ballantine Books.

Nielsen, S. L. (1994). Rational-emotive behavior therapy and religion: Don't throw the therapeutic baby out with the holy water. *Journal of Psychology and Christianity, 13,* 312–322.

Nystul, M. S. (2011). *Introduction to counseling: An art and science perspective.* Upper Saddle River, NJ: Pearson Education.

O'Donohue, W. (Ed.). (1998). *Learning and behavior therapy*. Boston, MA: Allyn & Bacon.

Polanski, P. J. (2002). Exploring spiritual beliefs in relation to Adlerian theory. *Counseling and Values, 46,* 127–136.

Polkinghorne, D. E. (2001). Managed care programs: What do clinicians need? In B. D. Slife, R. N. Williams, & S. H. Barlow (Eds.), *Critical issues in psychotherapy: Translating new ideas into practice*. Thousand Oaks, CA: Sage.

Prochaska, J. O., & Norcross, J. C. (2010). *Systems of psychotherapy: A transtheoretical analysis* (7th ed.). Pacific Grove, CA: Brooks/Cole.

Rogers, C. (1961). *On being a person*. Boston, MA: Houghton Mifflin.

Ross, L. (1977). The intuitive psychologist and his shortcomings: Distortions in the attribution process. In L. Berkowitz (Ed.), *Advances in experimental social psychology* (Vol. 10). New York, NY: Academic Press.

Russell, M. (1984). *Skills in counseling women*. Springfield, IL: Thomas.

Sands, T. (1998). Feminist counseling and female adolescents: Treatment strategies for depression. Journal of Mental Health Counseling, 20, 42–55.

Sharf, R. S. (2012) *Theories of psychotherapy and counseling: Concepts and cases* (5th ed.). Belmont, CA: Brooks/Cole.

Sherman, A. C., & Simonton, S. (2001). Assessment of religiousness and spirituality in health research. In T. G. Plante & A. C. Sherman (Eds.), *Faith and health: Psychological perspectives*. New York, NY: Guilford Press.

Slife, B. D., & Reber, J. S. (2001). Eclecticism in psychotherapy: Is it really the best substitute for traditional theories? In B. D. Slife, R. N. Williams, & S. H. Barlow (Eds.), *Critical issues in psychotherapy: Translating new ideas into practice*. Thousand Oaks, CA: Sage.

Smith, L. D., & Peck, P. L. (2004). Dialectic behavior therapy: A review and call to research. *Journal of Mental Health Counseling, 26,* 25–38.

Staton, R. D. (2000). The national health care economic context of psychiatric practice. In P. Rodenhauser (Ed.), *Mental health care administration: A guide for practitioners*. Ann Arbor: University of Michigan Press.

Stevens, M. J., & Morris, S. J. (1995). A format for case conceptualization. *Counselor Education and Supervision, 35,* 82–94.

Sturdivant, S. (1980). *Therapy with women*. New York, NY: Springer.

Swales, M. A. (2009). Dialectical behaviour therapy: Description, research, and future directions. *International Journal of Behavioral Consultation and Therapy, 5,* 164–177.

Thorne, B. M., & Henley, T. B. (2005). *Connections in the history and systems of psychology* (3rd ed.). Florence, KY: Cengage Learning.

Walborn, F. S. (1996). *Process variables: Four common elements of counseling and psychotherapy*. Pacific Grove, CA: Brooks/Cole.

White, M., & Epston, D. (1990). *Narrative means to therapeutic ends*. New York, NY: Norton.

Williams, R. N. (2001). The biologicalization of psychotherapy: Understanding the nature of influence (pp. 51–68). In B. D. Slife, R. N. Williams, & S. H. Barlow (Eds.), *Critical issues in psychotherapy: Translating new ideas into practice*. Thousand Oaks, CA: Sage.

Wolpe, J. (1990). *The practice of behavior therapy* (4th ed.). New York, NY: Pergamon Press.

Young, J. E., Klosko, J. S., & Weishaar, M. E. (2003). *Schema therapy: A practitioner's guide*. New York, NY: Guilford Press.

Young, J. S., Cashwell, C., Wiggins-Frame, M., & Belaire, C. (2002). Spiritual and religious competencies: A national survey of CACREP-accredited programs. *Counseling and Values, 47,* 22–33.

Part 2

The Credentialing and Practice of Clinical Mental Health Counseling

Education, Licensure, and Certification

OUTLINE

So you want to be a licensed professional or mental health counselor. What a great vocational choice! You can already envision the setting of your practice and the clientele you will serve.

For most of you, two important hurdles lie between your present status and the ability to practice independently: training and licensure. These are not inconsequential. Academic training entails earning a graduate degree in counseling. With diploma in hand, you then engage in professional practice under the supervision of a qualified mental health professional. Upon working the appropriate number of hours under qualified supervision, you have only one major hurdle to cross: passing the licensure exam. After passing the exam, you enter the promised land.

But things happen and plans change. Having practiced as a licensed mental health counselor for several years, you choose to move and set up your professional practice in another state. You discover that you cannot practice with your out-of-state license and must apply for a new license. There is no "license portability"! The sands of the promised land have shifted beneath your feet!

This chapter discusses academic preparation, licensure, and certification. Your understanding of the material in this chapter is a critical element in establishing your professional identity as a clinical mental health counselor. It is also necessary knowledge if you are to attain licensure and engage in professional practice.

First, the chapter explores the training model for clinical mental health counselors set forth by CACREP (the Council for Accreditation of Counseling and Related Educational Programs). The model's components provide a solid foundation of knowledge and skills for entry-level practitioners. The chapter then discusses the licensure and certification processes. Through these processes, CACREP and the individual states regulate the mental health counseling profession.

Ideally, licensure and certification rest on an interactive dynamic among professional practice, the training model, and professional identity. Figure 5.1 presents this complex relationship and its operation within the ecological context.

Clinical mental health counselors perform specific tasks in a variety of occupational settings. In these settings, they work alongside other mental health and human service professionals. The profession of clinical mental health counseling exists because it brings to the table a unique perspective and contribution to the treatment process. Its training model provides students with working knowledge and skills that set it apart from those trained in social work, psychology, or marriage and family therapy programs. In addition, the training model stays within the boundaries of the definition of the profession while being responsive to client and community needs in the ever-changing ecological context of service provision. The viability and vitality of the mental health counseling profession are ensured to the extent that licensure reflects the unique training and contributions of licensees relative to members of the allied mental health professions.

Licensure and certification, then, define the professional identity, training, and practice of clinical mental health counselors.

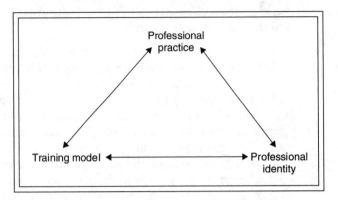

FIGURE 5.1 Interaction of Practice, Training Model, and Professional Identity

ACADEMIC PREPARATION OF CLINICAL MENTAL HEALTH COUNSELORS

Numerous paths are available for persons seeking to pursue training and licensure in counseling-related professions. In 2000, Hollis and Dodson noted that 542 departments of higher education currently offer one or more programs in counselor preparation. These programs represent a vast array of counseling-related professions and specializations, each of which has set academic standards for the specialized accreditation of graduate training programs in its profession. Specialized accreditation is a voluntary process in which academic programs demonstrate that their curriculum, department, faculty and staff, and institution meet high professional standards.

For example, the American Psychological Association Council on Accreditation (APA-CoA) serves as the national accrediting authority for professional education and training in psychology. It does not accredit bachelor's or master's programs but focuses on doctoral programs only. The Council on Social Work Education Commission on Accreditation (CSWE-CoA) sets the standards for the professional preparation of social workers. The CSWE-CoA reviews and accredits bachelor's and master's social work programs. The American Association for Marriage and Family Therapy (AAMFT) has established the Commission of Accreditation for Marriage and Family Therapy Education (COAMFTE). This organization accredits master's degree, doctoral degree, and postgraduate degree programs in marriage and family therapy. The national standards for the training of clinical mental health counselors are established by CACREP, which is the largest specialized accreditation body for master's and doctoral programs in professional counseling.

THE CACREP MODEL OF TRAINING FOR CLINICAL MENTAL HEALTH COUNSELORS

A brief history and description of CACREP was given in Chapter 1 of this text. As you may recall, CACREP is an independent agency recognized by the Council for Higher

Education Accreditation. Its mission is to promote the professional competence of counseling and related practitioners through the development of preparation standards, the encouragement of excellence in program development, and the accreditation of professional preparation programs (CACREP, 2009a). The standards are established to ensure that students develop a professional counselor identity and master the knowledge and skills necessary to practice effectively within their chosen area of specialization.

Established in 1981, CACREP accredits over 590 graduate counseling programs at over 250 academic institutions (Bobby & Urofsky, 2011). CACREP sets standards for and renders accreditation decisions on the following programs: addiction counseling; career counseling; clinical mental health counseling; marital, couple, and family counseling; school counseling; student affairs and college counseling; and counselor education and supervision (doctoral level only). The standards assess the overall quality of the academic institution and its administrative structure and organization; the program's objectives, curriculum, and clinical instruction; the faculty and staff; program organization and administration; and evaluation procedures.

The general curricular model established by CACREP consists of three general components: a common core curriculum, standards for the specializations, and professional practice experiences. Figure 5.2 illustrates the general design of graduate training programs for clinical mental health counselors that follow the CACREP model.

FIGURE 5.2 The General Curricular Model of CACREP

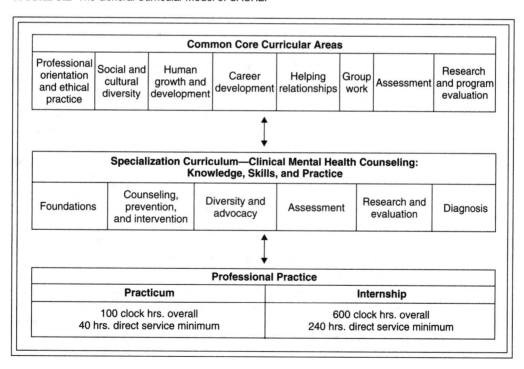

The categorization of the curriculum leaves the false impression that the content areas are encased in specific courses. This is not necessarily the case. Instead, the CACREP model takes an infusion approach that integrates the contents of core areas throughout the curriculum rather than compartmentalizing it in unique courses. Thus, for example, instruction in the core area of assessment occurs not only in the assessment course but in other courses, such as human development, research and program evaluation, psychopathology, and practicum/internship. As a result, students gain exposure to core contents in a variety of courses throughout their academic program.

Common Core Curriculum. It is vital that all counselors possess specific knowledge and skills regardless of specialization. CACREP has identified eight common core areas of study that are required of all students in counseling programs (CACREP, 2009).

- *Professional Orientation and Ethical Practice*—Studies that provide an understanding of the history and philosophy of the counseling profession, professional roles and functions, organizations and credentialing, supervision models, advocacy processes, and ethical and legal considerations.
- *Social and Cultural Diversity*—Curricular experiences in which students gain an understanding of multicultural contexts and trends; issues, strategies, and theories for working with culturally diverse individuals, groups, and families; development of multicultural competencies; ethical and legal issues; and social justice and advocacy skills.
- *Human Growth and Development*—Studies focusing on the nature and processes of physical, cognitive, socioemotional, and family development across the lifespan; normal and abnormal human behavior; effects of disaster, crises, and other trauma-causing events; exceptionality; addictions; and strategies for enhancing optimal development.
- *Career Development*—Studies that explore career selection, decision making, and development; program-delivery-systems development and evaluation; career assessment guidance and counseling (including technology-based approaches); and work-context interactions (e.g., family, life roles, and multicultural issues).
- *Helping Relationships*—Studies that provide knowledge of and skills in counseling and consultation processes such as predominant models of counseling; orientation to wellness and prevention; family systems models; crisis intervention and suicide prevention models; counselor/counselee characteristics and relationships; interviewing and counseling skill development; and technological strategies.
- *Group Work*—Studies that provide knowledge and skills for understanding, facilitating, and providing leadership in the development and evaluation of various forms of group work; principles of group dynamics, theories, and techniques; and the direct experience of group participation (minimum of 10 hours over one academic term).
- *Assessment*—Studies that provide knowledge of the history and meaning of assessment; theories, principles, and psychometric and statistical concepts for understanding individual and group approaches to assessment; and basic skill development in the selection, administration, scoring, and interpretation of assessment devices.

- *Research and Program Evaluation*—Studies that provide knowledge and skills in research methodology, statistical analysis (including application of statistical software), needs assessment, and program evaluation; use of research to inform evidence-based practice; and ethical and culturally relevant strategies.

Although these categories are described as core curricular *areas of study*, most graduate programs in counseling organize them as content for specific courses. Thus, a survey of accredited programs reveals a common set of eight core courses that are required for all students in graduate counseling programs with specializations in mental health and community counseling.

The core courses provide a foundation on which the specializations and clinical experiences rest. Through these curricular experiences, clinical mental health counselors become knowledgeable in the nature and promotion of mental health and wellness as well as the assessment and treatment of emotional disorder. In addition, they gain an understanding of the social factors that influence personal and systemic well-being. Finally, mental health counselors acquire a basic knowledge of what it means to be a licensed mental health or professional counselor by becoming familiar with their professional associations, codes of ethics, and standards of preparation, licensure, and certification.

CACREP STANDARDS FOR CLINICAL MENTAL HEALTH COUNSELING PROGRAMS

In addition to coursework covering the eight core curricular areas, clinical mental health counseling students are required to have academic experiences that cover critical areas of their specialization . The standards for clinical mental health counseling programs are listed in Figure 5.3. Overall, students in clinical mental health counseling programs are required to complete a minimum of 60 semester credit hours of study, covering the core areas, specialization-related knowledge and skills, and clinical areas.

As you can see, the CACREP standards for clinical mental health counseling specialization (CACREP, 2009a) consist of six components: foundations; counseling, prevention, and intervention; diversity and advocacy; assessment; research and evaluation; and diagnosis. Each of these components is further divided into sets of knowledge and skills/practices.

Foundations. Students in clinical mental health programs are expected to gain an understanding of the underlying structures, processes, and trends relevant to the professional practice of their specialization. Their studies include history and systems of clinical mental health counseling; relevant professional organizations and related ethical and legal codes; contemporary roles and functions; the economic and cultural forces influencing the practice of clinical mental health counselors; and the management of mental health programs, delivery systems, and emergency operations. Furthermore, clinical mental health counselors are trained to practice legally and ethically, and to

FIGURE 5.3 CACREP Standards for Clinical Mental Health Counseling Programs

Standards for the Specialization of Clinical Mental Health Counseling: Foundations	**Knowledge** 1. Understands the history, philosophy, and trends in clinical mental health counseling. 2. Understands ethical and legal considerations specifically related to the practice of clinical mental health counseling. 3. Understands the roles and functions of clinical mental health counselors in various practice settings and the importance of relationships between counselors and other professionals, including interdisciplinary treatment teams. 4. Knows the professional organizations, preparation standards, and credentials relevant to the practice of clinical mental health counseling. 5. Understands a variety of models and theories related to clinical mental health counseling, including the methods, models, and principles of clinical supervision. 6. Recognizes the potential for substance use disorders to mimic and coexist with a variety of medical and psychological disorders. 7. Is aware of professional issues that affect clinical mental health counselors (e.g., core provider status, expert witness status, access to and practice privileges within managed care systems). 8. Understands the management of mental health services and programs, including areas such as administration, finance, and accountability. 9. Understands the impact of crises, disasters, and other trauma-causing events on people. 10. Understands the operation of an emergency management system within clinical mental health agencies and in the community. **Skills and Practices** 1. Demonstrates the ability to apply and adhere to ethical and legal standards in clinical mental health counseling. 2. Applies knowledge of public mental health policy, financing, and regulatory process to improve service delivery opportunities in clinical mental health counseling.
Standards for the Specialization of Clinical Mental Health Counseling: Counseling, Prevention, and Intervention	**Knowledge** 1. Describes the principles of mental health, including prevention, intervention, consultation, education, and advocacy, as well as the operation of programs and networks that promote mental health in a multicultural society. 2. Knows the etiology, the diagnostic process and nomenclature, treatment, referral, and prevention of mental and emotional disorders. 3. Knows the models, methods, and principles of program development and service delivery (e.g., support groups, peer facilitation training, parent education, self-help). 4. Knows the disease concept and etiology of addiction and co-occurring disorders. 5. Understands the range of mental health service delivery —such as inpatient, outpatient, partial treatment and aftercare —and the clinical mental health counseling services network. 6. Understands the principles of crisis intervention for people during crises, disasters, and other trauma-causing events. 7. Know the principles, models, and documentation formats of biopsychosocial case conceptualization and treatment planning. 8. Recognizes the importance of family, social networks, and community systems in the treatment of mental and emotional disorders. 9. Understands profession issues relevant to the practice of clinical mental health counseling.
Standards for the Specialization of Clinical Mental Health Counseling: Diversity and Advocacy	**Knowledge** 1. Understands how living in a multicultural society affects clients who are seeking clinical mental health counseling services. 2. Understands the effects of racism, discrimination, sexism, power, privilege, and oppression on one's own life and career and those of the client. 3. Understands current literature that outlines theories, approaches, strategies, and techniques shown to be effective when working with specific populations of clients with mental and emotional disorders. 4. Understands effective strategies to support client advocacy and influence public policy and government relations on local, state, and national levels to enhance equity, increase funding, and promote programs that affect the practice of clinical mental health counseling. 5. Understands the implications of concepts such as internalized oppression and institutional racism, as well as the historical and current political climate regarding immigration, poverty, and welfare. 6. Know public policies on the local, state, and national levels that affect the quality and accessibility of mental health services.

FIGURE 5.3 (*Continued*)

	Skills and Practices
	1. Maintains information regarding community resources to make appropriate referrals. 2. Advocates for policies, programs, and services that are equitable and responsive to the unique needs of clients. 3. Demonstrates the ability to modify counseling systems, theories, techniques, and interventions to make them culturally appropriate for diverse populations.
Standards for the Specialization of Clinical Mental Health Counseling: Assessment	**Knowledge** 1. Knows the principles and models of assessment, case conceptualization, theories of human development, and concepts of normalcy and psychopathology leading to diagnoses and appropriate counseling treatment plans. 2. Understands various models and approaches to clinical evaluation and their appropriate uses, including diagnostic interviews, mental status examinations, symptom inventories, and psychoeducational and personality assessments. 3. Understands basic classifications, indications, and contraindications of commonly prescribed psychopharmacological medications so that appropriate referrals can be made for medication evaluations and so that the side effects of such medications can be identified. 4. Identifies standard screening and assessment instruments for substance use disorders and process addictions. **Skills and Practices** 1. Selects appropriate comprehensive assessment interventions to assist in diagnosis and treatment planning, with an awareness of cultural bias in the implementation and interpretation of assessment protocols. 2. Demonstrates skill in conducting an intake interview, a mental status evaluation, a biopsychosocial history, a mental health history, and a psychological assessment for treatment planning and caseload management. 3. Screens for addiction, aggression, and danger to self and/or others, as well as co-occurring mental disorders. 4. Applies the assessment of a client's stage of dependence, change, or recovery to determine the appropriate treatment modality and placement criteria within the continuum of care.
Standards for the Specialization of Clinical Mental Health Counseling: Research and Evaluation	**Knowledge** 1. Understands how to critically evaluate research relevant to the practice of clinical mental health counseling. 2. Knows models of program evaluation for clinical mental health programs. 3. Knows evidence-based treatments and basic strategies for evaluating counseling outcomes in clinical mental health counseling. **Skills and Practices** 1. Applies relevant research finds to inform the practice of clinical mental health counseling. 2. Develops measurable outcomes for clinical mental health counseling programs, interventions, and treatments. 3. Analyzes and uses data to increase the effectiveness of clinical mental health counseling interventions and programs.
Standards for the Specialization of Clinical Mental Health Counseling: Diagnosis	**Knowledge** 1. Knows the principles of the diagnostic process, including differential diagnosis, and the use of current diagnostic tools, such as the current edition of the Diagnostic and Statistical Manual of Mental Disorders (DSM). 2. Understands the established diagnostic criteria for mental and emotional disorders, and describes treatment modalities and placement criteria within the continuum of care. 3. Knows the impact of co-occurring substance use disorders on medical and psychological disorders. 4. Understands the relevance and potential biases of commonly used diagnostic tools with multicultural populations. 5. Understands appropriate use of diagnosis during a crisis, disaster, or other trauma-causing event. **Skills and Practices** 1. Demonstrates appropriate use of diagnostic tools, including the current edition of DSM, to describe the symptoms and clinical presentation of clients with mental and emotional impairments. 2. Is able to conceptualize an accurate multi-axial diagnosis of disorders presented by a client and discuss the differential diagnosis with collaborating professions. 3. Differentiates between diagnosis and developmentally appropriate reactions during crises, disasters, and other trauma-causing events.

Note: The parts of the CACREP Standards reproduced in this work represent only selected parts of the 2009a CACREP Standards. Inclusion of the CACREP Standards in this work is in no way intended to imply CACREP endorsement or approval of this work, and use of this work as a teaching tool does not establish or connote compliance with CACREP Standards for purposes of determining CACREP accreditation of any education program.

constructively modify their professional delivery of services in light of the constant changes in public policy, the economy, and the regulation of their profession.

Counseling, Prevention, and Intervention.   Students in clinical mental health counseling programs learn theories and skills that enable them to practice along the full continuum of mental health services, including remedial services, wellness enhancement, consultation, advocacy, prevention, and psychoeducational services to individuals, families, groups, and organizations in inpatient settings, intensive outpatient settings, community mental health programs, behavioral health care, emergency/crisis care, and community settings. As can be seen in Figure 5.3, competent practice requires a wide array of skills in these areas.

Diversity and Advocacy.   Knowledge, skills, and practices in diversity and advocacy build upon those established in the core area of study described in the previous section. Students of clinical mental health counseling must demonstrate skill in the culturally sensitive delivery of services to diverse populations. They must therefore have an in-depth appreciation of the full range of ecological forces that interact with the personal qualities and experiences of diverse clients. For example, barriers to accessing treatment are understood within the context of discrimination, injustice, and oppression. Furthermore, students learn how to integrate the unique strengths and resources of diverse clients into culturally sensitive treatment plans and service delivery systems.

Assessment.   This set of knowledge, skills, and practices encompasses the range of assessment activities necessary for the practice of clinical mental health counseling. Included are the development of accurate case conceptualizations and diagnoses; the selection, administration, and scoring of mental status exams, symptom and clinical scales, and personality inventories; and skills for making appropriate referrals for psychiatric consultations.

Research and Evaluation.   Specialization-based knowledge and skills in research and evaluation are very important for the survival of clinical mental health counselors in the contemporary practice environment. Clinical mental health counselors must, of course, be able to understand the available research in order to give their practice a dynamic, evidence-informed base. Although not all mental health counselors will themselves be researchers, they must be skilled consumers of the literature. Furthermore, funding sources increasingly call on practitioners to document the effectiveness of the services and programs they deliver. A good working knowledge of research and statistical methods and program evaluation models, as well as the demonstration of evidence-based practice, can set clinical mental health counselors apart from master's-level practitioners of other mental health professions.

Diagnosis.   Mental health counselors have a long history of using diagnostic systems in their professional practice (Cannon & Cooper, 2010; Hansen, 2003; Pistole & Roberts, 2002). Understanding and being able to apply diagnostic systems, such as the American Psychiatric Association's *Diagnostic Statistical Manual* (*DSM*), in the vast array of treatment contexts is a prerequisite for those mental health counselors who want to practice in community mental health settings or on multidisciplinary treatment teams. Training in accordance with the CACREP standards enables students to conceptualize developmentally and clinically appropriate multiaxial diagnoses that are ecologically informed.

PROFESSIONAL PRACTICE STANDARDS IN THE TRAINING OF CLINICAL MENTAL HEALTH COUNSELORS

The clinical training of mental health counselors is the most important component of academic preparation. It is in the applied, practical setting that classroom learning takes on reality. Increasingly, counselor education programs are including hands-on counseling experience throughout their curriculum. By trying on the counseling role, students can better assess their goodness of fit with the profession.

Two types of clinical experience are required: practicum and internship. The practicum consists of a minimum of 100 clock hours in an appropriate setting. This time must include:

- At least 40 hours of direct service to clients, including experience in individual and group counseling;
- An average of 1 hour weekly of individual or triadic supervision, typically provided by a program faculty member or a person supervised by a program faculty member;
- An average of 1.5 hours of group supervision, again typically provided by faculty members or people under the supervision of the faculty.

There must be a site supervisor who has a minimum of a master's degree in counseling or a related profession, at least 2 years of experience, and appropriate licenses or certifications.

The supervised internship requires 600 clock hours, which can begin following the successful completion of the practicum. Frequently, the internship serves as the capstone of the student's graduate program. It is here that students have the opportunity to pull together all components of their previous graduate training and experience the joys and frustrations of professional practice in a community setting. To have an optimal training experience, students should take the time and energy to identify internship settings and supervisors that will promote their personal and professional development. Many students find internships to be the most critical and exhilarating learning experience of their educational program.

Within this 600-hour requirement, the internship includes:

- 240 hours of direct service with appropriate clientele;
- Weekly 1-hour sessions of individual or triadic supervision, typically conducted by the site supervisor;
- Weekly 1.5-hour sessions of group supervision, typically conducted by program faculty.

As in practicum, site supervisors must have master's degrees in counseling or a related discipline, at least 2 years of experience, and appropriate licenses or certifications.

Few studies have investigated the impact or benefits of receiving counselor education from a CACREP-approved program (Schmidt, 1999). Vacc and Loesch (2000), though, note several positive consequences of graduating from such programs. First, the inherent strength of a program is communicated by its accreditation relative to programs that have not attained or attempted to achieve accreditation. Second, graduates from CACREP-approved programs are increasingly provided advantages when seeking counselor-related credentials. For example, the processing of state licensure applications may be expedited when the academic program is CACREP accredited. In addition, graduates from CACREP-approved programs can sit for the National Certification Exam (NCE) in the final semester of their program of study and before completing their postgraduate supervised experience. The NCE is a comprehensive exam consisting of 200 multiple-choice questions covering the eight CACREP core content areas and an additional five work behavior areas: fundamentals of counseling, assessment and career counseling, group counseling, programmatic and clinical intervention, and professional practice issues. With passing scores on the NCE, students are eligible for certification pending completion of the other requirements.

Adams (2006) compared the NCE test results of CACREP-accredited program test-takers with non-CACREP-program test-takers. She found that those test-takers who graduated from CACREP-accredited programs scored significantly higher than nonaccredited test-takers. Thus, preliminary evidence supports the assertion that the CACREP model of what is taught, how it is taught, and what is necessary is important in establishing professional credibility.

THE CREDENTIALING OF CLINICAL MENTAL HEALTH COUNSELORS

Credentialing follows the successful completion of the appropriate academic program. Since holding proper credentials is critical to being able to practice in the profession, students entering clinical mental health counseling programs should be sure that the program's curriculum fulfills the academic requirements of the relevant credentialing bodies.

Sweeney (1995) defines *credentialing* as a process that identifies individuals by professional group. Three basic methods are used: registry, certification, and licensure. Of these, *registry* is the simplest and least restrictive. To be listed on a registry, one can often simply provide the necessary information and pay a small fee. Although it is least useful in regulating the profession, being listed on a registry can provide useful information to consumers and professionals seeking to make referrals.

Certification, generally speaking, is a credentialing process by which a specific group or profession seeks to set standards to ensure quality within itself. Gladding (2011) defines *certification* as "the process by which an agency, government, or association officially grants recognition to an individual for having met certain professional qualifications that have been developed by the *profession*" (p. 28). Thus, counselors who are certified have gone through a voluntary process to confirm that they meet or exceed the minimum standards for practice as set by the profession. Certification restricts use of the professional title to those who have met the established standards but does not regulate, govern, or ensure the quality of professional practice.

Various types of certification are available to clinical mental health counselors. The most visible and highly recognized national counselor certification is issued by the National Board of Certified Counselors (NBCC; Schweiger, Henderson, McCaskill, Clawson, & Collins, 2011). Established in 1982, the NBCC offers certifications of both general practice and specialties. The National Certified Counselor (NCC) credential signifies that practitioners have met specified requirements for general practice in training, experience, and performance (Remley & Herlihy, 2010). These requirements include a graduate degree in counseling of at least 48 semester hours, completion of coursework that reflects the CACREP core content, and postgraduate clinical experience of at least 3,000 hours and 100 hours of face-to-face supervision over at least 2 years since graduation (NBCC, 2012a). In addition, applicants are required to attain a passing score on the NCE.

Qualified clinical mental health counselors who have attained the NCC may seek specialty certification as CCMHCs (Certified Clinical Mental Health Counselors) or MACs (Master Addictions Counselors). The CCMHC was established by AMHCA (American Mental Health Counselors Association) in 1979 and merged with NBCC in 1992 (Sweeney, 1995). In addition to holding the NCC, professionals seeking the CCMHC must demonstrate the following (NBCC, 2012b):

- Sixty hours of graduate coursework, including theories of counseling, psychotherapy, and personality; abnormal psychology and psychopathology; human growth and development; professional orientation and ethics for counselors; research; appraisal; and social/cultural foundations;
- An academic program of study that includes 9–15 semester hours of clinical training in supervised practica/internships in settings relevant to the practice of mental health counseling;
- A passing score on the National Clinical Mental Health Counseling Examination (NCMHCE). This exam presents examinees with 10 clinical vignettes typically encountered by mental health counselors and assesses the counselor's ability to apply knowledge, information-gathering and decision-making skills related to assessment, diagnosis, referral, treatment, evaluation, and aftercare;
- Submission of an audio- or videotape of a clinical counseling session for review following the successful passing of the NCMHCE.

The MAC is a certification for counselors specializing in the treatment of substance abuse and dependence. In addition to the NCC certification, counselors seeking the MAC credential must be able to document a minimum of 12 semester hours of graduate credit in the area of addictions *or* 500 hours of continuing education units, 3 years of supervised experience as an addiction counselor (with no fewer than 20 hours per week and 2 of the 3 years completed after the master's degree was conferred), and a passing score on the Examination for Master Addiction Counselors (EMAC)(NBCC, 2012c). Many clinical mental health counselors work in addiction settings and find the MAC a relevant certification option.

In contrast, *licensure* is a statutory process whereby the state regulates the counseling profession. Thus, licensure is a legal process and may regulate the use of a professional title (e.g., licensed mental health counselor, licensed professional counselor) and/or the scope of practice in that state (i.e., an identified set of techniques and practices that is limited to those professionals holding the counselor license). A clinical mental health counselor who is licensed can legally use the specific professional title accepted by that state and engage in the activities of the profession defined by the law. Licensure is viewed as the most desirable form of regulation of a profession because it demarcates the uniqueness of the profession and regulates both the use of the title and the practice of the profession (Corey, Corey, & Callanan, 2011).

Counselor licensure laws typically share several general components. First, the law contains several legal definitions relevant to the licensed profession. For example, basic concepts of the profession, such as *appraisal, counseling, professional counseling, counselor, mental health counselor, qualified supervisor,* and *the practice of mental health counseling* may be defined in very specific terms in state statutes. It is important that licensed mental health and professional counselors understand and practice within legal definitions of *appraisal* and not go beyond their scope of practice.

Second, state licensure laws establish a licensure board and set rules regarding its structure and responsibilities. The responsibilities of a licensure board include the development of administrative rules regarding professional practice, the application for and renewal of licenses, the approval of providers of continuing education, the administration of licensure exams, and the enforcement of the ethics code. A list of the state licensure boards for mental health and licensed professional counselors is found in Appendix B.

Third, the law specifies the precise requirements for licensure within the particular state. These include requirements for education, clinical experience and supervision, examination of applicants, continuing education, and licensure fees. Although the states have many requirements for licensure in common, they also vary in specific requirements. For example, the official professional titles used vary from state to state. Although the majority of states use the title of Licensed Professional Counselor (LPC), some have chosen variants of the mental health counseling designation (e.g., LMHC, or Licensed Mental Health Counselor). In addition, certain states require graduate programs of 48 semester hours, whereas others require 60 semester hours of graduate training in counseling. Furthermore, the number of required hours of practicum/internship, clinical experience, and postgraduate supervised experience differs. Even the criteria for determining acceptable supervision and the number of supervision hours vary.

Thus, it is highly recommended that students closely study the licensure laws of the state in which they desire to practice. It is vital that they enroll in or construct for themselves programs of study containing academic and clinical experiences that meet the specific state's licensure requirements. Too often, I have been approached by persons who have graduated from well-respected programs in counselor education who discovered after graduation that the state in which they desired to practice had set requirements that their academic program did not fulfill. These are often very fine points that are easily overlooked by the counselor trainee. Faculty advisers and specialization coordinators can assist students in making sense of the maze of licensure requirements. But it is ultimately the student who must be aware of the specific requirements of the state in which he or she wants to practice.

Corey et al. (2011) have identified arguments for and against the licensure and certification of counselors. It is generally held that the welfare of consumers is safeguarded more with licensure laws than without them. Professionals are required to demonstrate their ability to work at a specific level of competence and are held accountable if they do not. Furthermore, licensure helps to distinguish the various mental health professions so consumers can choose the most appropriate practitioner for their specific needs. Also, licensure makes counseling services more accessible because third-party reimbursers tend to cover the fees for services rendered by licensed professionals. Finally, licensure laws enable professions to regulate themselves.

However, some question the altruistic motives supporting professional licensure (Corey et al., 2011). They argue that professional licensure is more about protecting the "turf" of a profession and is therefore self-serving. Too often, the allied mental health professions are pitted against each other in efforts to protect the scope of their practice with little or no regard for the needs of consumers. In a survey of AMHCA branch presidents conducted to assess the level of interprofessional cooperation concerning licensure, Goldin (1997) found that the greatest support for the efforts of the mental health counseling profession came from the AAMFT, followed by the National Association of Social Workers, the American Psychological Association, and the American Psychiatric Association. Interprofessional cooperation is most likely when the respective professional organizations see it as beneficial to their own interests. Furthermore, once legal definitions and scope of practice are in place, the profession becomes less responsive to changes in the socioeconomic-political environment. Thus, the profession may become less capable of adapting to the changing needs of the clientele and communities it serves.

CONTEMPORARY ISSUES IN EDUCATION AND CREDENTIALING OF COUNSELORS

As noted at the beginning of this chapter, a complex relationship exists among counselors' academic training model, credentialing, and professional practice. This dynamic relationship is seen clearly in several contemporary issues facing the profession.

LICENSURE FOR MENTAL HEALTH COUNSELORS IN ALL 50 STATES: WHAT COMES NEXT?

The journey toward establishing counselor licensure in the United States began in 1976 in Virginia. It ended at the intended destination on October 11, 2009, when the governor of California signed into law the ordinance establishing the profession of Licensed Professional Clinical Counselor. With this act, clinical mental health and professional counselors are licensed professionals in all 50 states.

However, the impact of licensure on the profession has been paradoxical. On the one hand, as noted previously, it has brought mental health counselors together as they both seek and qualify for state licensure. On the other hand, licensure is regulated by the state and, as noted earlier, each state has the right to regulate the profession as it chooses. A survey of the various licensure laws reveals numerous state-specific paths to licensure. The number of credit hours required in an academic program, as well as the hours of direct service, supervision, and postgraduate work all vary among the states. Although passing scores on the NCE or NCMHCE exams are required in most states, several states have devised their own licensure exams. Furthermore, the states vary in the professional titles they use (e.g., licensed professional counselor, licensed mental health counselor, licensed professional counselor of mental health). Kaplan (2012) reports 45 different titles for professional counselors. One licensing board reports using five different titles to regulate the profession (Kaplan, 2012). This incoherence contributes to professional identity confusion among students, consumers, the general public, and members of allied mental health professions. So, now that we have licensure in all 50 states, can order be brought to this land of confusion?

Portability.   One consequence of the inconsistencies described is the inability to simply "transfer" a license from one state to another. *Portability* of licenses refers to one state's honoring another state's license. The ability of licensed mental health and professional counselors to move across state lines is hindered by the variations in the states' regulation of the profession. The profession of clinical psychology has moved to implement a system of *reciprocity,* in which certain states have negotiated agreements with other states so that the license in one state would be automatically accepted in the others, as long as the appropriate fees are paid. In contrast, efforts toward the portability of mental health and professional counselor licenses and state reciprocity have lagged far behind. However, realization of licensure portability has recently moved closer to reality through the implementation of the National Credential Registry of the American Association of State Counseling Boards (AASCB) (Williams, 2005).

The right of states to regulate professions reflects the general protection of a state's autonomy relative to the national government; states' rights are fundamental to our system of government. Thus, it is unlikely that the states will give up this right of professional regulation by passing the responsibility to the federal government or a professional organization. The present situation, though, makes it difficult for licensed practitioners to move from one state to another. And as Kaplan (2012) notes, individual states must attend to portability as a public protection issue created, in part, by lack of the standards necessary to facilitate the interstate mobility of counselor licenses.

Controversies and Growing Pains.   The recognition of the clinical mental health counseling specialization is due, in part, to CACREP's recognition of the blurred boundary between two former specializations: mental health and community counseling. In many ways, this bold move strengthens professional identity by merging two training models that were competing within the profession. Furthermore, professional identity is advanced by having licensure laws in all 50 states. Moving on, though, carries with it change and loss.

These advances do not necessarily put to rest all of the associated controversies. Allegiance to the former training models and related professional identities does not simply go away with revised CACREP standards and increased recognition in all 50 states. One recent survey of 295 CACREP counselor educators found significant differences of opinion regarding the recent CACREP revisions (Cannon & Cooper, 2010). Specifically, disagreement regarding the number of credit hours, the number of required clock hours for internships, and the requirement that full-time faculty graduate from counselor education programs fall along the lines that formerly demarcated community and mental health counseling specializations.

These allegiances also find expression as practitioners take up positions regarding the two contemporary issues facing the profession: portability and TRICARE provider status. The discussions reflect the complexities of bringing increased unity and coherence to the profession.

The issue of portability and its significance were discussed in the previous section. Nearly all mental health counselors strongly support the general goals of establishing portability of licenses and facilitating reciprocity between states. However, resolution of the complex issues is necessary before actual mechanisms can be put in place to make these things happen. Given the variations among the states in professional titles, scopes of practice, educational requirements, licensure exams, and required postgraduate supervised hours, it is no surprise that the resolution process stagnates while the political tug-of-war plays out. Collaboration, compromise, negotiation, and a problem-solving focus are integral strategies if progress is to be made. How might conflicts be resolved so that, at the very least, the position of mental health counselors is maintained relative to that of allied professions in matters of professional practice and public policy? The ACA (American Counseling Association) proposes to use the *20/20* definition of counseling, presented in Chapter 1, as a unifying point of departure.

A second source of controversy arises regarding TRICARE, a health care program of the U.S. Department of Defense. It provides civilian health care benefits to military personnel, retirees, their dependents, and some members of the military reserve. Recently, the Department of Defense established licensed mental health counselors as approved independent providers of mental health services to TRICARE beneficiaries (TRICARE: Certified Mental Health Counselors, 2011). This is a major accomplishment! But, it has stirred controversy within the profession. The rule specifies that to be eligible service providers, the licensed mental health counselors must be licensed at the highest tier in their respective state, must have passed the Clinical Mental Health Counselor Exam (CMHCE), *and* must have graduated from a CACREP-approved clinical mental health counseling program. Its wording reflects the current CACREP standards for the Clinical Mental Health Counseling Standards (CACREP, 2009a) and the 2011 AMHCA Standards for the Practice of Clinical Mental Health Counseling (AMHCA, 2011a). This rule leaves behind, for example, licensed counselors who graduated from a 48-hour program, did not graduate from a CACREP-approved program or pass the CMHCE, or do not possess the highest tier of license in their state. The rule does establish a transition period and grandfather provision for current practitioners (Finley, 2011/2012).

CONCLUSION

Through the hard work of many individuals in cooperation with local, state, and national professional organizations, the profession has, finally, reached maturity and attained the recognition that it deserves. Or has it? The contemporary issues just noted illustrate controversies about professional identity that linger despite licensure in all 50 states and a unified training model. Indeed, growing pains continue as mental health counselor identity proceeds into the next stage of professional development. Much has been attained; still more lies ahead. The challenge for the mental health professions is that their training models and credentialing bodies stay current with the constant changes in contemporary behavioral health care.

In recognition of the need to keep pace with new developments while maintaining rigorous educational and clinical practice standards, AMHCA has periodically put forth a set of professional standards (AMHCA, 2011a). The most recent revision, the 2011 *AMHCA Standards for the Practice of Clinical Mental Health Counseling*, continues the efforts of the professional association "to advocate for and seek to advance the practice of clinical mental health counseling" (p. 4). This document establishes standards for the following areas:

- Educational and predegree clinical training
- Faculty and clinical supervisors
- Clinical practice

It is noteworthy that the 2011 AMHCA Standards for Practice (AMHCA, 2011a) go beyond the standards identified by CACREP and recommend specialized knowledge and skills in the following areas:

- Biological Bases of Behavior—the organization of the central nervous system (CNS) and its role in mental health disorders; the role of neurobiology in thinking, emotion, and memory; an understanding of early childhood development, including the role of attachment and of the social environment in brain development; plasticity and the recovery of brain functioning across the lifespan; psychopharmacology; basic screening approaches to CNS functioning;
- Specialized Clinical Assessment—the purposes, strengths, and limitations of objective clinical mental health assessment in establishing goals and treatment plans; applications to diverse and special populations; the use of assessment tools and methodology in the formative and summative evaluation of treatment and mental health programs;
- Trauma Training—the ability to assess and differentiate the clinical impact of various trauma-causing events; evidence-based trauma resolution practices; the application of wellness and resiliency practices; sensitivity to differences across populations and stages of development;
- Co-occurring Disorders—the epidemiology, etiology, and neurological bases of co-occurring and substance use disorders; the interpretation of basic lab results; a foundational understanding of how drugs work (routes of administration,

distribution, dependence, withdrawal, dose response and interactions); techniques of the transtheoretical model and motivational interviewing. (pp. 12–18)

Application of these recommendations can prepare future clinical mental health counselors for placement in integrated behavioral health care and managed care environments.

While discussion about portability, TRICARE, and the interactions of the training model and professional credentialing with approved provider status continue among professional leaders, many LMHCs and LPCs working in the trenches still find themselves competing with more privileged therapists and clinicians who sit at the table of the allied mental health professions. Social workers continue to have a political advantage in the job market and in reimbursement by third parties. Too often, the mental health counseling profession is simply overlooked when consultations regarding state mental health policy take place. Furthermore, the public perception of counselors in relation to other mental health professions is mixed (Fall, Levitov, Jennings, & Eberts, 2000). Fall et al. found that their sample of 190 participants selected social workers most frequently as their choice to provide mental health services. However, the participants in this study had the least confidence in social workers' ability to successfully treat adjustment disorder, marital problems, psychotic depression, posttraumatic stress disorder, and borderline personality disorder relative to psychologists, psychiatrists, and master's- and doctoral-level professional counselors. In addition, master's-level professional counselors were ranked above psychiatrists and psychologists in perceived ability to treat adjustment disorders and marital problems.

We can conclude that licensure and the CACREP training model have helped place the mental health counseling profession as a key player in the field of mental health professions. But the profession has not achieved equal status in the eyes of other professionals or the general public. The strengths of our training model and product (i.e., services provided by clinical mental health counselors) continue to be well-kept secrets. Professional excellence and advocacy must be our primary tools if we are to receive consistent invitations to sit at the table with, gain a hearing with, and receive respect from the other mental health professions.

DISCUSSION QUESTIONS

1. To what extent do you see the training standards and licensure laws as able to adapt to the ever-changing environment of contemporary treatment? Discuss the importance of professional advocacy in establishing training standards and licensure codes that reflect the current needs of practicing mental health professionals. What can *you* do to advocate for your profession?

2. As you think about the training model for the profession, to what extent do you believe counselors in training can gain the knowledge and skills necessary to be effective in the contemporary treatment environment?

3. How, specifically, could you use your knowledge of the CACREP model in marketing yourself for professional positions in counseling when competing with social workers, marriage and family therapists, or psychologists?

4. In your opinion, who does professional licensure protect more—consumers of counseling services or the professional rights of the professional relative to the allied professional groups?

SUGGESTED ACTIVITIES

1. Obtain a copy of the counselor licensure law in the state in which you live or want to practice. What specific steps are involved in completing an application for licensure? What professional title may be used by licensees in that state? What educational, clinical, supervision, and exam requirements must the prospective licensee fulfill?

2. Compare and contrast the licensure laws of states using the term *licensed professional counselor* and those using *licensed mental health counselor*. What noteworthy similarities and differences can you identify?

3. Compare and contrast the scope of practice in the licensure laws pertaining to licensed professional counselors and licensed clinical social workers in the state in which you live or want to practice. What noteworthy similarities and differences can be identified?

4. Find the Web sites for the ACA, the AMHCA, and your state professional associations. Toward what specific professional issues related to licensure, professional recognition, and scope of practice are they directing their advocacy efforts? How specifically might you get involved?

REFERENCES

Adams, S. A. (2006). Does CACREP accreditation make a difference? A look at NCE results and answers. *Journal of Professional Counseling: Practice, Theory, and Research, 33,* 60–76.

American Mental Health Counselors Association. (2011a). *Standards for the practice of clinical mental health counseling.* Alexandria, VA: American Mental Health Counselors Association.

Bobby, C. L., & Urofsky, R., I. (2011). Thirty-something and aging well. In W. K. Schweiger, D. A., Henderson, K. McCaskill, T. W. Clawson, & D. R. Collins, *Counselor preparation: Programs, faculty, trends.* New York, NY: Routledge.

Cannon, E., & Cooper, J. (2010). Clinical mental health counseling: A national survey of counselor educators. *Journal of Mental Health Counseling, 32,* 236–246.

Corey, G., Corey, M. S., & Callanan, P. (2011). *Issues and ethics in the helping professions* (8th ed.). Belmont, CA: Brooks/Cole.

Council for the Accreditation of Counseling and Related Educational Programs. (2009a). *2009 Standards.* Alexandria, VA: Author.

Fall, K. A., Levitov, J. E., Jennings, M., & Eberts, S. (2000). The public perception of mental health professions: An empirical examination. *Journal of Mental Health Counseling, 22,* 122–134.

Finley, J. K. (December 2011/January 2012). TRICARE releases rules authorizing independent practice for CMHCs. *The Advocate,* pp. 6–7.

Gladding, S. T. (2011). *The counseling dictionary: Concise definitions of frequently used terms.* Upper Saddle River, NJ: Pearson Education.

Goldin, E. C. (1997). Interprofessional cooperation concerning counselor licensure: A survey of American Mental Health Counselor Association branch presidents. *Journal of Mental Health Counseling, 19,* 199–205.

Hansen, J. T. (2003). Including diagnostic training in counseling curricula: Implications for professional identity development. *Counselor Education and Supervision, 43,* 96–107.

Hollis, J. W., with Dodson, T. A. (2000). *Counselor preparation 1999–2001: Programs, faculty, trends* (10th ed.). Philadelphia, PA: Taylor & Francis; Greensboro, NC: National Board for Certified Counselors.

Kaplan, D. (2012). *Licensure reciprocity: A critical public protection issue that needs action.* Keynote address presented at the Annual Conference of the American Association of State Counseling Boards, Charleston, SC.

National Board for Certified Counselors. (2012a). Requirements for the NCC certification. Retrieved from http://www.nbcc.org/Professional/NCCReqs

National Board for Certified Counselors. (2012b). Certified clinical mental health counselor. Retrieved from http://www.nbcc.org/Specialties/CCMHC

National Board for Certified Counselors. (2012c). Master Addictions Counselor (MAC). Requirements for the NCC certification. Retrieved from http://www.nbcc.org/Specialties/MAC

Pistole, C. M., & Roberts, A. (2002). Mental health counseling: Toward resolving identity confusions. *Journal of Mental Health Counseling, 24,* 1–9.

Remley, T. P., & Herlihy, B. (2010). *Ethical, legal, and professional issues in counseling* (3rd ed.). Upper Saddle river, NJ: Pearson Prentice Hall.

Schmidt, J. J. (1999). Two decades of CACREP and what do we know? *Counselor Education and Supervision, 39,* 34–46.

Schweiger, W. K., Henderson, D. A., McCaskill, K., Clawson, T. W., and Collins, . (2011). *Counselor preparation: Programs, faculty, trends* (13th ed.). New York, NY: Routledge.

Sweeney, T. J. (1995). Accreditation, credentialing, professionalization: The role of specialties. *Journal of Counseling and Development, 74,* 117–125.

TRICARE: Certified Mental Health Counselors. (2011, December). *Federal Register, 76,* 80741–80744.

Vacc, N. A., & Loesch, L. C. (2000). *Professional orientation to counseling* (3rd ed.). Philadelphia: Brunner-Routledge.

6

Ethical and Legal Issues in Clinical Mental Health Counseling

OUTLINE

The Significance of Ethical Codes and the Law

The Relationship Between the Law and Codes of Ethics

Foundational Principles of Ethical Codes

Codes of Ethics

The Role of the ACA Ethics Committee and Investigation of Alleged Violations

Specific Ethical and Legal Issues

Conclusion

Nowhere is the interaction of self, training, and practice more critical in counseling than in the promotion of ethical and legal behavior. A working knowledge of professional and legal issues is essential for establishing a professional identity and engaging in effective professional practice. Counselors-in-training get this knowledge from learning about the law, the codes of ethics, and the various institutions and professional organizations that regulate the practice of counseling.

However, knowledge of the law and ethics by itself cannot guide the conduct of practitioners. In sessions with clients, counselors must often determine which course of action best supports these clients' interests and well-being. Counselors' schemas, which includes their worldview, values, and biases, are activated, along with their working knowledge of ethics and the law, *in situations*. These schemas, in interaction with the processing of data gathered throughout the counseling interview, lead, ideally, to effective therapeutic responses that are both legal and ethical.

Too often, ethical and legal issues are taught from a negative perspective. Students learn the list of "thou shalt nots" in order to avoid the ethical and legal landmines in the fields of professional practice. For example, students may understand the need to avoid certain types of dual relationships. They are less likely to learn in their coursework how, specifically, to successfully manage underlying transference or countertransference in ways that preserve the therapeutic relationship.

Ethical and legal practice is really about professionalism and excellence, that is, having the right combination of attributes and skills to facilitate beneficial change and growth in clients. Welfel (2013, p. 3) identifies five dimensions that ethics encompass:

1. Possessing adequate knowledge, skills, and judgment to produce effective interventions;
2. Respecting the dignity, freedom, and rights of the client;
3. Using power inherent in the counselor's role judiciously and responsibly;
4. Conducting oneself in such a way that promotes the public's confidence in the profession;
5. Maintaining the client's welfare as the highest priority of the mental health professional.

Both the ACA (American Counseling Association, 2005) and the AMHCA (American Mental Health Counselors Association, 2010) have devised codes of ethics that inform and regulate the behavior of their members. CACREP (Council for Accreditation of Counseling and Related Educational Programs, 2009a) includes a study of the ethical standards of the ACA and the AMHCA and the application of ethical and legal principles in professional practice as key criteria for fulfilling the core requirement of professional identity. Not only are these criteria central to the development of one's professional identity as a counselor (CACREP, 2009a), but they are also pervasive and extend into all other core areas of study and specialization in counselor education. In addition, local, state, and federal laws specify the profession's scope of practice and specify the minimal standards for professional behavior. Indeed, ethical and legal considerations are a part of practically every task performed by professional counselors.

THE SIGNIFICANCE OF ETHICAL CODES AND THE LAW

Understanding and acting in accordance with ethical codes and the law are important for several reasons. First, acting ethically and within the law promotes professionalism and excellence. Ethical behavior is conduct judged good or right for counselors who practice professionally (Remley & Herlihy, 2010). The ethical code expresses the profession's intent to regulate the behavior of its members. In contrast, legal codes express standards of behavior enforced by governmental agencies. Ideally, ethics and the law guide mental health and community counselors to regulate their professional behavior in ways that promote the well-being of others and prevent harm. Counselors striving for professional excellence rise above merely fulfilling the demands of codes and continually try to be the best counselor they can possibly be.

Second, mental health and professional counselors encounter many situations and dilemmas that defy easy resolution. Often, the break-even point at which a specific course of action will benefit the client is unclear. For example, reporting suspected child abuse may protect the child. Yet doing so jeopardizes any positive counseling relationship established between the counselor and the family. How is the counselor to proceed if the goal is to promote the client's welfare? What happens if the family reacts to the allegation by withdrawing from treatment? Or how should the counselor respond when offered an expensive gift by a client? Is it always appropriate to follow social convention and be a gracious receiver? Or is it sometimes ethically or clinically expedient to explore the action's potential meaning and, when indicated, choose not to accept the gift, even when a refusal might hurt the client's feelings (Gerig, 2004)? Although codes of ethics do not prescribe courses of action for many specific therapeutic events, they do provide principles that identify appropriate courses of action.

Third, consumers of counseling services are protected from those mental health counselors who are impaired, make poor decisions, misapply power and influence, and engage in overt misconduct. Unfortunately, the history of the mental health professions is littered with incidents in which consumers have been victimized by professionals' bad judgment or inappropriate behavior. An early study (Kardener, Fuller, & Mensh, 1973) surveyed 114 psychiatrists in Los Angeles and found that 10% admitted to sexual contact with patients. In a later study, Holroyd and Brodsky (1977) found that 5.5% of the male psychologists and 0.6% of the female psychologists had engaged in sexual intercourse with a client. Of these, 80% admitted to intercourse with more than one client. Illustrations of less extreme poor judgment and inappropriate behavior include the release of confidential information about counseling contacts, failure to contact potential victims of a client who is dangerous, and improper billing practices. Again, ethical and legal codes cannot prevent such actions. However, they clarify the standards to be used by professional organizations or legal authorities when allegations are made. When allegations against practitioners are substantiated, professional organizations impose specific sanctions to habilitate the impaired practitioner or, in extreme cases, to suspend or revoke the practitioner's license. In this way, counselors who represent a danger to consumers are removed from the profession.

Finally, we live in a highly litigious society. Mental health counselors find some protection from litigation by adhering to ethical and legal codes. As the mental health professions experienced significant professional growth and public recognition in the mid-1970s, the number of malpractice claims more than doubled (Montgomery, Cupit, & Wimberly, 1999). Montgomery and colleagues noted the following activities that may prompt malpractice litigation: sexual misconduct, incorrect treatment, financial loss from diagnosis and evaluation, breach of confidentiality, failure to warn, client suicide, and child custody decisions. Mental health professionals are sued most frequently for having sexual relations with clients. It appears that the second most frequent reason for taking counselors to court is clients' attempted or successful suicide (Remley & Herlihy, 2010).

It is difficult for researchers find the accurate number of ethical and legal violations. Self-report surveys, of course, are likely to provide low estimates. Furthermore, reports of ethical violations investigated by professional associations (e.g., the ACA Ethics Committee) offer only a limited picture of the ethical practices of counselors because they review only those cases that involve either current members or professionals who were members at the time of the alleged incident (ACA Governing Council, 2005). However, when considered alongside data reported from other sources, certain trends can be identified (Neukrug, Milliken, & Walden, 2001). General conclusions drawn from these sources have led counselor educators to include risk management strategies in courses covering legal and ethical issues. The goal is to help counselors practice legally and ethically and to avoid or lessen the impact of malpractice litigation.

THE RELATIONSHIP BETWEEN THE LAW AND CODES OF ETHICS

Society and the professions have established various processes to protect consumers from incompetent, unlawful, or unethical counselor practices. These include criminal law, civil litigation of malpractice complaints, federal regulations, and peer control mechanisms (Hess, 1980).

Criminal law embodies what the federal and state governments regard as illegal behavior. It also specifies how violations are to be punished. Most violations of criminal law involve such social crimes as murder, larceny, theft, assault, and rape and are prosecuted by local, state, or federal officials (i.e., county prosecutors and attorneys general). Typically, an act is judged criminal when the person committing the act intended to do something wrong. The state seeks to punish only those persons who are morally blameworthy. For example, a state-licensed professional counselor who practices outside the scope of practice specified by the state's licensure law has engaged in illegal behavior and may be prosecuted for a misdemeanor. Fines, jail terms, and probation can be consequences for professionals convicted of illegal activity.

In contrast, *civil law* covers controversies between two or more people. The focus is not the violation of a statute but the possible harm one person has caused another. When harm is judged to have occurred, the offended party is awarded an amount of money. No criminal sentence is imposed because the focus is not violation of the law. For example, a counselor might be successfully sued for emotional harm caused by an improper, though legal, dual relationship with a client. In such a case, no sentence is imposed because no law has been broken. However, the counselor must compensate the injured party financially for emotional damages.

Sometimes mental health professionals are subject to *federal regulations*. For example, the provisions of the Health Insurance Portability and Accountability Act (HIPAA) have had an enormous effect on how mental health and medical professionals gain informed consent and transfer information electronically. This federal law and its regulations, implemented on April 15, 2003, require that practitioners who transfer client records electronically comply with procedures regulating the informed-consent process. Furthermore, the regulations define what are considered therapy notes and how they are to be secured (Gillman, 2004). Penalties for failing to comply with the regulations are $100 for each violation and up to $25,000 per year for each requirement. Furthermore, penalties for the wrongful disclosure of information may include prison time (General Penalty for Failure to Comply with Requirements and Standards, 2001).

Finally, *peer control mechanisms* are implemented by professional groups that seek to monitor the activities of their group members. The most relevant peer group mechanisms for clinical mental health counselors are the ethics committee of the professional organization and its development and application of that profession's code of ethics. The Ethical Practice Committee of the ACA (then the American Personnel and Guidance Association, or APGA) was established in 1953, one year after the establishment of the organization (Walden, Herlihy, & Ashton, 2003). The first draft of the association's code of ethics was reviewed by members in 1950 and adopted in 1961 (Allen, 1986). The code has been revised every 7 years, on the average, to reflect changes in professional practice, in the needs and issues of clients, and in American society (Walden et al., 2003). Hubert and Freeman (2004) noted that the most recent ACA Code Revision Task Force was reviewing the previous code (ACA, 1995) and was looking at the integration of existing standards for Internet online counseling (ACA, 1999). In addition, the task force was charged with developing revisions related to multiculturalism, diversity, and social justice (Hubert & Freeman, 2004). These mandates were realized with the publication of the 2005 Code of Ethics (ACA, 2005).

Obviously, there is a significant amount of overlap between ethics codes and the law. The underlying purpose of both is to encourage harmonious social relations. Ideally, they allow professionals to act autonomously while also protecting the rights of others.

There are times, though, when ethics and the law conflict. For example, U.S. racial segregation laws were overturned when they were determined to violate human rights and personal well-being. Counselors may encounter such conflicts when subpoenaed by the court for copies of a client's clinical record. The counselor who refuses to release confidential information to the court in order to protect the best interests of a client can be found in contempt of court.

Finally, ethical codes often address issues that are not concerns of the law. For example, the professor who lectures from notes yellowed by years of use may be acting unethically, though not illegally, in not presenting current information to students. Generally speaking, ethical codes of professional conduct are more stringent than the legal standards.

FOUNDATIONAL PRINCIPLES OF ETHICAL CODES

Various authors have identified moral principles that are the foundation of professional codes of ethics (Beauchamp & Childress, 1989; Meara, Schmidt, & Day, 1996; Remley & Herlihy, 2010). These principles include autonomy, nonmaleficence, beneficence, justice, fidelity, and veracity.

Autonomy means facilitating increased independence and self-direction in clients. We respect the inherent freedom and dignity of each person and therefore recognize his or her freedom to choose. As a result, we must always insure that our clients are thoroughly informed about the counseling process. Counselors avoid behaving paternalistically and creating dependence that needlessly prolongs therapy. Instead, clients are encouraged to think, feel, decide, and act for themselves and to take responsibility for doing so. Sometimes counselors find it necessary to help clients develop important skills, such as accurate cognitive appraisal of situations, self-awareness, and assertiveness, that serve as a foundation for increased autonomy.

Nonmaleficence refers to avoiding doing intentional or unintentional harm. This avoidance requires clinical mental health counselors to be sensitive to and evaluate the potential risks of the process and outcome of counseling. This principle applies not only to doing therapy but also to teaching and conducting research. Thus, counselors are required to act when clients present a threat to themselves and others or when they suspect children are being physically abused. In addition, counselors avoid potential harm by not using therapeutic approaches or directives that run counter to the fundamental values of the culturally different client.

Beneficence means promoting good for others. Clinical mental health counselors provide services that promote personal well-being, growth, and relief from unhappiness and distress. In general, the identified goals of counseling guide clients toward more effective and productive lives. For example, counselors recognize and work within the boundaries of their expertise, selecting interventions wisely, based on the professional outcome literature. This principle applies not only to direct services to clients but also to larger networks, institutions, and processes of the ecological setting. It supports the use of indirect services, such as consultation and advocacy, as means to promote the well-being of groups, organizations, cultures, and societies.

Justice has to do with fairness and equality of treatment (Corey, Corey, & Callanan, 2011). Persons are entitled to equal access to and quality of treatment regardless of race, ethnicity, gender, sexual orientation, or religion. The application of this principle extends beyond the counselor-counselee relationship to the development and implementation of agency policy and procedures. For example, counseling agencies engage in hiring practices that do not discriminate, and they provide services that are sensitive to persons whose "difference" is relevant (e.g., culturally diverse or physically disabled clients).

Fidelity relates to honoring commitments and keeping promises, which are basic to the development and maintenance of trust. Contracts are honored. This includes adhering to fee arrangements, keeping scheduled appointments, and conducting the counseling according to a mutually agreed upon therapeutic plan. In addition, commitments made to the client are honored even when the originally assigned counselor becomes unavailable due to prolonged illness or relocation.

Finally, *veracity* has to do with honesty and genuineness. Counselors act with integrity rather than deception and covert manipulation of clients. They represent their training, credentials, and qualifications accurately and do not make reports to accrediting bodies, third-party reimbursers, peers, or clients that are untrue, biased, or distorted.

CODES OF ETHICS

As noted previously, the primary way a professional organization monitors and regulates the behavior of its members is through the development and enforcement of a code of ethics. A number of professional organizations and codes are relevant to the practice of counseling. Most relevant for clinical mental health counselors are the codes developed by the ACA (2005) and the AMHCA (2010). In addition, the National Board of Certified Counselors (NBCC) has put forth a code to be used by mental health professionals who have been awarded licensure as National Certified Counselors (NCCs), Master Addictions Counselors (MACs), and Certified Clinical Mental Health Counselors (CCMHCs). Other codes of ethics have been developed by the American Psychological Association (2010), the National Association of Social Workers (2008), and the American Association of Marriage and Family Therapists (2001). Finally, state licensure laws frequently include a section within the legal statute identifying standards for ethical practice.

According to Herlihy and Corey (1996), the codes of ethics fulfill three primary objectives. First, they educate members about the components of sound professional conduct. By reading and reflecting on the codes, mental health and community counselors increase their sensitivity to the presence and nature of the ethical issues embedded in their ongoing work with clients. Knowledge of the codes guides counselors in dealing with the challenges and dilemmas faced in professional practice. Second, the codes identify a set of standards to which professional counselors are accountable. By virtue of their professional membership, mental health counselors are obliged to monitor their own professional behavior as well as that of their peers. Third, the codes of ethics can act as catalysts for improving counseling services. Once sensitive to the content of the ethical codes, mental health counselors analyze their professional conduct and direct it toward best practice.

The ACA Code of Ethics (2005) consists of a preamble, a purpose statement, and eight sections, each of which covers a specific area of ethical behavior:

1. *The counseling relationship*—Specifies the ethical dimensions of the counselor-counselee relationship. The primary responsibility of respecting the dignity and promoting the welfare of clients is emphasized. Specific areas discussed include dual relationships, fees and bartering, termination issues, client rights, and respect of diversity.
2. *Confidentiality, privileged communication, and privacy*—Focuses on the need to respect the privacy of clients and clinical records. Special applications of this

standard include research and training, consultation, and working with groups, families, and minors.

3. *Professional responsibility*—Discusses standards of training, credentialing, and professional competence. Included are responsibilities toward the general public and other professionals, as well as ethical practices of advertising and the solicitation of prospective clients.
4. *Relationships with other professionals*—Notes standards of ethics relating to employers, employees, and consultees.
5. *Evaluation, assessment, and interpretation*—Specifies principles for ethical use of assessment techniques, including the selection, administration, scoring, interpretation, and storage of tests.
6. *Supervision, training, and teaching*—Provides specific guidelines for counselor educators, students, supervisors, supervisees, and other trainers.
7. *Research and publication*—Discusses specific ethical issues for research involving human participants and the reporting and publication of results. This section emphasizes the importance of gaining informed consent and protecting participants from any potential harm or side effects of their involvement in projects.
8. *Resolving ethical issues*—Communicates the responsibility of counselors to possess knowledge of the ethical code. In addition, this section outlines how suspected violations of the code should be handled.

The code concludes with a glossary of terms.

The Code of Ethics of the AMHCA (2010) begins with a preamble and provides detailed guidance to mental health counselors in the following sections:

1. Commitment to Clients
2. Commitment to Other Professionals (Relationship with Colleagues; Clinical Consultation)
3. Commitment to Students, Supervisees, and Employee Relationships
4. Commitment to the Profession (Teaching; Research and Publications; Service on Public or Private Boards and Other Organizations)
5. Commitment to the Public (Public Statements; Advertising)
6. Resolution of Ethical Problems

The AMHCA Code of Ethics is posted on the association's Web site (https://www.amhca.org/assets/news/AMHCA_Code_of_Ethics_2010_w_pagination_cxd_51110.pdf).

THE ROLE OF THE ACA ETHICS COMMITTEE AND INVESTIGATION OF ALLEGED VIOLATIONS

The ACA Ethics Committee promotes sound ethical behavior within the counseling profession by monitoring the professional conduct of ACA members. The responsibilities of this committee include educating members about the ACA Code of Ethics, periodically reviewing and recommending revisions to the code, receiving and processing complaints of alleged ethical violations of ACA members, providing interpretations of the ethical standards of the code, and recommending reasonable disciplinary actions to be taken against members where violation of ethical standards is substantiated (ACA Governing Council, 2005).

The ACA Ethics Committee receives complaints from persons who believe an ACA member has violated the ACA Code of Ethics (ACA Ethics Committee, 2010). When a complaint is accepted, evidence and documents supporting the complaint are provided to the charged member, who is then asked to respond to the complaint. Once these responses have been received, the committee members get copies of the complaint, the supporting evidence, and the related documents sent to the charged member and the responses received from the charged member. The committee then determines if any standard of the code has been violated. If it is determined that violations have occurred, the committee imposes one or a combination of the following possible sanctions (ACA Governing Council, 2005), listed by increasing levels of severity:

1. The ethics committee may choose to mandate specific *remedial requirements* to be completed within given time limits.
2. The member might be placed on *probation* for a specified length of time. Often, the remedial requirements must be completed within the probation period.
3. The professional might be *suspended* for a specified length of time. In addition, completion of remedial requirements within that time period is often required.
4. The professional might be *permanently expelled* from the ACA. For this sanction to be implemented, a unanimous vote among the committee members is required.

The ethics committee monitors a suspended member's compliance with the sanctions and may expel the member upon failure to fulfill the remedial requirements. The committee seeks to act in an educative and remedial, not a punitive, manner. Other possible corrective actions in addition to the preceding sanctions include further education and training, supervision, or personal evaluation and treatment.

SPECIFIC ETHICAL AND LEGAL ISSUES

COMPETENCE AND SCOPE OF PRACTICE

The establishment of trust is the cornerstone of an effective therapeutic relationship. And establishing competence is central to any discussion of trust and trustworthiness, because most clients will not enter into a counseling relationship if the counselor cannot demonstrate competence. Expectation of the counselor's competence enables clients to place trust in the counselor quite early in the counseling process.

It is essential that mental health counselors practice within their boundaries of competence. However, defining and assessing competence are difficult. The ACA Code of Ethics (2005) clearly states the centrality of competent practice in Section C.2.a:

> Counselors practice only within the boundaries of their competence, based on their education, training, supervised experience, state and national professional credentials, and appropriate professional experience. Counselors gain knowledge, personal awareness, sensitivity, and skills pertinent to working with a diverse client population. (p. 9)
>
> Reprinted from ACA Code of Ethics, Section C.2.a, p. 9 © 2005 The American Counseling Association. Reprinted with permission. No further reproduction authorized without written permission from the American Counseling Association.

Mental health counselors are competent to use particular techniques of assessment and intervention to the extent they have qualified through education, training, and experience (AMHCA, 2010). The application of such techniques must demonstrate cultural competence and sensitivity. In addition, counselors themselves seek professional services if they believe their ability to provide competent services is compromised by their mental or physical state. In such cases, it may be necessary to limit, suspend, or terminate service provision to clients until the counselor's condition is remediated.

However, a question arises: What particular criteria determine competence. What valid evidence of professional competence should be communicated to prospective clients? How can we determine a professional's level of competence in a specialized area? For example, after how much training and experience may a professional legitimately refer to himself or herself as a cognitive or play therapist?

Clearly, academic transcripts and diplomas, state license and professional certification, continuing education certificates, and evidence of supervised experience serve as accurate indicators of competence (AMHCA, 2010). It is important to distinguish between minimal competence and mastery. Education, licensure, and supervised experience demonstrate that the person has met or exceeded the minimal standards for practice of the profession. But advanced degrees and licenses do not necessarily guarantee that the professional engages in best practice, consults with more experienced practitioners, or stays current in his or her area of specialization. At a minimum, practicing within one's boundaries of competence requires the counselor to be sensitive to his or her strengths and weaknesses and in humility to seek additional training, supervision, and consultation throughout his or her career.

State licensure laws identify the *scope of practice* for a professional group. The scope of practice outlines those professional roles and tasks that the person licensed under the law can legally perform. The legally defined scope of practice generally reflects the knowledge and skills of the profession's training model (i.e., the CACREP standards). However, many states add their own nuances to their definitions of scope of practice. Thus, from a legal perspective, licensed professionals are bound to practice within their areas of competency *as identified by the state law*. For example, while the 2009 CACREP standards include the development of knowledge and skill for diagnosis based on the American Psychiatric Association's *Diagnostic and Statistical Manual of Mental Disorders (DSM),* some states have not included diagnosis in the scope of practice of professional counselors. In such states, mental health counselors must practice within the parameters established by the law. Mental health professionals who diagnose in these states violate a legal statute and can be taken to court by consumers or relevant professional organizations even though they can document the requisite training experiences.

INFORMED CONSENT: CLIENT'S RIGHTS AND RESPONSIBILITIES

Informed consent refers to the right of clients to be clearly informed regarding the nature of their counseling and to make autonomous decisions regarding it (Corey et al., 2011). Its practice demonstrates counselors' respect for the dignity, autonomy, and human rights of their clients and is fundamental to the development of the counseling contract (Hall & Lin, 1995). Although it is a critical component in the initial stages of counseling, the principle of informed consent is applicable to all stages of the counseling process.

Consideration of the principle of informed consent raises several concerns. First, the word *informed* implies that specific types of information should be provided to clients. The ACA Code of Ethics is clear:

> A.2.a. Informed Consent. Clients have the freedom to choose whether to enter into or remain in a counseling relationship and need adequate information about the counseling process and the counselor. Counselors have an obligation to review in writing and verbally with clients the rights and responsibilities of both the counselor and the client. Informed consent is an ongoing part of the counseling process, and counselors appropriately document discussions of informed consent throughout the counseling relationship. (ACA, 2005, p. 4)
>
> Reprinted from ACA Code of Ethics, Section A.2.a, p. 4 © 2005 The American Counseling Association. Reprinted with permission. No further reproduction authorized without written permission from the American Counseling Association.

The AMHCA Code of Ethics (2010) specifies that the "information includes but is not limited to: counselor credentials, issues of confidentiality, the use of tests and inventories, diagnosis, reports, billing, and therapeutic process. Restrictions that limit clients' autonomy are fully explained" (p. 4).

It is good counseling practice to have *written* informed-consent forms presented to clients before beginning treatment (Moline, Williams, & Austin, 1998). Indeed, the 2005 ACA Code of Ethics (ACA, 2005) requires that information be presented in *both* verbal and written forms. The following information should be included:

- The nature of the treatment, including the counselor's preferred theoretical perspective
- The time parameters for the sessions
- The method of payment
- No-show/cancellation policy
- The nature of and limitations on confidentiality
- The potential risks and/or side effects of treatment
- The qualifications of the counselor

Clinical mental health counselors include a *professional disclosure statement* and *client bill of rights* as part of the informed-consent process. The counselor gives the client a professional self-disclosure statement that summarizes the professional qualifications of the counselor, the nature of treatment, the fees, and the client's rights and options of recourse (Gladding, 2011). A sample professional disclosure form is found in Figure 6.1.

FIGURE 6.1

Sample
Professional
Disclosure
Form

Professional Disclosure Statement

Joel Yooper, MA, LPCC

Hiawatha Behavioral Health

3865 South Mackinaw Trail, Sault Sainte Marie, Michigan 49783

906/635-2805—jyooper@sault.com

Thank you for choosing Hiawatha Behavioral Health to pursue mental health services. This Professional Disclosure Statement will help you become familiar with my professional background and the nature of the services I provide.

Professional Credentials

I have been practicing as a Mental Health Counselor for over 20 years and specialize in individual and family counseling. My Master of Arts degree in Clinical Mental Health Counseling was earned from Western Michigan University (1989). I attained my Bachelor of Arts degree in Psychology from Lake Superior State University (1985). I am licensed as a Professional Clinical Counselor in the state of Michigan (#G000001111a). In addition, I have received intensive training in suicide prevention, mental health and wellness recovery, and the treatment of anxiety, depression, conflict management, and family system substance abuse assessment. I have extensive experience in the areas of crisis intervention, juvenile behaviors, co-occurring disorders, depression, and psychosis. I am a member of the American Mental Health Counselors Association (AMHCA), the American Counseling Association (ACA), and the Michigan Mental Health Counselors Association (MMHCA). My professional behavior is in full accord with the ethical codes of these organizations.

Philosophical and Counseling Approaches

I believe the provision of mental health services should be strength-based and seek to enhance the person's ability to flourish in his or her life situation. It is my desire that each person with whom I work fully live his or her life, rather than his or her diagnosis. Counseling provides you with a safe place to share in a private setting those areas of living that are problematic that you seek to resolve and to identify the goals you seek to attain. We will explore the environmental settings in which you live, your relationships, how they affect your current situation, and how they may be utilized as you seek to achieve your goals.

I tend to view the person within his or her context and to use Acceptance and Commitment Therapy as a primary approach to treatment. From this perspective, each person makes choices and takes responsibility for his or her behavior. Clients are encouraged to take an objective view of their life situation, embrace rather than resist what they feel and think, identify what they truly value, and direct their behavior in value-oriented directions.

Counseling Services

Several factors influence the processes and outcomes of counseling. A supportive counselor-client relationship characterized by openness, trust, feeling understood and accepted is a necessary foundation. The development and implementation of a treatment plan is a product of the counselor-client relationship. The client identifies

FIGURE 6.1

(continued)

the goals, vision, and dreams that he or she desires to attain as a result of counseling. A plan is then, developed by the counselor and the client and becomes the roadmap to be followed in the journey from the client's present location to where he or she wants to be as a result of successful treatment. The client's full involvement and motivation influence treatment efficiency and effectiveness.

Services offered by Hiawatha Behavioral Health include individual, group, and family counseling; case management; assertive community treatment; crisis intervention, including walk-in and 24-hour hotline service; peer-directed services; psychological testing; and medication service. One or more of these services are available to you, based on your level of need and the goals you have identified. At all points, the client collaborates with the counselor to ensure that treatment fits with the identified needs and desires. All services are voluntary, and clients have the right to discontinue them at any time.

Client Rights

The welfare of clients is our primary responsibility. You have the right to be treated with dignity and respect in all interactions with your counselor and other agency staff. We will be sensitive to issues of language, culture, and relevant indigenous practices of spirituality and healing.

As your counselor, I respect your right to privacy and will avoid any unwarranted disclosure of confidential information. Only in following instances will any personal or counseling-related information be released: when a client becomes a serious threat to self or others, when there are indicators of child or elder abuse, when mandated by law, or upon insurance company's request for information related to reimbursement of fees.

You are encouraged to become familiar with your rights as a consumer of our service. A full statement of your personal rights is provided on the HBH Web page (www. hbhcmh.org). Click on the Recipient Rights Policy. Please let me know if you have any questions. Should you believe your rights have been violated in any manner, please consult with the HBH Recipient Rights Officer, who can assist you in filing a grievance.

By your signature below, you are indicating that you have read and understood the contents of this statement and that any questions you have about this statement of services offered at HBH have been answered to your satisfaction. Your signature indicates agreement and compliance with the aforementioned conditions and rights.

Counselor's Name	Print Name	Date
Client's/Guardian's Name	Print Name	Date

This written form can build rapport and trust in the initial session and can invite the client to actively participate in a collaborative process. Furthermore, it conveys respect for the client's dignity and right of self-determination.

For consent to be truly informed, it is vital that clients understand the concepts, procedures, and implications conveyed. Special consideration must be given to the reading level of the materials. According to the National Assessment of Adult Literacy

(2003), the mean reading level of U.S. citizens is lower than high school, whereas the typical informed-consent form requires a Grade 12 reading level (Welfel, 2013). Thus, it is not sufficient merely to provide clients with a sheet of information and have them sign on the dotted line indicating that they have read the material. Ethical counselors seek evidence to confirm that the client fully comprehends the information prior to giving consent. This principle also applies to participants in research projects.

Second, the client gives consent for treatment. It is legitimate to raise the question, "Who is the client?" Consider, for example, the complexities of conducting marriage or family counseling. When working with multiple participants in a session, who specifically gives consent? The 2005 ACA Code of Ethics (A.7. Multiple Clients) provides the following guidance:

> When a counselor agrees to provide counseling services to two or more persons who have a relationship, the counselor clarifies at the outset which person or persons are clients and the nature of the relationships the counselor will have with each involved person. If it becomes apparent that the counselor may be called upon to perform potentially conflicting roles, the counselor will clarify, adjust, or withdraw from roles appropriately. (p. 5)

Reprinted from ACA Code of Ethics, Section A.7, p. 5 © 2005 The American Counseling Association. Reprinted with permission. No further reproduction authorized without written permission from the American Counseling Association.

At the outset, participants in family therapy should understand what is meant by the statement that the system or family unit is the focus of treatment, rather than its individual members. Furthermore, the counselor must be clear regarding who should attend. The family should know if all members are required to attend all sessions. Finally, family members should know the limits of confidentiality, a topic discussed later in this chapter. For example, the counselor must explain how individual secrets will be dealt with in the context of family therapy.

Third, informed consent occurs when the client makes a voluntary, autonomous decision. However, not all identified clients are capable of giving informed consent. A minor can enter into a therapeutic contract (a) by parental or guardian consent; (b) involuntarily at a parent's insistence; or (c) by order of the juvenile court (Lawrence & Kurpius, 2000). The primary exceptions occur if the child is considered emancipated (i.e., under the age of 18 and living separately from parents and managing personal financial affairs) or, in some states, if waiting to gain parental consent would create a life- or health-endangering condition (Lawrence & Robinson Kurpius, 2000). In cases of divorce, the custodial parent must grant consent for the treatment of his or her children. Consent from both parents is recommended if custody is shared (Welfel, 2013). While the consent of children and adolescents is not mandated, it is good clinical practice to seek their *assent* to treatment.

Furthermore, the ability to give autonomous, informed consent assumes the client has the psychological capacity to do so. For example, certain clients may be so impaired that they are unaware of their need for treatment. In such extreme cases, guardians, significant others, or the state may petition for the involuntary commitment of the client for inpatient treatment. In other cases, the consent of parents or guardians is required when mental retardation limits the client's capacity to make an informed, autonomous decision.

CONFIDENTIALITY AND PRIVILEGED COMMUNICATION

Confidentiality and privileged communication relate to the fundamental right of the client to privacy, that is, the right of persons to determine what information about them will be shared with or withheld from others (Remley & Herlihy, 2010). *Confidentiality* refers to the ethical responsibility to safeguard client-related information gained through the professional relationship and to disclose it only when fully informed clients freely give their consent. In legal proceedings, a related concept, privileged communication, refers to the legal obligation to protect clients against the forced disclosure of information conveyed in the context of the professional relationship (Corey et al., 2011).

The assurance of confidentiality is central to the counseling process (Hackney, 2000) and is a primary obligation of mental health counselors (AMHCA, 2010). The U.S. Supreme Court recognized its centrality in the 1996 *Jaffee v. Redmond* decision:

> Effective psychotherapy ... depends upon an atmosphere of confidence and trust in which the patient is willing to make a frank and complete disclosure of facts, emotions, memories, and fears. Because of the sensitive nature of the problems for which individuals consult psychotherapists, disclosure of confidential communications made during counseling sessions may cause embarrassment or disgrace. For this reason, the mere possibility of disclosure may impede development of the confidential relationship necessary for successful treatment. (p. 10)

Information protected by confidentiality includes all information related to the counseling contacts, words spoken in sessions, business records, clinical record, test results, and client-related information received from other parties.

However, the right to confidentiality is not absolute. Certain modalities of treatment make the guarantee of confidentiality impossible. The potential for unauthorized disclosure occurs when multiple clients are seen in treatment. For example, Corey and colleagues (2011) note that privileged communication does not typically apply to group counseling, unless there is a statutory exception. Furthermore, although group counselors should clearly define and express the importance of confidentiality, they cannot prevent group members from revealing information outside the group setting. The counselor should communicate this risk of unauthorized disclosure when seeking to obtain informed consent from prospective group clients.

Decisions must be made by the counselor on the extent to which confidentiality can be honored or broken in the counseling of minors. Children and adolescents are most often seen at the request of parents, teachers, or some other adult (Slovenko, 1998). Particularly problematic situations involve unwanted pregnancies, substance abuse, crimes against property, sexual behavior, and dangerousness to self or others (Isaacs & Stone, 2001). Generally speaking, four possible options are available (Hendrix, 1991): (a) complete confidentiality with no disclosure to parents, (b) limited confidentiality, in which minors waive in advance the right to know what may be disclosed, (c) informed forced consent when a child is provided advance notice that information will be revealed to parents, and (d) no guarantees made about confidentiality at all. Each option presents potential ethical and legal dilemmas. Isaacs and Stone (2001) found that mental health counselors tended to grant greater autonomy to minor clients as the age of the clients increased. As the age of clients increased, counselors tended to break confidentiality only in the most serious instances of imminent risk of dangerous behavior. Finally, the personal values of the counselor (e.g., liberal versus conservative, prochoice versus prolife) interact with the previously mentioned factors when the mental health counselor is deciding whether to breach confidentiality with a minor client.

PROTECTION OF CLIENTS OR OTHERS FROM HARM

Confidentiality must be breached when a risk of harm to clients or others exists. This circumstance includes suspected abuse or neglect of children, clients who pose a danger to themselves, clients who pose a danger to others, clients who have a communicable disease and whose behavior puts others at risk, and, in some states, suspected abuse of the elderly. The specific responsibilities of the mental health counselor in such situations include the duties to warn, to protect, and/or to report (Remley & Herlihy, 2010). Because the counselor makes a deliberate choice to break confidentiality, the decision to do so requires compelling evidence. These are among the most stressful situations faced by professional counselors (C. J. Deutsch, 1984; Farber, 1983).

Taking Action When Child or Elder Abuse or Neglect Is Suspected. The AMHCA Code of Ethics (2010) states:

> The release of information without consent of the client may only take place under the most extreme circumstances: the protection of life (suicidality or homicidality); child abuse, and/or abuse of incompetent persons and elder abuse. Above all, mental health counselors are required to comply with state and federal statutes concerning mandated reporting. (Principle I. A. 2. C., p. 2)

Indeed, all 50 states have statutes requiring that suspected abuse be reported to law enforcement. The specific time frame in which a report must be made varies according to the jurisdiction. The role of clinical mental health counselors is to report suspicions rather than hypotheses or hunches. Furthermore, the counselor need not conduct an investigation to substantiate the suspicion. When uncertain as to whether to report, mental health professionals should consult with their supervisors and colleagues.

Protecting Clients Who Pose a Danger to Themselves. Clients pose a danger to themselves when a suicide attempt is clear and imminent. Mental health counselors are ethically and legally required to break confidentiality when their clients represent a clear and imminent threat to themselves. To determine risk of self-destructiveness, the counselor conducts a *lethality assessment,* considering the following signs (Hoff, Hallisey, & Hoff, 2009; Jackson-Cherry & Erford, 2010):

- Presence of a suicide plan*
- Past history of suicide attempts*
- Absence of preventive psychological and social resources*

- Communication (i.e., relative isolation of client)*
- Experience of recent loss
- Physical illness
- Chemical abuse
- Unexplained changes in behavior
- Depression
- Social factors or problems
- Mental illness
- Statistical predictors—age, gender, race, marital status, sexual identity

The four signs followed by asterisks indicate very high risk, and the level of risk increases as the number of signs increases. (Hoff, 1995, p. 199). Appropriate interventions range from having the client sign a no-suicide contract to having the client involuntarily committed to a psychiatric facility. In addition, mental health professionals should always seek consultation with supervisors and colleagues to determine a path of action that is both ethically and legally sound.

Clients Who Pose a Danger to Others. Mental health professionals are required to contact law enforcement agencies when they determine that a client poses a high risk of assault or homicide. In addition, and based on principles of the *Tarasoff* case (*Tarasoff v. Board of Regents of the University of California*, 1976), potential victims of homicide must be warned. The following guidelines are useful in assessing the risk of assault or homicide (Hoff et al., 2009, p. 440):

- History of homicidal threats
- History of assaults
- Current homicidal threats and plan
- Possession of lethal weapons
- Use or abuse of alcohol or other drugs
- Conflict in significant social relationship (e.g., infidelity, threat of divorce, work-related problems)
- Threats of suicide following homicide

The mental health professional responds in measure to the degree of risk presented. Interventions can range from the development of a contract to involuntary commitment to a psychiatric institution. Furthermore, the mental health professional must take appropriate measures to protect herself or himself from danger. Playing the Lone Ranger is not recommended in such a situation.

Clients with Communicable Diseases Whose Behavior Poses a Danger to Others. One of the most controversial applications of the *Tarasoff* decision has emerged in relation to AIDS. The duty to warn may apply where HIV-positive clients engage in unprotected sex or share needles with unsuspecting third parties (Cohen, 1997). The ACA Code of Ethics (ACA, 2005) states:

> When clients disclose that they have a disease commonly known to be both communicable and life threatening, counselors may be justified in disclosing information to identifiable third parties, if they are known to be at demonstrable and high risk of

contracting the disease. Prior to making a disclosure, counselors confirm that there is such a diagnosis and assess the intent of clients to inform the third parties about their disease or to engage in any behaviors that may be harmful to an identifiable third party. (Section B.2.b., p. 7)

Reprinted from ACA Code of Ethics, Section B.2.b, p. 7 © 2005 The American Counseling Association. Reprinted with permission. No further reproduction authorized without written permission from the American Counseling Association

The code states that counselors "may be justified in disclosing information," which falls short of requiring the warning of vulnerable third parties. The AMHCA Code of Ethics adds that mental health counselors must confirm the diagnosis "with a medical provider" (AMHCA, 2010, Section I. A. 2. p. 3). The dilemma for mental health practitioners involves deciding the extent to which the duty to warn outweighs the need to protect confidentiality. In addition, states differ not only in requiring the disclosure of confidential information to a vulnerable third party, but also in who is required to disclose.

Cohen (1997) identifies the following conditions for justifiable disclosure:

- Conclusive medical evidence indicates that the client is HIV seropositive;
- The third party is placed at a high risk for contracting HIV, according to current medical standards, due to unprotected, ongoing sexual intercourse with the client;
- No other person is likely to disclose to the third party;
- The third party may be identified and contacted by the counselor with no intervention of law enforcement or other investigative agencies.

Counselors must be cautious and seek legal and professional consultation in determining the appropriate ethical and legal path to follow. Although justified in disclosing, mental health counselors must be mindful of the ethical, legal, and professional principles of maintaining confidentiality.

PROFESSIONAL BOUNDARIES AND DUAL RELATIONSHIPS

When asked to identify the most significant ethical problem related to professional boundaries, most persons, will place sexual contact or intercourse between counselors and clients at the top of the list. However, a wide range of issues sets boundaries between counselor and client. The boundaries are defined by the context of their occurrence, the specific dimension(s) involved, and the rules in operation. The boundaries crossed may be physical, psychological, emotional, or social. For example, physical boundaries are crossed when touch occurs in treatment.

Counselors may cross an emotional boundary when they become incapacitated by taking on the emotional pain of their clients.

Dual relationships are boundary issues that occur when a counselor assumes two or more roles concurrently or sequentially with a person seeking help (Pearson & Piazza, 1997). For example, a dual relationship exists when the counselor dates a current client or when the exchange of gifts between counselors and clients blurs personal and professional roles (Gerig, 2004). Often, the least extreme boundary issues are the most difficult to handle. I have much more difficulty in determining how to respond to a current client who approaches me while shopping at the mall with my family than in deciding whether it is ethical to accept an expensive gift from a client.

Pearson and Piazza (1997) identify several categories of multiple relationships:

- Circumstantial multiple relationships
- Structured multiple professional relationships
- Shifts in professional roles
- Personal and professional role conflicts
- Predatory professionals

Although professionals uniformly agree that sexual contact between counselors is unethical, they differ regarding their position regarding nonsexual multiple roles and boundary issues. In general, counselors are advised to avoid dual relationships when possible, especially when there is potential for exploitation or impaired clinical judgment (ACA, 2005, Section A.5.a.). Certain multiple relationships represent significant conflict of interests and roles and must therefore be avoided if the well-being of the client is to be promoted. However, it is awkward and perhaps harmful to avoid less extreme multiple relationships. For example, it is probably unnecessary to change the church I attend because one of my clients attends the same church. Or if the only teller window available is staffed by my current client, it is better for me to do my banking business at that window (assuming, of course, that the transaction does not involve cashing checks that reveal the names of other clients).

Indeed, the ACA Code of Ethics (ACA, 2005) notes the possibility that certain counselor-client nonprofessional interactions might be beneficial (Section A.5.d.). Mental health counselors should seek consultation and supervision, provide adequate information for the clients' informed consent, and adhere to credible decision-making models before entering into nonprofessional relationships with clients (AMHCA, 2010). The counselor should document in case records the rationale for engaging in such a relationship in advance, when feasible, and provide evidence that clients are not exploited.

To minimize risk to clients, mental health counselors are advised to set healthy boundaries early in the therapeutic relationship. Informed consent and open, ongoing communication regarding the nature of the treatment process provide added protection for clients. Consult with supervisors to maintain an objective perspective on the therapeutic relationship. And when a dual relationship becomes problematic, work under close supervision, and document the nature of this supervision in your records along with a detailed account of your interactions with the client.

ELECTRONIC COMMUNICATION AND E-THERAPY

In December 2000, an estimated 361 million persons, or 5.8% of the world's population, were using the Internet. In a little more than a decade, the number of Internet users has mushroomed to 2.267 billion users representing around 32.7% of the world's population (Internet World Stats, 2012). According to the 2012 results of the Pew Internet American Life Project, 80% of American adults and 93% of American teens use the Internet (Pew Research Center, 2012). The results of the Pew survey reveal the following patterns of Internet usage among American adults:

- 92% use a search engine to find information
- 91% send or read e-mails
- 84% search for a map or driving instructions
- 80% look for health/medical information
- 22% participate in an online discussion, a listserv, or other online group forum that helps people with personal issues or health problems.

Indeed, we have seen the distance between places shrink and the global village become a reality.

The implications and applications of the Internet and e-communication among the mental health professions have been profound. The provision of distance behavioral health services began as early as 1959, when the Nebraska Psychiatric Institute used a television link for consultation (Center for Substance Abuse Treatment, 2009). Riemer-Reiss (2000) found no reports in the mental health counseling literature discussing the direct applications of distance communication. Technologies hardly in use at the turn of the century are now commonly used for diagnosis, counseling, data management, transfer of counseling-related information, education, and supervision. Novel counseling-related applications of technology include use of mobile technology to enhance interventions (Warren, 2012) and virtual reality (second world) as an environment for group therapy and continuing education (Riva, 2005).

The 2010 AMHCA Code of Ethics provides detailed information about the role of technology in the practice of mental health counseling. The 2005 ACA Code of Ethics contains "educational, visionary, and inspirational" statements regarding the use of technology in Standard A.1. It is well beyond the scope of this section to provide an in-depth discussion of all the related legal and ethical aspects. Rather, my purpose is to call your attention to key ethical concerns that arise when mental health counselors use electronic communications and e-therapy as part of their service delivery.

Promoting the welfare of the client is the primary responsibility of counselors (ACA, 2005). Establishing and retaining secure virtual environments is essential when conducting distance counseling. As in any form of counseling, clients should be informed of its process and procedures. What types of formats are to be used? What are the benefits and risks of e-therapy? How, specifically, are client crises managed? What level of technical skill is required of e-therapy clients? What computer specifications are required to ensure the minimal interruption of sessions? The answers to these and other questions should be included in the informed-consent process.

Issues also arise regarding counselor competence. What special training is required to deliver counseling services electronically? How does the mental health counselor demonstrate adequate training and skill in computer technology or the delivery of specific techniques and interventions over the Internet? For example, does a Certified Cognitive Therapist possess the requisite knowledge and skills to deliver in vivo anxiety management techniques? Does your state license allow you to practice e-therapy across state lines? As of 2005, at least 18 states had enacted legislation related to the use of e-therapy (Center for Substance Abuse Treatment, 2009). Most practitioners must hold a license in each state or province in which they deliver services. In addition, they are legally obligated to practice within the scope of practice of that jurisdiction's license.

Unique concerns regarding boundary issues and dual relationships arise with the use of the Internet. Given the power differential in the counselor-client relationship, mental health counselors must take care in their use of e-mail communication with clients. The lack of visual cues can be a source of role confusion (Bradley, Hendricks, Lock, Whiting, & Parr, 2011). Limits should be placed on the type and frequency of e-mail communications between the client and the counselor. Policies should define what constitutes a professional exchange of information via e-mail and under what circumstance such an exchange may be considered a billable service. Boundaries are easily crossed and confidentiality compromised when counselors responds to practice-related e-mails from home. In addition, counselors should manage their use of social media and other instances of their Internet presence. Accepting clients as friends on your Facebook account amounts to a dual relationship. Be aware of what personal information is accessible to your clients via the Internet. While it is impossible to prevent public access to all personal information, reasonable precautions should be taken to limit the availability of your photograph, your home address, or links to close family members. Finally, searching the Internet for client-related information might be considered a serious violation of clients' rights and privacy. When taken to the extreme, such counselor behavior can be viewed as predatory.

CONCLUSION

A number of models for making ethical decisions are found in the professional literature (Corey et al., 2011; Cottone & Claus, 2000; Garcia, Cartwright, Winston, & Borzuchowska, 2003). A useful step-by-step model for making ethical decisions is presented by Welfel (2013):

1. Develop ethical sensitivity.
2. Clarify facts, stakeholders, and the sociocultural context of the case.
3. Define the central issues and the available options.
4. Refer to professional standards and relevant laws/regulations.
5. Search out ethics scholarship.
6. Apply ethical principles to the situation.
7. Consult with supervisor and respected colleagues.
8. Deliberate and decide.
9. Inform supervisor, implement and document decision-making process and actions.
10. Reflect on the experience. (p. 30)

If a counselor is called before an ethics committee for alleged violation, an inability to demonstrate the application of an ethical decision-making model in connection with the allegation becomes, in itself, an ethical problem (Welfel, 2013).

It is prudent to be mindful of the difference between ethical decision making and ethical or moral behavior. Rest (1983) identifies four components of moral behavior that must be present if moral action is to occur. First, the counselor must exhibit *moral sensitivity,* a recognition of situations that have implications for the welfare of the client. Second, the counselor must be able to engage in *moral reasoning,* that is to recognize and think through the moral dimensions involved in the specific ethical problem or dilemma. Third, counselors must *decide to carry out the moral alternative* by evaluating the options available and then implementing the most moral of them. Fourth, the counselor *implements the moral action,* enacting the desired behaviors *in context.* It is essential that clinical mental health counselors embody the highest ideals of professional practice and not see ethics as a simple matter of rule adherence.

DISCUSSION QUESTIONS

1. You are employed at a local community mental health center and lead a group of adolescent males who have been mandated into the conduct disorder group that you facilitate. A lack of participation by any member of the group is viewed as a violation of the probation criteria and is to be reported to the probation officer. What are the implications of informed consent when you are working with involuntary clients? Suppose you have four group members who choose to remain silent. They attend, but they do not participate in group activities. What are the ethical dilemmas for you, and how would you respond?

2. In what ways do counselors' personal sets of values interact with their ability to behave professionally and ethically? To what extent can a counselor's personal set of values be incongruent with the set of ethics he or she is required to adhere to?

3. Counselors frequently work with clients who express suicidal ideation. How would you assess the level of risk presented by a client? At what point is it necessary for a counselor to break confidentiality to protect the client? What specific steps would you take in such a situation?

4. What type of boundary issues or dual relationships will tend to be most difficult for you to manage? Discuss what they are and how you would choose to manage them.

SUGGESTED ACTIVITIES

1. How specifically would you discuss the ethical concerns of confidentiality and informed consent with your clients? Practice your skills with one or two peers. Then discuss the significance and limitations of confidentiality and informed consent by doing a role-play. Assign the roles of counselor and counselee. How would your discussion differ if you were conducting family or group counseling?

2. Suppose you choose to work in a private practice upon licensure. Develop a self-disclosure statement that you might provide to new clients as a way of introducing them to who you are, what your areas of specialization are, and what services you offer.

3. Suppose you operate a small, privately owned counseling practice. Develop a Web page to advertise your services. What ethical issues require special consideration when one is promoting a counseling service in this manner?

4. Develop several ethical dilemmas that you are likely to face as a professional counselor. Then apply the steps of ethical decision making (e.g., Welfel, 2013) to assist you in resolving the dilemmas.

REFERENCES

American Counseling Association Ethics Committee. (2010). Ethics committee summary–FY 2010. Retrieved from http://www.counseling.org/Files/FD.ashx?guid=e6bace0b-9a5e-4006-b01c-2eccbad6a1b4

American Counseling Association Governing Council. (2005). ACA policies and procedures for processing complaints of ethical violations. Retrieved from http://www.counseling.org/Resources/CodeOfEthics/TP/Home/CT2.aspx

American Counseling Association. (2005). *ACA code of ethics.* Alexandria, VA: Author.

American Counseling Association. (1999). *ACA ethical standards for internet on-line counseling.* Alexandria, VA: Author.

Allen, V. B. (1986). A historical perspective of the AACD Ethics Committee. Special Issue: Professional Ethics. *Journal of Counseling and Development, 64,* 293.

American Mental Health Counselors Association. (2010). *Code of ethics of the American Mental Health Counselors Association–2010 revision.* Alexandria, VA: Author.

American Psychological Association. (2010). *Ethical principles of psychologists and code of conduct: 2010 Amendments.* Washington, DC: Author. *American Psychologist, 44,* 703–708.

Beauchamp, T. L., & Childress, J. F. (1989). *Principles of biomedical ethics* (3rd ed.). Oxford, England: Oxford University Press.

Bradley, L. J., Hendricks, B., Lock, R., Whiting, P. P., & Parr, G. (2011). E-mail communication: Issues for mental health counselors. *Journal of Mental Health Counseling, 33,* 67–79.

Deutsch, C. J. (1984). Self-reported sources of stress among psychotherapists. *Professional Psychology: Research and Practice, 15,* 833–845.

Center for Substance Abuse Treatment. (2009). *Considerations for the provision of e-therapy.* HHS Publication. No. (SMA) 09-4450. Rockville, MD: Center for Substance Abuse Treatment, Substance Abuse, and Mental Health Services Administration.

Cohen, E. D. (1997). Confidentiality, HIV, and the ACA code of ethics. *Journal of Mental Health Counseling, 19,* 349–364.

Corey, G., Corey, M. S., & Callanan, P. (2011). *Issues and ethics in the helping professions* (8th ed.). Belmont, CA: Brooks/Cole.

Cottone, R. R., & Claus, R. E. (2000). Ethical decision-making models: A review of the Literature. *Journal of Counseling and Development, 78,* 275–283.

Council for the Accreditation of Counseling and Related Educational Programs. (2009a). *2009 Standards.* Alexandria, VA: Author.

Farber, B. A. (1983). Psychotherapists' perceptions of stressful patient behavior. *Professional Psychology: Research and Practice, 14,* 697–705.

General Penalty for Failure to Comply with Requirements and Standards, 42 USC § 1320d–5. (2001).

Gerig, M. S. (2004). Receiving gifts from clients: Ethical and therapeutic issues. *Journal of Mental Health Counseling, 26,* 199–210.

Gillman, P. B. (2004, February). A new era of documentation in psychiatry: Advice on psychotherapy, progress notes. *Behavioral Healthcare Tomorrow, 13*(1), 48–50.

Gladding, S. T. (2011). *The counseling dictionary: Concise definitions of frequently used terms.* Upper Saddle River, NJ: Pearson Education.

Hackney, H. (2000). *Practice issues for the beginning counselor.* Needham Heights, MA: Allyn & Bacon.

Hall, A. S., & Lin, M. (1995). Theory and practice of children's rights: Implications for mental health counselors. *Journal of Mental Health Counseling, 17,* 63–80.

Hendrix, D. H. (1991). Ethics and intrafamily confidentiality in counseling children. *Journal of Mental Health Counseling, 13,* 323–333.

Herlihy, B., & Corey, G. (1996). *ACA ethical standards casebook* (5th ed.). Alexandria, VA: American Counseling Association.

Hess, H. F. (1980). Procedures, problems, and prospects. *Professional Practice of Psychology, 1,* 1–10.

Hoff, L. A. (1995). *People in crisis: Understanding and helping* (4th ed.). San Francisco: Jossey-Bass.

Hoff, L. A., Hallisey, B. J., & Hoff, M. (2009). *People in crisis: Clinical and diversity perspectives* (6th ed.). New York, NY: Routledge.

Holroyd, J. C., & Brodsky, A. M. (1977). Psychologists' attitudes and practices regarding erotic and non-erotic physical contact with patients. *American Psychologist, 32,* 843–849.

Hubert, R. M., & Freeman, L. T. (2004). Report of the ACA ethics committee: 2002–2003. *Journal of Counseling and Development, 82,* 248–251.

Internet World Stats. (2012). Internet growth statistics. Retrieved from http://www.internetworldstats.com/emarketing.htm

Isaacs, M. L., & Stone, C. (2001). Confidentiality with minors: Mental health counselors' attitudes toward breaching or preserving confidentiality. *Journal of Mental Health Counseling, 23,* 342–356.

Jackson-Cherry, L. R., & Erford, B. T. (2010). *Crisis intervention and prevention.* Upper Saddle River, NJ: Pearson.

Kardener, R. R., Fuller, M., & Mensh, I. N. (1973). A survey of physicians, attitudes and practices regarding erotic and nonerotic contact with patients. *American Journal of Psychiatry, 130,* 1077–1081.

Lawrence, G., & Robinson Kurpius, S. E. (2000). Legal and ethical issues involved when counseling minors in nonschool settings. *Journal of Counseling and Development, 78,* 1360–136.

Meara, N. M., Schmidt, L. D., & Day, J. D. (1996). Principles and virtues: A foundation for ethical decisions, policies, and character. *Counseling Psychologist, 24*(1), 4–77.

Moline, M. E., Williams, G. T., & Austin, K. M. (1998). *Documenting psychotherapy: Essentials for mental health practitioners.* Thousand Oaks, CA: Sage.

Montgomery, L. M., Cupit, B. E., & Wimberly, T. K. (1999). Complaints, malpractice, and risk management: Professional issues and personal experiences. *Professional Psychology: Research and Practice, 30,* 402–410.

National Association of Social Workers. (2008). *Code of ethics for the National Association of Social Workers.* Washington, DC: Author.

Pearson, B., & Piazza, N. (1997). Classification of dual relationships in the helping professions. *Counselor Education and Supervision, 37,* 89–99.

Pew Research Center. (2012). Pew internet and American life project. Retrieved from http://www.pewinternet.org/

Remley, T. P., & Herlihy, B. (2010). *Ethical, legal, and professional issues in counseling* (3rd ed.). Upper Saddle River, NJ: Pearson Prentice Hall.

Rest, J. R. (1983). Morality (pp. 556–629). In J. H. Flavell & E. M. Markman (Eds.), *Handbook of child psychology: Vol. 3. Cognitive development.* New York, NY: Wiley.

Riemer-Reiss, M. L. (2000). Utilizing distance technology for mental health counseling. *Journal of Mental Health Counseling, 22,* 189–203.

Riva, G. (2005). Virtual reality in psychotherapy: Review. *CyberPsychology and Behavior, 8,* 220–230.

Slovenko, R. (1998). *Psychotherapy and confidentiality: Testimonial privileged communication, breach of confidentiality, and reporting duties.* Springfield, IL: Thomas.

Walden, S. L., Herlihy, B., & Ashton, L. (2003). The evolution of ethics: Personal perspectives of ACA ethics committee chairs. *Journal of Counseling and Development, 81,* 106–110.

Warren, J. M. (2012). Mobile mind-mapping: Using mobile technology to enhance rational emotive behavior therapy. *Journal of Mental Health Counseling, 34,* 72–81.

7

Employment Settings: Where Clinical Mental Health Counselors Work and What They Do

OUTLINE

Application of the Clinical Mental Health Counseling Paradigm

Stages of Helping

The Traditional Continuum of Mental Health Care and Expanded Settings of Professional Practice

Clinical Mental Health Counselors on the Job

Conclusion

As part of the admission process to programs that award a Master of Arts in counseling, prospective students are often required to interview with faculty who teach in their chosen area of specialization. Among other things, it is vital that persons entering the program know what, specifically, they are getting into, because their expectations regarding the profession often guide their decision to enter one specialization (e.g., mental health counseling) instead of the another (e.g., marriage and family counseling/therapy). So, early in the interview, applicants are asked, "What do mental health counselors do?"

The responses I have received to this question reveal certain myths and stereotyped beliefs regarding the profession. Frequently, the applicant responds, "Mental health counselors work with individuals and, primarily, diagnose and treat mental illness. They usually work in an office setting for sessions that are around 50 minutes in length."

Although such responses are accurate up to a point, they fail to capture the breadth and depth of clinical mental health counselors' scope of practice. In many ways, the nature of the profession continues to be one of mental health care's best-kept secrets. This chapter considers the dimensions of professional practice by exploring where mental health counselors work and what they do. Certainly, no text can provide an exhaustive review of the contemporary work environment. The creativity with which my colleagues engage in their professional endeavors knows few boundaries or limitations. I will therefore limit my focus to several examples that will help you grasp the breadth, depth, and significance of the mental health counseling profession. The foundations model presented in Chapter 3 will serve as an organizing template to guide this discussion. In this chapter, you will catch a glimpse of the exciting possibilities that await as you anticipate professional practice.

APPLICATION OF THE CLINICAL MENTAL HEALTH COUNSELING PARADIGM

In Chapter 3, a paradigm for clinical mental health counseling was presented. Professional practice was described as having three dimensions: mental health/wellness, mental illness/dysfunction, and ecological context. All client systems and services can be plotted along these interacting dimensions.

There are four contemporary trends in the counseling profession (McAuliffe & Eriksen, 1999), each of which interfaces with the clinical mental health counseling paradigm:

- A move of the primary locus of client issues from the individual to the ecological context in which the individual is embedded;
- An increased emphasis on strength and development rather than on deficits and pathology;
- An increased acceptance of multiple and subjective realities rather than empirically based, objectively defined truth;
- An increased reliance on education and prevention and a decreased emphasis on remediation.

By applying the clinical mental health counseling paradigm to professional practice, clinical mental health counselors resist the pressures of the traditional medical model and third-party reimbursers to take a narrow view of professional practice. For example, it is an error to assume that the definition of *client system* is necessarily limited to individuals, groups, and families. Although these are certainly legitimate foci for assessment and intervention, we must be alert to the needs and possibilities of intervention that exist in larger networks, such as the extended family, the peer group, formal and informal organizational structures and processes, the neighborhood, the community, the subculture, or society at large. In addition, the clinical mental health counseling paradigm alerts mental health counselors to consider the variety of interactions among the multiple ecological levels in the client's world and their influence on the client's presenting concerns.

The paradigm shows the vast array of the community counseling model's direct and indirect services (Lewis, Lewis, Daniels, & D'Andrea, 2003), which are available in a variety of service delivery settings. These services seek to promote wellness and treat dysfunction using assessment and intervention strategies that cut across the interacting levels of the ecological context.

STAGES OF HELPING

Several primary modalities of intervention used by clinical mental health counselors are discussed in a later section. Regardless of the modality used, the people-helping process consists of five primary stages (Hackney & Cormier, 2013):

1. establishing the relationship;
2. assessing or defining the presenting problem;
3. identifying and setting goals;
4. choosing and initiating interventions; and
5. planning and introducing termination and follow-up.

ESTABLISHING THE RELATIONSHIP

As I noted in Chapter 3, many counselors see the therapeutic relationship as being the primary curative factor in the treatment process. Although numerous definitions have been put forth, two fundamental characteristics of effective counseling relationships stand out (Martin, 2000).

First, a positive relational bond is developed, characterized by personal warmth, empathy, and acceptance. The effective counselor communicates a focused interest in and acceptance of the client as worthwhile and significant. The counselor communicates these elements from the start, and they become the foundation of a trust that allows genuine self-disclosure. Depending on the modality in use, the term *client* may refer to an individual, a family, a group, an organization, or a community. That is, the term refers to the specific unit that is the focus of assessment and intervention.

Second, a counseling relationship establishes a mutual commitment to the collaborative process and goals of counseling (Martin, 2000). Productive change is unlikely if clients do not understand what to expect in the counseling process. Furthermore, clients need to know "who does what" in order to make change happen. They are more likely to commit to the "work" of counseling when they know what to expect and what is expected of them. For this reason, mental health counselors seek to obtain the client's informed consent to treatment early in the process of developing the counseling relationship. The counseling relationship, then, becomes a working alliance that combines both the relationship in itself and the relationship as a means of achieving the desired outcome (Egan, 2010).

Motivational interviewing (Miller & Rollnick, 2002) is an evidence-based approach that assists the counselor in establishing a supportive counseling relationship (Sciacca, 2012). The three concepts basic to this approach are collaboration, evocation, and autonomy (Miller & Rollnick, 2002). The term *collaboration* expresses the valuing of an egalitarian relationship that treats the experiences and perspectives of the client with respect. *Evocation* emphasizes the use of the client's inherent resources, strengths, and intrinsic motivation for change. *Autonomy* highlights the client's capacity and right to self-direction and being an informed consumer of the service. These concepts promote the development of a positive working alliance that empowers the client for change (Kress & Hoffman, 2008).

The counseling relationship is established when clients perceive that they are viewed as significant and valued; understand the nature, process, and mutual responsibilities of counseling; and consent and commit to that process. Once the relationship is established, the potential of a successful outcome is increased, and counseling can proceed to the next stage.

ASSESSING OR DEFINING THE PRESENTING PROBLEM

Often, when working with couples in conflict, I note that they come into the initial session feeling very stuck. They want to tell me about the various futile attempts they have made to solve their problem. However, as they discuss the nature of the problem, it soon becomes apparent that each person has a different perspective. The couple has failed to develop a coherent, mutually held view of their problem. How can they solve the problem if they have not clearly determined what it is they need to resolve?

Entry-level counselors often make the same mistake. Studies have shown that when given an hour to diagnose a client, mental health practitioners tend to come to their diagnostic conclusions in a matter of minutes and then spend the remaining time selectively abstracting data supporting their initial determination (Cozolini, 2004). That is, after hearing the client's brief description of the presenting complaint, they move quickly to the resolution phase without collaborating with the client to develop mutually agreed-upon goals. Strategies of change are much less likely to succeed when the client and the counselor lack a clear, collaborative view of the precise nature of the problem.

Two tasks are primary in assessment: information gathering and decision making. These tasks are woven throughout the entire process of counseling. In the initial phases, information gathering helps the counselor and the client gain a better, more accurate view of the presenting problem. The information obtained in assessment provides the raw material for a conceptualization of the problem and, in some settings, a formal diagnosis of the client's condition, using criteria and codes in the fourth revised edition of the *Diagnostic and Statistical Manual of Mental Disorders (DSM-IV-TR;* American Psychiatric Association, 2000). Furthermore, the information gathered assists the counselor and the client in plotting a course of action or a formalized treatment plan. Finally, continuing assessment provides important data for determining whether or not the implemented strategies are having their desired effect.

The Initial Interview and Assessment.   The transition to problem identification, assessment, and goal setting is frequently marked by an unstructured invitation extended by the counselor to the client, such as "How can I help you?" Basically, the counselor is seeking an answer to the question, "What's going on? (Egan, 2010). The answer becomes what might be called a *functional diagnosis,* a current picture of how the client is navigating in his or her niche. It is here that the client's problem is placed in context.

Counselors must be flexible in their approach to problem identification and assessment to ensure that they are responsive to and respectful of the cultural diversity of clients. The culturally sensitive counselor moves with caution by regulating the amount of structure within the session, the depth of personal exploration requested, and the nature of directives. As Egan (2010) notes,

> The more helpers understand the broad characteristics, needs, and behaviors of the populations with whom they work—African Americans, Caucasian Americans, diabetics, the elderly, drug addicts, the homeless, you name it—the better positioned they are to adapt . . . the counseling process itself to the individuals with whom they work. (p. 50)

Within the warmth, safety, and empathic understanding the counselor conveys, clients soon discover an opportunity for exploration and sharing unlike most interpersonal relationships they have encountered before.

Counselors use a variety of ways to solicit information and encourage clients' expression of feelings (Hackney & Cormier, 2013), including open- and closed-ended questions, requests for clarification, paraphrasing, acknowledgment of nonverbal behaviors, reflection and summarization of feeling, statements of summary, and "Columbo-type" incomplete statements. These latter statements reflect a style of information gathering used by the main character of an old television detective show. Columbo came across as a rather bumbling and confused investigator, but his questions and incomplete sentences drew out critical information and metaphors that would lead to the solving of the case. Counselors can use this style of communication to gain critical information for constructing case conceptualizations.

Although counselors often open a session with an unstructured question, they must assume control over the direction and pace of the interaction. It is, after all, conversation with a purpose. In most settings, counselors seek to gather the following types of information in the first session:

1. *Identifying and demographic information:* It is vital that counselors have accurate identifying information such as clients' names, addresses, and phone numbers for business operations of the agency and in the event that the counselor must

contact the client between sessions. Counselors also gather information regarding demographic variables such as age, gender, ethnicity, race, marital status, vocation, and educational status.

2. *Presenting problems:* It is critical to obtain a description of the problems experienced by the client and to record them in the client's own words. Often, clients present with complex situations with several problems occurring at various levels. Counselors want to determine who is involved in the problem; its specific, objective description, including its antecedents and consequences; and the client's related thoughts and feelings. In addition, information is gathered that enables counselors to conceptualize clients and their presenting problems in the ecological context. This includes gaining an understanding of how the client and the problem(s) interact with family and social relationships and with academic and vocational performance. The strengths and deficits of subgroups, community, formal and informal institutions and supports, and the larger social and cultural (including economic and political) context are also assessed.

3. *Current life setting and functioning level:* Answers to the following questions help the counselor better understand the client's overall quality of life: How adaptive is the client in daily functioning? What is a typical day and week for the client? To what extent are wellness practices a part of this client's routine and repertoire? Mental health counselors are mindful of the complex interacting components of the client's particular ecological context as they seek answers to such questions. For example, it is important to determine how the client's internal strengths and resources interact with the varying levels of wellness or pathology existing in the family, the peer group, the subculture, and the community. Does the soft discrimination of low expectations of significant others place artificial caps on the client's *zone of proximal development* (Vygotsky, 1962)?

4. *Client's biopsychosocial history:* Clients' history sheds light on their current circumstances. Counselors gather information regarding the following: medical history (e.g., unusual illness, injuries, or hospitalization), educational history (academic achievement and extracurricular interests), past vocational experience, past social and sexual relationships, partnerships and marriages, divorces, traumatic experiences (e.g., physical, sexual, or emotional abuse and neglect, or natural disasters), and substance use/abuse patterns.

5. *Family history and constellation:* The family plays an important role in the client's development. Patterns of behavior and relating often cross generational boundaries. McGoldrick (1999) notes that persons can be compared to music in that the individual notes are understood only as we perceive them in conjunction with each other, our memory of the combination of notes played in the past, and the anticipation of what notes will played next. Useful family information includes strengths of relationships between family subsystems (including relative level of differentiation, disengagement, and enmeshment); histories of emotional disturbance, substance abuse, significant physical illness, and losses; vocational patterns; and residential locations and moves. Genograms are useful for gathering and organizing such family information and provide a means of presenting the data visually so that significant patterns of behavior and relating within the family can be discovered and explored (Nichols, 2009).

6. *Behavioral observations:* Counselors pay careful attention to clients' behavioral and nonverbal presentations to assess their current level of functioning. This includes physical appearance, dress, posture, communication skill and style, gestures, facial expressions, degree of self-awareness, level of cognitive and sensoriperceptual functioning, and general level of vocabulary and comprehension.

In clinical settings, counselors may systematically gather this information by conducting a *mental status exam.* This global assessment of a client's mental functioning is to the mental health practitioner what the general physical examination is to a medical practitioner. Figure 7.1 lists the types of information gathered in a thorough mental status exam.

<table>
<tr>
<td>

FIGURE 7.1

Major
Components
of a Mental
Status Exam

</td>
<td>

Whereas a psychosocial history is a record of the client over the course of his or her life, a mental status exam is an evaluation of the client at one point in time. During the clinical interview, the counselor should make note of the following:

1. *Appearance*—a general description of overall appearance, dress, grooming, unusual features or gestures, posture (rigid, slumped, etc.);

2. *Motor activity*—gait position, bizarre postures, overall level of activity, any twitches, mannerisms, tics, agitation, clumsiness, rigidity, combativeness;

3. *Attitude*—level of cooperation, boredom, seductiveness, hostility, openness, defensiveness, guardedness, playfulness, and so on;

4. *Speech*—rapid or slow, pitch, pressured, hesitant, emotional, monotonous, volume, slurred, mumbled, relevance, spontaneity;

5. *State of consciousness*—alertness, responsiveness to environment, ability to carry out tasks (simple, then complex—e.g., touching nose with finger, then touching another body part simultaneously);

6. *Affect*—mood is client's internal emotional state, whereas affect is the outward expression of the internal state; congruity between client's description of mood and counselor's observation of affect; appropriateness to situation, anxiety level, stability of affect;

7. *Perception*—hallucinations (false perceptions of a sensory stimulus in the absence of a sensory stimulus); illusions (the misinterpretation of a true sensory stimulus); depersonalization and derealization;

8. *Thinking process*—abstract reasoning, loose associations, tangential thinking, circumstantiality, blocking, perseveration, echolalia, flight of ideas;

9. *Content of thought*—delusions, obsessions, suicidal, homicidal, paranoid ideation;

10. *Judgment*—extent to which the client understands the consequences of his or her actions;

11. *Memory*—ability to recall and/or recognize remote and recent past;

12. *Intelligence*—assessment of general level of intellectual functioning (average, above or below average);

13. *Concentration and attention span*—client's ability to attend and focus;

14. *Orientation* $\times$ 3—assessment of client's orientation to time (time, date, year), place (where client is), and person (who client is and who clinician is).

</td>
</tr>
</table>

What do counselors do with this mass of information? First, the data are organized in a manner that describes the client's *story*. Counselors document the assessment stage by writing an intake report, which becomes a part of the client's clinical file. In writing this document, counselors present the information concisely and coherently and stick to the facts presented by the client, avoiding professional jargon, elaborate inferences, and biases.

For many clinical mental health counselors, making a clinical diagnosis is a primary objective in conducting the initial assessment interview. As the client's presenting problem, current situation, and background information are explored, counselors are trained to pick up on behavioral indicators of significant emotional or behavioral patterns associated with the client's present distress. The counselor then considers these patterns in relation to criteria that define recognized categories of emotional and mental disorders. When a good fit between the displayed patterns of the client and recognized categories occurs, the counselor makes a tentative diagnosis. Technically, the diagnosis of a client is always a conceptualization in progress and subject to revision upon the receipt of additional information.

The professional literature bears witness to the widespread acceptance among counselors and counselor educators of client diagnosis (Mead, Hohenshil, & Singh, 1997; Ritchie, Piazza, & Lewton, 1991; Seligman, 1999). However, the practice remains somewhat controversial within the counseling profession. Some see the profession's emphasis on normal human development and mental health promotion as incompatible with diagnosis, which is part of the traditional medical model of clinical psychology (Vacc, Loesch, & Guilbert, 1997). In contrast, others see knowledge and skills in diagnosis as essential for clinical mental health counselors if they are to render reimbursable services in the contemporary treatment environment. Increasingly, students in CACREP-approved clinical mental health counseling programs are receiving in-depth training in diagnosis.

By far, the most widely used diagnostic system for classifying mental disorders is the *Diagnostic and Statistical Manual of Mental Disorders*. The text revision of its fourth edition (*DSM-IV-TR;* American Psychiatric Association, 2000) is in current use but is to be replaced by the fifth edition (*DSM-V*) by May 2013 (Ginter, 2012). According to the *DSM-IV-TR,* mental disorder is characterized by:

- A clinically significant behavioral or psychological syndrome occurring in an individual;
- Experienced distress or impairment in adaptive functioning in one or more major life areas;
- The syndrome exceeds expected or culturally approved responses to specific events;
- Deviant behaviors or conflicts between an individual and society, in themselves, are not considered mental illness unless such behaviors are functions of a mental illness. (American Psychiatric Association, 2000)

DSM-IV-TR attempts to use objectively based criteria for defining the various disorders included in its classification system. A specified number of symptoms and criteria must be present before a diagnosis can be made. This is a *categorical* approach to diagnosing, which assumes that specific forms of mental illness can be reliably distinguished from other forms, based on the unique sets of observable symptoms. However, research has shown that the significant overlap in the symptoms of specific diagnostic categories results in relatively low reliability (Ginter, 2012). In response, the proposed *DSM-V* is moving toward a *dimensional* approach to diagnosing, where each symptom is seen as lying on a continuum of severity or intensity. For example, substance abuse and dependence are collapsed into a single diagnosis, with specifiers indicating its level of severity (e.g., 2–3 criteria = moderate; 4 or more = severe). Other *DSM-IV-TR* categories that are likely to become spectrum-based disorders in the *DSM-V* include autism spectrum disorders, certain affective disorders (e.g., clinical depression and bipolar disorder), and schizophrenia.

In addition, the *DSM-IV-TR* assesses the presenting condition according to five dimensions. Its authors note that

> the use of the multiaxial system facilitates comprehensive and systematic evaluation with attention to the various mental disorders and general medical conditions, psychosocial and environmental problems and level of functioning that might be overlooked if the focus were on assessing a single presenting problem. (American Psychiatric Association, 2000, p. 27)

These dimensions, or axes, are described as follows:

Axis I: The Clinical Disorders and Other Conditions That May Be a Focus of Clinical Attention. This axis includes the major categories of mental illness, such as Early Childhood Disorders, Substance Abuse Disorders, Schizophrenia and other Psychotic Disorders, Mood Disorders, Anxiety Disorders, Eating Disorders, Sexual and Gender Identity Disorders, Impulse-Control Disorders, and Adjustment Disorders.

Axis II: Personality Disorders or Mental Retardation. The category of personality disorders includes a variety of pervasive and long-standing patterns of inflexible and maladaptive behaviors that interfere with the client's social and/or occupational functioning. Specific diagnostic classifications include borderline, antisocial, narcissistic, dependent, paranoid, and schizoid personality disorders.

Axis III: Current Medical or Physical Condition. On this axis, counselors list current medical conditions relevant to the understanding or managing of the client's mental disorder.

Axis IV: Severity of Psychosocial Stressors. Counselors report any psychosocial or environmental factors that might influence the course of the mental disorder, its treatment, and its prognosis. Both negative and positive stressors require clients to adjust to the demands placed on them and are considered on this axis.

Axis V: Global Assessment of Functioning. On this axis, counselors report the client's general level of psychological, social, and occupational functioning, using the Global Assessment of Functioning (GAF) Scale. This scale provides a system for rating the client's level of general functioning on a hypothetical continuum of mental illness–mental health that ranges from 0 to 100 (American Psychiatric Association, 2000)

It is being proposed for the *DSM-V* that Axes I–III be collapsed into a single level of diagnosis that includes clinical, personality, and medical categories (Ginter, 2012).

This approach fits with the recommendation that the new *DSM* be more closely aligned with the International Classification of Disease (ICD), which is the diagnostic system developed by the World Health Organization and used by the international health community.

Clinical mental health counselors approach the diagnostic process from a wellness perspective. Figure 7.2 is a diagram of this process. The person is viewed holistically. The clinical, personality and medical dimensions are understood as interacting in such a way that the person is viewed as a whole system rather than as consisting of component parts. The whole person, then, participates in interaction with his or her particular ecological context. In other words, the person (Axes I–III) is in a complex relationship with the environment. The assessment and impact of personal levels of wellness and personal-environmental strengths and resources are given careful consideration in developing an accurate diagnostic picture. Problems that clients (i.e., Axes I–III) experience as they interact within their ecological niche are expressed on Axis IV. The degree to which clients are flourishing or languishing (i.e., the general assessment of their functioning) is rated on Axis V.

It is important that clinical mental health counselors be aware of the specific scope of professional practice as defined in the state in which they practice. Although all mental health counseling programs abiding by CACREP standards require a working knowledge of the diagnostic process and systems, individual state licensure laws vary in what is legally permissible professional behavior. Many states include diagnosis in the scope of practice of licensed mental health and professional counselors. However, other states limit diagnosis to other mental health professions, typically psychiatry, psychology, and social work. Although licensed counselors in these latter states can submit diagnostic impressions or evaluations to third-party reimbursers, they must be

FIGURE 7.2 An Ecologically Informed View of a *DSM-IV-TR* Diagnosis

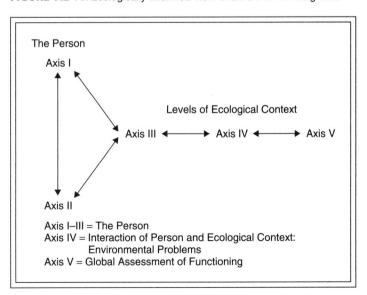

careful to utilize appropriate terminology and not overstate their areas of competence. A few states, such as Indiana, have chosen to use the word *evaluation* rather than *diagnosis* in their licensure law.

IDENTIFYING AND SETTING GOALS

With an accurate grasp of the problem, the counselor and the client are in a good position to specify the desired outcomes. Some clients come into counseling knowing what they want from the service. Mental health counselors must assist other clients in developing a vision of what life might look like in the absence of the concerns and problems that brought them into counseling. Bertolino and O'Hanlon (2002) have found the following questions useful in moving clients to think in more positive, goal-oriented ways:

- How will you know when things are better?
- How will you know when the problem is no longer a problem?
- What will indicate to you that therapy has been successful?
- How will you know when you no longer need to come to therapy?
- What will be happening that indicates to you that you can manage things on your own? (p. 91)

Frequently, the goals of clients contrast with their problem statements. For example, a client might complain of feeling overanxious in a variety of settings. In identifying a goal, the client might simply state that he desires to feel calm and relaxed. Through a collaborative process, the counselor and the client arrive at a concise and precise statement of what it would look and feel like to be calm and relaxed in specific settings. This process helps both the client and the counselor understand their purpose for meeting and to better recognize when they no longer need to meet.

Thus, goal statements are products of the assessment data. They specify the focus of ongoing assessments throughout treatment to determine the extent to which the desired outcomes are being attained. Goal statements should include the following six components:

1. *Who:* Who specifically will be performing the behavior?
2. *Direction:* Does the goal involve an increase, decrease, or maintenance of a specific behavior?
3. *Behavior, thought, or affect:* What is the observable activity that the identified person is to do? As noted previously, a goal statement specifies what the client should rather than should not do.
4. *Conditions:* What is the specific setting(s) in which the observable activity is to be performed? In other words, what are the trigger events or antecedent conditions that will provide the context for the new behavior, thought, or emotion?
5. *Degree:* What is the level of performance desired? Because realistic goals rarely entail perfect performance at all times, the counselor and the client determine the quality (level of proficiency), quantity (frequency), and level of stability that is to be present for the client to conclude that counseling is no longer necessary.
6. *Time frame:* What is the estimated length of time expected for the goal to be attained, assuming the client works in treatment according to the plan?

For example, for clients seeking to lose weight, merely setting a goal in pounds to be lost is not particularly helpful because the specific antecedents, thoughts, and behaviors necessary to accomplish the weight loss are not specified. Consider the following goal statement:

- Judy will lose 20 pounds over the next 3 months.

Although losing 20 pounds might be a very good thing, Judy has not identified exactly what she must do in order to lose those 20 pounds and maintain that weight. In contrast, consider this alternative: Judy will

- eat three meals each day until the goal of 20 pounds lost is attained and maintained for 3 weeks;
- limit caloric intake to 1,800–2,000/day for the first week and 1,400–1,700/day for succeeding weeks until weight loss of 20 pounds is attained;
- jog or exercise-walk at least five times per week for 20 minutes per session; and
- eat snacks only when physically hungry.

Goals specified in this manner are defined in terms of specific behaviors that can be integrated into Judy's daily routine. As these specific behaviors are developed and strengthened, Judy's lifestyle becomes more supportive of the long-term maintenance of her goals. In counseling, such goal statements enable the counselor and the client to identify the specific therapeutic activities that will be most helpful and efficient in attainment of the client's goals.

CHOOSING AND INITIATING INTERVENTIONS

The process of counseling can be likened to going on a journey. From the client's perspective, the question is "How do I get from *where I am* to *where I want to* go?" Once the counselor and the client have determined their current location (i.e., problem identification and/or diagnosis) and destination (i.e., treatment goals), it is much easier to decide which specific path to take in order to get from here to there. Selecting this path requires an individual approach. While numerous paths might lead to the desired destination, certain paths work better for some than for others. Mental health counselors draw upon their knowledge of the immense outcome literature to identify which particular theory and technique are likely to work best and for whom. Furthermore, a truly collaborative approach increases the likelihood that selected interventions will be culturally sensitive.

Taken together, the concise statement of the presenting problem and diagnosis, the identified goals, and the selected strategies form the components of a therapeutic contract. The general form of therapeutic contracts is shown in Figure 7.3. Such contracts become roadmaps allowing clients and counselors to see where they started, where they are now, and where they are going. The information contained in therapeutic contracts is also fundamental to establishing the client's *informed consent* for the proposed treatment, an essential ethical element for the counseling process.

Modalities of Intervention. Clinical mental health counselors select from among the many specific techniques derived from traditional and contemporary counseling theories (see Chapters 3 and 4) as strategies of change. The primary modalities used

FIGURE 7.3
Treatment Plan
and Contract

Treatment Plan

Client Name:

Case #:

Date:

Summary of Presenting Problem(s):

Provisional Diagnosis:

      Axis I:

      Axis II:

      Axis III:

      Axis IV:

      Axis V:

Justification for Diagnosis:

Date of Review:

Signatures

      Counselor: Date:

      Supervisor: Date:

      Consultant: Date:

Service Plan

Problem Statement	Goals/Objectives
1.	1.
2.	2.
3.	3.
4.	4.
5.	5.
6.	6.
7.	7.

FIGURE 7.3
(Continued)

Treatment Recommendations and Rationale:

Signatures:

      Client(s):   Date:

      Counselor(s):   Date:

      Supervisor: Date:

include individual, group, and family counseling; consultation; and advocacy. Often, more than one modality is implemented to modulate the intensity of treatment and facilitate desired outcomes.

Individual Counseling. In the minds of most laypersons and some counselors, the process of counseling is viewed as involving an interaction between the counselor and one client. Indeed, a number of traditional theories were designed to fit this one-to-one model. The individual format is familiar to counselors and most incoming clients and ensures the relative privacy that is so critical to the establishment of trust. It provides an intimate yet flexible structure for establishing an effective counseling relationship that meets the varying demands and characteristics of the particular client.

Group Work. Group work comprises a broad array of strategies that have in common the application of procedures to a collection of two or more individuals who meet in face-to-face interaction to achieve mutually agreed-upon goals. The Association for Specialists in Group Work (ASGW), a division of the American Counseling Association (ACA), defines *group work* as

> a broad professional practice involving the application of knowledge and skill in group facilitation to assist an interdependent collection of people to reach their mutual goals, which may be intrapersonal, interpersonal or work related. The goals of the group may include the accomplishment of tasks related to work, education, personal development, personal and interpersonal problem solving, or remediation of mental and emotional disorders. (ASGW, 2000, p. 330)

Specific forms of group work include task and work groups, psychoeducational groups, group counseling, and group psychotherapy (Corey, Corey, & Corey, 2010).

Frequently, mental health counselors working in agency settings are assigned specific responsibilities that include task- or work-related groups. For example, a community mental health agency may have a standing committee whose purpose is to ensure that the policies and procedures of its various programs are compliant with the standards of specific federal programs, such as Medicaid. The task of the group's members is first to understand the specific requirements of Medicaid, which are subject to continual revision. The members then are charged with developing appropriate intra-agency standards, forms, and instructions to enable agency staff to provide a standard of care and documentation that fulfills Medicaid's requirements. The work of such groups is critical to the financial well-being of the mental health center because fulfillment of these standards enables the center to bill and collect funds for services provided to Medicaid-eligible clients.

Sometimes communities set up task forces in which a variety of representatives from community agencies meet to identify problems, set goals, and develop programs to meet the needs of specific target populations. For example, Sault Ste. Marie, Michigan, a community located on the U.S.-Canadian border, had a well-recognized problem with transients who would hitchhike up the interstate highway only to find that they could not cross over into Canada. Some of these persons were homeless and without funds and placed a burden on the limited resources of community human service organizations. To address these concerns, a Homelessness Task Force was set up to assess needs and community resources and make specific recommendations on ways agencies and organizations could assist these persons. After conducting a community needs assessment, the task force recommended that a homeless shelter be created. Financing from a variety of sources was pooled to support the shelter, which was staffed by volunteers. In addition, community agencies and organizations developed an interagency support network that organized existing systems to assist transient homeless persons in finding needed mental health, substance abuse, and crisis intervention services. Mental health counselors, along with members of other helping professions, played key roles throughout the program's development.

Psychoeducational groups are group experiences intentionally structured to teach knowledge and skills for wellness and the prevention of relational, psychological, and educational problems. These groups provide the clients with relevant information and skills in a context that encourages discussion and sharing; the goal is to enhance important skills for living. Specific themes for psychoeducational groups include parent skill training, stress management, anger control, relationship enhancement, and social skill development. Group participants learn specific types of knowledge and skills and are better prepared to cope with future stressors. As the participants' resources are bolstered, vulnerability and risk decrease.

Group counseling involves the application of group processes and techniques to help participants resolve difficult but normal problems of living. The focus is on personal growth and the prevention and remediation of nonclinical problems. Typical topics include management of chronic pain, adaptation to divorce, maintenance of sobriety, development of coping skills for adults who were abused as children, and personal wellness/growth issues. Group counseling may be offered in community mental health settings and also at schools, college dorms, women's shelters, churches, group homes, and juvenile detention centers. Although some counseling groups have open-ended structures and no specific time limits, many use brief, time-limited formats, the number of sessions ranging from 6 to 12 (Erford, 2011). Ideally, groups are composed of five to eight participants who commit to consistent, voluntary attendance for the duration of the group.

Psychotherapy groups use group processes and techniques to treat psychological disturbance. Research has demonstrated the advantages of group psychotherapy over individual therapy for specific diagnostic categories, on the basis of both time efficiency and outcome effectiveness (McKay & Paleg, 1992). In addition, group psychotherapy can be used as an adjunct to individual counseling for mild to moderate depression, social phobia, panic, substance abuse/dependence, and adjustment disorders. Typically, participants in such groups have been diagnosed as having mental or emotional disorders. Thus, leaders of these groups must have specialized skills in assessment, diagnosis, treatment planning/evaluation, and specific models of group intervention. Group leaders must be able to take sessions deep enough to involve each participant in therapeutically meaningful experiences. Commonly applied approaches in group psychotherapy are cognitive-behavioral therapy, gestalt therapy, interpersonal therapy, and transactional analysis. In addition, crisis management skills are required to help clients manage acute stressors and in-session or between-session episodes of decompensation (i.e., gradual or sudden breakdowns in defenses marked by increased levels of depression, anxiety, or psychotic symptoms).

Knowledge and skills in conducting group work are foundational to the counseling profession and are identified as a core area of study by CACREP (2009a). Training and experience in group work are critical for the counselor's professional survival in the contemporary mental health climate, where cost containment and treatment efficiency are demanded by employers, clients, and managed care organizations.

Family Counseling. Clients often describe their presenting problems in individualistic terms and anticipate that their treatment will follow a stereotyped one-to-one format. However, persons and the problems they experience do not exist in a vacuum. Family counseling assumes that the family is the most basic emotional unit and is therefore the most appropriate target for intervention. With a jigsaw puzzle as a metaphor, if one of the pieces seeks to reconfigure itself, the adjacent pieces must adapt. From the family counseling perspective, human change is accomplished most efficiently when all of the puzzle pieces are on the table.

Numerous presenting concerns lend themselves to family systems interventions. In fact, it can be argued from an ecologically informed perspective that all presenting problems have family dimensions. For example, families who have children with attention deficit disorder (ADD) are confronted with numerous behavioral, academic, social, and developmental challenges (Erk, 1997). Clinical mental health counselors must not err by believing that ADD is an individual entity requiring individual treatment. Family stress, relational and communication patterns, and family rules and roles influence and are influenced by the ADD child. In general, family counseling is recommended for the following conditions: families with a member who has a chronic mental illness; families with acting-out adolescents; families with multiple presenting issues; clients with problems related to family structure or family relational processes; and families with marital problems. Numerous empirical studies have demonstrated the general effectiveness of family counseling, although it has not been clearly determined which specific disorders or clients are most likely to benefit (Nichols, 2009).

As noted in Chapter 3, numerous theories and techniques guide family assessment and treatment. Family counseling differs from individual counseling on both conceptual and pragmatic levels (Beamish & Navin, 1994). Unfortunately, many mental health counselors lack in-depth training in family counseling and may be called on to make difficult treatment and ethical decisions for which they have been poorly prepared. For example, who exactly is the client—the symptom bearer or the family unit itself? How do the systemic assessment and diagnosis relate to the *DSM* diagnostic categories? How does one gain informed consent when treatment involves all family members, some of whom (e.g., children or adolescents) may not be especially interested in participating? To what extent can confidentiality be maintained? How does the counselor manage information learned from different family members (e.g., knowledge of an extramarital affair)? It is critical that mental health and community counselors receive adequate training and supervised experience before attempting family counseling.

Consultation. In contrast to the modalities discussed up to this point, consultation is an indirect form of problem solving. It is a helping process in which a specialized professional (the consultant), such as a mental health counselor, assists another party (the consultee) in carrying out work- or role-related activities (Dougherty, 2009). Clinical mental health counselors can work with individuals, organizations, or entire communities in consultant-consultee relationships (Lewis et al., 2003).

Several important characteristics of consultation are identified in this definition. First, the goal of consultation is *problem solving*. The interactions between the consultant and consultee have a specific problem and solution focus. Obviously, a very wide range of concerns can be the focus of the consultant-consultee relationship. For example, an elementary school teacher may consult with a mental health counselor to explore alternative ways of managing the behavior of a particular student or class. Or the director of a small, private human service organization may want to evaluate the effectiveness of specific programs. In the latter case, the mental health counselor is hired as a consultant to assist in designing an evaluation process that enables the director to learn the extent to which program goals are being attained.

Second, consultation is typically a *tripartite relationship* (i.e., it involves three parties): the consultant, the consultee, and the consultee's client or client system: The consultees hire the consultants to assist them with specific problems in the client system.

Third, consultation is an *indirect helping relationship*. As noted previously, the consultant does not provide direct interventions but provides assistance to the consultee, who then implements the plan in collaboration with the client system. For example, a local church is experiencing rapid growth, and a number of new families are introducing specific issues, such as past abuse, family dysfunction, parenting concerns, and life adjustment issues. The pastor and the staff are overwhelmed and are also limited in their ability to meet these new congregational needs. The services of a consultant are sought to explore ways in which the church may minister more effectively to its members. The goal of consultation, as illustrated in this example, is not for the consultant to intervene in the lives of the church attendees. Rather, the consultant works with the pastor and the staff of the church, which will, in turn, develop a support system to facilitate personal growth among the church members.

A number of specific models of consultation are used in practice (Dougherty, 2009): organizational, mental health, behavioral, and school-based consultation. It is beyond the scope of this text to discuss these models. However, a generic model that provides a framework for consultation services (Kurpius & Fuqua, 1993) consists of six phases: preentry; entry, problem exploration, and contracting; information gathering, problem confirmation, and goal setting; solution searching and intervention selection; evaluation; and termination. Often, it is necessary to recycle through these stages, especially when information gathered at a later stage provides insights necessitating the revision of the identified goal. In this model, the consultant-consultee relationship is egalitarian, democratic, and collaborative. The consultant has faith in the consultee's ability to identify the problem and generate potential solutions. The primary goal of the consultant is to provide an environment that facilitates the problem-solving process.

As consultants, mental health counselors take a broad range of roles: advocate, expert, trainer/educator, collaborator, fact finder, and process specialist (Dougherty, 2009). As *advocates*, consultants may persuade the consultee to do something that the consultant deems desirable, such as using a specific approach to facilitate intra-agency relationships. In another example of appropriate advocacy, the consultant sees discrepancies between how an organization purports to treat clients and how it is actually treating them. The consultant may advocate to the consultee on behalf of the clients by recommending change strategies to bring organizational behavior in closer alignment with expressed organizational values. However, consultants serving as advocates must avoid participating in unhealthy triangles and alliances that may be a part of the organization's dysfunctional dynamics. Self-awareness, skills in organizational assessment, and an objective problem-solving focus help the counselor-consultant stay within appropriate role boundaries.

Consultants also serve as *experts* or technical advisers. For example, a small, private mental health agency seeking accreditation may want a mental health counselor to conduct an independent audit of its services and programs to determine the agency's readiness to proceed with the accreditation process.

Consultants may act as *educators* to provide in-service training in an organization. A mental health agency may seek the assistance of a consultant to train its staff in the use of the revised *DSM*. To serve in this role, consultants must have the knowledge and skills to fulfill the specific educational needs of the organization.

Consultants often work as *collaborators* with the consultee to accomplish a specific task within a given time (Dougherty, 2009). The consultant and consultee might gather data independently, share observations, brainstorm alternative solutions to the problem, select and implement a specific alternative, and monitor the result. In this role, the consultant provides a level of objectivity that the consultee may be less able to attain.

Consultants also serve as *fact finders* (Dougherty, 2009). They gather information, analyze it, and provide accurate feedback to the consultee (Lippitt & Lippitt, 1986).

Finally, consultants may function as *process specialists* (Dougherty, 2009). In this role, they serve as outside observers and facilitators to assess how a particular process is working. They then provide the consultees feedback that can be used to increase the efficiency of the process or remediate glitches in the service delivery system.

Advocacy. Grounded in ecological theory, mental health counselors recognize that the problems clients face are embedded in an ecological context. Unfortunately, too many persons in our society are subjected to forms of injustice, inequity, and stigmatization. Although counselors encourage clients to take appropriate responsibility for their wellness, they also recognize that barriers inhibiting wellness are sometimes institutionalized. Thus, it is necessary for counselors to work for change not only in the behavior of clients but also in the attitudes and actions of the larger systems.

Advocacy is an indirect approach to helping clients by engaging in the process of "arguing or pleading for a cause or proposal" (Lee, 1998, p. 8). Generally, there are three types of advocacy: case advocacy, class advocacy, and professional advocacy. In *case advocacy*, counselors represent the interests of the clients they serve. For example, a counselor may confer with school administrators to gain access for a client to specific services available to persons with special needs. Or counselors may advocate on behalf of a young client who, because of her family's practice of religion, is forced by the school to participate in holiday rituals at school that go against the teachings of her faith. Mental health professionals sometimes work indirectly by intervening at a higher level in the system to bring about client empowerment.

In *class advocacy*, counselors represent the interests and rights of an entire group. March (1999), for example, documents the inaccurate images of mental illness that are depicted across the mass media and suggests how counselors as advocates can act as agents of social action by calling attention to how these distorted depictions are a source of oppression. In this way, counselors intervene on behalf of clients by being agents of change at the ecological levels of the mesosystem, exosystem, and macrosystem. Advocacy can take place with and on behalf of individuals and their communities (Ratts, 2011). Such efforts often foster sociocultural change to meet the needs of clients and communities (AMHCA, 2010).

The legitimacy of such advocacy efforts by clinical mental health counselors rests on ethical principles that guide professional behavior. The primary ethical principle obligates counselors to respect the worth and dignity of all clients, as mandated by the American Mental Health Counselors Association (AMHCA; 2010). This respect is apparent when counselors

- ensure that clients possess the right to choose freely and can act autonomously;
- avoid doing harm;
- promote clients' welfare;
- seek fair treatment of clients regardless of gender, race, religion, and so on.

In addition to being directly involved in advocacy efforts, mental health counselors can help consumers of mental health services become advocates for change. The trend in which mental health consumers help themselves as advocates has been termed the *quiet revolution* (Carling, 1995). A number of consumer mental health advocacy groups exist at the national, state, and local levels. Among these are the National Alliance for the Mentally Ill, where the family members of the mentally ill have become sophisticated advocates for change to improve the lives of the mentally ill (Citron, Solomon, & Draine, 1999). The National Mental Health Consumers Association is a network of over 500 self-help groups that focuses on the protection of human rights, the promotion of consumer-run professionally operated community mental health services, the elimination of stigma and discrimination, and improvement in the responsiveness and accountability of mental health services (Carling,

1995). Indeed, the advocacy efforts of clients have their foundation in the philosophy of recovery in mental illness, which intertwines hope, empowerment, and social connection (Sowbel & Starnes, 2006).

In order to produce effective advocates on behalf of those served, the profession of mental health counseling must be understood, well received, and respected by both the general public and the other mental health professions. Thus, *professional advocacy,* or advocacy on behalf of the profession itself, is imperative (Myers, Sweeney, & White, 2002). Myers and colleagues (2002) propose seven actions necessary for a strong professional advocacy effort:

1. Agreement on a common professional identity;
2. Development and implementation of a national initiative to increase public awareness of the unique role of counselors as mental health providers;
3. Intraprofessional collaboration on issues of concern regarding clients and the profession;
4. Inclusion of advocacy in counselor training;
5. Outcome studies on counseling work of mental health counselors that demonstrate strengths of counselor training model and credentials;
6. Development of curricular materials and resources for both professional and client advocacy;
7. Development and implementation of a comprehensive advocacy plan for the profession. (p. 398)

Advocacy, then, is best viewed as an indirect, multidimensional effort in which mental health counselors seek to promote the well-being of others. The effectiveness of this approach requires a strong, highly respected profession whose voice draws the attention of relevant power holders to the needs and concerns of the mentally ill and other consumers of mental health services. The benefits to the client and the profession are interactive and reciprocal when case, class, and professional advocacy efforts are interconnected and well integrated into professional practice.

PLANNING AND INTRODUCING TERMINATION AND FOLLOW-UP

Many counselors in training feel rather overwhelmed as they consider the many nuances of providing mental health services to individuals, groups, couples, and families. At first, it may seem difficult to look so far down the therapeutic path. Yet, one of the paradoxes of professional counseling is having in view the *end* of a counseling relationship from its start.

For most clients, counseling is a significant life event. Good counselors join with their clients at the start, forming strong, supportive bonds that often become safe havens during turbulent times. Mental health counselors must recognize the important role they have played in the lives of their clients. Therefore, they need to manage the termination of the counseling relationship with sensitivity, intentionality, and good therapeutic judgment. Hackney and Cormier (2013) suggest that as much time in session be spent on termination concerns as were spent on rapport building.

Either the client or the counselor may initiate termination. For example, the client may believe that the goals of counseling have been attained and the presenting issues have been resolved. Circumstances such as relocation, new jobs, or shifting family schedules may lead to a premature termination. Sometimes, clients simply fail to keep a scheduled appointment and no further contact occurs.

Mental health counselors have professional and ethical obligations regardless of the type of client-initiated termination. If the client initiates a premature termination, the mental health counselor should advise the client of the risks and provide referral information (ACA Governing Council, 2005). A detailed termination report should be written and placed in the client's file. The counselor should record the reason for termination (if known), the clinical status at the time of termination, the progress noted, and any treatment issues that remained unresolved.

Regardless of who initiates the termination, the client and the counselor should spend some time assessing and summarizing how much progress the client has made toward goal attainment, as well as how the gains made might generalize to other life situations. The possibility of relapse should be considered and constructive responses explored. The counselor and the client should identify, assess, and develop a plan for handling difficult times (Marlatt & Gordon, 1985).

Contact does not necessarily end with termination. One or more follow-up sessions may be scheduled. Such *booster sessions* soften the finality of termination and allow the client to check-in, report on how the therapeutic gains have been maintained, and engage in brief problem-solving interventions as needed. Typically, the client is invited to contact the counselor should a need for future services arise.

THE TRADITIONAL CONTINUUM OF MENTAL HEALTH CARE AND EXPANDED SETTINGS OF PROFESSIONAL PRACTICE

Mental health counselors serve the needs of clients in a variety of settings. The Community Mental Health Centers Act of 1963 mandated the development of a nationwide network of community-based mental health clinics in every community around the country. These clinics were required to provide five essential services: inpatient counseling (short term), outpatient counseling, emergency services, crisis stabilization, and consultation/education (Lourie, 2003). These essential services gave rise to what is referred to as the *continuum of mental health care* (Hoff & Adamowski, 1998), illustrated in Figure 7.4.

One of the factors that determines the appropriateness of treatment concerns the delivery of effective interventions in ways that place minimum restrictions on the client's freedom. Services are arranged on the continuum of mental health care from the least to the most restrictive. In general, the services that provide clients the greatest amount of independence are the least costly to both the client and society (Hoff, Hallisey, & Hoff, 2011). In recent decades, the clear trend has been toward the least restrictive treatment in community-based settings. Hospitalization is reserved primarily for persons who are experiencing acute, severe episodes of mental illness, or who are extremely lethal and in need of stabilization.

FIGURE 7.4 Continuum of Mental Health Care

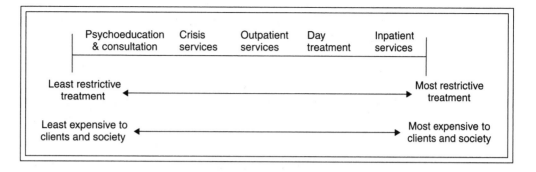

Clinical mental health counselors are employed in the full range of settings along the mental health care continuum. In a recent nationwide survey of AMHCA members, Normandy-Dolberg (2010) found the most common work setting to be private solo practice (over 50%), followed by outpatient settings (over 30%). Other settings included private group practices, public and private agencies, inpatient mental health centers, hospitals, in-home, and substance treatment facilities. Respondents reported providing services for individuals (children, adolescents, and adults), couples, and families. Normandy-Dolberg found that about 50% of her respondents participated in managed care, with equal numbers filing their own claims by mail and electronically by an office administrator. Hollis and Dobson (2000) reported that 58% of community counselors and 52% of mental health counselors take jobs in agencies the first year after graduation.

MENTAL HEALTH AND COMMUNITY COUNSELORS ON THE JOB

This section briefly describes the work of mental health and community counselors performed in several specific settings. Through this description, you will gain a better idea of the range of potential roles available to mental health and community counselors. You will also discover how the training and experiences of clinical mental health counselors enable them to make unique professional contributions that facilitate mental health and wellness for the clients they serve.

AGENCY/COMMUNITY MENTAL HEALTH CENTERS

I have alternated between community mental health and higher education throughout my professional career. When possible, I have contracted with community agencies to provide direct individual and family counseling when I was primarily employed at colleges and universities. Early in my career, I served as the outpatient program director for a small community mental health center (CMHC) in the Upper Peninsula of Michigan.

Located in Sault Sainte Marie, a city with a population of around 17,000, the CMHC served two large but sparsely populated counties. The agency offered a wide range of services, including outpatient individual, group, and family counseling; 24-hour crisis intervention; testing; assertive community treatment; and day treatment for the chronically mentally ill and the developmentally disabled. A diverse population was served, and a large population of Native Americans resided in the catchment area.

This position provided me with a wide array of professional opportunities and experiences. Indeed, no two days were ever the same. My primary responsibilities revolved around overseeing the operations of the outpatient program, supervising the master's-level counselors, and providing direct services to individuals and families. The agency offered extensive supervision. I provided individual and group supervision to eight counselors. Although some supervisory time was spent reviewing ever-changing policies and procedures, our primary focus was monitoring problem identification/diagnosis, treatment development and implementation, and specific questions regarding treatment and professional development. Personally, I carried a caseload of around 20 to 25 clients. I worked with a wide range of diagnostic categories using primarily the cognitive-behavioral and Bowenian theoretical frameworks. The majority of clients presented with depression, anxiety, substance abuse, and domestic violence/abuse–related issues. The agency's clinical director supervised my counseling and supervision. Sometimes the services I rendered were part of a more comprehensive treatment plan involving staff from other programs within the agency. For example, I provided family counseling as part of a multidisciplinary team with one family whose 8-year-old was being treated for autism. My treatment goals for this family included strengthening communication and support within the family, increasing conflict management skills in the marital dyad, and reinforcing of the home-based interventions directed toward the child.

After a 12-year stint in higher education, during which time I provided contracted services, I engaged in full-time employment as the manager of crisis services for Hiawatha Behavioral Health, of Sault Sainte Marie, Michigan. I supervised a small staff of full-time professionals who provided crisis intervention services around the clock in a three-county region. The typical work rotation for crisis staff was a 72-hour shift followed by 7 days off. When on duty, workers carried pagers. After-hours calls were answered by an independent hotline service and were forwarded to the crisis worker. On some nights, the frequency and intensity of calls were light. Other nights, however, were quite busy, and the crisis worker was paged for the crises of current agency clients, as well as of persons in the public, the city lockup, or the hospital emergency room. Although no two calls were alike, a rather standard process of triage was followed to determine quickly the immediate needs of the client and to assess whether an emergency response was required. For example, calls were received from the jail or the emergency room requesting a crisis worker to do a prescreening to determine level of lethality and need for hospitalization. If the person was presenting a clear and imminent risk to self or others, arrangements were made for the immediate transport to a psychiatric hospital for brief, intensive treatment. If the risk was not clear and imminent, a crisis management plan was devised in collaboration with the client to ensure his or her safety and management of the current crisis. Often, referrals were made to counseling agencies to link the client to the support of individual, group, or family counseling. In addition, psychiatric consultations were sometimes required when severe symptoms were part of the clinical picture.

In addition to managing the crisis intervention program, I also supervised the agency's crisis stabilization and jail diversion programs. The crisis stabilization program provided an intensive service to clients experiencing severe crises but not requiring hospitalization. Such clients received these 24-hour services in the community setting. Our jail diversion program worked with persons who were in contact with the corrections system but who were not likely to benefit from incarceration because they had severe and persistent mental illness. Arrangements were made for them to receive intensive mental health services in lieu of incarceration. In addition, our jail diversion specialist provided brief, focused counseling services to persons incarcerated in the city and county jails. This program gave inmates an opportunity to express their thoughts and feelings and to develop coping strategies not typically available in a corrections setting.

In addition to my clinical, supervisory, and crisis work, I served on several agency and community committees, such as the agency's quality management committee and its recovery committee. I had the opportunity to develop a comprehensive three-county suicide prevention program. Finally, I served on several community committees: the community housing committee, the interagency collaborative committee, and the community crisis response team committee. In these various areas of responsibility, I found that my training as a mental health counselor had given me a unique combination of knowledge and skills to address issues of wellness and pathology from an ecological perspective. My experience in these settings was exhilarating and gave depth and breadth to my understanding of the profession.

PRIVATE PRACTICE

After working in agency settings for 10 years, Jim chose to develop a private practice. He is now self-employed as an independent, full-time counselor. His counseling practice is housed in a suite of offices, where a central reception and business operation are shared with other practitioners—a psychologist, a financial adviser, and a chiropractor. The expenses for the services of a receptionist and an office manager are shared. Beyond that, Jim functions with almost total autonomy. His services include individual, group, marriage, and family counseling; consultation; and psychoeducational programming for church groups, parent-teacher organizations, and local/regional professional organizations.

In a typical week, Jim works in the office approximately 50 to 55 hours. He schedules four to five individual, marital, or family sessions Monday through Friday and an additional three on Saturday. To be successful as a private practitioner, he must be responsive to the scheduling needs of his potential clientele. Thus, most sessions are conducted in the late afternoons and evenings to accommodate family schedules. In addition, he runs a brief, structured group on Tuesday nights. His areas of special expertise include parent skill training, anxiety, depression, self-management, and self-esteem. He has built a professional reputation that has enabled him to establish a strong referral network. In addition, Jim offers an ongoing group on Thursday evenings for adults who were abused as children. He spends his morning hours on the administrative tasks involved in maintaining a business, and on service-related paperwork such as intakes, treatment plans, 30-day case reviews, and case-closing reports.

Although he enjoys his current autonomy and variety, Jim readily identifies a number of drawbacks to being a full-time private practitioner. First, it's difficult for him to find the relevant and required continuing-education hours that are offered outside his peak office hours. In addition, the costs of attending the national conferences offered by his professional association are prohibitive. For him, time is money, and taking time off can cause a significant cash flow problem. Second, although having your own private practice might appear to some to be the way to riches, the operating costs are extensive. Consider the costs of reasonable auto, health, life, and professional liability insurance; vacation and sick days; holidays; professional dues; continuing education; office rental; equipment maintenance; and salaries and benefits for support staff. Add to this amount your desired salary, and you quickly discover the type of pressure Jim experiences to generate enough income simply to break even or make a small profit.

Although Jim clearly enjoys and finds fulfillment in his work, he recognizes that building and maintaining a private practice is hard work. Self-care skills are essential if the mental health practitioner is to survive and thrive. He advises those considering going this route to keep their heads up and eyes open. If one's professional path can be likened to a journey, one must be aware that the traffic is moving at a fast rate and is subject to slowdowns and detours. But the scenery can be grand, and in many ways the trip itself often brings as much pleasure as the arrival at the destination.

SUBSTANCE ABUSE TREATMENT PROGRAMS

Linda serves as primary counselor in an intensive outpatient program for substance abuse. She earned her Master of Arts degree in counseling with a specialization in mental health counseling. In addition, she is a licensed professional counselor and holds the master addictions counselor certification. Currently, she provides assessments and individual and group counseling for substance-dependent and dually diagnosed (i.e., co-occurring substance abuse disorder and mental illness) populations. She has worked in personal recovery for over 15 years, and she is passionate about her vocation. The work is demanding and she carries a very large caseload.

A multidisciplinary team makes the initial assessments. Linda conducts mental status examinations in the context of structured clinical interviews. She writes up intake reports that summarize clients' presenting problem, psychosocial history, and readiness for change. In collaboration with other team members, Linda develops provisional diagnostic impressions and treatment plans. Clients are provided with information regarding the nature of the presenting problem, treatment options, and potential benefits/side effects. The input of clients is given significant consideration in the development of the individualized treatment plans.

Linda provides individual counseling to persons admitted to the intensive outpatient program. Although her clients may be in a great deal of emotional pain at the onset of treatment, many resist or deny their need for treatment. Linda finds it necessary to provide a balance of warmth and unconditional acceptance with varying amounts of confrontation. She has found advantages-disadvantages analysis (Beck, Wright, Newman, & Liese, 1993) and "spitting in the client's soup" (Dinkmeyer & Sperry, 2000, p. 107) to be helpful in moving clients to a psychological place where they are more aware of the problems brought on by their substance abuse. She also uses psychoeducational techniques to enhance her clients' understanding of chemical addiction and its clinical picture if left untreated. Linda relies heavily on cognitive-behavioral strategies in helping clients identify triggering events, emotions, and memories that elicit the craving of substances. She then works with her clients to develop and implement strategies to deal effectively with the identified situations and specific triggers.

Linda also works as a cotherapist for several groups that are key components of the program. In the anger management group, clients develop an awareness of anger issues, interpersonal boundaries, and triggering events and cognitions. The participants then work on strategies and develop skills in assertiveness and effective problem solving. Linda also cofacilitates relapse prevention groups. Clients learn the role of situational factors and "hot" cognitions in precipitating relapse. They develop strategies to prevent relapses and limit the damage when they revert to old patterns of thinking and using.

Professionals working in substance abuse treatment centers are especially at risk for burn-out. Clients are often resistant to treatment. High attrition and relapse rates can lead to feelings of discouragement. Linda has found it vital to take care of herself in order to survive and thrive in this professional niche. She attends to her personal wellness through consistent, healthy dietary practices; physical exercise; and focused practice in spiritual disciplines. These, along with her strong desire to make differences in the lives of others, help her maintain a faith in the human capacity to make positive changes toward greater levels of functioning.

SMALL COLLEGE COUNSELING CENTER

Cynthia was trained as a community counselor and is currently employed at a small, private liberal arts college in the Midwest. In this position, she serves in four different capacities: counselor at the college counseling center, adjunct professor, adviser for the community service program, and an academic support professional for the student retention program.

As counselor, Cynthia meets with traditional and adult students who encounter a variety of problems while pursuing academic degrees. The counseling center provides brief counseling services and refers those experiencing severe mental disorders. Cynthia works with a wide range of emotional and behavioral problems, such as depression, anxiety, self-mutilation, eating disorders, posttraumatic disorders, and self-esteem issues. In addition, she provides premarital counseling and works with female students who have unplanned pregnancies. Cynthia enjoys working with the variety of presenting issues seen at the college counseling center and finds them similar to those seen in other clinical settings.

Cynthia also teaches a course for the Department of Education titled "Diversity in the Classroom." In this course, her training and experiences enable her to help future K–12 educators learn about the needs of the diverse students they will serve. She sees it as vital that they become aware of their own biases and helps them work toward breaking down any stereotypes and prejudices they hold that may prevent them from being effective teachers.

The college encourages its students to engage in volunteer work around the community, doing such diverse tasks as painting houses or cleaning parks, alleys, and riverways. As adviser for the community service program, Cynthia organizes these opportunities and monitors and oversees the volunteer work of students, staff, and faculty.

Finally, Cynthia provides services in the retention program, for students at risk of dropping out of college, by linking them to the available campus resources. She receives a list of the names of students who are failing three or more courses at mid-term, meets with them, and assesses the problems related to their poor academic performance. These problems may include interpersonal problems with roommates, financial problems, health-related issues, adult attention deficit hyperactivity disorder (ADHD), and learning disorders. She collaborates with students in developing an individualized plan that integrates the available services such as mentoring, coaching, tutoring, counseling, and financial assistance.

Through her position at the college, Cynthia has been able to pursue a variety of personal and professional interests with community agencies and programs. For example, she serves on the board of a local home for teenage mothers. In addition, she has become involved with Community United Religious Efforts, a task force that assists persons of diverse backgrounds in getting to know, understand, and embrace one another. Finally, Cynthia works closely with the House of Higher Learning, an on-campus house where students work through issues of racial reconciliation.

Cynthia believes her broad-based training in counseling has uniquely prepared her to serve in these various roles. The pace is fast, and each day brings a new set of challenges and opportunities. She finds great fulfillment as she assists students in enhancing their lives while pursuing their academic goals.

UNIVERSITY HEALTH SERVICE

Suzanne works at the Sexual Assault Crisis Service (SACS), a unit within the Department of Counseling and Psychological Services (CaPS) at the health center of a large state university. The health center has approximately 180 employees, including 11 full-time and 3 part-time counselors, 1 full-time psychiatrist, 2 part-time psychiatrists, and 7 support staff workers who work exclusively for CaPS.

The SACS was created in 1988 to meet the unique counseling needs of individuals with sexual assault issues. It offers individual and group counseling, advocacy, a 24-hour crisis line, referral resources, and educational programming. The service is open to all students, faculty, and staff of the university.

All clients seen by Suzanne have some presenting issue involving sexual assault. It may be a recent incident or it may stem from childhood or adolescent experiences. Clients may identify sexual assault as the reason for seeking counseling, or they may present with psychological symptoms that are attributable to sexual assault. Frequently, clients present with depression, anxiety, eating disorders, academic issues, interpersonal conflict, or somatic symptoms and, upon intake, reveal a history of sexual assault. Therefore, patients enter either by scheduling an appointment at SACS, as a crisis response, or as a referral from other counseling staff or health center personnel.

Suzanne takes a thorough psychosocial history at intake that includes a description of the presenting problem, symptoms, family history, medical/psychological history, social/developmental history, and a mental status exam. This information provides the foundation for creating a diagnostic impression. She then develops a treatment plan with the client. It may include individual counseling, a group for individuals who have been sexually assaulted, referral to other counseling groups, and/or referral to needed medical or legal resources.

Suzanne's position is full time, although she is normally in the office for only 25 hours a week. She is compensated additional hours for serving on call, which requires her to carry a pager 2 weeks per month and to respond to crisis calls. During the day, Suzanne sees persons in her office who have requested crisis intervention. After hours, most of her responses are returning phone calls to individuals who have been victimized or to other concerned parties. The remainder of her time is divided among clinical work, outreach, consultation, and administrative duties. Overall, she sees an average of 10 clients a week for individual counseling during the academic year, and she occasionally facilitates a group. In addition, she is a member of a multidisciplinary peer review team, the county domestic violence task force, the network of campus service providers, and the university's commission on personal safety, where she chairs a subcommittee.

Suzanne is engaged in professional activities beyond her job. She is active in state professional organizations. In addition, she develops educational programs and workshops, designs fliers and pamphlets, presents visiting lectures in a variety of academic units, and has moderated a live call-in television program that broadcasts on the campus cable system.

Suzanne has worked in this setting since 1988. Her academic preparation includes a Bachelor of Arts degree in sociology and a Master of Science degree in counseling, with a specialization in community counseling. Prior to being employed at SACS, she worked in agencies that dealt primarily with abused and neglected children. In addition to her academic preparation, she has gained much knowledge about the treatment of sexual assault victims through research, workshops, and experience. Overall, she believes her current position works well for her. The variety and flexibility it offers offset the stress of the position.

IN THE BARN: EQUINE THERAPY

Terrie is a licensed mental health counselor who engaged in postgraduate training to become certified as an equine therapist. She is now co-owner of Reins and Rainbows, Inc., which is located in Wabash, Indiana. She also works at a private residential center that serves troubled youth and their families. She provides an average of 6 hours of equine therapy per day to clients who are referred to her by the juvenile justice system, the Indiana Department of Children and Family Services, and regional school systems. Frequently, these children and adolescents display significant behavioral problems and have difficulty in relationships. Most have experienced physical abuse, sexual abuse, and neglect. The goals of her work are to decrease the frequency and intensity of behavioral disturbance, to increase the client's ability to engage in and maintain stable and supportive relationships, and to work toward the reunification of the family.

She describes her work as consisting of "a lot of cognitive-behavioral approaches integrated with the hands-on, experiential work that occurs in equine therapy." Terrie notes one myth regarding equine therapy is that "horse riding" is the primary tool used for intervention. In fact, horse riding is rarely used as part of therapy. Terrie estimates that 98% of her equine therapy occurs "on the ground." Riding creates a power differential between the person and horse, where the horse can no longer see the rider but is expected to function in a subservient role to its "master." It is much more common for the client to stand alongside or in front of and facing the horse.

Equine therapy is much more than a metaphorical process for establishing secure, emotional attachments. It is a collaborative effort and consists of two components: equine-assisted therapy and equine-assisted learning. The horse becomes a tool for emotional growth and learning in each component.

When doing equine-assisted therapy, Terrie works alongside a certified horse professional. Together they work with troubled adolescents, whose emotional and behavioral problems have resulted in their removal from family, school, and community. Treatment takes place in a barn that contains a heated arena. The adolescent establishes a relationship with the horse, which becomes a way of talking about and processing personal feelings. Through interactions with the horse, the teen gains an understanding of how his or her behavior affects others. They learn through experience that horses do not respond well to yellng, pushing and pulling, or other forms of coercive or power-assertive approaches. For example, Terrie may have the horse stand in the middle of the arena. The youth is given the task of getting the horse to move outside a large circle without using of any physical contact. Horses will show visible indicators of dismay and sometimes nip at persons they do not trust. They also seem quite adept at sensing when the teen's verbal behavior, nonverbal behavior, and actions are incongruent. The client also discovers that the best way to lead the horse is being in a side-by-side position rather than in front of or behind the horse. Such therapeutic experiences help the teen to develop ideas on the nature and consequences of relationships characterized by reciprocal and respectful interactions, where boundaries are honored.

Throughout therapy, Terrie uses her mental health counseling skills to process the ongoing interactions and the underlying relational dynamics. As treatment progresses, family members enter and participate in the treatment. She has found that her clients experience increases in self-confidnce, self-efficacy, self-concept, effective communication and problem-solving skills, impulse control, and boundaries. What is learned in a relationship with a horse is readily generalized to the underlying processes in the teen's primary relationships with family, peers, and the community.

Terrie sees a good fit between equine therapy and the mental health counseling paradigm. Working with horses is a positive, wellness-oriented approach that can assist clients in enhancing their levels of well-being while addressing underlying symptoms of pathology.

HOME-BASED THERAPY

Lisa works for a youth service bureau, a nonprofit organization that provides emergency care to children and youth removed from their homes. While the organization originally provided residential facilities with the primary goal of establishing the reunification of the family, it now offers a vast array of services, including supervised visitation, home-based casework, and home-based therapy. Referrals come from the department of child services and juvenile probation.

On the average, Lisa carries a caseload of 8 to 10, but it can vary depending on the presenting needs of the families. For example, one family might be referred because their child has extermely poor school attendance, which may improve with only a few hours of individual and family counseling over several weeks. In contrast, a family may be unable to control their acting-out teenage children, so 4 to 6 hours a week of individual therapy for each child, couples therapy, and a family session, over the course of several months, are required.

Lisa provides services in the home or at school. Seeing her clients during the school day gives her more flexibility with scheduling. But she also finds that the therapeutic content can sometimes be too emotionally intense and can interfere with the child's schoolwork. Caseload management and scheduling become problematic when too many clients require evening hours.

When assigned a case, Lisa first gathers background information and the desired goals from the referral source. While the family is her client, her services are contracted for by the referral source that is mandating counseling for the client system. Successful treatment often involves goals that are identified by the juvenile justice system or child protective services as well as the client. Thus, the ability to coordinate diverse goals and establish a collaborative interagency process is critical if treatment is to proceed. Lisa also has to sign the necessary authorizations for the release of confidential information.

Lisa notes that at initial contact, the families are often at the lowest points of their lives. Thus, she sees her initial task as establishing rapport and instilling a sense of hope and trust with her clients. The referral source sets the number of hours of service she can devote to each case. She budgets the allotted time based on the specific goals and objectives identified, the intensity of treatment required, and the modalities to be used. She might meet with her clients in their home, at school, or in community settings such as parks, restaurants, or the homes of the family's friends. Personal safety is of utmost importance in doing home-based thrapy, and Lisa is careful not to put herself or her clients in potentially dangerous situations.

In a typical day, Lisa meets with four to six clients. In addition, she gives the referral sources updates, makes appointments, reschedules no-shows and cancellations, and makes collateral contacts with physicians, case managers, and school personnel. She also meets with the family team, members of the multidisciplinary treatment team, and her supervisor. The remainder of her time is spent on writing up progress notes, mileage records, and billing tickets for third-party reimbursement, and onother miscellaneous tasks.

Lisa believes her training in clinical mental health counseling has been essential to being able to perform her job. When working with a "client," she is attending not only to an "identified client" and the family unit, but to the prescribing medical specialist, the school team, the referrer, the case manager, the visitation supervisor, and other outside service providers. The ecological perspective, along with the family systems and addictions components, have been essential for conceptualizing these complex cases and providing efficient assessment and treatment.

Lisa likes home-based therapy and sees it as a privilege to be made a part of the family's life at one of the most difficult times for them. The hours are long and clients can be rather resistant at first. But it is very gratifying to see them grow through therapy and become a better functioning, emotionally healthy family unit.

CONCLUSION

Kottler (2003) has learned some important lessons from ocean surfing that apply to the work of counselors, supervisors, and teachers. First, he notes that "no matter how ready I am to ride a wave, or help a client, there's little that can be accomplished until the timing is right. It doesn't have to be perfect, because you can take a wave a little early or late and compensate accordingly, but you must wait patiently for the opportunities as they arise" (p. 27). Second, he has discovered that catching a wave is much like counseling. You may have some idea where things will end up, but frequently, you go someplace totally unexpected but not necessarily less desirable.

So be patient. You may be starting out on the journey or taking a trip down a side road. Enjoy the scenery! Take the time to know your surroundings. Don't be so overly focused on your destination that you miss the pleasures and lessons found along your way. Take on passengers—mentors, colearners, and colleagues. Growing into the profession is a developmental process. Make use of the numerous resources that surround you.

Finally, take care of yourself. Graduate study and professional life can become black holes that consume all that surround them. Maintain a balanced lifestyle that facilitates physical, emotional, social, and spiritual development. Build health-promoting behaviors into your daily routine. Above all, find the time to enjoy the journey and those persons who you are fortunate enough to encounter on your path.

DISCUSSION QUESTIONS

1. The text states that motivational interviewing skills can be useful in the process of establishing the counseling relationship. Identify three components of motivational interviewing, and discuss how you would use them to increase your effectiveness in professional practice.
2. This chapter notes that a common error of the novice counselor is to jump into the problem resolution stage prematurely. Why do you think this error occurs so frequently? What personal and situational factors could lead you to such behavior? What steps might you take to prevent premature jumps into problem resolution?
3. To what extent are you comfortable diagnosing clients? To what extent do you see diagnostics as a necessary skill for the contemporary mental health and community counselor? How would you avoid using diagnostic labels in ways that could be personally demeaning or harmful to the clients you serve?

4. To what extent do you see the role of consultant as part of your future job description? Give several examples of counseling situations and settings where consultation might be a useful or important tool in your professional practice.

SUGGESTED ACTIVITIES

1. Imagine you are a licensed professional counselor in private practice. Design an informed-consent form to be used with the clients you serve. Your instructor might provide you with useful models to guide you in developing this form.
2. Survival in the counseling professions requires the utilization of wellness practices in one's daily routine. To what extent are you currently practicing wellness? Can you identify specific wellness practices from which you could benefit? Develop a self-management plan to assist you in implementing the identified practices in your personal routine.
3. The class separates into triads. Practice conducting intake sessions. Assign the roles of counselor, client, and observer. Learn to gather the pertinent information, conduct mental status exams, and develop a complete diagnosis. Use the questions identified by Bertolino and O'Hanlon (2002, p. 91) to develop client-identified goals. The observer is to provide objective feedback to the counselor and assess the extent to which the client felt comfortable throughout the process. As time permits, rotate roles. (Several class sessions may be required to complete this activity.)
4. Interview several professional counselors to gain a better understanding of their professional roles and the issues they face in professional practice.

REFERENCES

American Counseling Association Governing Council. (2005). ACA policies and procedures for processing complaints of ethical violations. Retrieved from http://www.counseling.org/Resources/CodeOfEthics/TP/Home/CT2.aspx

American Mental Health Counselors Association. (2010). *Code of ethics of the American Mental Health Counselors Association–2010 revision.* Alexandria, VA: Author.

American Psychiatric Association. (2000). *Diagnostic and statistical manual of mental disorders* (4th ed., text revision). Washington, DC: Author.

Association for Specialists in Group Work. (2000). Professional standards for the training of group workers. *Journal of Specialists in Group Work, 25,* 327–342.

Beamish, P. M., & Navin, S. L. (1994). Ethical dilemmas in marriage and family therapy: Implications for training. *Journal of Mental Health Counseling, 16,* 129–143.

Beck, A. T., Wright, F. D., Newman, C. F., & Liese, B. S. (1993). *Cognitive therapy of substance abuse.* New York, NY: Guilford Press.

Bertolino, B., & O'Hanlon, B. (2002). *Collaborative, competency-based counseling and therapy*. Boston, MA: Allyn & Bacon.

Carling, P. J. (1995). *Return to community: Building support systems for people with psychiatric disabilities*. New York, NY: Guilford Press.

Citron, M., Solomon, P., & Draine, J. (1999). Self-help groups for families of persons with mental illness: Perceived benefits of helpfulness. *Community Mental Health Journal, 35,* 15–30.

Corey, M. S., Corey, G., & Corey, C. (2010). *Groups: Process and practice* (8th ed.). Belmont, CA: Brooks/Cole.

Cozolini, L. (2004). *The making of a therapist: A practical guide for the inner journey*. New York, NY: Norton.

Dinkmeyer, D., Jr., & Sperry, l. (2000). *Counseling and psychotherapy: An integrated, individual psychology approach*. Upper Saddle River, NJ: Prentice Hall.

Dougherty, A. M. (2009). *Psychological consultation and collaboration in school and community settings* (5th ed.). Belmont, CA: Brooks/Cole.

Egan, G. (2010). *The skilled helper: A problem-management and opportunity-development approach to helping* (9th ed.). Belmont, CA: Brooks/Cole.

Erford, B. T. (2011). *Group work: Processes and applications*. Upper Saddle River, NJ: Pearson Education.

Erk, R. R. (1997). Multidimensional treatment of attention deficit disorder: A family oriented approach. *Journal of Mental Health Counseling, 19,* 3–22.

Ginter, G. (2012, February). *DSM-5 is progressing to the finish line. The Advocate,* pp. 10–12.

Hackney, H. L., & Cormier, S. (2013). *The professional counselor: A process guide to helping* (7th ed.). Upper Saddle River, NJ: Pearson.

Hoff, L. A., & Adamowski, K. (1998). *Creating excellence in crisis care: A guide to effective training and program designs*. San Francisco, CA: Jossey-Bass.

Hollis, J. W., with Dodson, T. A. (2000). *Counselor preparation 1999–2001: Programs, faculty, trends* (10th ed.). Philadelphia, PA: Taylor & Francis; Greensboro, NC: National Board for Certified Counselors.

Kottler, J. A. (2003, January). Learning to surf. *Counseling Today,* pp. 25, 27.

Kress V. E., & Hoffman, R. M. (2008). Non-suicidal self-injury and motivational interviewing: Enhancing readiness for change. *Journal of Mental Health Counseling, 30,* 311–329.

Kurpius, D. J., & Fuqua, D. R. (1993). The consulting process: A multidimensional approach. *Journal of Counseling and Development, 71,* 601–607.

Lee, C. C. (1998). Counselors as agents of social change. In C. C. Lee & G. R. Walz (Eds.), *Social action: A mandate for counselors* (pp. 3–14). Alexandria, VA: American Counseling Association.

Lewis, J. A., Lewis, M. D., Daniels, J. A., & D'Andrea, M. J. (2003). *Community counseling: Empowerment strategies for a diverse society* (3rd ed.). Pacific Grove, CA: Brooks/Cole.

Lippitt, G., & Lippitt, R. (1986). *The consulting process in action* (2nd ed.). La Jolla, CA: University Associates.

Lourie, I. S. (2003). A history of community child mental health. In A. J. Pumariega & N. C. Winters (Eds.), *The handbook of child and adolescent systems of care: The new community psychiatry*. San Francisco, CA: Jossey-Bass.

March, P. A. (1999). Ethical responses to media depictions of mental illness: An advocacy approach. *Journal of Humanistic Counseling, Education and Development, 38,* 70–80.

Marlatt, G. A., & Gordon, J. (Eds.). (1985). *Relapse prevention: A self-control strategy for the maintenance of behavior change*. New York, NY: Guilford Press.

Martin, D. G. (2000). *Counseling and therapy skills* (2nd ed.). Prospect Heights, IL: Waveland Press.

McAuliffe, G. J., & Eriksen, K. P. (1999). Toward a constructivist and developmental identity for the counseling profession: The context-phase-stage-style model. *Journal of Counseling and Development, 77,* 267–280.

McGoldrick, M. (1999). History, genograms, and the family life cycle. In B. Carter, & M. McGoldrick (Eds.), *The expanded family life cycle: Individual, family, and social perspectives* (3rd ed.). Boston, MA: Allyn & Bacon.

McKay, M., & Paleg, K. (1992). *Focal group psychotherapy.* Oakland, CA: New Harbinger.

Mead, M. A., Hohenshil, T. H., & Singh, K. (1997). How the *DSM* is used by clinical counselors: A national study. *Journal of Mental Health Counseling, 19,* 383–401.

Miller, W. R., & Rollnick, S. (2002). *Motivational interviewing: Preparing people for change* (2nd ed.). New York, NY: Guilford Press.

Myers, J. E., Sweeney, T. J., & White, V. E. (2002). Advocacy for counseling and counselors: A professional imperative. *Journal of Counseling and Development, 80,* 394–402.

Nichols, M. P. (2009). *Family therapy: Concepts and methods* (9th ed.). Upper Saddle River, NJ: Pearson Education.

Normandy-Dolberg, J. (2010, September). AMHCA survey results: Concerns cited with managed care, and with funding retirement. *The Advocate,* pp. 6–7.

Ratts, M. (2011). Multiculturalism and social justice: Two sides of the same coin. *Journal of Multicultural Counseling and Development, 39,* 24–37.

Ritchie, M. H., Piazza, N. J., & Lewton, J. C. (1991). Current use of the *DSM-III-R* in counselor education. *Counselor Education and Supervision, 30,* 205–211.

Seligman, L. (1999). Twenty years of diagnosis and the *DSM. Journal of Mental Health Counseling, 21,* 229–239.

Sowbel, L. R., & Starnes, W. (2006). Pursuing hope and recovery: An integrated approach to psychiatric rehabilitation. In J. Rosenberg & S. Rosenberg (Eds.), *Community mental health: Challenges for the 21st century.* New York, NY: Routledge.

Vacc, N. A., Loesch, L. C., & Guilbert, D. E. (1997). The clientele of certified clinical mental health counselors. *Journal of Mental Health Counseling, 19,* 165–170.

Vygotsky, L. S. (1962). *Thought and language.* Cambridge, MA: MIT Press.

8

Appraisal and Research in the Practice of Clinical Mental Health Counseling

OUTLINE

Appraisal

Ethical Practice in Appraisal

Research and Program Evaluation

Ethical Practice in Research

Conclusion

In Chapter 3, I began with a statement, "I am a mental health counselor," and then went on to quote Gibson and Mitchell (2003), who noted that we call ourselves counselors because that is what we do. Although career development, advocacy, and consultation may be roles we fill, counseling is central to our professional identity. This close identification with counseling leads students to wonder sometimes why they must have a working knowledge of appraisal and research. As Hadley and Mitchell (1995) observe, those entering the counseling profession tend to be socially oriented and motivated to help others. They are not pursuing a counseling degree due to a strong desire to gather data, test hypotheses, or crunch numbers.

Traditionally, mental health professionals have been viewed as scientist-practitioners. In other words, counselors are expected to be competent to conduct and publish research as they provide direct services to clients. They *make* as well as *apply* knowledge. Indeed, the Council for Accreditation of Counseling and Related Educational Programs (CACREP) identifies *assessment* and *research and program evaluation* as two of the eight core areas required of all students in graduate-level counseling programs. In addition, appraisal and research content appear on the certification exams of the National Board of Certified Counselors (NBCC) and the licensure exams of most states.

However, the "why" question lingers. Many practicing counselors do not find the scientific research in professional journals to be particularly relevant to their work. Why might this be so? Much of the problem has to do with the extent to which research conditions in the laboratory are artificial and sterile. In the world of professional practice, the lack of control over extraneous variables is the rule, not the exception. For example, an empirical study investigating the response of depressed clients to cognitive-behavioral therapy (CBT) will attempt to control for all extraneous variables in order to isolate the effect of the independent variable (CBT) on the dependent variable (level of depression). However, clients do not live in vacuums and are influenced by numerous factors in addition to the treatment administered by their counselors. Thus, counselors rarely have the opportunity to treat a case of "pure depression." In addition, basic research tends to compare the differences between the means of groups, whereas counselors treat individuals. To what extent, then, do the results and conclusions from empirical research generalize to the counseling context? Do such results and conclusions really apply to what counselors do? To conclude that appraisal and research methods are irrelevant to mental health counselors, though, is akin to throwing the baby out with the bath water. Knowledge and skills in appraisal and research are vital for several reasons. First, mental health professionals must be able to determine the extent to which their interventions are truly effective. For example, a mental health counselor might apply for and receive a grant from a federal agency to provide parent skill education within the catchment area of the community mental health center. Typically, in a grant proposal, the applicant must include a plan for measuring the effectiveness of the program. Once the grant is awarded, the grantee is expected to be a good steward of the grant money and must use appraisal and research in reporting to the granting agency how the funds were used in the development, implementation, and outcomes of the program. In addition, third-party reimbursers often require evidence of the mental health professional's ability to achieve successful and efficient clinical outcomes if the practitioner is to remain in good standing on the provider list.

Second, discussions of new therapeutic techniques and preventive psychoeducation in the professional literature introduce mental health professionals to ideas that they can apply in their practice. The understanding of psychometric and research concepts and principles enables mental health counselors to discern whether the reported approaches will generalize to other populations. Such a determination requires a knowledge of sampling procedures. Furthermore, counselors need a firm grasp of psychometric and research concepts and principles to achieve outcomes similar to those described in the professional literature.

Finally, to deal with the deluge of reports of the latest and greatest therapeutic breakthroughs, counselors sometimes must use their knowledge of appraisal and research methods as if donning hip waders to move through these mucky wetlands to solid ground.

APPRAISAL

THE USES OF TESTS

Tests can be defined as measurement devices that quantify a sample of an individual's behavior. Basically, tests systematically assign numbers to individuals to concisely represent a characteristic of that person. If tests are to be useful, the construction, administration, scoring, and interpretation must follow prescribed procedures that ensure their results are valid (i.e., they accurately reflect the characteristic being measured) and reliable (i.e., the results can be replicated).

We encounter many situations that require answers to very specific questions about the nature of the person. Clinical interviews typically are sufficient for diagnosing and devising a treatment plan. But what if we need to assess whether a person could benefit from specialized rehabilitative services? And further, what if our assessment would determine whether the client could procure financial assistance to pay for the needed services? What if a court requests your input concerning arrangements for custody, child placement, or juvenile probation? Although a clinical interview will yield important contributions to the decision-making process, conclusions can be more solidly based on the focused, objective results from carefully chosen tests.

Sometimes, counselors request information from other institutions or agencies for clients who have received services there. These files may contain results and conclusions from psychological testing, so the requesting counselor must be able to assess the meaning, validity, and reliability of these test results in order to use them appropriately in the construction of a treatment plan.

KEY CONCEPTS AND PRINCIPLES IN APPRAISAL

Classical True-Score Theory. Classical test score theory assumes that any observed score (X) on a given test consists of two components: the true score (T) and the error score (*E*) (Whiston, 2013). Stated as a formula, $X = T + E$. On any given psychological variable, classical test score theory assumes that there is an actual true score (a level that is stable for the particular individual) but that random and unsystematic error influences the obtained score so that it varies from the individual's true score on any given day. Factors that can contribute error to an obtained score are changes in mood, level of fatigue, conditions in the testing environment, and subtle changes in the procedures of test administration. When the error is truly random, it is assumed that with repeated administrations of the test, the mean of the summed *X*s will approach *T*. The *standard error of measurement* communicates how much an observed score varies from the true score. It can be used to estimate the reasonable limits of a person's true score, given an obtained score.

Reliability.   In testing, *reliability* refers to the degree to which scores obtained on tests are consistent, dependable, and repeatable (Drummond & Jones, 2010). The reliability of a test increases as the sources of random error are controlled.

You should be familiar with three basic types of reliability. *Test-retest reliability* is the consistency of the scores when an examinee takes a test at two different times. For example, when a person takes an intelligence test on two different occasions, his or her scores should be consistent. If he or she got exactly the same score each time, the reliability coefficient would be 1.0. In contrast, when the two scores are completely unrelated, the reliability coefficient would equal 0.0.

Internal reliability is the extent to which the test items measure the same thing, that is, the variable that the test claims to measure. Again, internal reliability is reported by the calculation of a coefficient. For example, a test can be divided into two parts: even/odd items or first half/second half. The correlation between the obtained responses on the two halves indicates the extent to which they consistently measure the variable they claim to measure. For example, if a test purports to measure level of depression, a strong positive correlation should be found between the answers to the even items and the answers to the odd items.

Sometimes, appraisal involves the direct observation of behavior. For example, when two or more counselors act as judges to rate the on-task versus off-task behaviors of the children in a classroom, there should be a significant agreement between their ratings. This agreement is referred to as *interrater reliability*. The resulting reliability coefficient reflects the proportion of agreement among raters, and not content-sampling or time-sampling error (Drummond & Jones, 2010).

So, what is the acceptable reliability coefficient for all tests? Unfortunately, it depends on the nature of the test and the construct it purports to measure. Generally, reliability should be equal to or greater than .90 when the test is used in clinical or high-stakes decision-making situations. Otherwise, reliability coefficients of .70 or higher are acceptable (Drummond & Jones, 2010).

Validity.   Generally speaking, *validity* refers to the extent to which an instrument accurately measures what it says it measures. You can be confident in the results of a test only if there is a high degree of agreement between the test score and the quality being measured.

Several methods are used to determine the validity of tests. *Content validity* refers to the extent to which a test measures the skills or subject matter that it is supposed to measure. In its simplest form, content validity is assessed by expert opinion. For example, in developing a licensure exam for mental health counselors, a group of experts would review the items to determine the extent to which the instrument covers the specific areas of knowledge and skills deemed basic to the practice of mental health counseling. Although it is essential, content validity must be supplemented by other forms of validity because of its reliance on subjective judgment.

Criterion-related validity is the correlation between a test score and some performance measure. Relatively high correlation coefficients increase the predictive power of the test. For example, the Graduate Record Exam (GRE) is often used to predict students' success in graduate school programs. The criterion-related validity of the GRE rests on the correlation between attained GRE scores and measures of academic success (e.g., grade point average).

Construct validity refers to the extent to which a test accurately measures a specific theoretical concept. The construct validity of an instrument is established when the results of the test lie in the direction of what has been predicted by an underlying theory. For example, the cognitive theory states that the thought process of depressed persons is characterized by cognitive distortions and negative self-statements. The construct validity of a specific test measuring cognitive distortions is established when scores on these instruments correlate highly with measures of depression (e.g., the Beck Depression Inventory–II).

Standardization.   Suppose you completed a life adjustment scale and the counselor reported that you obtained a score of 35. I suspect you would immediately ask, "What does that mean?" An individual score on a test is meaningless unless it is accompanied by additional interpretive information. An important component of test construction is obtaining data on the performance of a sample of persons representative of those with whom the test will eventually be used. This process is referred to as *test standardization.* Its primary purpose is to establish the distribution of raw scores in the standardization group (or norm group). It also establishes a set of standard procedures for the administration of the test. The obtained scores are then converted into percentile ranks, grade equivalents, or standard scores (*norms*). Most test manuals contain tables of raw and converted scores established by standardization. The scores of examinees take on meaning when evaluated according to the table of norms for their appropriate group. Thus, norms are the frame of reference used to interpret the raw scores by indicating how the test taker's score compares to the scores of persons of similar age, gender, or grade (Whiston, 2013).

CATEGORIES OF APPRAISAL TECHNIQUES

Intelligence Tests.   The area of intelligence testing represents somewhat of a paradox for the counseling professions. On the one hand, the measurement of intelligence has a long history and played a foundational role in the development of psychology as a profession with practical applications beyond teaching and research (Whiston, 2013). On the other hand, the conceptualization and definition of intelligence has proven to be among the most elusive in the area of appraisal (Kaplan & Saccuzzo, 2012). Generally, *intelligence* refers to one's capacity to learn and ability to reason, judge, and adapt effectively to one's environment. Intelligence tests measure the examinee's ability to think abstractly and use verbal, numerical, and abstract symbols (Drummond & Jones, 2010).

Intelligence testing originated in 1905, when Alfred Binet, a French psychologist, was asked to develop a process for identifying children not likely to benefit from a public school education. Originally, Binet developed a scale that was age related and used mental age (MA) as an index to indicate the level of intellectual functioning possessed by an average child at a given chronological age. Terman (1916) further developed the concept by introducing the intelligence quotient (IQ), computed by dividing one's mental age by his or her chronological age and then multiplying the quotient by 100 (to remove decimals). The IQ has become the standard index of intelligence, although it is now determined by means of the *deviation IQ,* which assumes a normal distribution of IQ in the general population.

Intelligence tests have been developed for administration to individuals and to groups. For example, the Wechsler scales are individually administered inventories with age-related versions for preschoolers (the Wechsler Preschool and Primary Scale of Intelligence–III, or WPPSI–III; Wechsler, 2002), for primary and secondary schoolers (the Wechler Intelligence Scale for Children–IV, or WISC–IV; Wechsler, 2003), and for adults (the Wechsler Adult Intelligence Scale–IV, or WAIS–IV; Wechsler, 2008). On the Wechsler tests, the examinee takes specific subtests, some of which require verbal responses and some of which are more performance oriented. The raw scores obtained on these subtests are converted to scaled scores, each of which has a mean of 10 and a standard deviation of 3. The scores attained on the subscales are summed to produce four index scores: Verbal Comprehension (VCI); Perceptual Reasoning (PRI); Working Memory (WMI); and Processing Speed (PSI). These scores are then summed to give the Full Scale Intelligence Quotient (FSIQ), which has a mean of 100 and a standard deviation of 15. Figure 8.1 shows the relationship of the various subtests on the WAIS–IV to the calculation of four indices and the FSIQ.

Intelligence tests are used to make decisions regarding the placement of children in school programs and for the diagnosis of mental retardation and learning disability. In addition, performance on intelligence tests provides valuable information on individuals' information-processing skills.

However, the use of intelligence tests continues to be controversial. Because of the widespread disagreement regarding the concept of intelligence, opinions differ greatly on the weight of intelligence test scores in basic decisions that seriously affect examinees' lives. When making important client-related decisions or testing clinical hypotheses, clinical mental health counselors base their conclusions on multiple sources of data, such as clinical interviews, direct observation, and standardized tests. Their conclusions take into consideration the convergence of the various results and data.

FIGURE 8.1 Relationship of Subtests to Indices and FSIQ on the WAIS–IV

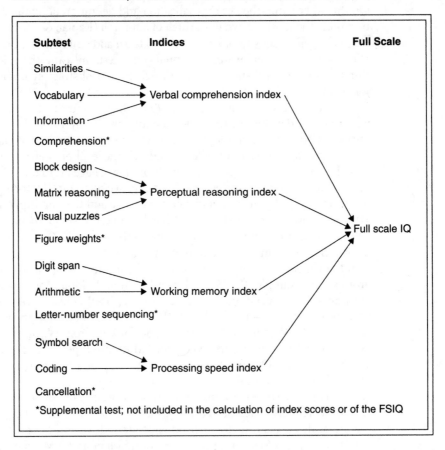

Achievement Tests. Of the varieties of appraisal instruments, achievement tests are by far the most numerous. They include teacher-made tests in primary and secondary school, standardized tests administered at various grade levels across school systems, comprehensive exams administered to graduate students as they near completion of their academic programs, and minimum competency exams used by states as part of licensure requirements. Generally, achievement tests are appraisal instruments that measure a person's degree of learning in a specific subject.

Until the 20th century, the primary method of measuring achievement was by oral exam, for example, the oral interrogation of students by visiting examiners. The Boston Public School System began to substitute written exams in 1845 (Anastasi & Urbina, 1997). It was not until 1864 that George Fisher, of England, developed an objective test for measuring achievement in spelling, and by the early 1900s, objective testing became the norm (Aiken, 2003). Recently, though, there has been a marked increase in the construction of standardized achievement tests using an essay format.

Achievement tests serve a number of purposes. Traditionally, they have been the primary tools for determining the level of students' academic achievement. The results of these tests provide instructors with useful feedback on the effectiveness of their classroom instruction. In addition, the public is increasingly demanding that school systems be held accountable for the services they provide. The outcome measures derived from the results of achievement testing are used in determining the extent to which a given teacher, school, or system is living up to the stated objectives.

You might ask, "What relevance do achievement tests have for mental health and community counselors?" Frequently, achievement tests provide counselors with useful information on the young client's current level of functioning and what can reasonably be expected of him or her. Such information is useful in establishing what Vygotsky (1962) called the person's "zone of proximal development," which is the range of tasks that a child can master with verbal guidance and modeling by a more skilled child or by an adult. Achievement tests also yield information that counselors can use to assist the child and his or her teachers and parents in adapting to each other's reciprocal requirements (Santrock, 2010).

Furthermore, a school's response to a mental health counselor's request for the release of a client's confidential information may include scores on achievement tests that are critical in case conceptualization, diagnosis, and treatment planning. For example, a diagnosis of learning disorders requires a significant discrepancy between scores obtained on intelligence and achievement tests. For example, a child who attains an IQ of 100 on the WISC–III but a 70 on the fourth edition of the Wide Range Achievement Test (WRAT–IV; Wilkinson & Robertson, 2007) might be diagnosed with learning disability because the differential between the scores is 2 standard deviation units. The results of other tests will show not only the child's general level of achievement but also the degree of strength or weakness in specific subskills. And further testing may reveal the precise nature of the learning disorder and suggest useful approaches for therapeutic intervention.

Aptitude Tests and Interest Inventories. Aptitude tests are used in a variety of settings to predict what people can learn (Drummond & Jones, 2010). A number of specialized aptitude tests are used in the selection of candidates for academic programs. The Scholastic Aptitude Test (SAT) and the American College Testing (ACT) program are used by many colleges and universities in their undergraduate admissions decisions. The SAT consists of two major sections. The first assesses verbal and mathematical reasoning; the second includes an English essay. The ACT contains a series of subtests that cover the following subjects: mathematics, social studies, and natural sciences.

Other exams are used to guide decision making for graduate school admissions. Examples are the GRE, the Medical College Admissions Test (MCAT), Graduate Management Admissions Test (GMAT), Law School Admissions Test (LSAT), and the Millers Analogies Test (MAT).

Other aptitude tests are designed to measure the skills necessary for successful on-the-job performance. Some are measures of general skills, such as mechanical ability, manual dexterity, or spatial relations. For example, the Purdue Pegboard test consists of five tasks that measure fine hand and finger movement. On one part of the test, examinees put small pins into holes and place a small washer and collar over the pin. This task is repeated, and the entire task takes from 5 to 10 minutes. Times scores are compared to those of machine operators, production workers, and general factory applicants. In contrast, some aptitude tests measure skills for specific professional groups such as tests of clerical, artistic, musical, or computer aptitude. The Clerical Aptitude Test is a pencil-and-paper test and measures the ability to check numbers, names, dates, and addresses.

Interest inventories are self-report tests on which the examinee expresses his or her likes and dislikes for a variety of activities and attitudes. These are compared to the interest patterns of the members of different occupational groups, and the results are used by professional counselors to assist persons in finding jobs that match their interests.

As we learned in Chapter 2, the vocational counseling movement and the development of interest inventories were central in the establishment of counseling as a profession. Today, interest inventories are administered for a variety of purposes and in high schools, colleges, and rehabilitation contexts. They are also used to assist persons in making midlife career changes and pre/postretirement decisions. Although school counselors and career counselors are among the most frequent users, consumers of interest inventories also include industrial consultants and human resources personnel (Aiken, 2003).

The Strong Interest Inventory® (SII®; Donnay, Morris, Schaubhut, & Thompson, 2005) is a widely used interest inventory that integrates the personality theory of John Holland (Whiston, 2013). It is designed to help persons make educational and vocational decisions and retirement plans and to reveal employees' job satisfaction or dissatisfaction. All occupations are viewed as falling into one of six types: realistic, investigative, artistic, social, enterprising, and conventional. These form the basis for the General Occupational Theme Scale. In addition to identifying the predominant occupational types of the examinee, the SII includes 30 basic interest scales, 244 occupational scales, and 5 personal style scales. Comprehensive computer-generated reports synthesize the wealth of data to provide counselors and examinees with relevant information to facilitate career decision making.

Personality Tests.   *Personality* can be defined as the relatively stable and distinctive characteristics of behavior that reflect the person's reactions to the environment and unique adjustment to life. Personality tests attempt to assess the following characteristics:

- *Personality traits* —Relatively enduring tendencies to act, think, and feel in a certain manner in any given situation;
- *Personality states* —Emotional reactions that vary from situation to situation;
- *Personality types* —General descriptions of personal styles, such as high social interest, high activity levels, and subjective styles of personal decision making;
- *Self-concept* —The person's view of self.

Frequently, personality tests are used in clinical settings to provide useful data for diagnosing or gaining insight into the client's problems. However, numerous personality tests tap into the personal strengths and generally healthy characteristics of examinees. These can provide insight into client's behaviors and style of relating for the purpose of growth enhancement. In addition, personality tests are used in numerous research studies.

Several strategies are used in personality assessment. Often, a structured, objective format consisting of true/false or multiple-choice items is used. These items present structured, unambiguous stimuli, and the interpretation of responses is fairly evident and specific. For example, the Myers-Briggs Type Indicator® (MBTI®), authored by Isabel Briggs Myers and Katherine C. Briggs, uses an objective item format and is based on the personality theory of Carl Jung. Its purpose is to determine where examinees fall on the introversion-extroversion continuum and, in addition, to identify the primary way in which the examinee experiences or comes to know the world: sensing, intuiting, feeling, or thinking. In contrast, the Minnesota Multiphasic Personality Inventory–2 and California Personality Inventory also use objective formats but are constructed by the criterion-group strategy. Items were selected for inclusion on these tests on the basis of how the standardization group responded and not on the basis of mere item content.

Other personality tests use a projective format. These tests present examinees with relatively unstructured stimuli such as inkblots, ambiguous pictures, or play materials. The underlying assumption is that examinees will project personal thoughts, feelings, and interpretations onto the stimulus that is seen. Examples of projective personality tests are the Rorschach Inkblot Test, the Thematic Apperception Test, and the House-Tree-Person "drawing."

Self-Report Clinical Scales.   Hundreds of self-report scales have been developed since the 1990s and are routinely used in clinical settings. Often, clinical mental health counselors must assess clients along specific cognitive, emotional, or behavioral dimensions to determine the frequency or intensity of the symptoms being treated. Such assessment may be required to measure pretreatment levels of the presenting symptoms, to monitor progress during counseling, and to measure outcomes.

Clinical scales focus on specific dimensions of the client's experience, such as depression, anxiety, anger, assertiveness, or hopelessness. Because most have been developed for efficient administration, scoring, and interpretation, self-report clinical scales are usually brief and written in objective formats. The intent of the items is apparent to the examinee and therefore create the potential for faking good or bad.

The Beck Depression Inventory–II (BDI–II; Beck, Steer, & Brown, 1996) is a widely used self-report clinical scale. It consists of 21 items, each of which contains four statements relating to the symptoms of depression. The following is an illustration of an item on the BDI–II:

A. 0 I have not experienced recent difficulty falling asleep.
   1. I have recently experienced some difficulty in falling asleep.
   2. Frequently, I am unable to fall asleep.
   3. I am never able to fall asleep.

The examinee selects the response that most closely reflects his or her recent experience. The responses are then summed. The total score can range from 0 to 63. Normal mood fluctuations are indicated by scores of 1 to 10; mild mood disturbance, 11 to 16; borderline clinical depression, 17 to 20; moderate depression, 21 to 30; severe depression, 31 to 40; over 40, extreme depression (Beck et al., 1996).

Although such appraisal instruments share the weaknesses of other self-report measures, they do provide an efficient means of monitoring client progress and outcome. In addition, these tools are useful for gathering data when one is conducting program evaluations. Thus, mental health counselors should have a working knowledge of the vast array of self-report clinical scales so that they know how to establish the effectiveness of their professional practice.

ETHICAL PRACTICE IN APPRAISAL

The ethical practice of appraisal encompasses five specific tasks: test selection, administration, interpretation, reporting, and storage of test-related materials (ACA, 2005; AMHCA, 2010). In addition, mental health counselors must attain and maintain professional competence in appraisal skills to protect the client's welfare. Only professionals who have adequate education, training, and experience can select, administer, score, and interpret test responses. Typically, test publishers use a rating scale of test administrators' academic and professional credentials to regulate the purchase of tests. The purchase of certain tests requires that prospective purchasers demonstrate they have successfully completed courses in assessment or have attained a terminal degree. Those who fail to recognize and practice within professional boundaries can cause great harm to clients. Such unethical practice can result in legal action or restrictive sanctions against the counseling professional.

Test Selection. In selecting specific appraisal instruments, professional counselors take into consideration the specific question(s) to be answered and the unique characteristics of the examinee. To find the appropriate instruments, they must have a working knowledge of the vast array of instruments. In addition, a number of sources of information are available that can validate the use of a particular test in a specific situation. Test manuals provide useful information on the purpose, construction, and psychometric properties of the test. Reference tools such as *Tests in Print VII* (Murphy, Impara, & Plake, 2006) and *The Sixteenth Mental Measurements Yearbook* (Plake & Spies, 2005) contain publisher information, concise overviews, and reviews of specific tests. The methodology sections of many journal articles often discuss specific tests and their specific applications. But to make sense of this information, mental health counselors must understand the psychometric theory and techniques that justify their test selection.

In addition, the selection process must be sensitive to the specific needs and characteristics of the client. The client's age, gender, cultural background, and cognitive developmental level must be considered. The mental health and community counselor needs to be sure the specific test has been standardized and has norms that produce valid, reliable, and generalizable test results.

Test Administration.   Great care is taken in the administration of tests. Counselors must carefully follow the test instructions to ensure administering the test in standard conditions. Often, the test manual provides sets of instructions that are to be read verbatim to the examinees. A comfortable yet professional setting for test taking includes adequate lighting, seating, noise control, privacy, and temperature. Control of all extraneous environmental factors that might contribute to unexplained variance is vital. Test administration should be postponed if client illness or extraordinary events might influence the results. Any physical disabilities, such as limitations in seeing or hearing or eye/hand coordination, should be ascertained so that they can be adequately accommodated. Finally, adequate time must be allowed for completion of the test.

Test Interpretation.   Procedures for scoring tests are usually clearly explained in the test manual. The professional is responsible for the accurate scoring of tests, and for accurate interpretation even when it is based on computerized scoring. Any conclusions must be solidly based on and justified by empirical evidence. Because the data from testing are a sample of only some of the examinees' behaviors, overall conclusions are never based solely on test results. Rather, the results are always considered in connection with the client's specific situation and also take into account the test-taking circumstances and cultural factors. If tests lack sufficient validity and reliability, only tentative conclusions can be based on their results. In addition, preconceptions and examiner biases must not be allowed to influence test interpretation.

Test Reporting.   The results and conclusions from testing must be communicated ethically and professionally. Although counselors test their clients for their own purposes in diagnostic and treatment decision making, the results and conclusions are frequently directed to other professionals who are working with the client. In addition, clients should be informed of the rationale for the testing and of the results.

Thus, test reports are written to meet the demands of various audiences. The bottom line, of course, is clarity and directness in communicating the rationale for and the conclusions derived from testing. Professional jargon should be avoided; conciseness and precision are virtues. The writer's professional reputation is enhanced by good style, readability, and grammatical correctness. Clients have a right to receive feedback regarding how they performed on the test, how the test results will be used, and who will have access to the information (ACA, 2005). Again, counselors who communicate this information to their clients must be sensitive to language and cultural differences.

All documents related to the client's testing are confidential, and any release of such information requires the client's informed consent. Electronic transfer of test results can occur only upon guarantee that the information-transferring devices can limit the delivery of the data to the intended receivers. Staff involved in typing, filing, and mailing test reports must be trained in the importance of maintaining confidentiality.

Finally, mental health counselors are responsible for the security of test materials, data, and reports. Test materials should be stored in a secure file cabinet and room. Adequate office management requires that the location of test-related files and documents be known at all times. Counselors should avoid leaving files containing test results open on desktops, where others can see them. In general, ethical practice in appraisal maintains and supports the integrity and well-being of those served.

RESEARCH AND PROGRAM EVALUATION

Basically, research is a systematic process of obtaining data for the purpose of answering questions, resolving problems, and gaining greater understanding concerning specific phenomena. The systematic process used is often referred to as the *scientific method.* It consists of the following stages:

1. The researchers construct a concise statement of the problem or research question, that is, a statement of what they are proposing to investigate and why it is significant. They identify specific variables to be explored, including dependent, independent, intervening, and potentially confounding variables.
2. Based on the existing information, the researchers construct a hypothesis, and of which direction the gathered data will take.
3. A specific plan is developed for gathering information to answer the research question. This plan details who will participate in the study, what specifically is to be measured, and what procedures will be used in gathering the information.
4. The researchers carry out this plan.
5. The data are analyzed and interpreted, that is, transformed into numbers for statistical analysis and examined for their meaning. The researchers determine whether the data support the initial hypothesis.
6. The researchers come to conclusions with regard to the original research questions. In addition, they note the limitations of the study and identify directions for further research.

Relatively few practicing mental health counselors spend significant time and energy on basic research. Rather, they find themselves working in the trenches of direct service delivery. They are more likely to use research methods to determine the extent of clinical progress, measure outcomes, determine the effectiveness of psychoeducational programs, and conduct needs assessments as part of program development. The results of such studies have immediate relevance to practitioners. But because such studies take place in the real world, they lack the "sterile" conditions that are typical of pure theoretical research.

KEY CONCEPTS AND PRINCIPLES IN RESEARCH

Sampling.   Counselors are rarely able to have access to all the members of a population or the entire range of potential behaviors. *Sampling* refers to the techniques used to gather data from a subset of the entire population or set of behaviors in such a way that the data gathered are representative of the population. If I conduct an empirical study to determine the extent to which interpersonal therapy decreases symptoms of depression, I will limit my study to a selected sample of persons who are representative of the entire population of depressed persons. This is accomplished by taking a *random sample* of participants, where each person in the population has an equal opportunity of being selected for the study. When more than one variable has the potential to confound the outcome of the study, researchers sometimes use *stratified random sampling.* For example, the outcome might be influenced by differences in the age or gender of the participant and there is a risk that the experimental and placebo groups might be imbalanced according to these variables. Using stratified random sampling, the researcher subdivides the sample according to the identified variables and then randomly samples each variable separately. This allows the characteristics of the sample to resemble more closely the characteristics of the population.

Sometimes extraneous variables operate within the selected group that are beyond the direct control or awareness of the researcher. The operation of these variables may go undetected and influence the outcome of the study. The easiest way for researchers to overcome this problem is through the *random assignment* of participants to the groups. For example, we might take the group of depressed persons and randomly assign them to either interpersonal treatment or placebo groups in such a way that each person has an equal opportunity to be placed in either group and the placement of any particular participant does not affect the probability of another from being assigned to a group.

Validity.   *Validity* refers to the accuracy of definitions and research methods. Actually, two types of validity must be considered simultaneously—internal and external validity. *Internal validity* refers to the extent to which the results of a study can be interpreted accurately. Suppose we are interested in comparing the effectiveness of cognitive and interpersonal therapies in treating depression. To do so, we assign student volunteers to either the cognitive or the interpersonal group. Each group receives 10 sessions of treatment, delivered in a group modality, in which counselors, self-identified as either cognitive or interpersonal therapists, follow protocols developed by the researchers. Data are gathered and the researchers conclude that cognitive therapy is more effective than interpersonal therapy in decreasing levels of depression. To what extent can or should we have confidence in the accuracy of this conclusion? Due to the lack of control over extraneous variables or initial levels of depression in participants, we have no way of knowing whether the results obtained are, in fact, due to the interventions. The impact of delivering counseling through group modalities introduces dynamics into the design that might add to or detract from the power of the identified independent variables. The results of such a study cannot be interpreted accurately due to a lack of internal validity.

External validity exists to the extent that the results of a study can be generalized to other populations and conditions. Why might the study in the previous example lack external validity? To what extent can the results of the study be generalized to persons who are clinically depressed? Because the participants in the study were volunteer students, we have no way of knowing whether the quality of affect in the experimental groups resembles that in clinical populations. Furthermore, administering treatment in group modalities limits the extent to which the results would generalize to the treatment of individuals.

Reliability. A concept closely related to validity is reliability. In fact, reliability is a necessary characteristic for validity (Heppner, Wampold, & Kivlighan, 2008). When we consider reliability in research, the focus is on the consistency of methods, conditions, and results. *Internal reliability* deals with the extent to which the methods of data collection and the analysis and interpretation of the results are consistent within a study. In contrast, *external reliability* refers to the extent to which independent researchers using the same methods can obtain the same or similar results.

Operational Definitions. Many of the variables of interest to counselors are often defined in subjective terms that defy direct, concise measurement. If the researcher is interested in investigating or assessing aggressive behavior in children, an agreed-upon definition must be constructed that provides an accurate description of the phenomenon under study. Furthermore, *aggression* must be defined in such a way that independent raters agree on the presence or absence of the aggressive behavior.

Operational definitions are used in research and appraisal to safeguard against threats to the validity and reliability by defining concepts and variables in terms of the specific operations in which they can be measured. For example, mental health counselors may want to determine their effectiveness in treating anxiety. If they use operational definitions, anxiety can be defined in terms of a test score, observations of social withdrawal, and specific behavioral indicators of the activation of the sympathetic nervous system. Such definitions guide researchers toward more precise measurement of the constructs being investigated and reduce measurement error, therefore increasing the validity and reliability of the study.

SPECIFIC MODELS OF RESEARCH DESIGN

Direct Observation. *Observational research* refers to methods in which the researcher observes and records the ongoing behavior of participants but does not seek to exert influence on the situation or manipulate the behavior in any way. For example, in classic research on attachment using the Strange Situation (Ainsworth, Blehar, Waters, & Wall, 1978), researchers observed the behaviors of young children in a playroom alone, with a stranger, and upon unification with their primary caregivers. The conclusions provided data for the creation of specific research questions and hypotheses that, upon further investigation, led to the discovery of secure and insecure attachment relationships.

Observational research can take two general forms. In *naturalistic observation*, data collection occurs in the existing context with no manipulation of the environment. The researcher measures the behavior of individuals in their natural environment. In contrast, *participant-observer research* takes place when the researcher joins and participates in the group under study. Researchers using observational methods must control for the *Hawthorne effect:* Knowledge of being observed sometimes leads participants to behave differently than when in natural settings.

Clinical mental health counselors may use observational methods as part of assessment and treatment monitoring. A school system might refer a third-grade student who is frequently unmanageable in classroom settings. To understand the nature of the presenting problem, the counselor may identify operational definitions of *unmanageable behavior* and then conduct an observation to assess the behavior in context. Or an agency may be interested in determining the effect of implementing a peer/consumer support component in an existing day treatment program. Data gathered through direct observation of clients' behavior would be important in evaluating the relative benefits of the program.

If observational research is to be valid and reliable, counselor-researchers must attend to several factors. First, the behavior or phenomenon under study must be well defined. This is the only way the researcher can know what to count and what not to count. If, for example, the variable being observed is "aggressive behavior," those rating the behavior must have an operational definition that can facilitate high interrater agreement on its relative presence or absence. Second, it is important for researchers to specify the exact conditions in which the observations are made. In other words, what are the antecedent conditions potentially supporting the behavior? Does the aggressive behavior take place during instructional time, recess, lunch, or immediately prior to dismissal? Such information places the behavior in context and assists in the construction of case conceptualizations and treatment plans. Third, researchers must decide how to "count" the behavior. For example, a simple frequency count of the displays of aggressive behavior might be used as the measure of the dependent variable. But does the report of mere quantity deliver the quality of data desired? To what extent should levels of intensity or severity be considered? Do aggressive actions against inanimate objects count? What about verbal aggressiveness? Clearly, valid and reliable observational studies require operationally defined variables that accurately reflect the characteristic being investigated.

Survey Methods. Research studies using survey methods are concerned primarily with determining *what is* and are much less interested in finding explanations. In addition, survey methods are used to gather information on how people feel, think, perceive, or behave in specific contexts. Typical applications include consumer satisfaction surveys, needs assessments in program development, determination of levels of interests or preferences, and program evaluations.

A variety of methods are available for survey research. Structured and unstructured interviews can be conducted in person or over the phone. But in either case, an oral exchange takes place between the interviewer and the interviewee. In contrast, questionnaires can be used to elicit numerous forms of responses. For example, checklists, Likert scales, multiple choice, and brief written responses each have unique strengths and weaknesses. These kinds of questionnaires can be administered to individuals or groups and can be delivered by mail or electronically by online survey systems such as Survey Monkey™. The researcher weighs these strengths and weaknesses in selecting the approach that best serves his or her purposes.

Correlational Methods. Correlational research seeks to explore the relationship between two or more variables. For example, a researcher may be interested in the relationship between religiosity and mental health. Although it would be extremely difficult to establish a causal relationships between religious orientation (e.g., Allport's intrinsic, extrinsic, and indiscriminately proreligious orientations) and level of mental health, it is possible to explore how mental health covaries with religious orientation.

The strength of the relationship is communicated by a correlation coefficient, which may range from -1.0 to $+1.0$. A positive correlation exists when levels of mental health increase as levels of intrinsic religious orientation increase. If an inverse relationship exists, a negative correlation between the two variables is present.

It is beyond the purpose and scope of this text to discuss the statistical procedures. The statistical analysis of data is greatly facilitated by statistical packages for computers, such as SPSS (Statistical Package for the Social Sciences) or R Commander (Hogan, 2010).

If a relationship between two or more variables can be established, it is theoretically possible to predict how a person will perform on one variable based on his or her performance on the other variable. For example, decisions regarding the admission of students to a graduate program can be partially based on the relationship among graduate GPA (grade point average) and scores on the GRE, undergraduate GPA, and ratings of performance in the admissions interview. Or scores obtained on measures of negative self-statements and cognitive distortions might be used to predict one's level of depression. In both examples, multivariate methods (e.g., multiple regression analysis) are required because more than two variables are being correlated.

Experimental Methods. In simple experiments, a researcher deliberately manipulates or varies one or more variables (i.e., the independent variables) and measures the effect on one or more other variables (i.e., the dependent variables). When control is exerted over potentially confounding variables, a true experiment is conducted that is capable of detecting cause-effect relationships. Ideally, clinical studies attempt to control for all critical variables other than the type of treatment. For example, a researcher may seek to answer the following research question: "Which of several prominent treatment regimens is most effective in decreasing levels of social phobia in clinical populations?" In order to test the hypothesis, the researcher randomly selects members of clinical populations diagnosed with social phobia and assigns them to person-centered, cognitive-behavioral, strategic family, and placebo groups. Treatment manuals are used to ensure that the implementation of the treatments is accurate and consistent. The outcome data for the groups are analyzed to establish if statistically significant differences occur.

Sometimes, though, researchers are unable to exert the level of control over variables that is necessary for true experimentation. For example, the researcher may be interested in determining if significant differences in diagnosis occur between males and females or among individuals of various socioeconomic classes presenting with similar symptoms. Because it is impossible to create groups through random selection assignment, the researcher relies on random selection of participants from within existing populations. Such studies are described as using quasi-experimental methods. No experimental manipulation occurs because the differences between groups are based on preexisting characteristics of the participants. The importance in the distinction between experimental and quasi-experimental approaches lies in the ability of the former to detect causal relationships.

Within-Subject Designs. In a variety of situations, it is desirable to focus on individual participants. Frequently, mental health counselors are interested in determining the effect of treatment on individual clients. Within-subject designs investigate individuals under both experimental (i.e., treatment) and nonexperimental conditions and are sometimes known as $N = 1$ studies. These approaches are characterized by the single-subject rule, which means that only one variable is manipulated at a time. All other variables are held constant. This is necessary to ensure that the results of treatment can be attributed to the treatment. In a simple A-B design, the participant is observed until a stable rating of the dependent variable can be established over a set length of time. This period of "no treatment" is referred to as the baseline condition (A). After the baseline is established, the treatment (i.e., independent variable) is introduced and measured at intervals equal to those in the baseline. Interpretation of results is based on the assumption that changes noted in the dependent variable are due to the action of the independent variable.

Within-subject designs have numerous applications in the practice of clinical mental health counseling. For example, Joe was referred to the college counseling center because of poor undergraduate academic performance. In collaboration with his counselor, Joe developed and implemented a self-management program to enhance his studying of his coursework. To establish a baseline, he operationalized the dependent variable in terms of minutes spent studying per night. He gathered baseline data for 1 week. He then implemented a plan that involved removal of television while studying. The effect on minutes of study was monitored for 1 week. This was followed by the implementation of a token system in which points were earned for a specific number of minutes spent in study and could be used toward the purchase of a CD. The plan was effective in significantly increasing the amount of time spent in study. As the new behavior stabilized over time, Joe weaned himself from his self-management plan while continuing to monitor the dependent variable for indicators of relapse.

Qualitative Methods.   Increasingly, researchers are utilizing methods that are less reliant on quantitative measures. Qualitative methods use words rather than numbers to describe phenomena. Studies using qualitative methods are often descriptive and exploratory and are less concerned with testing specific hypotheses or establishing the validity of theories or techniques. Frequently, as a means of gathering data, this method uses direct observation, in which the researcher is a participant-observer. Examples of qualitative methods include case studies, ethnography, and phenomenological investigations. Software packages, such as NVivo 9 (NVivo 9, 2011), enable researchers to organize written data, conduct content or cluster analyses, and construct tree diagrams.

PROGRAM EVALUATION

Program evaluation is a form of applied research that systematically investigates the effectiveness of intervention programs. Frequently, mental health counselors must report on whether agency programs are producing the positive benefits that they purport to promote. Funding organizations, mental health boards, taxpayers, and consumers need to distinguish effective from ineffective programs. Programs failing to live up to expectations must be revised, replaced with more productive alternatives, or simply eliminated. Systematic evaluation of programs serves as a basic feedback mechanism enabling program managers to devise and implement corrective measures that will ensure consumer benefits from program participation.

Program evaluation involves, first, a thorough description of the entity to be evaluated and then the establishment of standards or criteria by which the performance of the program is to be judged (Rossi, Freeman, & Lipsey, 1999). Two general approaches are *formative* and *summative evaluation. Formative evaluation* is research activity undertaken to provide useful information that will inform decisions on how to improve the operation of a program. It focuses on all operations of the service delivery system. In contrast, *summative evaluation* is research activity designed and implemented to determine the overall effectiveness of the program. Thus, summative evaluation is concerned with outcomes.

Well-designed programs have several important characteristics. First, the needs and wants of the intended recipients must be accurately assessed. Based on an accurate understanding of community needs, program developers can develop a mission statement that expresses the vision and purpose of the program. In addition, the identified program goals and objectives are anchored in the belief that their attainment will lead to the fulfillment of the identified needs. The program then becomes the step-by-step means by which the specific goals and objectives are attained. Furthermore, the staff of a well-designed program have the working knowledge and skills necessary to carry out the program successfully. Finally, the delivery system must have the necessary backup supports for successful implementation and maintenance of the program. These include human resources, equipment, physical facilities, and technical supports.

Numerous research methods are used in conducting program evaluations. Their selection depends on the specific purpose of the evaluation, the needs and expectations of the stakeholders, and the specific nature of the questions being asked. For example, surveys using interviews or questionnaires may inform the initial needs assessment. In addition, survey research is used in measuring program delivery processes or level of consumer satisfaction. Sometimes information from the organization's existing data management systems provides an efficient means of obtaining information regarding the day-to-day operations of the program. Participant-observer methods are useful in gathering qualitative data for formative evaluation. Quasi-experimental methods can be used to assess how much program recipients benefit from their participation in the program by comparing scores on outcome measures with those of a control or waiting-list group.

Given the immense number of variables involved in implementing and evaluating programs, researchers must choose the best possible design from a scientific perspective. But they must also consider the potential uses and importance of the results, the practicality of the various design options, and the likelihood that the selected method will produce credible results (Rossi et al., 1999). The results of program evaluation may lack the validity and reliability of true experiments, but with appropriate rigor, program evaluations enable program managers to assess the quality of service provided in the context of the real world.

ETHICAL PRACTICE IN RESEARCH

Clinical mental health counselors who conduct research must always act within the ethical standards put forth by the ACA (2005) and the AMHCA (2010). The most basic responsibility is to respect the dignity of participants and promote their welfare. Colleges, universities, and many counseling-related organizations have human subjects review boards—for example, institutional review boards (IRBs)—whose mandate is to ensure the protection of participants in research conducted at the respective institution. Formal research proposals must be presented to and approved by such boards before the actual study can be conducted. Every effort is made to protect participants from potential harm, misuse, and discomfort. The principles of informed consent and confidentiality are especially applicable for counselor-researchers.

Informed consent is a fundamental right of participants in a research study: They must be given an accurate description of all features of the investigation. Researchers must openly communicate the purpose and procedures of the study, the potential risks of harm or discomfort, and potential benefits. Furthermore, it must be made clear that participation is voluntary and participants are free to withdraw from the study at any point without repercussions. If deception is used, researchers explain the necessity of this procedure as soon as possible. Following the collection of data, the researchers fully debrief the participants to dispel any potential misconceptions. Finally, the right to informed consent is extended to sponsoring or participating agencies, organizations, and institutions.

Mental health counselors understand that any gathered data or information pertaining to the participants is confidential. The personal identity of the participants must be protected. Researchers gather data in such a way that they cannot be linked to the identity of any one participant. Any possibility that personal information might be divulged to others should be fully explained as part of the informed-consent process.

Finally, counselors must report results of their investigations ethically. They must take care to communicate their results accurately. The limitations of the investigation and possible alternative interpretations of the results should be stated clearly so that readers will not be misled in any way. Due recognition should be given to students/research assistants and others who made significant contributions to the design or conducting of the investigation.

CONCLUSION

Now that you have been introduced to the role of appraisal and research in the practice of clinical mental health counseling, the question that may linger is "So what?" After reading the previous pages, you may be convinced that tasks of appraisal and research are peripheral to the professional role you anticipate. Thus, you do not see such skills as having a significant impact on your professional identity.

However, our involvement in research and appraisal has much to do with the integrity of our profession. With little or no concern about the empirical validation of the procedures we use, little foundation exists for our claims of therapeutic efficacy. If consumers are to benefit from counseling, and if counselors are to survive this era of increased accountability, the mental health counseling profession must act to promote interventions of proven effectiveness (King & Heyne, 2000).

How would you defend your practice against the accusation that it foists on consumers a product that is suspect (Koop, 2004)? That is, that counselors do not actually do what they claim to do. Several basic skills are required to advocate to consumers, the general public, legislators, and third-party reimbursers on behalf of the profession. First, mental health counselors must be familiar with and understand the current literature on empirically validated therapies. Counselors must therefore have a working knowledge of literature searches and must be able to review the relevant research on its psychometric and methodological merits. Second, mental health practitioners must be able to evaluate their own professional practice. In most cases, this evaluation entails the ability to design and carry out $N = 1$ research and program evaluation. In addition, this research needs to be more qualitative and contextually sensitive if conclusions are to reflect accurately the realities of our clinical worlds.

Most mental health professionals agree that there is much more to determining whether a particular approach to treatment is valuable than simply demonstrating that it can produce statistically significant outcomes under controlled conditions (King & Heyne, 2000). Consumers of our services expect positive outcomes. We must meet clients where they are, gain an accurate understanding of their situation, identify their goals, and implement a plan devised to achieve these goals. Competent clinical mental health counselors use appraisal and research skills to achieve these ends.

DISCUSSION QUESTIONS

1. In your own words, what is meant by the term *scientist-practitioner*? To what extent does your understanding of this term fit with what you see as the primary function of mental health counselors?
2. What specific limits do you see on mental health counselors' ability to be scientist-practitioners? Do these limits influence the quality or quantity of original research and theory emanating from the mental health counseling profession?
3. To what extent will you depend on standardized appraisal instruments to inform yourself of the presenting problems of your clients? In what specific clinical situations do you believe appraisal instruments are necessary components of assessment?
4. In what specific ways might research inform your clinical practice? At what particular times in your future practice of counseling might you engage in empirical research? Identify ways in which having a research orientation will strengthen your effectiveness as a counselor.
5. What training and clinical experiences would you need to be considered an expert in the use of a particular psychological test (e.g., the current version of the Minnesota Multiphasic Personality Inventory, or MMPI)?

SUGGESTED ACTIVITIES

1. Read the section of your state's licensure law that discusses scope of practice for licensed mental health or professional counselors. Does it specifically define or specify any limitations regarding the use of psychological tests or appraisal instruments?
2. Locate the most recent edition of *Tests in Print* and *The Mental Measurements Yearbook*. Select a specific test and review the information about it provided by these important reference tools.
3. Look through recent issues of the *Journal of Counseling and Development* and the *Journal of Mental Health Counseling*. What topics are the subjects of empirical research? To what extent would you be able to apply the findings of these journals' articles to your professional practice? What topics would interest you to

investigate empirically? Would you consider publishing your results in a professional journal? Why or why not?

REFERENCES

Aiken, L. R. (2003). *Psychological testing and assessment* (11th ed.). Boston, MA: Allyn and Bacon.

American Counseling Association Governing Council. (2005). ACA policies and procedures for processing complaints of ethical violations. Retrieved from http://www.counseling.org/Resources/CodeOfEthics/TP/Home/CT2.aspx

Ainsworth, M. D., Blehar, M. C., Waters, E., & Wall, S. (1978). *Patterns of attachment.* Hillsdale, NJ: Erlbaum.

American Mental Health Counselors Association. (2010). *Code of ethics of the American Mental Health Counselors Association–2010 revision.* Alexandria, VA: Author.

Anastasi, A., & Urbina, S. (1997). *Psychological testing* (7th ed.). Upper Saddle River, NJ: Prentice Hall.

Beck, A. T., Steer, R. A., & Brown, G. K. (1996). *Beck Depression Inventory II.* San Antonio, TX: Psychological Corporation.

Donnay, D. A. C., Morris, M. L., Schaubhut, N. A., & Thompson, R. C. (2005). *Strong Interest Inventory manual.* Mountain View, CA: Consulting Psychologists Press.

Drummond, R. J., & Jones, K. D. (2010). *Assessment procedures for counselors and helping professionals* (7th ed.). Upper Saddle River, NJ: Pearson Education.

Gibson, R. L., & Mitchell, M. H. (2003). *Introduction to counseling and guidance* (6th ed.). Upper Saddle River, NJ: Merrill Prentice Hall.

Hadley, R. G., & Mitchell, L. K. (1995). *Counseling research and program evaluation.* Pacific Grove, CA: Brooks/Cole.

Heppner, P. P., Wampold, B. E., & Kivlighan, D. M. (2008). *Research design in counseling* (3rd ed.). Belmont, CA: Thomson Brooks/Cole.

Hogan, T. P. (2010). *Bare bones R: A brief introductory guide.* Thousand Oaks, CA: Sage.

Kaplan, R. M., & Saccuzzo, D. P. (2012). *Psychological testing: Principles, applications, and issues* (8th ed.). Belmont, CA: Wadsworth.

King, N. J., & Heyne, D. (2000). Promotion of empirically validated psychotherapies in counseling psychology. *Counselling Psychology Quarterly, 13,* 1–13.

Kongstvedt, P. R. (1996). *The managed health care handbook* (3rd ed.). Gaithersburg, MD: Aspen.

Koop, V. (2004, Spring). The search for Christian integrity. *CAPS Report, 33*(1), 5.

Murphy, L. L., Impara, J. C., & Plake, B. S. (Eds.). (2006). *Tests in print VII.* Lincoln: University of Nebraska Press.

NVivo 9 [Computer software]. Cambridge, MA: QSR International.

Plake, B. S., & Spies, R. A. (Eds.). (2005). *The sixteenth mental measurements yearbook.* Lincoln: Buros Institute of Mental Measurements, University of Nebraska.

Rossi, P. H., Freeman, H. E., & Lipsey, M. W. (1999). *Evaluation: A systematic approach* (6th ed.). Thousand Oaks, CA: Sage.

Santrock, J. (2010). *Life-span development* (13th ed.). New York, NY: McGraw-Hill.

Sarason, S. B. (1984). If it can be studied or developed, shouldn't it be? *American Psychologist, 39,* 477–485.

Terman, L. M. (1916). *The measurement of intelligence.* Boston, MA: Houghton Mifflin.

Vygotsky, L. S. (1962). *Thought and language.* Cambridge, MA: MIT Press.

Wechsler, D. (2002). *Wechsler Preschool and Primary Scale of Intelligence* (3rd ed.). San Antonio, TX: Psychological Corporation.

Wechsler, D. (2003). *Wechsler Intelligence Scale for Children* (4th ed.). San Antonio, TX: Psychological Corporation.

Wechsler, D. (2008). *Wechsler Adult Intelligence Scale* (4th ed.). San Antonio, TX: Psychological Corporation.

Whiston, S. C. (2013). *Principles and applications of assessment in counseling* (4th ed.). Belmont, CA: Brooks/Cole.

Wilkinson, G. S., & Robertson, G. J. (2007). *Wide Range Achievement Test 4.* Lutz, FL: Psychological Assessment Resources.

Professional Practice in Multicultural Contexts

OUTLINE

Diversity and Multiculturalism in America

Multiculturalism as the Fourth Force in Counseling

Key Definitions and Concepts

Barriers to Effective Multicultural Counseling

Foundational Principles in Multicultural Counseling

The Culturally Competent Counselor

Conclusion

W e had invited a small group of students to our home for a fish fry. As Antowine and Anika approached the small town in which we lived, a police car pulled out from a parking lot and began to follow them. After making several turns and still being followed, Antowine decided to take a more indirect route to our home, turning several times and going into other neighborhoods. The police car stayed behind several car lengths, not missing a turn. Finally, as Antowine turned into our driveway, the police car slowly drove on.

Upon their arrival, Antowine told us about touring our town while being followed. The couple took it in stride and noted that they have come to expect such "welcomes." As young African- and Asian Americans, they had experienced similar episodes as they ventured into small-town America. Yes, we are all created equal, but unfortunately, and in the words of George Orwell, some are created more equal than others. Much has changed since the civil rights movement of the 1960s, but the "problem of race" is still with us (Jones, 1997, p. 2). Simply reflect on the public debates concerning health care reform, access to adequate medical care and mental health services, securing national borders from illegal entry into the United States, or disparity among economic classes. Often, issues involving race, ethnicity, and diversity are interwoven throughout these discussions in overt and covert ways.

The multicultural perspective is foundational to the practice of contemporary clinical mental health counseling. Clearly, diversity in race and culture is the rule and not the exception in our society. Multiculturalism tolerates and even supports alternative views of mental health, taking into account not only differences in race and ethnicity but also differences in nationality, education, sexual orientation, religion, age, geographic location, and socioeconomic influences. This acceptance is a logical consequence of being ecologically minded. Thus, mental health professionals who embrace the multicultural perspective are able to work with persons of different backgrounds without assessing recognized differences between themselves and their clients in terms of being right and wrong, superior and inferior.

This chapter introduces the implications of diversity and multiculturalism for the profession of mental health counseling. First, the chapter describes the current multiracial, multicultural face of America and the necessity for skilled mental health counselors to demonstrate multicultural competence. Second, foundational principles for respectful counseling of diverse populations are discussed. Competent counselors must be aware of numerous barriers to effective cross-cultural counseling and significant influences of their personal cultural self. In addition, a working knowledge of the implications of racial/cultural identity development theory, within- versus between-group differences, and the convergence of multiple identities helps counselors recognize and work with the diversity in various groups of people.

DIVERSITY AND MULTICULTURALISM IN AMERICA

The face of America has changed. The nation is not becoming diverse or multicultural, it *is* diverse and multicultural. This reality makes it vital that counselors develop multicultural knowledge and skills if they are to work effectively with the vast array of people in their communities.

Although the U.S. population has always been multicultural in its composition, its diversification has rapidly increased in recent decades as minority populations have increased at higher rates than white non-Hispanic populations (U.S. Census Bureau, 2010b). At 64% of the total population in 2010, there are more white non-Hispanics in the U.S. population than ever before. But their proportion of the total population declined by 5% from 2000 to 2010. In contrast, the Hispanic population has grown from 4.5% in 1970 to 16% of the U.S. population in 2010; it is now the largest minority population in the country. African American, Asian/Pacific Islanders, and American Indian/Alaska Natives make up about 13%, 5%, and 2% of the U.S. population, respectively. These various racial and ethnic groups are not evenly distributed throughout the United States (U.S. Census Bureau, 2010b). In 2010, nearly one-half (47%) of the West's population was minority. California, Texas, Hawaii, New Mexico, and the District of Columbia have current populations where "minorities" have become the majority.

Other important demographic differences, such as educational attainment, labor force participation, and poverty can be noted among these groups (U.S. Census Bureau, 2010a). Nearly 88% of white non-Hispanics have completed high school, compared to 89% of Asian Americans, 84% of African Americans, and 63% of Hispanics. However, 52.4% of Asian Americans have earned at least a bachelor's degree, compared to 30% of white non-Hispanics, 19.8% of African Americans, and 13.9% of Hispanics. Generally speaking, married couples have lower poverty rates than other types of family structures. However, all minority groups are more likely to live in poverty than are white non-Hispanics (U.S. Census Bureau, 2010a): In 2009, 9.4% of white non-Hispanics, 25.8% of African Americans, 25.3% of Hispanics, and 12.5% Asian Americans were living in poverty.

Dividing the population into the aforementioned groups masks the complex multicultural fabric of contemporary society (U.S. Census Bureau, 2003). For example, within the category of Hispanic population are Mexicans, Puerto Ricans, Cubans, and South and Central Americans. Similarly, American Indian is a broad category encompassing descent from various tribes, such as Cherokee, Chippewa, Navajo, Choctaw, and Sioux. As we shall see in later sections of this chapter, conceptualizing race and ethnicity in such broad constructs obscures the extent to which within-group and individual differences operate. The well-intentioned but straightforward application of a simple knowledge of the general differences among these groups without more refined ecological reflection can result in stereotyping and counselor insensitivity. Mental health counselors must carefully view each client in his or her milieu. Given the interactional nature of the counseling process, it is appropriate to conclude that all counselor-client relationships are, in fact, multicultural (APA, 2004).

MULTICULTURALISM AS THE FOURTH FORCE IN COUNSELING

It is common to speak of the counseling profession as having been influenced by specific forces that have emerged in chronological order. The first three forces are Freud and the psychoanalytic perspective, behaviorism, and humanistic psychology (Locke, 1992).

Clinical mental health counselors have become alert to the changing face of America and the extent to which basic Western assumptions about the person and the helping process are deeply woven into the fabric of the theory and techniques that have historically guided counselors' work. Contemporary trends and the composition of American society have led the counseling profession to view the multicultural orientation as integral to the work of mental health counselors. As a result, multiculturalism is rightly recognized as the fourth force in counseling (Pedersen, 1990).

The multicultural emphasis grew out of several social trends of the late 1950s and the 1960s. The decade of the 1960s was marked by social turmoil and incremental change. While President John F. Kennedy announced his vision of a New Frontier, the attention of the nation was being called to the deep inequities in U.S. society along the lines of race, culture, and gender. Rosa Parks, Martin Luther King Jr., and many others took a stand against patterns of unfairness, prejudice, and subjection by acting according to a higher set of moral principles. As the industrial era gave way to a multicultural, urban society of the information age, the "melting pot" gave way to a vision of a "mosaic." The globe was shrinking and America was becoming increasingly diverse.

It is from this context that increased sensitivity to issues of race, ethnicity, and culture emerged. By the late 1960s, counselors from minority groups were expressing concern that the practice of counseling ethnically different clients without special training was unethical. In 1973, the Vail Conference Follow-Up Commission of the American Psychological Association (APA) declared that the provision of counseling services to persons of culturally diverse backgrounds by persons lacking in knowledge and skill in servicing such groups was unethical. Furthermore, it was considered unethical to deny such persons service due to a lack of trained staff. Thus, it became the obligation of mental health agencies to employ culturally competent staff or provide opportunities for continuing education to prepare staff to meet the needs of the culturally diverse population served (Korman, 1973, cited in Midgette & Meggert, 1991).

It is no longer possible (or permissible) for counseling professionals to ignore the implications of their own culture or the culture of their clients. They must increase their cultural sensitivity if they are to work effectively with and meet the needs of the diverse members of their communities. This process entails becoming more knowledgeable about their personal background and the backgrounds of the specific cultural groups with whom they work. It also requires the development of counseling skills that are culturally sensitive and relevant to their clients.

The requirements of nondiscrimination and the need for multicultural competence are now codified in the ethical standards of the ACA and the American Mental Health

Counselors Association (AMHCA). The AMHCA Code of Ethics specifies that its members not engage in any form of discriminatory behavior based on the client's "age, color, culture, disability, ethnic group, gender, race, religion, sexual orientation, marital status, or socioeconomic status" (AMHCA, 2010, p. 9). Furthermore, the Preamble to the ACA Code of Ethics (2005) states, "Association members recognize diversity and embrace a cross-cultural approach in support of the worth, dignity, potential, and uniqueness of people within their social and cultural contexts" (p. 3). These principles have specific applications in the ongoing counseling process. In addition, clinical mental health counselors respect diversity and resist discriminatory practices when conducting research or when serving as supervisors, employers, or instructors.

Counselor educators share responsibility in developing and enhancing multicultural awareness and competence among mental health counselors. First, and as noted in Chapter 5, the standards for the accreditation of graduate school training programs in counseling as specified by the Council for Accreditation of Counseling and Related Educational Programs (CACREP) identify social and cultural diversity as one of the common core areas (CACREP, 2009a, Section II.G.2.). Second, it is important that practicum and internship experiences provide students with opportunities to work with populations that reflect the racial, ethnic, cultural, and demographic diversity of their communities (CACREP, 2009a, Section III.). Third, graduate students in counseling programs gain important knowledge and skills in relating the many facets of multiculturalism to the specific practice of their specialization (i.e., clinical mental health counseling) (CACREP, 2009a, pp. 111–112). Finally, academic programs are called on to design recruitment and retention strategies for the employment of faculty members who reflect the diverse backgrounds in U.S. society (CACREP, 2009a, Section I.J.).

KEY DEFINITIONS AND CONCEPTS

Before moving farther along in our discussion, it is helpful to define several foundational terms and concepts that appear repeatedly in any discussion of multiculturalism. Although these are familiar, their interchangeable use masks subtle distinctions that, when recognized, can lend clarity to the subject. The misuse of these terms in certain contexts is sometimes interpreted as cultural insensitivity.

Can clear, precise distinctions be made among the terms *race, ethnicity,* and *culture*? Much confusion exists because of the overlap in specific dimensions of each concept. *Race,* for example, may be defined as a biologically based classification system of people groups based on visible physical characteristics (e.g., skin pigmentation, facial features, texture of hair). Clearly, the identification of racial differences based on differences of physical appearance is one of the most prominent boundary markers used in the construction of individual and group identities. However, given that the Human Genome Project found 99.9% of the 30,000 human genes shared by everyone (Anderson, 2003), to what extent are such biologically based distinctions truly valid or meaningful? Furthermore, Zuckerman (1990) found the major component of genetic diversity to be between persons of the same tribe or nation (84%), with race and geographic region accounting for 10% and 6%, respectively. Thus, any attempt to anchor racial categories to a biological foundation is misguided. Race may carry popular meaning as a social construct and status variable, but counselors must avoid using the term in any way that supports forms of prejudice or discrimination (Robinson-Wood, 2012).

Ethnicity is a related term that carries several interpretations (Baruth, & Manning, 2012). In a broad sense, *ethnicity* refers to a group of persons who identify with one another by virtue of sharing common ancestry, religion, language, skin color, and/or culture. When used in this manner, the term is interchangeable with *race*. The more narrow sense focuses on the setting apart of groups of persons on the basis of national origin and distinctive cultural patterns.

Culture can be defined as "a way of living that encompasses the customs, traditions, attitudes, and overall socialization in which a group of people engage that are unique to their cultural upbringing" (Gopaul-McMicol & Brice-Baker, 1998, p. 5). These are shared patterns of learned behavior and are transmitted across generations by members of the group. Culture is a dynamic force that is ever changing while simultaneously providing its members with a sense of commonality and consistency that allows for the development of a common identity.

It naturally follows, then, that a multicultural orientation is inclusive and provides the opportunity for persons of differing backgrounds to celebrate similarities and differences without requiring the determination of rightness, wrongness, or rankings of superiority/inferiority. As we shall see, multiculturalism has implications not only for the training and practice of mental health counselors but also for the larger discipline of counselor education. Counselor education must be fundamentally committed to contributing to the betterment of the human condition for *all* people.

Clinical mental health counselors must be able to understand and empathize with persons from diverse groups who have experienced devaluation, disadvantage, disregard, and unfair treatment because of their racial/ethnic identities. The terms *prejudice, racism,* and *discrimination* are frequently used to describe such treatment. *Prejudice* is "an attitude, judgment or feeling about a person that is generalized from attitudes or beliefs held about the group to which the person belongs" (Jones, 1997, p. 10). When prejudice operates, people are judged by the color of their skin and according to preconceived stereotypes. When prejudices are held by mental health professionals, the risk significantly increases for potential inaccurate assessments and mistreatment.

In contrast to prejudice, racism builds on prejudice by assuming the superiority of one's race/ethnic group over others. *Racism,* generally speaking, refers to the use of power and position, overtly or covertly and intentionally or unintentionally, to treat others differently on the basis of perceived racial differences between them and oneself. It has two forms: individual and institutional (Baruth & Manning, 2012). *Individual racism* occurs when a single person's belief in his or her racial superiority leads to discriminatory acts against others viewed as racially inferior. In *institutional racism* social policies and laws have the intentional or unintentional consequence of positioning one racial/ethnic group over other groups in privilege, power, and advantage.

Finally, *discrimination* refers to biased treatment of a person based on the view one holds of the group to which that person belongs. For example, a white middle-class female may be given special privileges over persons of other groups in the rescheduling of missed appointments. Whereas the stated excuses of the white client may be accepted at face value, similar excuses from a young African American female might be viewed as a form of resistance (Tidwell, 2004). Discrimination is likely to have been experienced by many if not most ethnic minority clients. The special significance for the mental health counselor is that perceived discrimination has been found to be related to decreased mental health (Cokley, Hall-Clark, & Hicks, 2011).

Clinical mental health counselors should be prepared to skillfully address racism and discrimination, whether it is part of implicit institutionalized practices, the presenting problem, or the client's life history. Self-awareness and honesty are necessary if mental health counselors are to recognize the operation of discrimination in their private or agency practices. Consultation and advocacy services may be useful to victims or vulnerable populations.

Various definitions of *cross-cultural counseling* are found in the professional literature. Atkinson, Morten, and Sue (2003) define it as "any counseling in which two or more of the participants are *racially/ethnically* different" (p. 21). When the mental health professional assumes the ecological perspective, there is a sense in which all counseling work is multicultural (Pedersen, 1991).

BARRIERS TO EFFECTIVE MULTICULTURAL COUNSELING

Specific barriers, such as the implications of the concepts discussed in the previous section, must be overcome if effective cross-cultural counseling is to be achieved. Additional barriers that deserve mention include cultural encapsulation of the counselor, systemic barriers within counseling delivery systems, misapplication of traditional theories of counseling, miscommunication, and mistrust.

CULTURAL ENCAPSULATION

Historically, the profession of counseling tended to assume the appropriateness of the universal application of its concepts, principles, and techniques. In doing so, culturally specific alternatives were excluded from serious consideration. For example, Evans, Valadez, Burns, and Rodriguez (2002) note that mental health counselors tend to choose traditional therapeutic approaches that are in accordance with their own cultural experience. In contrast, minority mental health counselors hold more favorable views of nontraditional techniques. Furthermore, traditional counseling theories and techniques have been developed primarily by persons of non-Hispanic white, Western, male, middle-class heritage.

Wrenn (1962) coined the term *cultural encapsulation* to describe the tendency of counselors to (a) define and dogmatically cling to viewing reality according to their own sets of cultural assumptions to the exclusion of alternative interpretations, (b) demonstrate insensitivity to persons of other cultural backgrounds who hold alternative perspectives, (c) resist or simply not recognize the necessity of testing the validity of one's underlying assumptions, and therefore (d) become trapped in what may be described as a cultural tunnel vision (Corey, Corey, & Callanan, 2010). Too often students enter graduate training programs wearing monocultural lenses and quickly subscribe and adhere to specific theories as doctrinal truth. As Pedersen (1994) notes, good counselors can no longer ignore through their own encapsulation the fundamental role culture plays in their lives and the lives of their clients.

MISAPPLICATION OF TRADITIONAL THEORIES AND TECHNIQUES

Frequently, the theories and techniques of counseling are presented and accepted as special sets of insights, principles, and approaches that have universal application for the understanding and treatment of the human condition. These are accepted as though they carry the strength of divinely inspired truths. They are so much a part of the predominant culture's landscape that their presence and the implications of their operation are ignored. Only recently has the profession begun to unpack the cultural baggage encased in the traditional "tool kits" provided to graduates of counselor education programs. Historically, it has been common practice of many graduate programs to offer a single course with a multicultural emphasis rather than to integrate the insights of multiculturalism across the curriculum (Das, 1995). Current standards for clinical mental health counseling encourage infusion of diversity and multicultural knowledge, skills, and practice across the curriculum (CACREP, 2009a).

A number of fundamental presuppositions undergirding traditional models of counseling can be identified. These models hold implicit assumptions that reflect the world view of predominant western culture:

1. *Individualism* There tends to be an unquestioned acceptance of the autonomous, self-preoccupied individual as being the primary psychological entity in the assessment, conceptualization, and treatment of the human condition. What the client thinks and feels represent the realities on which problems and therapeutic goals are based. Frequently, self-will and self-advancement are emphasized without an accompanying concern for others. When stuck in the treatment process, counselors-in-training are taught to move deeper in the psyche of the individual rather than expand the therapeutic system by actively including relevant ecological factors that take a client-in-situation/context orientation (Cook, 2012). Although human ecology may be given lip service, the theories and techniques of intervention, as used in professional practice, remain firmly entrenched in a very narrow individualistic perspective.

2. *View of normalcy and pathology* Most theories of counseling hold views of what constitutes normal and abnormal behavior. These views reflect a Western, Euro-American perspective and can stand in stark contrast to views held by other cultures. Indeed, the major distinction most theories make between physical and psychological/psychiatric disorders is not universally held. Mental health professions and members of the predominant Western culture commonly talk about being anxious, depressed, or stressed and may attribute these conditions to non-physical causes. This assumption may not be strongly held among persons of

different cultures (Angel & Williams, 2000). Such clients might, therefore, question the rationale for the existence of autonomous professions that treat "emotional disorders." Rather, it might make more sense within their cultural framework to be seen by a medical doctor, religious leader, or good friend. Indeed, concepts of mental health and mental illness are highly variable across cultures (Lefley, 2010). And these conceptualizations can determine the nature of resources dedicated to their service. For example, "talking out" or "working through" related/underlying issues to relieve emotional distress may seem odd to the culturally different client, who might be expecting a more direct intervention such as medicine, advice, or specific directives. Finally, the cross-cultural literature is replete with descriptions of unique *culture-bound syndromes*, in which patterns of disordered or psychotic behaviors cluster in unique ways that are found only in particular cultural settings (Lefley, 2010; Smart & Smart, 1997). Discussions of such syndromes are absent in the contents of traditional theories of counseling.

3. *Functional agnosticism and antireligiousness* Spirituality, organized religion, spiritual beliefs, and the role of priests and spiritual leaders may be central to the functioning and worldview of clients from different cultures. Although spirituality is much more in vogue these days in our profession, most theories and techniques fail to acknowledge and integrate religious/spiritual dimensions into professional practice in ways that are respectful to indigenous people groups. Furthermore, mental health counselors receive more lip service than actual skills-building training in the integration of religion and spirituality.

4. *Personal happiness as a legitimate goal of counseling* In our culture, people often see the possession of personal happiness as an unalienable right and, thus, seek it as a measurable outcome in counseling. Being pleased with personal physical appearance or feeling good about self are important to many persons in Western culture but may be nonissues among those living in or emigrating from third world countries. Instead, persons from other cultures might place more value in the pursuit of personal contentment with their situation. Furthermore, the acceptance of one's situation within the context of that person's understanding of the common good may be viewed as a more legitimate goal.

5. *Insight and process of change* The traditional theories and techniques of counseling rely on self-awareness and insight as important change agents. It is assumed that personal adjustment can be enhanced by increasing knowledge and awareness about self, others, and the situation. The success of many approaches hinges on the client's willingness and ability to engage in activities that can facilitate and enhance the client's insight and awareness. However, many cultural groups do not value insight and self-exploration and, in fact, might see "thinking about it too much" as a causative factor of one's emotional distress (Sue & Sue, 2008).

SYSTEMIC BARRIERS WITHIN COUNSELING DELIVERY SYSTEMS

A number of widely accepted conventions are built into traditional delivery systems of counseling. The scheduling of a one-to-one meeting of a counselor and client, sometimes made several weeks in advance, for a 50-minute session occurring at a frequency of approximately once a week at the counselor's office to explore presenting problems and one's innermost thoughts is rarely questioned. These and other structures and processes of the traditional delivery of mental health services may act as barriers that keep the culturally different from receiving needed treatment.

The fact that children, adolescents, and families of color have been underserved by most public and private human service delivery systems in the United States is well documented (Hernandez, Isaacs, Nesman, & Burns, 1998). When socio-demographic profiles and need for care are taken into account, African Americans receive mental health services at one-half the rate of Whites (Walton, Berasi, Takeuchi, & Uehara, 2010). Magnitude of poverty, family disintegration, community disorganization, family and community violence, chemical abuse, illiteracy, and teenage pregnancy interact with and contribute to the development and maintenance of emotional distress. Geographic location of mental health services, unavailability of affordable transportation, inconvenient office hours, and lack of minority staff converge to create systems of mental health services that discriminate against certain groups. Numerous indirect, systemic interventions are required if the problem of underserved populations is to be remedied.

LANGUAGE BARRIERS AND MISCOMMUNICATION

The effectiveness of counseling relies on the transmission of meaning through verbal, nonverbal, and written communication. The counselor's language, as well as his or her observations of the client's use of language, influences all aspects of the counseling process. The grammatical structure delineates how various pieces of reality fit together (Dell, 1980). Furthermore, words assist persons in perceiving and understanding reality. They are used as labels and become symbols representing persons, places, and objects. Indeed, it can be argued that one's vocabulary shapes one's views of reality and worldview (Sanchez, 2001).

Problems in communication between clients and counselors can prevent minorities from using appropriate services (Sherer, 2002). Adequate command of the spoken language is necessary for accurate information gathering, assessment, identification of goals, treatment planning, and treatment. Members of the predominant culture in the United States have become comfortable with psychological jargon. The Dr. Phils and Lauras of the media have captured the fascination of the country and toss out words and concepts that laypeople understand.

Unfortunately, mental health counselors may mistakenly assume that clients from minority racial/ethnic groups who communicate reasonably well in other social situations can accurately express and comprehend the meaning of words exchanged in counseling settings. Counselors may use slang or colloquialisms that confuse minority clients. Furthermore, clients may not understand the use and meaning of common words when used in unique contexts. For example, one client was fluent in conversational English but encountered difficulty when attempting to complete the MMPI. He encountered terms such as *constipation* and *bowel movement* in specific questions and became confused regarding their precise meaning when in the context of a psychological test. He responded to the items in an arbitrary manner, which resulted in a test proto-col with questionable validity.

MISTRUST

In multicultural counseling situations, the potential presence of mistrust must be assessed and dealt with early in the counseling relationship. It can take various forms and be directed toward individuals or institutions. In addition, feelings of mistrust can be reciprocal.

Counselors may hold preconceived notions and assumptions that impede the estab-lishment of effective therapeutic relationships. Social psychologists have noted the general tendency for people to underestimate contextual influences and overestimate dispositional influences in explaining the behavior of others. This tendency is so basic that it is referred to as the fundamental attribution error (Jones & Harris, 1967). For example, in attempting to explain why I failed to meet a deadline for writing this text, I might point to having to prepare for new courses, dealing with several clients who went into crisis, and remedying problems with my computer. However, when attempt-ing to explain the similar behavior in another person, I commit the fundamental attri-bution error if I attribute his or her behavior to laziness, irresponsibility, or ethnicity.

Certain underlying assumptions supported by Western culture strengthen our pro-pensity to commit fundamental attribution errors. As we have noted, Western culture places a high value on individualism and personal autonomy. It supports the belief that each person is self-sufficient and can be successful by taking personal responsibil-ity and making good choices. Thus, we assume people cause events, and we pay less attention to interacting situational factors (Myers, 2010). We encourage others by say-ing, "You can make it if you try!" It naturally follows from this perspective that those who struggle or fail to get ahead did not try hard enough, are irresponsible, or are lazy. Too often, such faulty reasoning becomes the basis for stereotypes and prejudiced behavior.

The bottom line is that culture and the operation of fundamental attribution errors can be a foundation for the mistrust of certain minority groups. Mental health coun-selors of the predominant culture must refute flawed personal assumptions that oper-ate without question if they are to view each client accurately for the uniqueness the client brings to the counseling situation.

In addition, many minority clients may come into counseling with varying degrees of mistrust. Mistrust may be directed primarily at the counselor, who becomes a sym-bol of the dominant culture or the holders of societal power. Too often, non-Hispanic whites fail to appreciate the impact of history in the lives of other ethnic groups. Sev-eral students in my social and cultural diversity classes have gotten defensive when confronted with racial and ethnic inequities and state, "It is unfair for you to perceive me or other members of my race as though we have personally committed wrongs toward you or persons of your race. I have never owned a slave and do not hold any bigoted attitudes!" Such statements can be considered as *microaggressions* (Sue, 2010) and reveal the extent to which members of the dominant group do not understand the commonplace "verbal, behavioral, and environmental indignities, whether intentional or unintentional, that communicate hostile, derogatory, or negative racial, gender, sexual-orientation, and religious slights and insults" to minority message recipients. Unfortunately, microaggressions are ways minority mistrust receives reinforcement in contemporary society. Thus, culturally sensitive mental health counselors recognize that the caution, hesitancy, or guardedness displayed in initial sessions by the culturally different may reflect the generalization of mistrust into the clinical setting.

The roots of mistrust among many minority clients may lie in a lack of information regarding the nature of services provided or inappropriate referrals and treatment. Immigrants or members of minority groups often enter counseling as a result of being referred to an agency by school personnel or human service agencies (Gopaul-McNicol & Brice-Baker, 1998). They may not have a clear understanding of the reasons for the referral. Sometimes such clients do not have accurate information about the roles of agencies or the nature of services to be provided. For example, one female, single parent who was a recent immigrant was concerned about her fifth-grade child, who was being teased by other children on the school bus. Not knowing where to turn for assistance, she looked for resources in the yellow pages of her phone book and saw "Child and Family Assistance Agency Services." Not knowing much about this agency or its primary role, which was Child Protective Service (CPS), she naively contacted the agency, saying that she "was having difficulties with [her] child" and that the situation was "out of control." She was interviewed by a CPS worker and noted in response to a question that she did, at times, use corporal punishment to discipline her child. Alarmed at this admission, the CPS worker promptly removed the child from the home and placed her in the temporary custody of foster parents. It was mandated that the mother complete a "parent skill training" program before the mother could regain custody. Language and cultural differences were obstacles for this young mother, and she did not regain custody of her child for over a year. Such intermittent occurrences serve as powerful reinforcers of avoidant behavior. It is not surprising that no-show rates are higher among minority clients (Tidwell, 2004).

FOUNDATIONAL PRINCIPLES IN MULTICULTURAL COUNSELING

Culturally sensitive counselors are continually mindful of a number of foundational principles. These include the activation of schema and confirmatory bias; awareness; between- versus within-group differences; racial/cultural identity development; and multiple identities.

ACTIVATION OF SCHEMAS AND CONFIRMATORY BIAS

As noted in Chapter 3, each person possesses schema and a set of values that are formed through developmental processes taking place within specific cultural contexts. The schema and values include sets of personal attitudes and assumptions that are activated in specific interpersonal contexts. Once activated, schema and associated values held by the counselor and client, respectively, flavor how each perceives and interacts with the other.

When the counselor and client engage in interpersonal communication, which is central to the process of counseling, the perceiver in the interaction integrates not only what is said and related cues (e.g., intonation, facial expression, and posture) but also information regarding the person's physical appearance, age, gender, and physical ability/disability (Kunda & Thagard, 1996). These incoming stimuli cue schema used to differentiate people according to observable characteristics. For example, once counselors categorize a client as black or white, male or female, the content of that particular schema influences what counselors perceive, how quickly they perceive it, and their interpretation of what is noticed (Fiske & Taylor, 1991).

Consider the following scenario (adapted from Payne & Cameron, 2010, p. 446):

> Counselor Sam is white and client Jay is black. Together they interact in the initial session with the best of intentions. However, Sam holds implicit biases. These are not revealed through his verbal behavior. Instead, it is recognized through subtle microbe-haviors such as less direct eye contact, increased blinking, speech errors, and less open posture and verbal friendliness (Payne & Cameron, 2010). Sam is not conscious of these subtle behaviors, but Jay picks up on them and judges Sam to be less friendly and unworthy of his full trust. If Sam holds an underlying belief that blacks tend to be aggressive, his behaviors toward Jay may be influenced, who may react with some mild "resistance" or hostility. And since Sam is not aware of his underlying beliefs, he will tend to see Jay's reaction as uncalled for and having no basis in the context. The setting up of a self-fulfilling prophesy will have the tendency to reinforce Sam's stereotype of "black males as aggressive."

To the extent that the environmental context is made hostile by the minority members' awareness of the biases that surround them, the context can function to reinforce the very stereotypes that feed them (Payne & Cameron, 2010)!

These principles of social cognition have important implications for clinical mental health counselors engaged in multicultural practice. First, schemas play critical roles in organizing persons we encounter into in-group and out-group categories. In-groups tend to be more highly valued, trusted, and favored. It is common to have biases and stereotyped attitudes about persons from out-groups, who in our society might be persons from minority groups. Because our schemas operate beyond conscious awareness, counselors must be aware of and sensitive to their personal attitudes and underlying assumptions, which may be more culturally biased than they believe.

Second, mental health professionals must recognize the potential for *confirmation bias*. This refers to a human tendency to search for information that confirms one's preexisting conceptions (Myers, 2010). For example, a counselor who holds a biased view regarding the behavioral patterns of a minority group will tend to seek out data during the assessment phase that confirm his or her preexisting schemas. Mental health counselors should carefully stay in the present and recognize when their clinical hypothesis-making moves them from observable, in-session data.

The preceding discussion highlights the necessity that mental health professionals possess accurate self-awareness and the ability to be honest with self. These skills are vital if counselors are to avoid the potential pitfalls presented by confirmatory bias and our tendency toward making in-group/out-group distinctions. Being sensitive to these tendencies helps clinical mental health counselors fulfill their primary ethical responsibility of truly respecting the dignity and promoting the welfare of their clients (ACA, 2005).

BETWEEN- VERSUS WITHIN-GROUP DIFFERENCES

For years, the mental health professions have been aware of the ethnic differences among the clients they serve. Clients raised in and who have assimilated the values of non-predominant cultures often display different customs, traditions, attitudes, and behavioral styles that are expressed in situations. Evans-Pritchard (1962) character-ized the differences between Christian and Muslim faiths this way: "A Christian man shows respect for his religion by taking off his hat and keeping on his shoes, while a Muslim man in an Arab country will show similar respect by keeping on his hat and removing his shoes" (p. 2). The implications for mental health counselors are obvious. Behaviors, similar in appearance, displayed by different clients can carry different meanings. To assume and act according to the accepted meaning of the predominant culture is a sure path leading to misunderstanding between counselor and client and, potentially, misdiagnosis and misguided interventions. Thus, mental health profes-sionals must possess baseline knowledge of the differences in and implications of the cultural backgrounds of their clients.

Yet it is risky simply to act on differences assumed to exist between the counselor and client. On practically every socially meaningful category, there are as many within-group differences as there are between-group differences. For example, it is helpful to borrow from principles of behavioral statistics. For any characteristic of a given popu-lation, we can identify a particular range, mean, and standard deviation of scores. Often, when graphed, the obtained scores take on the appearance of a normal curve. We use inferential statistics when investigating the differences that may exist between groups. Technically, a difference between groups on a given characteristic is judged as being statistically significant when the difference (or variance) between groups is greater that the difference within each group.

As noted, important differences *do* exist among the groups we serve. However, to focus only on the between-group differences while ignoring very real within-group differences opens up the potential for misunderstanding, misdiagnosis, and mistreat-ment due to counselor insensitivity to the specific client system. Functioning from the ecological perspective is the best way to find a balanced way to navigate through the sometimes erratic waters created by perceived differences between and within groups.

RACIAL/CULTURAL IDENTITY DEVELOPMENT

Persons vary in the extent to which they personally identify with their particular race or culture. Thus, one factor contributing to within-group variations is individual dif-ferences in clients' racial/cultural identity development (Atkinson et al., 2003; Sue & Sue, 2008). This model identifies five stages of identity development persons may experience as they attempt to come to terms with their minority culture in relation to the predominant culture. At each stage, personal identity is characterized by four corresponding attitudes regarding self, others of the same minority, others of different minorities, and persons of the dominant culture. Not all persons in a specific minority group experience each of the stages. Furthermore, moving through the earlier stages is not a prerequisite to being in the later stages. For example, a young person may be in stage 5 without having moved through stages 1 through 4 by virtue of being born into a particular family of origin.

Persons in the first stage, *conformity,* tend to show strong preference for the values of the dominant culture. Thus, the minority person emulates and seeks to assimilate the role models, value systems, and lifestyles of the dominant culture while devaluing self as a member of the minority group. Personal attributes that serve as minority group identifiers may be viewed with contempt and become sources of distress.

Minority persons, though, tend to have experiences with the dominant culture that contradict the assumptions and conclusions held in the conformity stage. Thus, the second stage is characterized by *dissonance,* which stems from an increased awareness that one's minority culture has strengths and is not as bad as previously believed. In addition, minority persons begin to see problems in the dominant culture. The dissonance stage, then, is marked by a questioning and challenging of previously held beliefs.

The third stage, *resistance and immersion,* occurs as minority persons move toward and endorse the values and lifestyles of their minority group. They may experience shame and guilt at having previously sold out to the dominant culture and, in a sharp turnaround, express anger at the racism and oppression that they have experienced at the hands of the dominant group. As a consequence, they distrust and dislike dominant group members.

The fourth stage is characterized by *introspection.* Here, minority members are more comfortable with self and their own heritage. This frees them to be less compelled to view culture in a dichotomous manner. As their energies move from such strong investment in highlighting the minority group against the negatives of the dominant culture, persons find a balance between minority group identification and establishing personal autonomy. They are more willing to draw from those characteristics of both their minority culture *and* the dominant culture in moving toward a sense of self-fulfillment.

In the final stage of *integrative awareness,* minority persons experience greater flexibility and inner control. They can now examine the qualities of minority and dominant cultures and take positions on issues based on an objective analysis that reflects their personal values. The views of all groups can be considered with little or no need to take the position held by any particular group. Persons in this stage are motivated to work toward the elimination of racism, prejudice, and stereotyping in all expressed forms.

ACCULTURATION

Acculturation may be defined as "the gradual physical, biological, cultural, and psychological changes that take place in individuals and groups when contact between two cultural groups takes place (Cardemil & Battle, 2003, p. 280). In multicultural societies, it is common for individuals or groups from one culture to move into a region dominated by another cultural group. Pressure is exerted on those of the minority culture to conform with and accommodate the norms and mores of the dominant group while simultaneously abandoning and devaluing their own cultural roots.

People experience and navigate through these pressures differently (Cuellar, 2000). For some, both the ways and values of minority persons' own and dominant culture are valued. Such may be the case for the first-generation immigrant who experiences the economic and social benefits reaped through successful employment in U.S. urban settings. Yet the native language and practices of his or her culture are maintained in the home. For others, though, the dissonance between their own culture and the lifestyle and values of the dominant culture can be a source of individual and familial stress. Consider the eighth-grade student who masters English as a second language, establishes a strong social network of close friends who are native to the dominant culture, and actively participates in a wide range of school and extracurricular activities. However, in the home, the language and ways of the native culture are practiced. The child's parents might be alarmed at and discipline the child for the display of behaviors and attitudes that are widely accepted in the dominant culture but viewed as unacceptable within the perspective of their native culture. The accompanying revision stress can result in increased vulnerability to certain health problems and the development of psychological symptoms (Cuellar, 2000).

Clinical mental health counselors should be mindful of the ways in which acculturation-related issues can influence the process of counseling. For example, clients' preference for particular counselors might be influenced by the extent to which clients have assimilated the values of the dominant culture. Minority clients who devalue their original culture might actually desire to be seen by a counselor from the dominant culture. Furthermore, differing levels of cultural assimilation and accommodation among family members might be powerful dynamics underlying the presenting problem. Thus, a culturally insensitive conceptualization of the presenting problem might lead to treatment of the oppositional child with little consideration of the underlying conflict in cultural values. It is also possible that a child may be referred for counseling services when, in fact, the behaviors in question are socially appropriate when viewed through the lens of the family's native culture. In such instances, advocacy and psychoeducational interventions directed to referral sources might be indicated.

MULTIPLE IDENTITIES

Our ability to gain full and accurate understanding of the clients we serve will be incomplete if we take a narrow view of personal identity. One's racial/cultural identity, important as it may be, does not develop or express itself in a vacuum; nor does it define personal identity. As noted by Das (1995), there is simply no one-to-one correspondence between the ethnographic description of a cultural group and the psychological makeup of a particular individual belonging to that group. Differences in personal identities are best conceptualized by considering the manner in which a variety of identity constructs interact and converge to form one's unique personal identity. Thus, each person is best viewed as being composed of multiple identities (Robinson-Wood, 2012).

Arrendondo (Arrendondo, 1992; Arrendondo & Toporek, 1996) has identified three dimensions of personal identity that must be considered if assessment and treatment are to be effective. The A dimensions include those characteristics into which people are born, such as gender, sexual orientation, race, culture, socioeconomic status, and physical abilities/disabilities. In contrast, B dimensions include those personal characteristics that are less visible but are influenced by the person's achievements, such as work experience, academic background and performance, religion, hobbies, and marital status. The C dimensions are specific historical events that affect the direction and quality of the person's life.

The contents of the three dimensions as identified by Arrendondo (1992) may require modification in light of identity development and experiences of persons who have multiple heritage backgrounds. Until recently, racial classification systems have assumed single racial or ethnic identities. In such contexts, biracial or multiple race persons do not easily fit into existing race-related social constructs. What are the personal and developmental consequences for persons who sit on the lines that have historically demarcated racial identity? Henriksen and Paladino (2009) note how the multiple heritage individuals experience life and development differently than monoracial minority or majority persons. This plot thickens as one adds ethnicity, gender, and sexual identity into the mix, all of which is embedded in unique ecological contexts.

Henriksen and Paladino (2009) present a multiple heritage identify development model (MHID) to assist counselors in understanding, being sensitive to, and working with persons of multiple heritage. It takes into consideration several sources of personal identity including: ethnicity, gender, sexual orientation, national origin, religion/spirituality, indigenous heritage, and language. Each is expressed and interacts within persons as they interact in their environments. The following six stages are (Henrikson & Paladino, 2009, pp. 37–40):

1. *Recognition* Identification with multiple heritages;
2. *Transition* Inner search for identity;
3. *Experimentation* Seeking a group with which to identify;
4. *Awareness* Awareness of multiple identities;
5. *Acceptance* Recognize and accept basic differences between people;
6. *Neutrality* Lack of difference recognition.

Their model is not linear or age-related. Persons may cycle through and return to any of the stages, and may not experience each stage.

Although being mindful that the three dimensions of identity and related models described above can raise the counselor's awareness to issues of diversity, a truly holistic view of the client can be achieved only as the quality of interaction and integration among these constructs is understood. To do so, mental health counselors rely on the ecological perspective (Bronfenbrenner, 1979, 1989) and clinical mental health counseling paradigm (Chapter 3) as foundational pillars. Clients incorporate into their personal identities ideas, values, attitudes, and behaviors from their multileveled environmental contexts. The process is dynamic and interactive but not necessarily reciprocal.

Thus, the old adage that "the whole is greater than the sum of its parts" holds true for counselors striving to develop a holistic understanding of and appreciation for the diverse clients they serve. Knowing that a particular client is Hispanic/African American, male, Catholic, single, a father, and living in the south side of Chicago helps the counselor to grasp the complexity of the client's makeup. Knowledge of the generic descriptions of each descriptor and treating descriptors as though their boundaries are impenetrable creates a barrier to understanding the person. To understand and appreciate that unique person for who he or she is, the counselor must go beyond the superficial gathering of data regarding each characteristic. This is accomplished by listening to the client's story, seeking out information that clarifies the nature and quality of these interacting identities, and comprehending the personal meanings as they are perceived by the client from within his or her particular frame of reference.

THE CULTURALLY COMPETENT COUNSELOR

This chapter has discussed the changed face of American society, which is truly multicultural in its composition. In response, many counselors have become increasingly aware of numerous barriers to effective counseling that occur when traditional models and delivery systems are applied in a "one size fits all" manner to meet the needs of diverse populations. It is in this context that multicultural competencies have become necessary skills for effective professional practice.

In the early 1990s, the leadership of the Association of Multicultural Counseling and Development assumed responsibility for assisting "mental health professions in recognizing the assets of culture, ethnicity, race, and other social identities as indelible dimensions of every human being, and for addressing concerns about ethical practice" (Arrendondo & Toporek, 2004, p. 45). The then presidents of the AMCD directed the AMCD's Professional Standards Committee to prepare a set of Multicultural Counseling Competencies (Sue, Arrendondo, & McDavis, 1992) that were operationalized as specific beliefs, attitudes, knowledge, and skills (Arrendondo & Toporek, 1996).

Arrendondo (1999, p. 103) notes several operating premises running through the list of Multicultural Counseling Competencies:

1. All counseling is cross-cultural.
2. All counseling happens in a context influenced by institutional and societal biases and norms.
3. The relationships described are primarily between a white counselor and clients of ethnic racial minority status.
4. Constituencies most often marginalized and about which counselors have been least prepared to serve are from Asian, black/African American, Latino, and Native American heritage.
5. Counseling is a culture-bound profession.

Supporting this entire effort is the underlying assumption that the effectiveness and ethical conduct of mental health and community counselors are enhanced when training programs are culturally sound.

The Multicultural Counseling Competencies (Arrendondo et al., 1996; Sue et al., 1992) set standards for the development of beliefs and attitudes, knowledge, and skills in three specific domains: the counselor's self-awareness of personal beliefs, attitudes, values, and assumptions; understanding the worldview of the client; and the development of appropriate intervention strategies (Arrendondo, 1999). These are summarized in Table 9.1.

TABLE 9.1 Summary of the Multicultural Counselor Competencies		**Cultural Awareness of One's Assumptions, Values, and Biases**	**Understanding the Worldview of the Culturally Different Client**	**Developing Appropriate Intervention Strategies and Techniques**
	Beliefs and Attitudes	• Identifies own culture/cultural groups from which counselor derives significant beliefs and attitudes • Recognizes impact of one's beliefs on ability to respect persons of other groups • Identifies learned cultural attitudes that both demonstrate and hinder respect • Recognizes limits of their multicultural competencies	• Understands how personal assumptions can be similar to and different from members of that group, and how these influence counseling interactions • Understands how personal emotional reactions could influence counseling effectiveness • Understands how race, ethnicity, culture, and minority status influences personality development, display and recognition of normal/abnormal behaviors, and utilization of counseling services	• Respects client's religious and spiritual beliefs, values, and practices as they contribute to wellness, level of functioning, and the indigenous helping process • Values bilingualism • Recognizes operation of fundamental attribution errors (i.e., the tendency to blame others for their circumstances)

TABLE 9.1 (Continued)		Cultural Awareness of One's Assumptions, Values, and Biases	Understanding the Worldview of the Culturally Different Client	Developing Appropriate Intervention Strategies and Techniques
			• Recognizes the socio-political forces that influence the lives of racial and ethnic minorities	
	Knowledge	• Awareness of how their cultural heritage influences view of healthy and unhealthy mental health and behavior • Possesses understanding of oppression, racism, discrimination, and stereotyping and capability of acknowledging own racist attitudes, feelings, beliefs • Understands the social impact that personal communication style and relating has on those of diverse backgrounds.	• Can articulate differences in verbal and nonverbal behavior of the 5 major cultural groups • Describes 2 models of minority identity development • Explain history of ethnic groups • Identifies within group differences • Discusses viewpoints of other cultural groups regarding major issues • Becomes aware of how own cultural socialization shapes intolerance and disrespectful attitudes • Understand how race, culture, etc. may affect	• Can articulate context in which traditional theories have developed and inherent cultural biases contained in their underlying presuppositions and explicit goals and techniques • Aware of institutional barriers operating in the counseling service delivery system that inhibits utilization by racial/ethnic minority groups • Aware of potential cultural biases and misuses of traditional counseling appraisal and assessment tools • Possesses knowledge of diverse family/community structures and dynamics and their inherent strengths

TABLE 9.1

(Continued)

	Cultural Awareness of One's Assumptions, Values, and Biases	Understanding the Worldview of the Culturally Different Client	Developing Appropriate Intervention Strategies and Techniques
		personal formation	• Understands the nature of social and cultural prejudice and discrimination and its influence on personal well-being of clients
Skills	• Recognizes own limitations relative to culture and seeks out professional development experiences to improve understanding and skills in working with culturally different clients • Actively seeks to enhance understanding of diverse cultures and to develop a non-racist personal identity	• Familiar with pertinent and current research regarding mental health and illness as it relates to cultural diverse populations • Participates in multicultural activities outside of the counseling setting or vocation to promote an understanding of other ethnic groups and cultures that goes beyond mere academic training • Becomes involved with minority individuals outside counseling setting	• Skilled in application of various verbal and nonverbal helping responses in language of client • Able to apply counseling technique with flexibility so that specific approaches used are a good fit for the needs of the culturally different client • Able to apply systemic and advocacy interventions on behalf of the oppressed and victims of discrimination • Educates clients in counseling process, legal and ethical concerns

Culturally competent counselors share certain characteristics. First, they are aware of the underlying assumptions, values, beliefs, and attitudes they bring to the counseling relationship. They are in touch with their *cultural selves* and recognize the manner in which their attitudes, thoughts, feelings, and behaviors have been shaped by cultural forces. In addition, they grasp the extent to which forces of the predominant culture have influenced the course of their personal development and how these forces operate within their particular ecological context. And if they are white, non-Hispanic counselors, they understand the advantages of their privileged position in society and its association to power and overt/covert oppression. These attitudes and sets of knowledge and skills help mental health and community counselors relate to and empathize with the culturally different. As a consequence, their ability to establish and maintain an effective therapeutic relationship is enhanced.

Second, competent multicultural counselors assume the responsibility of becoming aware, knowledgeable, and skilled about other ethnic groups (Arrendondo, 1999). Counselors' self-awareness of their own culture forms the base for understanding the worldview of others. This is more than a mere academic exercise in which counselors-in-training learn about the worldview characteristics of specific cultural groups. Rather, all counselors learn about the ongoing, dynamic interactions among culturally different clients, their particular group, the various elements of their immediate sphere, and society. A working knowledge that expresses itself in practical skill is best developed when counselors step out of their cultural boundaries and actively participate in community events, celebrations, and meetings of other cultural groups. In other words, they benefit from seeing the culture of others in action rather than through the pages of a book. Thus, the goal is to gain knowledge of the worldview of the culturally different that is ecologically contextualized.

Third, culturally competent mental health and community counselors develop a repertoire of strategies and techniques that enable them to effectively and sensitively intervene in the lives of the culturally different clients they serve (Arrendondo, 1999). They recognize the limitations of traditional models of counseling, which has been prepared, cooked, and simmered in the kettle of the predominant culture. Such concoctions have left many ingredients out, resulting in a less flavorful and fulfilling product. Specifically, competent counselors acquire culturally sensitive interviewing skills, assessment techniques, and sets of intervention strategies that are sensitive to and effective in treating the *full* range of human behaviors expressed in its cultural context. Indigenous practices and referral resources can be important components of the comprehensive treatment plan.

The cultural competency guidelines (Arrendondo & Toporek, 1996; Sue et al., 1992) have not been met with universal acceptance. Thomas and Weinrach (2004; Weinrach & Thomas, 2002), in fact, have declared that the AMCD multicultural counseling competencies are extremely flawed. Specifically, they state that to focus exclusively on issues of race and ethnicity, in itself, is racist. Furthermore, they contend that the set of competencies lacks an empirical base. It is questioned whether any set of competencies should be imposed on mental health professionals (Thomas & Weinrach, 2004). Arrendondo and Toporek (2004) counter these arguments by noting that the competencies have been endorsed by the ACA and American Psychological Association. They conclude that multicultural competency "is becoming a way of life" for mental health professionals and anticipate a widespread positive response from counselors, educators, and researchers (Arrendondo & Toporek, 2004, p. 53).

CONCLUSION

In this chapter, we have moved from establishing the rationale that gave birth to the multicultural counseling movement to identifying foundational principles and specific competencies for its practice. Most multicultural counseling theorists and researchers conclude that the practice of multicultural counseling is much more than the application of intervention recipes from a techniques cookbook for application with members of specific racial or ethnic minorities. Most agree that the effectiveness of multicultural mental health interventions hinges on the application of specified skills with special sensitivity to the multiple identities of the particular client(s) being served. This is viewed as attending to the ecological context of culturally diverse clients.

It strikes me as odd, though, that given all of the rhetoric about being aware and sensitive to the operation of Western presuppositions in the practice of mental health counseling, we seem to stumble into the very trap that we warn against. Namely, our conceptualization of multicultural counseling seems too often to be laced with the individualistic bias that is so prominent in traditional theory and techniques.

What ultimate good do we accomplish if we, as counselor educators, produce mental health counselors who are multiculturally competent but who practice in settings whose structures, policies, and procedures exemplify the presuppositions, values, and worldviews of the predominant culture? This new breed of counselor could be extremely sensitive to and skilled in the treatment of clients from diverse groups. But if the cultural values and assumptions are, indeed, institutionalized, relatively few minority persons in need of our services will voluntarily seek them out. Is this fourth force in the counseling profession powerful enough to influence the many institutional barriers that prevent effective outreach to minority groups? Or has the individualized focus of our cultural lenses prevented us from developing ecologically relevant, systematic interventions to overcome these institutional barriers? Does our continuing emphasis on treating identified clients reflect the extent to which our "culturally sensitive talk" is much stronger than our "walk"?

For example, is not a cultural and institutional bias of the mental health system in operation when children of color are served in disproportionate numbers through special education and juvenile justice systems rather than through alternative community mental health options? In addition, numerous policies have institutionalized practitioner and agency behavior that predates contemporary concern over diversity issues. These policies and procedures should be revisited. It is no longer reasonable to have token representation in leadership roles of persons whose roots are in minority culture but who no longer maintain any direct tie to that culture (Mason, Benjamin, & Lewis, 1996). Members of the community should be allowed to make a larger contribution to the direction of agency policy and operations. The physical appearance of the agency, including its décor, locations, name, hours of operation, reading materials in the waiting room, and its furnishings can better reflect the diversity of the clients and, actually, "jump-start a positive relationship" (p. 177).

We do well to recognize the extent to which the profession of counseling is, in many ways, a unique culture. It has socialized many of us to view our worlds in particular ways. We have learned to speak a unique language with various nuances that carry specific meanings to its members. A particular set of values is held and advocated on that platform. The counseling culture also reflects a particular view of wellness and mental health and a process through which both may be attained.

From an ecological perspective, then, mental health community counselors need to recognize not only the interaction of cultures at the individualistic level as the counselor meets with a client. Although it is important that counselors bring multicultural competencies to the relationship, it is vital that they be aware of the clash among the culture of counselors, client systems, and that of the larger society. As we advocate for causes the counseling profession holds dear, we might experience frustrations that result from the unavailability of funding to update physical structures or change locations of our treatment facilities and the plodding bureaucratic process that prevents the development and implementation of policies and procedures more sensitive to the cultural variations of our constituencies. But when we have strong emotional reactions to such barriers to change, some of us for the first time in our lives might be coming face to face with and experiencing the dynamics of power, partiality, bias, prejudice, and discrimination that operate on us as members of a minority culture. We, indeed, have many lessons to learn.

DISCUSSION QUESTIONS

1. Discuss the following statement: "Given the interactional nature of the counseling process, all counselor-client relationships are multicultural." Do you agree with this statement? How, specifically, can a counseling interaction be truly multicultural when the counselor and client are members of the same culture?
2. In your future practice, to what extent will you seek to serve clients of diverse cultural backgrounds? If so, what specific steps will you take to ensure that your professional practice is culturally sensitive?
3. Identify and briefly discuss the four components of cultural encapsulation. Identify which component would be most difficult for you to overcome. Explain why.
4. Are there times in which it is appropriate and necessary to overstep the boundaries of the traditional delivery system of mental health services to meet the various needs of the culturally different client? Identify specific examples. How would you do so in ways that are ethically and professionally responsible?

SUGGESTED ACTIVITIES

1. Identify a civil rights leader or individual who is culturally different from you and who has influenced you personally. Name the specific characteristics of this person that you admire and which have been influential. In what ways have you attempted to live out the characteristics in your personal life?

2. Identify a person you know who is culturally different from you. Set a time to discuss with this person the ways in which you are similar and different from him or her. Consider perspectives on time, family, politics, spirituality, religions, sexuality, work and productivity, individuality, and consumerism. The goal of this activity is to increase your personal awareness of your cultural heritage relative to the heritage of others.

3. Conduct a class exercise in which each person brings to class and discusses an object that is symbolic or a metaphor of an important aspect of that person's culture. This can be a fun and informative way of learning more about the cultural diversity that surrounds you.

4. Invite the director of a community mental health center or mental health association to speak to the class about the cultural barriers to receiving adequate mental health services and efforts to make such services more accessible to culturally diverse populations.

REFERENCES

American Mental Health Counselors Association. (2010). *Code of ethics of the American Mental Health Counselors Association–2010 revision.* Alexandria, VA: Author.

Anderson, N. B. (2003). *Unraveling the mystery of racial and ethnic health disparities: Who, what, when, where, how and especially, why?* Boston, MA: Institute on Urban Health Research, Northeastern University.

Angel, R. J., & Williams, K. (2000). Cultural models of health and illness (pp. 25–44). In I. Cuéllar & F. A. Paniagua (Eds.), *Handbook of multicultural mental health.* San Diego, CA: Academic Press.

American Psychological Association. (2004). Guidelines on multicultural education, training, research, practice, and organizational change for psychologists. *American Psychologist, 58,* 377–402.

Arrendondo, P. (1992). Latina/Latino counseling and psychotherapy: Tape 1. *Cultural consideration for working more effectively with Latin Americans.* Amherst, MA: Microtraining and Multicultural Development.

Arrendondo, P. (1999). Multicultural counseling competencies as tools to address oppression and racism. *Journal of Counseling and Development, 77,* 102–108.

Arrendondo, P., & Toporek, R. (1996). Operationalization of the multicultural counseling competencies. *Journal of Multicultural Counseling and Development, 24,* 42–79.

Atkinson, D. R., Morten, G., & Sue, D. W. (2003). *Counseling American minorities* (6th ed.). New York, NY: McGraw-Hill.

Baruth, L. G., & Manning, M. L. (2012). *Multicultural counseling and psychotherapy: A lifespan approach* (5th ed.). Upper Saddle River, NJ: Pearson Education.

Bronfenbrenner, U. (1947). Research planning in neuropsychiatry and clinical psychology in the veterans administration. *Journal of Clinical Psychology, 3,* 33–38.

Bronfenbrenner, U. (1989). Ecological systems theory. *Annals of Child Development, 6,* 187–249.

Cardemil, E. V., & Battle, C. L. (2003). Guess who's coming to therapy? Getting comfortable with conversations about race and ethnicity in psychotherapy. *Professional Psychology: Research and Practice, 34,* 278–286.

Cokley, K., Hall-Clark, B., & Hicks, D. (2011). Ethnic minority-majority status and mental health: The mediating role of perceived discrimination. *Journal of Mental Health Counseling, 33,* 342–263.

Cook, E. P. (2012). *Understanding people in context: The ecological perspective in counseling.* Alexandria, VA: American Counseling Association.

Council for the Accreditation of Counseling and Related Educational Programs. (2009a). *2009 Standards.* Alexandria, VA: Author.

Cuellar, I. (2000). Acculturation and mental health: Ecological transactional relations of adjustment. In I. Cuellar & F. A. Paniagua (Eds.), *Handbook of multicultural mental health: Assessment and treatment of diverse populations* (pp. 45–62). New York, NY: Academic Press.

Das, A. K. (1995). Rethinking multicultural counseling: Implications for counselor education. *Journal of Counseling and Development, 74,* 45–53.

Dell, P. F. (1980). The Hopi family therapist and the Aristotelian parents. *Journal of Marital and Family Therapy,* **, 123–129.

Evans, M. P., Valadez, A. V., Burns, S., & Rodriquez, V. (2002). Brief and nontraditional approaches to mental health counseling: Practitioners' attitudes. *Journal of Mental Health Counseling, 24,* 317–329.

Evans-Pritchard, E. (1962). *Social anthropology and other essays.* New York: Free Press.

Fiske, S. T., & Taylor, S. E. (1991). *Social cognition* (2nd ed.). New York, NY: McGraw-Hill.

Gopaul-McNicol, S., & Brice-Baker, J. (1998). *Cross-cultural practice: Assessment, treatment, and training.* New York, NY: Wiley.

Henriksen, R. C., & Paladino, D. A. (2009). Identity development in a multiple heritage world. In R. C. Henrikson, & D. A. Paladino (Eds.), *Counseling multiple heritage individuals, couples, and families.* Alexandria, VA: American Counseling Association.

Hernandez, M., Isaacs, M. R., Nesman, T., & Burns, D. (1998). Perspectives on culturally competent systems of care. In M. Hernandez & M. R. Isaacs (Eds.). *Promoting cultural competence in children's mental health services.* Baltimore, MD: Paul H. Brooks.

Jones, J. M. (1997). *Prejudice and racism* (2nd ed.). New York, NY: McGraw-Hill.

Jones, E. E., & Harris, V. A. (1967). The attribution of attitudes. *Journal of Experimental Social Psychology, 3,* 2–24.

Kunda, Z., & Thagard, P. (1996). Forming impressions from stereotypes, traits, and behaviors: A parallel-constraint-satisfaction theory. *Psychological Review, 103,* 284–308.

Lefley, H. P. (2010). Mental health systems in a cross-cultural context (pp. 135–161). In T. L. Scheid, & T. N. Brown (Eds.), *A handbook for the study of mental health: Social context, theories, and systems* (2nd ed.). New York, NY: Cambridge University Press.

Locke, D. C. (1992). *Increasing multicultural understanding: A comprehensive model.* Newbury Park, CA: Sage.

Mason, J. L., Benjamin, M. P., & Lewis, S. A. (1996). The cultural competence model: Implications for child and family mental health services. In C. A. Heflinger & C. T. Nixon (Eds.), *Families and the mental health system for children and adolescents: Policy, services, and research.* Thousand Oaks, CA: Sage.

Midgette, T. E., & Meggert, S. S. (1991). Multicultural counseling instruction: A challenge for faculties in the 21st century. *Journal of Counseling and Development, 70,* 136–141.

Myers, D. G. (2010). *Social psychology* (10th ed.). New York, NY: McGraw-Hill.

Payne, B. K., & Cameron, C. D. (2010). Divided minds, divided morals: How implicit social cognition underpins and undermines our sense of social justice (pp. 445–460). In B. Gawroski, & B. K. Payne (Eds.), *Handbook of implicit social cognition: Measurement, theory, and applications.* New York, NY: Guilford Press.

Pedersen, P. (1990). The multicultural perspective as a fourth force in counseling. *Journal of Mental Health Counseling, 12,* 93–95.

Pedersen, P. (1991). Multiculturalism as a generic approach to counseling. *Journal of Counseling and Development, 70,* 6–12.

Pedersen, P. (1994). *A handbook for developing multicultural awareness* (2nd ed.). Alexandria, VA: American Counseling Association.

Robinson-Wood, T. L. (2012). *The convergence of race, ethnicity, and gender: Multiple identities in counseling* (4th ed.). Upper Saddle River, NJ: Pearson Education.

Sanchez, A. R. (2001). Multicultural family counseling: Toward cultural sensibility. In J. G. Ponterotto, J. M. Casas, L. A. Suzuki, & C. M. Alexander (Eds.), *Handbook of multicultural counseling* (2nd ed.). Thousand Oaks, CA: Sage.

Sherer, R. A. (March 2002). Surgeon general's report highlights mental health problems among minorities. *Psychiatric Times, 19*(3). Retrieved August 9, 2004, from http://www.psychiatrictimes.com/p020301a.html

Smart, D. W., & Smart, J. F. (1997). *DSM-IV* and culturally sensitive diagnosis: Some observations for counselors. *Journal of Counseling and Development, 75,* 392–398.

Sue, D. W., & Sue, D. (2008). *Counseling the culturally diverse: Theory and practice* (5th ed.). New York, NY: Wiley.

Sue, D. W. (2010). *Microaggressions in everyday life: Race, gender, and sexual orientation.* Hoboken, NJ: Wiley.

Sue, D. W., Arrendondo, P., & McDavis, R. J. (1992). Multicultural counseling competencies and standards: A call to the profession. *Journal of Counseling and Development, 70,* 477–483.

Thomas, K. R., & Weinrach, S. G. (2004). Mental health counseling and the AMCD multicultural counseling competencies: A civil debate. *Journal of Mental Health Counseling, 26,* 41–43.

Tidwell, R. (2004). The "no-show" phenomenon and the issue of resistance among African-American female patients at an urban health care center. *Journal of Mental health Counseling, 26,* 1–12.

U.S. Census Bureau. (2003). *People: Race and ethnicity.* Retrieved July 24, 2004, from http://factfinder2.census.gov/faces/nav/jsf/pages/index.xhtml

U.S. Census Bureau. (2010a). Income, poverty, and health insurance coverage in the United States: 2009. Retrieved from http://www.census.gov/newsroom/releases/archives/income_wealth/cb10-144.html

U.S. Census Bureau. (2010b). *2010 census shows America's diversity.* Washington, DC: U.S. Department of Commerce.

Walton, E., Berasi, K., Takeuchi, D. T., & Uehara, E. S. (2010). Cultural diversity and mental health treatment (pp. 439–460). In T. L. Scheid, & T. N. Brown (Eds.), *A handbook for the study of mental health: Social contexts, theories, and systems* (2nd ed.). New York, NY: Cambridge University Press.

Weinrach, S. G., & Thomas, K. R. (2002). A critical analysis of the multicultural counseling competencies: Implications for the practice of mental health counseling. *Journal of Mental Health Counseling, 24,* 20–35.

Wrenn, C. G. (1962). The culturally encapsulated counselor. *Harvard Educational Review, 32,* 444–449.

Zuckerman, M. (1990). Some dubious premises in research and theory on racial differences: Scientific, social, and ethical issues. *American Psychologist, 45,* 1297–1303.

Part 3

Contemporary Issues and Trends

10

Managed Care and Third-Party Reimbursement

OUTLINE

Managed Care in Context

What Is Managed Care?

Impact on the Practice of Mental Health Counseling

Conclusion: Surviving in the Era of Managed Care

I entered the counseling profession as an individual and family counselor in 1983. The small, not-for-profit, mental health agency that I worked for specialized in what was viewed as brief therapy. Clients were scheduled for sessions at varying intervals and might be seen over the course of a year or so. However, the average number of sessions scheduled for typical clients in outpatient counseling ranged from 12 to 20. The agency set fees on a sliding fee scale and billed insurance companies for services rendered. A copayment of 20% was the norm for most clients' insurance plans that provided mental health benefits. In addition, these plans set limits on the maximum benefit for outpatient treatment. Sometimes the number of sessions per year was limited to 50. Other policies set a maximum annual payout for outpatient treatment at $2,000.

Although insurance companies occasionally audited the agency's business and clinical recordkeeping practices, counselors at the agency were able to assess, diagnose, and treat clients with a great deal of autonomy. After conducting the initial interview and assessment, counselors devised a treatment plan and, collaborating with the client, set explicit goals and objectives and estimated time frames for accomplishing the goals and objectives. They also listed the specific treatment approaches they planned to use in the case. The resulting document, which was reviewed by our clinical supervisor, served as a therapeutic contract between the client and the counselor, guiding the treatment and monitoring the outcome. Insurance companies were billed and reimbursement occurred at regular intervals. The treatment process was within the control of the counselor.

The process just described seems like a distant memory for most veteran mental health care providers. Few would have predicted the shift in professional practice that has occurred due, in large measure, to the advent of managed care. Most practitioners have been required to alter how they conduct and manage counseling. A number of private practitioners have been forced out of business. The change in the profession has been so great that some refer to it as the "mental health care revolution" (Zimet, 1989).

This chapter addresses the contemporary practice of mental health counseling in the managed care environment. Responses to the following questions are explored: Was managed care a mental health care revolution and a radical shift that came "out of the blue"? Or was it a logical response to the rising costs in health care, which had reached crisis proportions? What is managed care? How does it, in fact, manage care? What procedures does it implement to control the costs of service? How have mental health practitioners reacted and responded to managed care?

MANAGED CARE IN CONTEXT

FINANCIAL RISK AND THE RISE OF INSURANCE COMPANIES

It is typically stated or inferred that the manner in which mental health care is now managed and delivered in the United States represents a radical shift from how business was once conducted. Several decades ago, procedures such as pretreatment authorization, utilization reviews, capitation, and other incentives for "efficient treatment providers" were not part of the mental health care environment. However, it is important to recognize the extent to which the history of third-party reimbursement for physical and mental disorders has contributed to the current situation.

Through the mid-1800s, society was much less fragmented. It was more rural and agrarian and less mobile. The population was less dense, and resources to meet the needs of society were virtually inaccessible for many. When unexpected needs arose, resources were pooled so that families and other small social units, such as churches or loosely woven community associations, were able to "take care of their own."

The Amish culture provides us with a contemporary model of social support that was much more common in the past. The Amish religion prohibits participation in insurance plans. Thus, when tragedy strikes, Amish people are on their own. Amish families support each other with money, goods, and services in times of crisis. For example, when a barn is ignited by lightning and burns to the ground, families from the surrounding area organize and assist in the cleanup and rebuilding of the structure. They have a barn raising and, in a matter of days, have the burned-out structure cleared away and a new barn constructed in its place. When a young child suffers from a heart condition and requires open heart surgery, Amish families band together and provide financial support for the required medical services. The social group operates according to the principles of modified communalism. Thus, financial risk is spread to all members of the group when a hardship besets any of its members.

By the mid to late 1800s, Western society was being influenced by increased industrialization and urbanization. Among the consequences were loosened kinship ties and a decreased sense of community and shared meaning (Cushman, 1995). People were much more vulnerable to the increased risk of injury and occupational hazard. Various sorts of insurance programs began to spring up by the mid-1800s to protect families by the pooling of financial risk. In this way, insurance plans began to fill the void created by loosened social and familial ties (Faulkner, 1960). Initially, accident insurance programs arose in England to cover medical expenses for injuries that did not lead to death (Throckmorton, 1998). In 1864, the Travelers Insurance Company of Hartford was established, and by 1866, 60 different insurers existed in the United States to provide coverage for injury as well as for health and sickness (Faulkner, 1960; Throckmorton, 1998).

In 1883, Germany became the first nation to legislate national health insurance. Other European countries soon followed suit (Throckmorton, 1998). In the United States, national health insurance was promoted by the Socialist Party as early as 1904. President Woodrow Wilson proposed a national health care plan in the 1920s in an attempt to improve labor-management relations (Numbers, 1984). However, his proposal failed. Although the American Medical Association supported such proposals initially, its support weakened considerably when limits on reimbursement for medical care were included in the package (Numbers, 1984).

Citizens of the United States were hard hit by the devastating impact of the Great Depression, and calls for national health insurance were renewed (Numbers, 1984). In this context, Congress experienced increased pressure to develop a national program that would provide at least minimal coverage for all citizens. The forerunner to Blue Cross/Blue Shield developed in 1929 when a group of schoolteachers arranged for Baylor University Hospital to provide health care in exchange for a monthly prepayment (Throckmorton, 1998).

This model took hold, and in 1937, the Health Service Plan Commission was established to oversee the Blue Cross plans, which were becoming more numerous across the country (Throckmorton, 1998). Blue Cross covered expenses for physician services in the hospital. Blue Shield was developed in 1939 and provided coverage for medical expenses for outpatient physician services outside. The success of Blue Cross/Blue Shield, the emergence of the United States from the Great Depression, and the nation's involvement in World War II led to a rapid increase in the number of health care insurers (Faulkner, 1960). During the 1950s and 1960s, insurance policies rapidly expanded the range of benefits. Policies could now be written that covered not only health issues, but also vision, dentistry, and prescriptions for medicine.

With the passage of the Community Mental Health Centers Act of 1963, increased acceptance of counseling and decreased stigma of the recipients of such services led to the coverage of mental health services in insurance plans. Mental health benefits have often taken center stage in the national discussion over rising health care costs (Wiggins, 1988).

THE PUSH TOWARD MANAGED CARE

Chambliss (2000, p. 26) notes that until the late 1970s, the delivery of health care in the United States was guided by two underlying assumptions: "The doctor knows best" and "We must spend whatever is necessary." By the 1980s, though, treatment guided by these principles was beginning to be viewed as "deluxe" and excessively expensive. The prevailing U.S. political philosophy under the Reagan administration emphasized decreased involvement of federal regulation and an increased role for the private sector in a free market to regulate health care costs. It was the prevailing economic and political context of the 1980s that facilitated the rapid development and expansion of managed care.

The costs of health care had become excessive. Mirin and Sederer (1994) note that, in 1965, payments for health care in the United States totaled approximately $42 billion. By 1985, these costs had multiplied 10-fold to $442.3 billion. In the next 7 years, health care costs doubled to over $800 billion. By the early 1990s, health care costs were rising at a rate three times greater than the rate of inflation and were consuming more than 14% of the gross national product (Polkinghorne, 2001). The typical American family spent 16.4% of its income on health care (H. B. Smith, 1999). In addition, the cost of mental health care had increased at a rate that exceeded the increased cost of health care in general (H. B. Smith, 1999). From 1987 to 1992, the annual benefit cost per employee for substance abuse and mental health coverage jumped from $163 to $400 (Mirin & Sederer, 1994). Of this amount, outpatient mental health care accounted for about 3% to 4%. As of 2008, the costs of health care were doubling every five years (Cummings & O'Donohue, 2008).

Employers bore the burden of this financial expense (Ceniceros, 2001). In 1963, employers were spending, on the average, between 4 and 8 cents per dollar of profit for employees' health care benefits. By 1990, that amount had increased to around 50 cents per profit dollar. These costs were projected to continue their upward spiral. Increasingly, employers are passing the costs of premiums on to employees, who are less likely to complain in the context of the current tough job market.

A second factor contributing to the move toward managed care was findings suggesting that unnecessary services were being provided and consequently billed to third-party reimbursers. Insurance companies had long suspected that diagnostic categories were being applied loosely, the claims for which were submitted for reimbursement. The findings of Vessey and Howard (1993) provided some support for the validity of such suspicions. Their study, in which data were pooled from a number of epidemiological surveys, reported that as many as 50% of persons being seen in psychotherapy were being treated for disorders that did not meet the diagnostic criteria in the *DSM* (the American Psychiatric Association's *Diagnostic and Statistical Manual of Mental Disorders;* (Vessey & Howard, 1993). What is sometimes referred to as *updiagnosing* occurs when the mental health practitioner gives a reimbursable diagnosis to a client who does not fully meet the *DSM* criteria so that the third-party reimburser will pay instead of the client (Cummings & O'Donohue, 2008). Such fraudulent practices are unethical and illegal.

The managed health care movement emerged from the aforementioned trends. This movement has been driven by the need to control spiraling health care costs. To control costs, managed care has replaced the traditional fee-for-service system and has placed limits on the amount and types of services rendered by providers (Segal, 2006). In doing so, managed care has made a significant impact on the way mental health services are delivered, regardless of discipline (Scheid, 2010; H. B. Smith, 1999). Experts from the managed care industry believe that the implementation of recent health care reform laws, such as the Patient Protection and Affordable Care Act (2010), will inspire an increase in efforts to cut the costs and improve the efficiency of service delivery ("Four Industry Insiders," 2011).

WHAT IS MANAGED CARE?

The bottom line of all managed care efforts is the containment of the costs of health services. Total health care costs may be calculated from the following formula (Broskowski & Marks, 1992):

$$\text{total costs} = \text{utilization} \times \text{cost per unit.}$$

Attempts at containing the costs of mental health care are directed toward managing the frequency with which specific services are used and the fees associated with those services.

Related to the goal of cost containment is the focus on accountability, to ensure efficiency and value (Chambliss, 2000). From the viewpoint of a third-party reimburser, the value of a service lies in a significant and positive outcome resulting from the investment of time and resources. The true value of a specific mental health service is determined by the nature and extent of client goal attainment and satisfaction in relationship to the cost of the particular service. The following formula is helpful in evaluating proposed services for clients (Chambliss, 2000):

$$\text{value} = \frac{\text{desired outcomes} - \text{adverse}}{\text{cost}}$$

As Chambliss (2000) notes, both the numerator and the denominator must be addressed if the value of a service is to be demonstrated. We are reminded here that clients are consumers of a service. And like most of us, they are always seeking a better value for their dollar (Cummings & O'Donohue, 2008). In practice, it is much easier to demonstrate reduction in cost than it is to provide definitive evidence regarding the quality of clinical outcomes. Thus, a primary function of managed care is to get a better deal (i.e., lower prices) from the mental health professional.

Managed care, then, is a general term used to describe a constellation of businesses, organizations, and practices that arrange for the financing and delivery of mental health services (Lawless, Ginter, & Kelly, 1999; Phelps, Eisman, & Kohout, 1998). Generally speaking, the term *managed care* is commonly used to refer to a range of programs and policies that control access to care, the types of care delivered, and the cost of care (Cuddeback & Morrissey, 2010). Managed care organizations (MCOs) have instituted several specific mechanisms for the purpose of cost containment. Generally, these mechanisms either reduce the overall utilization of mental health services or reduce the average price per unit of service.

When these mechanisms are organized and implemented coherently, various types of managed care programs emerge (Virk, 2011). *Health maintenance organizations* (HMOs) are the most common form of managed care system (Broskowski & Marks, 1992; Chambliss, 2000). The HMO may provide direct services or negotiate contracts with independent practitioners or group practices to provide direct services to consumers. HMOs typically have lower premiums and out-of-pocket expenses and no deductibles and are less comprehensive than other types of managed care systems (Virk, 2011). Preferred provider organizations (PPOs) are "networks of providers that collectively provide comprehensive health care coverage or an array of specialty care, such as mental health or substance abuse" (Broskowski & Marks, 1992, p. 31). Providers of care are invited to join a PPO based on quality of work, geographic location, or ability to provide specialty service. PPO providers tend to be reimbursed at a discounted rate *after* services are rendered. Point-of-service (POS) plans combine the best of HMO and PPO plans (Virk, 2011). A case manager or mental health professional serves as a gatekeeper and controls utilization of services. The consumer selects the provider at the point of service. Network providers are reimbursed on a capitation basis, an approach to cost containment that will be discussed later. Consumers enrolled in POS plans do have the option of selecting an "out-of-network" provider, who is reimbursed on a fee-for-service basis.

Community mental health centers are increasingly fitting the definition of managed care organizations (Gaver, 2000; Uttaro, Vali, Horwitz, & Henri, 1998).

PROCEDURES FOR REDUCING UTILIZATION

Managed care organizations use several procedures to reduce utilization of mental health services and thereby limit the total cost of mental health services to third-party reimbursers. These include pretreatment authorization of treatment, concurrent utilization reviews, incentives for efficient providers, and increased employer/user cost sharing.

Pretreatment Authorization of Treatment.   The goal of pretreatment authorization of treatment is to ensure that any treatment initiated has been determined to be medically necessary and appropriate (Feldstein, Wickizer, & Wheeler, 1988). This requires that the counselor call a review organization and gain approval for treatment prior to providing direct service to the client. Occasionally, a case manager of the MCO assists in assessing clients' needs, the degree of medical necessity, and the best provider of services. Thus, it is the HMO and not the mental health counselor who actually *authorizes* treatment (Wilcoxon, Magnuson, & Norem, 2008).

Typically, the basis for determining "medical necessity" is the valid diagnosis of the client using *DSM* criteria. Furthermore, authorization of treatment requires that the techniques used and the frequency and number of sessions be appropriate for the specific diagnostic category. Counselors must show the scientific basis for the specific treatment approach selected and demonstrate their ability to promote therapeutic gains for the particular client (Chambliss, 2000). Increasingly, authorization is contingent on a demonstration that the service to be provided has been scientifically validated as efficacious. In this way, managed care serves a gatekeeping function in the contemporary mental health care environment. A significant obstacle for the mental health professions is the double-edged sword of developing the valid and reliable diagnoses *and* demonstrating which specific type of treatment works for which specific type of client (Sheid, 2010). Each task is fraught with difficulties.

With the authorization of treatment, counselors usually receive assurance that they will be reimbursed for services rendered, provided that a valid claim is submitted (Broskowski & Marks, 1992). Although counselors are not necessarily limited to provision of authorized treatment, they risk not being reimbursed for any service that is not authorized.

Concurrent Utilization Reviews.   Concurrent utilization reviews answer the primary question "To what extent is it necessary for the client to continue in treatment beyond the original limits authorized?" (Broskowski & Marks, 1992). In the past, the answer to this question was based on the judgment of the counselor made in collaboration with the client. In the contemporary treatment setting, however, the counselor collaborates with a reviewer to justify continuation of treatment. The reviewer may be a highly skilled supervisor or a less skilled technician working from management service protocols. For example, to extend a patient's hospital stay, counselors working in inpatient settings must provide the reviewer with objective evidence that the patient remains a clear danger to himself or herself. Counselors working with a depressed client in an outpatient program are required to demonstrate that additional sessions using specific techniques are necessary for the client to reach an acceptable level of functioning. In either case, an independent reviewer employed by the mental health facility or the managed care organization serves as a consultant and assists the counselor in making treatment decisions and discharge plans (Broskowski & Marks, 1992). Counselors must have relevant data to support their request for an extension of the original authorization and must clearly communicate this rationale to the reviewer. Thus, the concepts of medical necessity and appropriateness of treatment are relevant throughout the entire therapeutic process.

Utilization reviews are controversial from a professional perspective. They threaten the autonomy of the counselor and collaboration of the counselor and the client in clinical decision making (Segal, 2006). Denials of authorization for additional sessions may be based on the average number of sessions recommended or conducted by other providers treating similar conditions. Denials can also result from the need to reduce utilization based on budgetary restraints and consequent administrative directives to cut costs.

To function adequately in the contemporary mental health setting, mental health counselors must possess a variety of foundational appraisal, therapeutic, and research skills. At the very least, mental health counselors must possess a working knowledge of basic research methodologies that can be applied in clinical settings to measure client progress. They must also be well read on the vast range of appraisal instruments available and must be skilled in their administration, scoring, and interpretation. Finally, skill development in evidence-based treatments, such as motivational interviewing, the transtheoretical model, and dialectical behavior therapy, is necessary if mental health counselors are to compete for jobs and function in managed care environments.

Several benefits of pretreatment authorization and concurrent utilization review processes have been noted (Chambliss, 2000). First, it is generally acknowledged that these procedures save a great deal of money by reducing the length and frequency of hospitalizations and outpatient treatment. In addition, some believe that these procedures have led to improved efficiency and effectiveness of treatment by forcing mental health professionals to apply a technical eclecticism in determining what will work best and for whom.

Incentives for Efficient Providers. As noted in the preceding discussion, managed care is built around principles that encourage the efficient provision of service. Specific policies provide incentives for practitioners to incorporate these principles into their practice. For example, MCOs screen prospective providers to determine if they meet company standards as providers of service. If they meet these standards, mental health professionals can be placed on the organization's list of accepted providers of service (i.e., the provider panel).

Additions to a panel require several things. First, there must be a need for additional panel participants in a given geographic region. Managed care organizations estimate that one provider of mental health services is needed for every 1,000 people they insure (Polkinghorne, 2001). If a particular area is adequately supplied with providers, the MCO has no need to recruit new counselors. In such situations, an appropriately credentialed counselor will not be eligible to receive reimbursement from that particular MCO. However, if the demand for counseling services increases, more providers may be recruited. Thus, gaining a position on a provider list is a competitive process. Unfortunately, members of various mental health professions are pitted against one another to attain provider status.

Second, mental health professionals must show that they follow acceptable diagnostic and treatment procedures and are willing to accept reduced fees (Polkinghorne, 2001). Counselors who do not abide by the protocols of the MCO or do not achieve the desired outcomes with their clients may be dropped from the provider list. The key incentive is that providers on specific panels receive a consistent flow of referrals from the MCOs in which they are members. Theoretically, then, this becomes a win-win situation for the mental health provider and the third-party reimburser.

Third, the net effect of pretreatment authorization and concurrent utilization review is to encourage the use of therapeutic approaches that are brief and goal oriented. The very nature of managed care requires that counselors address presenting problems through brief, problem-solving techniques (Bistline, Sheridan, & Winegar, 1991). Doing so helps to ensure that clients will attain the identified goals and objectives of treatment within the time frames approved through the authorization process. In addition, being a provider of efficient, time-limited services is an important factor in becoming a member of provider lists.

Increased Employee and User/Client Cost Sharing. Managed care organizations distribute the financial risk among employees, users/clients, providers, employers, and the MCO itself (Broskowski & Marks, 1992). Doing so helps to lower total costs and makes health care more affordable.

Increasingly, though, the burden of these cost-sharing efforts has moved to employees and clients. Employees are paying higher insurance premiums, regardless of whether they use their plan's benefits (Broskowski & Marks, 1992; Ceniceros, 2001). In addition, copayments and deductibles distribute financial risk by placing increased responsibility on users of services. Typically, the managed care organization sets a maximum limit for the financial risk of users (i.e., the total amount of copayments and deductibles) beyond which the MCO and provider share the remaining risk.

PROCEDURES FOR CONTROLLING PRICE PER UNIT

In addition to limiting utilization and increasing cost sharing, managed care seeks to lower total costs by exerting control over the cost per unit of service. Procedures used to accomplish this purpose include capitation, use of less expensive but equally effective treatment approaches, and retrospective claims reviews.

Capitation. Under capitation reimbursement procedures, counselors contract with the MCO to be reimbursed at a fixed rate for all medically necessary mental health services to be provided for 1 year for one health plan enrollee (Staton, 2000). Under such a reimbursement plan, a counselor's income is based on the number of persons enrolled in the plan rather than the type or frequency of service provided (Kongstvedt, 1996). For example, a managed care organization using a capitation framework might reimburse a practitioner at a rate of $0.55 per member per month regardless of the quantity or type of sessions conducted. Assuming that 2,500 persons carry the specific insurance plan, each becomes a potential client for the practitioner. In this example, the practitioner would receive $1,375 (55 cents × 2,500) in monthly reimbursement from the MCO. However, the counselor's rate of reimbursement per session under capitation depends on the actual utilization of the service. Thus, if the counselor sees 15 clients who are covered by the plan in a given month, reimbursement per session is $1,375 ÷ 15 = $91.67. However, if 25 clients are seen in that month, reimbursement per session is $55.00. To maintain a profitable practice/organization, practitioners working under such arrangements are influenced by an implicit incentive to withhold treatment and thus increase business/organizational profits (Staton, 2000).

Capitation, then, can have advantages for both the MCO and the counselor. For the MCO, costs for service become more predictable. A specific rate of reimbursement is set for each person covered by the plan. Regardless of actual types and frequencies of service rendered, each practitioner is reimbursed, typically on a monthly basis, according to the negotiated rate. Practitioners are guaranteed steady incomes under capitation. The burden of financial risk is shifted to the MCO, which receive incentive *if* clients use fewer mental health services. There is an obvious downside. If a significant increase in demand for service occurs, the mental health professional receives decreased income.

Less Expensive but Equally Effective Treatment Approaches. Managed care promotes the use of treatment approaches that cost less but have an outcome comparable to more expensive alternatives. This has been achieved in several ways. First, MCOs have tended to hire master's-level practitioners because they can be reimbursed at a lower rate than doctoral-level psychologists. Indeed, Crane and Payne (2011) conducted a longitudinal, retrospective investigation of CIGNA Health Care insurance claims for 490,000 persons over four years. After controlling for regional, gender, and diagnosis differences, they discovered that the average cost of therapy was lowest for mental health and professional counselors, marriage and family therapists, medical doctors, master's-level social workers, nurses, and psychologists, in that order from low to high. Furthermore, a number of studies (e.g., Smith & Glass, 1977; Strupp & Hadley, 1979) have concluded that the efficacy of treatment is unrelated to the therapists' credentials or level of academic degree. As a result, mental health counselors, master's-level social workers, and marriage and family therapists are now the primary providers of mental health services.

Second, managed care has promoted the use of medication over talking therapies when it can be demonstrated that no significant difference exists in the efficacy of treatments. In many cases, medication proves to be a less expensive alternative and is increasingly used for conditions for which psychotherapy and counseling have traditionally been viewed as viable alternatives.

Retrospective Claims Reviews. In retrospective claims reviews, an independent reviewer audits the clinical chart after the client's termination of treatment. The purpose of such reviews is to determine if the treatment authorized and submitted for reimbursement was, in fact, rendered. Infrequently, a retrospective review is also used when insurance fraud or abuse is suspected (Broskowski & Marks, 1992).

So, how do these various managed care practices play out in community mental health settings? The typical scenario begins at the client's initial request for service. Most mental health centers have single points of entry, delineated levels of care, and preauthorization, utilization management, and review procedures (Segal, 2006). The client first meets with a bachelor's-level social worker, who gathers intake information and determines if the client is eligible for the services available at the community mental health center. The eligible client is assigned to a mental health counselor or MSW, who conducts a full biopsychosocial assessment. The *level of medical necessity* is established on the basis of the resulting diagnosis and current level of functioning. This result, in turn, establishes the particular level of care and related services for which the client is eligible. For example, a person diagnosed as clinically depressed might be eligible for Level II Care, which entails receiving weekly outpatient individual/group counseling and psychiatric consultation for a specified time. In contrast, the person diagnosed with schizophrenia, being eligible for Level IV Care, gets assertive community treatment, including wraparound physical health care, psychiatric consultation and medication monitoring, day treatment, and peer support. In each case, authorization for additional services is subject to review at specified intervals.

This process may seem quite complex and intimidating. However, it is greatly facilitated by computer software that links diagnostic impressions, level of care, and available services. Complex treatment plans are developed as the mental health counselor inputs assessment results, follows computer-assisted decision trees, and cuts and pastes from a series of specific goals, objectives, and methodologies listed in drop-down boxes. Typically, a case manager is assigned to oversee the implementation of the various treatment components.

IMPACT ON THE PRACTICE OF MENTAL HEALTH COUNSELING

Managed care has caused "an upheaval in the practice community" (Acuff et al., 1999, p. 563). It is unlikely that mental health service providers will ever return to a simple fee-for-service structure. Changes have occurred in the nature of treatment, its delivery, and the management of the business of mental health service. More changes are anticipated with the gradual implementation of the Patient Protection and Affordable Care Act (2010). These include mandated coverage by benefit packages of mental health and substance abuse treatment; rehabilitation, prevention, and wellness services; and increased coordination and integration of medical, mental health, and substance abuse services ("Health Reform: Overview," 2010).

Many mental health counselors hold a negative opinion of managed care and indicate that it has adversely affected how they provide services (McClure, Livingston, Livingston, & Gage, 2005; Normandy-Dolberg, 2010). And the emotional reactions of counselors and other mental health professionals have sometimes been intense (Beier & Young, 1998; Danzinger & Welfel, 2001, p. 394). Although such intense reactions can spill over into the counseling process, our primary focus is on how counselors have coped with and adapted their practice in light of the managed care revolution.

Responding to managed care is complicated by the fact that the relationships between service providers and MCOs are constantly changing as a result of the interaction of consumer needs, the business needs and financial risks of employers, national and state legislation, and the shifting landscape of managed care (Lawless et al., 1999). Managed care organizations also feel under attack on many fronts and are experiencing enormous economic pressures (Davis, 1999). Price competition is fierce, and the administrative and network management overhead costs are enormous. In addition,

MCOs are beginning to feel a strong backlash from consumers, who charge that medically necessary care has been inappropriately limited under the current system (Davis, 1999).

These are indeed rapidly changing and turbulent times for mental health practitioners and administrators (Sullivan, 2013). The source of the stress is a moving target. The train bearing the baggage of managed care is upon us. The words of Will Rogers are instructive in this context: "Even if you are on the right track, you'll get run over if you just sit there." Sitting on our past laurels might temporarily inflate our professional self-esteem, but professional risk runs high without constructive interaction and response to the contemporary managed care environment. Mental health professionals and MCOs relate to one another in a context of ongoing uncertainty. Counselors are required to be especially vigilant in these changing times. The continued existence of their professional practice may depend on it.

Beier and Young (1998) borrow from Karen Horney's terminology in describing the responses of mental health professionals to the advent of managed care (Horney, 1945). The responses can be described as either "moving toward, moving away from, or moving against the changes in the system" (p. 198). For counselors moving toward managed care, few are running forward with open arms eagerly seeking to embrace a good friend. Rather, these counselors are doing what they have to do to survive in the current delivery system environment. Certainly, the activities of the American Mental Health Counselors Association (AMHCA) fit into this category. As if playing in a high-stakes card game, the professional organization is making a concerted effort to play with the cards it has been dealt. While working actively to lobby legislators and confront the disparity among service providers, AMHCA has collaborated with some of the largest MCOs in shaping credentialing criteria (Davis, 1999). If the profession is to survive and flourish, it must play according to the rules that currently set the parameters of how the game is played. Many counselors have integrated the various policies and procedures of managed care into their professional practice. For some professionals, obtaining multiple licenses has become a way of increasing the number of claims that are reimbursed (Geisler, 1995). In an unpublished study, Gerig (1999) surveyed members of the Indiana Mental Health Counselors Association to determine their rate of reimbursement success. He found that a number of Licensed Mental Health Counselors (LMHCs) in the state were using other credentials in addition to the LMHC to meet the credentialing criteria of specific MCOs.

Another group of counselors can best be described as moving away from the system. Many counselors in this category bypass third-party reimbursement. Gerig (1999) found that of those members of the Indiana Mental Health Counselors Association who were providing direct service to clients, about 50% were billing their clients directly and bypassing the third-party reimbursement option. Various reasons for maintaining a fee-for-service system abound. Zimpfer (1995) found that a number of licensed professional clinical counselors (LPCCs) in Ohio erroneously concluded that they were simply ineligible for insurance reimbursement and did not submit claims. Others expressed uncertainty regarding the prospect of attaining success in collecting claims. A third group professed to be "afraid to try." As Zimpfer (1995) notes, such beliefs are patently false because the results of his study give "credence to the status of counselors as eligible providers" (p. 109). In this study, 78% of the individual claims submitted were reimbursed.

Another reason not to seek reimbursement from MCOs concerns how the process conflicts with the nonmedical model that is an underlying philosophy of the mental health counseling profession. Diagnostic categorization of clients is contrary to a developmental emphasis on mental health and strength. Counselors who work on a fee-for-service basis are able to provide services regardless of whether clients fit the identified symptoms of a disorder specified in the *DSM-IV-TR* (the fourth revised edition of the *DSM*). In addition, such counselors are able to better integrate a wellness model into their practice.

A third group of professional counselors can be described as going against the managed care revolution. These are the ones who are fighting the system and actively seeking its overthrow. Many perceive MCOs as seeking to pay the smallest fees by using the least expensive service providers and obstructing client care by requiring pretreatment authorizations, capping the number of sessions, and blocking client access to qualified professionals by setting limits on provider lists (Beier & Young, 1998). Some mental health professionals have chosen to go on the offensive and engage in head-to-head combat with managed care. Unhappy about the extent to which HMOs have cut into their income and autonomy, psychologists from one state affiliated with the American Federation of Teachers, an organization of 140,000 members, to increase their lobbying clout (Talan, 2000). In 2000, the California Medical Association filed a federal suit against four of the state's largest health plans, claiming that these organizations had crippled the physicians' businesses and "cheated" their patients (Benko, 2000). Others are choosing to file legal suits against MCOs one at a time (Talan, 2000). Clearly, the fight is on. No one is sure, at this point, who is winning. But it is likely that this match will go to the final rounds. Too many see the profession and their livelihoods hanging in the balance.

CONCLUSION: SURVIVING IN THE ERA OF MANAGED CARE

All professional counselors are affected by managed care in some way. A number of counselors are attempting to cope with the contemporary situation. This can be likened to the fight or flight response to an identified stressor (Beier & Young, 1998). Others are discovering novel ways of adapting to the demands placed on them by managed care and are proceeding with varying degrees of resignation. But many are thriving in the current mental health care environment. How can mental health counselors survive and even thrive in the context of managed care?

First, counselor self-care skills are critical. The ability to cope with emotional reactions to managed care and its demands is necessary for counselors if they are to avoid the high risk of burnout. For private practitioners, the fight for survival breeds an ongoing uncertainty and fear, which become the "ground" on which the pressures and frustrations of day-to-day demands of doing business with MCOs become the "figure." Scheid (2010) found psychological burnout of mental health practitioners to be associated with increased bureaucratic control (e.g., increased paperwork and rules), a lack of professional pride in one's work (often, expressed in those finding their work meaningless), decreased job autonomy, and critical attitudes toward the cost containment policies of managed care. Counselors do well to implement and maintain a balanced lifestyle that promotes personal wellness. Keep a daily gratitude journal, and implement strategies for decreasing negativity and cultivating positivity (Fredrickson, 2009). Finally, a regimen of stress management techniques can be integrated into the professional's daily routine.

Second, surviving and thriving as a mental health counselor requires a working knowledge of the ins and outs of doing business in the managed care environment. Lawless and colleagues (1999) correctly note that two types of questions confront mental health counselors; both knowledge and skill acquisition are needed in constructing adequate responses. Specifically, the questions "Can you explain what capitation means?" and "How do I respond to utilization review in such a way as to gain maximum services for my clients?" call attention to the need for continuing education, accurate assessment of current skill levels, and recognition of regional variations in the operation of MCOs (Lawless et al., 1999).

Third, counselors also need specific knowledge skills if they are to conduct successful direct negotiations with MCOs (C. E. Anderson, 2000). For example, as noted earlier, counselors frequently work with a case manager or reviewer employed by the MCO for preauthorization of services and concurrent review of services. Establishing a positive and collaborative relationship based on mutual respect ensures that the welfare of the client will be primary. Skills in diagnosis and treatment planning are also prerequisites not only for effective clinical practice but also for communicating goals and objectives of treatment and how they are to be attained through the recommended intervention. The clear, precise use of language increases the likelihood that the case manager will understand and approve the counselor's recommendations. In addition, successful relations with MCOs are enhanced when correct procedural codes are used in completing paperwork and communicating with the case manager (C. E. Anderson, 2000; Puente, 1997).

Fourth, mental health counselors must possess a thorough knowledge and understanding of their code of ethics (i.e., American Counseling Association, 2005; AMHCA, 2010), the ways they interact with the policies and practices of managed care, and the process of ethical decision making (Danzinger & Welfel, 2001). Basic ethical considerations for counselors include the primacy of the client's welfare, counselor competence, confidentiality, and informed consent (Glosoff, Garcia, Herlihy, & Remley, 1999).

Fifth, mental health counselors may be required to make a paradigm shift from older, traditional models of service delivery. Cummings (1995) suggests that a catalyst model be followed if a practitioner is to succeed under the new system. This model includes the following characteristics (Polkinghorne, 2001):

1. Many clients are seen for brief episodes of treatment, frequently in nontraditional modes.
2. A brief and intermittent counseling process occurs throughout the lifespan of the client.
3. Counselors serve as catalysts for client change.
4. Healing resources from the community are mobilized.
5. Capitation and other reimbursement arrangements free counselors to provide services as needed regardless of client's ability to pay.

What Cummings (1995) refers to as a catalyst model appears to have much in common with presuppositions that underlie the profession of mental health counseling. As has been noted throughout this book, professional counselors see their practice as being developmental and as emphasizing mental health as well as mental illness. Mental health counseling is also guided by ecological theory (Bronfenbrenner, 1979), which supports the counselor's approach to assessment, treatment, and utilization of client support systems.

Thus, although other mental health professions may be facing significant adjustments in how they conceptualize their work, mental health counselors have a theoretical base that enables them to interact with clients as well as the current market forces in constructive ways. Generally speaking, then, mental health counselors possess a foundation for successful professional practice in the managed care environment.

DISCUSSION QUESTIONS

1. Define *managed care*. What is its goal and, generally speaking, how does it seek to attain that goal?
2. What specific procedures does managed care use to contain costs of mental health services? To what extent would you feel comfortable working within a managed care system? What specific skills would you need to work within such a setting?
3. To what extent do you see managed care as (a) a necessary correction of a system that was not working, (b) a necessary evil, or (c) an unethical system that does not have client welfare in mind? Explain your response.
4. As you consider your response to managed care, which of the following categories best fits your current position: moving toward, moving away, or moving against? Why?
5. To what extent do you believe that professional counselors have adequate preparation and skills to work within managed care environments?

SUGGESTED ACTIVITIES

1. Organize and conduct a panel discussion. Invite several LPCs (Licensed Professional Counselors) or LMHCs to class and explore their experiences in working in a managed care environment.
2. Conduct a survey of various mental health professionals in your region. Include psychiatrists, psychologists, clinical social workers, professional counselors, and marriage and family therapists. Explore the extent to which their practice or the agencies in which they work have been influenced by managed care. Consider getting on provider lists, working with reviewers, and obtaining reimbursement for services. Then compare variables across the various professional groups.

3. Visit the Web sites of several MCOs. Compare and contrast the services provided, the criteria for inclusion on the provider lists, and the procedures for preauthorization, concurrent review, and so on.

4. Interview an LMHC working at a community mental health center. Review the types of documentation (i.e., paperwork) required by Medicaid or other relevant MCOs. In what ways are these documents necessary to demonstrate that the mental health services provided are in full compliance with organizational standards?

REFERENCES

Acuff, C., Bennett, B. E., Bricklin, P. M., Canter, M. B., Knapp, S. J., Moldawshy, S., & Phelps, R. (1999). Considerations for ethical practice in managed care. *Professional Psychology Research and Practice, 30,* 563–575.

American Counseling Association Governing Council. (2005). ACA policies and procedures for processing complaints of ethical violations. Retrieved from http://www.counseling.org/Resources/CodeOfEthics/TP/Home/CT2.aspx

Anderson, C. E. (2000). Dealing constructively with managed care: Suggestions from an insider. *Journal of Mental Health Counseling, 22,* 343–353.

Beier, E. G., & Young, D. M. (1998). *The silent language of psychotherapy* (3rd ed.). New York, NY: Aldine de Gruyter.

Benko, L. B. (2000, July 10). Managed care under siege. *Modern Healthcare, 30*(28), 34–36.

Bistline, J. L., Sheridan, S. M., & Winegar, N. (1991). Five critical skills for mental health counselors in managed health care. *Journal of Mental Health Counseling, 13,* 147–152.

Bronfenbrenner, U. (1979). *The ecology of human development: Experiments by nature and design.* Cambridge, MA: Harvard University Press.

Broskowski, A., & Marks, E. (1992). Managed mental health care. In S. Cooper & T. H. Lentner (Eds.). *Innovations in community mental health.* Sarasota, FL: Professional Resource Press.

Ceniceros, R. (2001, October 22). Employees bear more costs. *Business Insurance,* pp. 3–4.

Chambliss, C. H. (2000). *Psychotherapy and managed care: Reconciling research and reality.* Boston, MA: Allyn & Bacon.

Crane, D. R., & Payne, S. H. (2011). Individual versus family psychotherapy in managed care: Comparing the costs of treatment by the mental health professions. *Journal of Marital and Family Therapy, 37,* 273–289.

Cuddeback, G. S., & Morrissey, J. P. (2010). Integrating service delivery systems for persons with a severe mental illness. In T. L. Scheid & T. N. Brown (Eds.), *A handbook of the study of mental health: Social contexts, theories, and systems* (2nd ed., pp. 510–528). New York, NY: Cambridge University Press.

Cummings, N. A., & O'Donohue, W. T. (2008). *Eleven blunders that cripple psychotherapy in America: A remedial unblundering.* New York, NY: Routledge.

Cummings, N. A. (1995). Impact of managed care on employment and training: A primer for survival. *Professional Psychology: Research and Practice, 26*(1), 10–15.

Cushman, P. (1995). *Constructing the self, constructing America: A cultural history of psychotherapy.* Reading, MA: Addison-Wesley.

Danzinger, P. R., & Welfel, E. R. (2001). The impact of managed care on mental health counselors: A survey of perceptions, practices, and compliance with ethical standards. *Journal of Mental Health Counseling, 23,* 137–150.

Davis, J. (1999, July/August). Annual managed care trends report: From Chaos to opportunity. *The Advocate, 22*(4), 1, 4–5.

Faulkner, E. J. (1960). *Health insurance.* New York, NY: McGraw-Hill.

Feldstein, P., Wickizer, T., & Wheeler, J. (1988). Private cost containment: The effects of utilization review programs on health care use and expenditures. *New England Journal of Medicine, 318,* 1310–1314.

Fredrickson, B. L. (2009). *Positivity.* New York, NY: Three Rivers Press.

Gaver, K. (2000). Mental health care delivery systems. In P. Rodenhauser (Ed.), *Mental health care administration: A guide for practitioners.* Ann Arbor: University of Michigan Press.

Geisler, J. (1995). The impact of the passage of a counselor licensure law: One state's experience. *Journal of Mental Health Counseling, 17,* 188–199.

Gerig, M. (1999). *Third-party reimbursement and the experiences of members of the Indiana Mental Health Counselors Association.* Unpublished manuscript.

Glosoff, H. L., Garcia, J., Herlihy, B., & Remley, T. P. (1999). Managed care: Ethical considerations for counselors. *Counseling and Values, 44,* 8–16.

Horney, K. (1945). *Our inner conflicts.* New York, NY: Norton.

Kongstvedt, P. R. (1996). *The managed health care handbook* (3rd ed.). Gaithersburg, MD: Aspen.

Lawless, L. L., Ginter, E. K., & Kelly, K. R. (1999). Managed care: What mental health counselors need to know. *Journal of Mental Health Counseling, 21,* 50–65.

McClure, R. F., Livingston, R. B., Livingston, K. H., & Gage, R. (2005). A survey of practicing psychotherapists. *Journal of Professional Counseling, Practice, Theory, and Research, 33,* 35–46.

Mirin, S. M., & Sederer, L. I. (1994). Mental health care: Cut-rent realities, future

Normandy-Dolberg, J. (2010, September). AMHCA survey results: Concerns cited with managed care, and with funding retirement. *The Advocate,* pp. 6–7.

Numbers, A. (1984). *Compulsory health insurance.* New York, NY: Basic Books.

Phelps, R., Eisman, E. J., & Kohout, J. (1998). Psychological practice and managed care: Results of the CAPP practitioner study. *Professional Psychology: Research and Practice, 29,* 31–36.

Polkinghorne, D. E. (2001). Managed care programs: What do clinicians need? In B. D. Slife, R. N. Williams, & S. H. Barlow (Eds.), *Critical issues in psychotherapy: Translating new ideas into practice.* Thousand Oaks, CA: Sage.

Puente, A. E. (1997). Reimbursement for professional psychological services. *Journal of Psychopathology and Behavioral Assessment, 19,* 91–99.

Scheid, T. L. (2010). Consequences of managed care for mental health providers (pp. 529–547). In T. L. Scheid, & T. N. Brown (Eds.), *A handbook for the study of mental health: Social contexts, theories, and systems* (2nd ed.). New York, NY: Cambridge University Press.

Segal, S. P. (2006). Social work in a managed care setting (pp. 209–220). In J. Rosenberg & S. Rosenberg (Eds.), *Community mental health: Challenges for the 21st century.* New York, NY: Routledge.

Smith, H. B. (1999). Managed care: A survey of counselor educators and counselor practitioners. *Journal of Mental Health Counseling, 21,* 270–284.

Smith, M. L., & Glass, G. V. (1977). Meta-analysis of psychotherapy outcome studies. *American Psychologist, 32,* 752–760.

Staton, R. D. (2000). The national health care economic context of psychiatric practice. In P. Rodenhauser (Ed.), *Mental health care administration: A guide for practitioners.* Ann Arbor: University of Michigan Press.

Strupp, H. H., & Hadley, S. W. (1979). Specific versus nonspecific factors in psychotherapy. *Archives of General Psychiatry, 36,* 1125–1136.

Talan, J. (2000, January/February). Fighting with care. *Psychology Today, 33*(1), 11.

Tarasoff v. Board of Regents of the University of California, 17 Cal. 3d 425,551. (1976).

Throckmorton, W. (1998). Managed care: "It's like deja-vu, all over again." *Journal of Psychology and Christianity, 17,* 131–141.

Uttaro, T., Vali, F., Horwitz, A. V., & Henri, W. F. (1998). Primary therapists' views of managed care. *Psychological Reports, 82,* 459–464.

Vessey, J., & Howard, K. (1993). Who seeks psychotherapy? *Psychotherapy, 30*(4), 546–553.

Virk, P. (2011, February 12). Tutorials in medicine: Managed care organizations. The Next Generation Retrieved from http://www.nextgenmd.org/archives/718

Wiggins, J. G. (1988). Psychology's inclusion in health benefits planning. *Psychotherapy in Private Practice, 6*(2), 129–134.

Wilcoxon, S. A., Magnuson, S., & Norem, K. (2008). Institutional values of managed mental health care: Efficiency or oppression? *Multicultural Counseling and Development, 36,* 143–154.

Zimet, C. N. (1989). The mental health care revolution: Will psychology survive?

Zimpfer, D. G. (1995). Third-party reimbursement experience of licensed clinical counselors in Ohio. *Journal of Mental Health Counseling, 17,* 105–113.

11

The Changing Face of Community Mental Health

OUTLINE

*C*ommunity mental health is a phrase and concept that members of the mental health profession use repeatedly. Yet I wonder how much we really grasp its meaning and implications. We may refer to the community mental health center or say that we work in community mental health, but are we really meaning what we say or saying what we mean? To what extent does our training model reflect a community mental health orientation? Furthermore, to what extent do we *do* community mental health, even those of us who work in community mental health centers?

The pursuit of mental health involves both a quest for optimal human functioning and a simultaneous movement away from emotional distress, dysfunction, and mental illness. These aspects of mental health may be viewed as lying within two distinct but interacting dimensions. If we add to this the idea of *community,* we see that we have entered the realm of interacting systems.

The clinical mental health counseling paradigm clearly reflects this perspective. The ecological perspective is foundational to the training and practice of clinical mental health counselors. The theoretical and practical issues related to defining *mental health,* as noted in Chapter 3, significantly increase in number and complexity when the descriptor *community* is added. Thus, community mental health is ecological by definition, and the mental health counseling profession should therefore be on the cutting edge of related theory making and practice by virtue of its theoretical foundation and training. This chapter explores the extent to which the delivery of community mental health services has been successful in maintaining an ecological focus.

This chapter discusses how services are delivered to individuals and related systems that seek to resist or overcome mental illness and to pursue optimal levels of functioning. First, the history of care for the mentally ill is summarized. Second, a general model of mental health care delivery systems is presented. Third, the fundamentals of grant writing are described. Fourth, several contemporary trends and approaches to service delivery are described. Finally, the chapter explores how specific mental health concerns are being addressed in the community.

The attainment of community mental health does not occur simply through the provision of services to individuals. The whole is truly greater than the sum of its parts. Thus, effective programs mobilize community resources to facilitate and maintain personal and community mental health. The relationship is dynamic and reciprocal.

COMMUNITY MENTAL HEALTH IN THE UNITED STATES

The community mental health movement in the United States is often seen as commencing with the Community Mental Health Centers Act of 1963. However, the movement has actually been a "slow train running" with origins dating back to the mid-1800s (Cutler, 1992; Suppes & Wells, 2003). Perhaps the most famous early advocate was Dorothea Dix, who in 1843 began to draw public attention to the deplorable living conditions of the mentally ill. Systematically documenting their plight, Dix presented a report to the Massachusetts legislature that became the impetus for state funding of hospitals to treat persons with mental illness (Suppes & Wells, 2003).

Unfortunately, the resulting development of mental hospitals failed to significantly influence the plight of persons with mental illness in the United States. The federal government's first major move toward addressing the needs of the mentally ill was the National Mental Health Act of 1946 (Public Law 79-487). Through this act, the National Institute of Mental Health (NIMH) was established and became the federal think tank and financial resource for innovative mental health programs through the 1970s (Cutler, 1992). The act also established a number of research and training programs that continue to this day.

As was noted in Chapter 2, flaws in the existing mental health service delivery system were being exposed by the mid-1950s. The population in mental hospitals peaked in 1955, when over 559,000 patients were being housed in prolonged-care hospitals for the mentally ill (Torrey, 2006). Up to this point, the guiding principle for the treatment of mental disorders was to move the disordered person from normal family, social, and community settings to a sheltered, institutionalized environment. But in recent years, the underlying philosophy has shifted toward community-based treatment, support, and rehabilitation. This philosophy is central to the concept of *deinstitutionalization,* which refers to the practice of transferring formerly institutionalized individuals to sheltered community environments or to homes in the community (Barry, 1998). By 1995, the inpatient population had decreased to 71,619 (Torrey, 2006). Today it is less than 60,000.

However, average daily census data may not reflect the activity level of inpatient facilities. For example, there were approximately 2 million admissions to inpatient treatment services in 1997 (Milazzo-Sayre et al., 2001). Many of these admissions reflected the increased reliance on brief 24- to 72-hour hospitalizations for those requiring acute stress management and crisis stabilization services. This practice gives rise to the *revolving-door phenomenon,* where those with mental illness may experience multiple relapses requiring brief, multiple hospitalizations in the context of their community-based treatment. Decreased patient counts, as shown in daily census data, also reflect current clinical and managed care practices that have reduced length of stay and increased patient turnover (Levine, Perkins, & Perkins, 2005).

The locus of residential treatment has moved to community outpatient settings. In 1997, according to Milazzo-Sayre et al. (2001), 5.5 million patients were admitted to outpatient care, along with an additional 171,000 admissions to community-based residential care. If we sum the total admissions to inpatient care (2 million), community-based outpatient care (5.5 million), and community-based residential care (171,000), we find a total of 7.67 million persons admitted for mental health treatment annually.

Several forces have played important roles in shaping the shift to community-based care (Barry, 1998). First, the development of a number of medications provides practitioners with effective means of decreasing the symptoms of major psychiatric disorders such as schizophrenia, bipolar disorder, and depression. Second, the available economic resources no longer support long-term, inpatient care for the mentally ill. Instead, emphasis has shifted to community models of outpatient care. Third, given the supply of mental health professionals from a variety of disciplines, multidisciplinary team approaches can be offered that provide a more comprehensive approach to outpatient mental health care than was previously available.

Other out-of-home settings must be considered as we attempt to comprehend the nature of and need for community mental health. The elderly comprise a frequently overlooked and underserved population. Although the population of persons housed in nursing homes has decreased in recent years due to improved community and in-home services, it is estimated that approximately 340,000 residents of nursing homes are in need of mental health services for psychiatric conditions (Levine et al., 2005). In addition, the criminalization of the mentally ill has been well documented, and a large number of persons with mental illness are housed in jails and prisons (Hiday & Burns, 2010). In 2000, more than 128,000 adolescents were housed in public and private juvenile justice facilities. Furthermore, nearly 542,000 children and adolescents resided in foster care, many of them victims of abuse or neglect (National Clearinghouse on Child Abuse and Neglect Information, 2003).

The focus of our discussion thus far has been the treatment of diagnosable populations. However, it is important for mental health counselors to understand the distinction between mental illness and problems in living (Levine et al., 2005). As noted in Chapter 3, placing diagnosable emotional/subjective distress and mental illness on the same continuum as mental health is an artifact of the medical model. The single-dimensional view directs us to conceptualize mental health interventions in terms of treating disorders rather than taking into consideration wellness and solution-focused approaches that are systemically based. The clinical mental health counseling paradigm takes a more holistic view of persons, which includes both levels of wellness and pathology operating within their particular ecological context. When this expanded view is taken, we gain sight of other significant mental health concerns in communities. These include homelessness, substance abuse, dually diagnosed populations, victims and perpetrators of abuse, education-related problems, problems in living for those with chronic illness and sexually transmitted diseases (STDs), crisis intervention and disaster relief, and addressing the special needs of rural/isolated communities and the underserved. Finally, we must add to our list issues related to normal human development or transitions and family living, such as vocational stress and decision making, relational enhancement, timely and untimely pregnancy, abortion, adoption, infant mortality and birth defects, foster care, divorce, remarriage, blended families, and personal loss/grieving.

Certainly, the listed concerns represent a mere sampling of the potential issues present in any given community. For community mental health services to be truly effective, programs and interventions must target real needs. According to the U.S. Surgeon General (2001), the mental health service delivery system consists of four sectors: the specialty mental health sector (psychiatrists, psychologists, and mental health counselors), the general medical/primary-care network (family physicians and general medical practitioners, nurses, and medical specialists), the human services sector (juvenile/criminal justice system, family services and social welfare, and faith-based and charitable services), and voluntary services (self-help groups and organizations). In addition to being frontline providers of mental health care, mental health counselors bring to the table an ecological focus on and a working knowledge of needs assessment and program evaluation. Thus, the mental health counseling profession is well positioned to take leadership roles in a variety of community mental health–related settings.

A MODEL OF MENTAL HEALTH DELIVERY SYSTEMS

Effective community mental health programs share a number of essential elements that operate in a fully integrated manner for the purpose of delivering services that meet specific needs of persons and systems living in an ever-changing environment. In their classic text *People in Systems: A Model for Development in the Human-Service Professions and Education,* Egan and Cowan (1979) present a model that responds to the question "On what logic is an effectively designed and functioning system based?" The essential components of Egan and Cowan's model are described in the following sections. Figure 11.1 displays the manner in which these components interact to create an effective, dynamic service delivery system.

FIGURE 11.1 A Model of a General Mental Health Delivery System

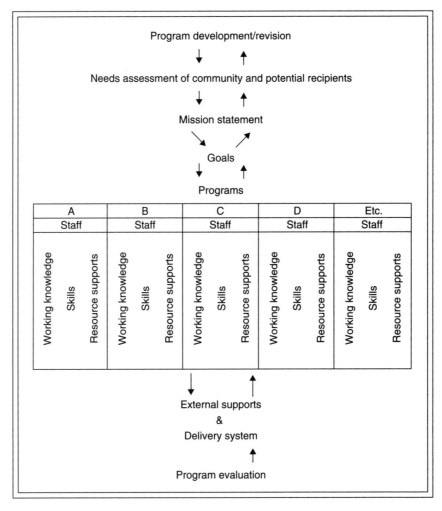

ASSESSMENT OF THE NEEDS AND WANTS OF SERVICE RECIPIENTS

Prior to developing and implementing a program to meet the purported mental health needs of a given population, effective service delivery systems carefully identify who are potential service recipients living in the particular locality. Needs are best viewed as an existing state in persons or communities that is the result of the difference or discrepancy between a "what is" condition and the "what should be" condition (Altschuld & Witkin, 2000, p. 7). Needs assessment, then, is a set of procedures used to gather valid and reliable data on the nature of problems affecting the particular population so that specific means can be designed and implemented to decrease or eliminate the needs. A comprehensive needs assessment is a critical ingredient in establishing a rationale for new or expanded programs and includes the following tasks: gathering community demographic data; conducting a community problem/asset analysis; performing a market analysis; and determining if, in fact, the need exists (Calley, 2011).

MISSION

Mental health professionals providing service in effective programs know what their program is all about (i.e., its reason for being). Effective programs are characterized by an overarching sense of purpose and vision that is expressed in a mission statement. Such statements communicate a general purpose of the service delivery system, its underlying philosophy, and the nature of products and services delivered. Program development follows directly from an accurate needs assessment.

GOALS

Effective mental health care delivery systems translate general mission statements into a statement of specific goals, whose attainment represents the fulfillment of the identified needs of recipients. These express the anticipated effects on participants resulting from participation in the intervention. Goals should be measurable, realistic, worthwhile, and adequate. They should be agreed upon by all stakeholders and viewed as important and feasible. Failure to create objective, measurable goals often results in mediocre programs, ones that have face validity but do not fulfill the expectations or needs of recipients.

PROGRAMS

Programs are the step-by-step means by which each specified goal is achieved. Sometimes there is a one-to-one correspondence among an identified need, a related goal, and a program. For example, a crisis management program might be developed to meet the emergency mental health needs of clients, the general public, organizations, or communities. In other instances, several programs might be designed to fulfill a specific goal, or one program may, in fact, fulfill several purposes. Thus, mental health, public health, and community assistance programs might combine resources to meet the multiple needs of the chronically homeless.

We can begin to see the continuity in well-developed delivery systems. Programs are developed and implemented to assist clients in attaining specific goals that fit into the general mission of the organization and were identified directly from the needs assessment.

WORKING KNOWLEDGE, SKILLS, AND RESOURCE SUPPORTS

Adequate human resources must be available if programs are to be effective. Leadership and professional/support staff must have both the working knowledge and the requisite skills to conduct the program. For example, a particular knowledge base and set of skills are necessary if the delivery of a parenting skill development program to adult referrals from Child Protective Services is to be effective. Adequate staff selection and training procedures must be in place to ensure that all persons responsible for the delivery of services have appropriate preparation and resources (e.g., time, financial supports, and credentials) to deliver the program content as intended. Program developers also identify what community resources are available and know how they can be accessed.

ENVIRONMENTAL SUPPORTS: TECHNOLOGY AND FACILITY

The best designed programs can fail miserably if little or no attention is paid to the backup supports necessary for successful program implementation. Required technical supports, such as reliable Internet, PowerPoint™, liquid crystal display (LCD) projectors, and participant resource materials, must be readily available as needed. Furthermore, the physical facility must be adequate to support the specific program needs and demands, such as comfortable seating, accessible location, available transportation, adequate parking, and appropriate room decor.

PROGRAM EVALUATION

Finally, managers and stakeholders of mental health programs seek confirmatory evidence gathered via program evaluation to ensure that the program is operating as intended and that the desired outcomes are being attained. Approaches to conducting formative and summative program assessment were discussed in Chapter 8. These are vital feedback mechanisms that ensure that programs stay on target in ever-changing recipient and environmental conditions.

FUNDING PROGRAMS THROUGH GRANTS

Tight budgets, decreased federal and state support, and strict financial accountability of managed care greatly affect how community mental health agencies develop, implement, and maintain programs. Moving forward with program development and implementation is totally contingent on acquiring adequate financial support for the program. Thus, community mental health organizations engage in a continual search for external funding sources to assist in the provision of their programs and the development of their facilities (Calley, 2011).

The process of successful grant writing involves at least seven basic steps. First, the individual or agency seeking external funding identifies needs or develops ideas that become the focal point of the proposal. Most fundable projects are related to a clearly documented need and an innovative solution that is cost effective.

Second, an appropriate funding source is identified. Generally, the primary sources for external funding are public, private, and community foundations; for-profit businesses and corporations; and federal and state government foundations.

Third, a grant proposal is prepared. The sections of a standard grant proposal are

1. The cover letter. It introduces your organization and its mission and states concisely what you are seeking. This letter should contain novel content and not simply regurgitate the content that follows.
2. An executive summary. Here you identify your organization, its mission, the key points of your grant proposal, the need for the proposed program, its cost and the amount you are requesting, the timeframe of the project, and the expected outcomes. Writing the summary is challenging because it needs to be both comprehensive and concise.
3. A statement of the existing problem or need or a description of the specific situation. In this section, the grant writer defines the issue and communicates that the specific organization is uniquely qualified to tackle the problem.
4. Working goals and plan. A clear and concise statement is made regarding what the organization plans to do about the problem. This section clearly identifies who is the intended audience, who is to deliver the program, and when and where the program delivery will take place.
5. Measurable outcomes and impact. Here the funding source is informed of what specific difference or change will take place as a result of successful program implementation. It is important to specify outcomes that are relevant, meaningful, and measurable.
6. Budget. An accurate, detailed budget is provided that includes an itemized list of all expected expenses and income.
7. Description of the organization. Be accurate, but spin a compelling narrative that lets funders know that your organization is best qualified to carry out the project(s) you have outlined. Include financial information, such as the organization's budget and annual donations.
8. Supplementary materials. The funding source may ask for specific materials, such as a letter declaring tax-exempt status, a list of the organization's board of directors, or an organizational financial statement. (Grantseeking in Minnesota, 2004)

Fourth, the proposal is submitted. It is extremely important to follow the submission instructions meticulously. Any deviations from the stated protocol can greatly decrease the likelihood that the grant proposal will be accepted.

Fifth, the proposal is either accepted or rejected. If the original grant proposal is not accepted, it is sometimes possible to revise it and resubmit it to the funding source. Finally, the grant is administered according to plan.

How does one learn the art and science of successful grant writing? Frequently, courses in grant writing are offered for credit through colleges and universities. In addition, numerous grant-writing seminars or continuing education experiences abound. However, the best way to learn grant writing is through engaging in the actual writing process under the guidance of an experienced mentor (Longo & Schubert, 2005). Such opportunities are often available for graduate assistants or in large community mental health or human services organizations. In the contemporary mental health care environment, grant-writing skills have become vital for the mental health counselor who seeks to develop innovative ideas into effective programs.

CONTEMPORARY TRENDS IN COMMUNITY MENTAL HEALTH

A number of contemporary trends can be identified that interact with and influence the structure and delivery of programs in community mental health. These function as contextual factors that influence the particular shape and direction that mental health delivery systems are taking. Among these are the postdeinstitutionalization era and the least restrictive treatment environment. In response, traditional programs have shifted toward increased application of case management models, such as assertive community treatment, recovery and the consumer movement, and evidence-based treatment.

THE POSTDEINSTITUTIONALIZATION ERA

Contemporary mental health delivery systems operate in the postdeinstitutionalization era. The decline in the rates of psychiatric patients treated in inpatient facilities was discussed in an earlier section. This decline can be attributed in part to shifts in treatment philosophy (Levine, 1981). Changes in funding and reimbursement policies are related to an increased emphasis on more cost-effective alternatives. In addition, changes in the law make it more difficult to commit patients to and retain them in hospitals involuntarily.

Providing adequate care for persons who formerly would have been serviced in inpatient facilities continues to present challenges for community mental health systems. Previously protected by the controlled environment of mental institutions, many are increasingly vulnerable to substance abuse and dependence, which has necessitated the development of effective programs for treating dually diagnosed populations. Furthermore, a large number of the chronically mentally ill with minimal supports have found independent living difficult. Some are homeless and live as street people. Many do not clearly see their need for or the benefits of mental health services. Still others, while recognizing their need for services, find the service delivery experience aversive and prefer to avoid it (Levine et al., 2005).

Clearly, creative approaches to mental health programming and delivery are required to fill the gaps in service provision in the postdeinstitutionalization era. In the sections that follow, unique approaches to service are described that avoid the "one size fits all" approach that too often characterized community mental health programs in the past.

LEAST RESTRICTIVE TREATMENT

A foundational concept supporting contemporary mental health services is *least restrictive treatment*. Basically, the idea is to match the prescribed treatment's level of intensity to the severity of the client's condition in such a way that restrictions to the client's personal freedom are minimal. Treatment is guided by the minimum sufficiency principle, whereby clients participate in programs exerting the least restriction necessary for the provision of the desired outcomes.

In the contemporary mental health service environment, this concept has been applied by dramatically decreasing clients' average lengths of stay in hospitals. Lengths of stay in state mental hospitals were 421 days in 1969 and 189 and 1978. Currently, the average hospital stay for psychiatric conditions is less than 8 days (Levine et al., 2005). Rather than emphasizing delivery of intense therapy, the contemporary goal of hospitalization is client stabilization. Once stabilized, clients are released to the care of community-based agencies and practitioners, where appropriate outpatient treatment plans are devised and implemented.

These shorter stays have given rise to the revolving-door phenomenon. Some clients are admitted, stabilized, released to outpatient care, and then readmitted. Too often, this becomes a repetitive cycle, an additional stressor on the client, and a burden not only for the service delivery systems but also for clients' families, who formerly found respite in more lengthy hospital stays. One troubling illustration of the revolving door is the story of Sylvia Frumkin, described in Susan Sheehan's book *Is There No Place on Earth for Me?* (1983), who experienced 27 admissions to eight different hospitals and 45 changes in treatment setting, all taking place in a period of 18 years!

For successful service delivery of the "least restrictive treatment" within the contemporary environment, functional interagency referral and communication networks across the community's continuum of mental health are prerequisites. Coordinating councils can be established to coordinate the delivery of mental health and adjunctive support services. Furthermore, mental health professionals must monitor the progress of their clients when in inpatient care and work closely with hospital staff to develop adequate discharge plans. Many community mental health centers employ peer support specialists, who can assist in providing a soft landing for persons returning to the community after a hospital stay. Such an approach characterizes the wraparound philosophy, the use of culturally competent, community-based supports and services to assist persons with severe mental illness as they seek to be safe, stay together, and maintain everyday adaptive functioning (Walker & Bruns, 2006).

ASSERTIVE COMMUNITY TREATMENT PROGRAMS

Persons with severe mental illness frequently require a variety of services, such as general medical care, mental health treatment, substance abuse treatment, housing services, and vocational rehabilitation. Many of these services were more centrally available at long-term-stay mental institutions and are fragmented in community settings. Those in most need of services demonstrate limited ability to advocate for themselves, to initiate provider contact, and to coordinate the complex scheduling demands when they are referred to multiple service providers. As a result, the chronically mentally ill have difficulty receiving the desirable or necessary services (Mechanic, 1991).

A case management model has emerged as a primary way to assist clients in accessing, coordinating, and integrating different services. Assertive community treatment (ACT) is perhaps the most comprehensive case management approach (Drake, 1998). It attempts to bring all of the functions of long-term hospitalization into a community-based system of care for persons with severe and persistent mental illness (Corrigan, Mueser, Bond, Drake, & Solomon, 2008). The foundational tenets of ACT (Test, 1998) are

1. The community is the proper location of care for persons with severe and persistent mental illness, since it is there where they face daily, ongoing stressors.
2. Community-based treatment and related supports must be comprehensive and capable of addressing all areas of the client's life.
3. Treatment must be flexible and individualized to meet the individual needs of persons within their unique ecological setting and across time.
4. Treatments and supports must be well organized and available 7 days a week, 24 hours a day.

A team of professionals representing the professions of counseling, social work, nursing, rehabilitation, and psychiatry provides comprehensive, community-based treatment, rehabilitation, and support to clients who have not historically responded well to traditional outpatient treatment. Often, clients served by ACT teams have co-occurring problems, such as homelessness, substance abuse, or involvement in the correctional/judicial system. The team's caseload is small and the responsibility is shared among team members. This arrangement allows wraparound services to be as flexible and intensive as needed.

The effectiveness of ACT is well established (Lehman, Steinwachs, & Co-Investigators of the PORT Project, 1998; Mueser, Bond, Drake, & Resnick, 1998; Salkever et al., 1999; Santos et al., 1993), and it has achieved status as an evidence-based treatment (discussed later) for persons with severe psychiatric disabilities (Corrigan et al., 2008).

With services such as medication delivery, rehabilitation, and behavioral training in basic adaptive living skills delivered in community living settings, the problems of nonattendance and lack of transportation are avoided. This is a costly service and is reserved for persons with severe psychiatric disabilities (Corrigan et al., 2008).

RECOVERY AND THE CONSUMER MOVEMENT

Consumers have become increasingly influential in shaping mental health policies and delivering services (Kaufmann, 1999). This consumer and self-help movement is an expression of the social justice movement that dates back to the mid-1800s. Reformers like Dorothea Dix worked tirelessly to call America's attention to the plight of poor, indigent persons with mental illness. Traveling across the nation, she raised consciousness of the deplorable conditions and treatment of the mentally ill and advocated for the creation of large hospitals to treat this population. Elizabeth Packard, released from a mental institution after having been committed against her will, initiated a national campaign to prevent the similar incarceration of others without a jury trial to determine their sanity (McLean, 2010). After having experienced two major hospitalizations, one lasting for 3 years, Clifford Beers (1908) wrote a book detailing abuses he had experienced and brought attention to the conditions of fellow patients. With the support of other clinicians, he established the National Committee for Mental Hygiene in 1909, which became known as the National Mental Health Association in 1950 (McLean, 2010).

The underlying assumption of the consumer and self-help movement is that persons with shared experiences can be more helpful and can provide more supportive environments than persons who have not experienced psychiatric treatment (Corrigan et al., 2008). Underlying this movement is the strong desire and effort of mental health consumers with chronic mental illness to develop appropriate control of psychiatric treatment and put an end to the oppressive stigma that accompanies such diagnostic classifications. The notable consequences of the consumer movement include consumer-developed and -managed systems of care, self-help groups, consumer advocacy organizations, and the recovery perspective, which is discussed later.

The number of self-help and consumer groups increased rapidly throughout the last quarter of the 20th century (Levine et al., 2005). Putnam (2000) noted that the growth of the self-help movement occurred at a time when membership in other types of social organizations, such as churches, political organizations, and even traditional neighborhoods, decreased. The number of Alcoholics Anonymous (AA) groups in the United States increased from around 50 in 1942 to well over 58,000 in 2012 (Alcoholics Anonymous, 2012). Parents Without Partners (PWP) started in 1957 with one group consisting of two women. It is promoted as the world's largest nonprofit membership organization focusing on the interests and welfare of single parents and their children (Parents Without Partners, 2012). The National Self-Help Clearinghouse was formed in 1976 and communicates information about the activities of the more than 500,000 self-help groups currently operating in the United States (Katz, 1993; White & Madara, 2002). Self-help groups focus on a wide array of issues, including addictions, abuse, bereavement, mental illness, physical disability, parenting, and other specific life stressors (White & Madara, 2002).

In addition to consumer-managed programs and self-help groups, a variety of consumer support groups have emerged to assist clients and their families as they deal with the symptoms and various consequences of mental illness (Fristad & Sisson, 2004). Frequently, these groups appear to meet three vital family needs: support, education, and empowerment (Marsh, 1996). Through these groups, families find assistance in mobilizing the available resources and managing complex emotional reactions as they support family members with mental illness. Furthermore, such consumer groups are vehicles for advocacy efforts to improve standards of professional practice and care. For example, the National Alliance for the Mentally Ill (NAMI) is a self-help support and advocacy organization whose members are consumers, families, and friends of persons diagnosed with severe mental illness (NAMI, 2005). It consists of over 1,000 local affiliates and 50 state organizations. The advocacy efforts of NAMI seek increased funding for research, housing, jobs, rehabilitation, and suitable health insurance.

Perhaps the most significant consequence for community mental health has been the rise of the recovery perspective. The U.S. government's Substance Abuse and Mental Health Services Administration (SAMHSA) defines *recovery* as "a journey of healing and transformation enabling a person with a mental health problem to live a meaningful life in a community of his or her choice while striving to achieve his or her full potential" (SAMHSA, 2006, p. 1). This definition describes an underlying philosophy for mental health services, an approach to treatment delivery, and the experience of consumers. Ten fundamental components of recovery philosophy are

- *Self-Direction* Recovery is directed by the consumer who best knows his or her personal life goals and can design a unique path for their attainment.
- *Person-Centered* Multiple paths are available in moving toward recovery, and the ongoing journey builds upon the consumer's unique strengths, resiliencies, needs, preferences, experiences, and cultural background.
- *Empowerment* Consumers have the right to choose speak for themselves and their needs, desires, and aspirations. Doing so enables them to gain control of their destinies and influences the role of societal structures in their lives.
- *Holistic* Recovery encompasses all aspects of the consumer's life and is not limited to his or her treatment.
- *Non-linear* Recovery is a process of journeying marked by steady progress, occasional setbacks, and growing through the experience.
- *Strength-based* Recovery builds upon the inherent and acquired resiliencies, strengths, coping skills, and worth of the person.
- *Peer Support* Other consumers in recovery create an invaluable social network and support system that facilitates social learning of skills and accompanying attitudes.
- *Respect* Mental health systems and community demonstrate respect and full inclusion of consumers. Efforts are directed toward the elimination of stigma and discrimination of persons with mental illness.
- *Responsibility* Consumers take responsibility of their personal journeys of recovery. Doing so provides self-understanding and increased meaning to their lives.
- *Hope* This is the fundamental and essential message of recovery. Persons can and do experience a better future, characterized by living their lives, and not their diagnoses. (SAMHSA, 2006, pp. 1–2)

Mental health services are transformed in fundamental ways as recovery philosophy is implemented across the service delivery system. Partnerships between consumers and mental health professionals in developing person-centered, collaboratively devised goals and methods supplant the use of power assertion and coercive procedures in the development of treatment plans and adherence. Consumers are viewed as capable and responsible persons rather than patients with "broken brains" who are needy, helpless, and dependent upon professional supports for their survival.

The lives of consumers *in recovery* become a deeply personal journey of healing, rediscovery, self-renewal, and transformation (Onken, 2006). Wellness strategies, such as journaling, visiting friends, exercising, nutritious eating, praying, meditating, doing acts of kindness, and practicing gratitude, are well suited to integration into recovery work (Fredrickson, 2009; Onken, Craig, Ridgway, Ralph, & Cook, 2007). Ridgway (1999) sees recovery as a three-part journey in which the consumer reclaims a positive sense of self, takes charge of the management of his or her psychiatric condition, and recovers personal roles and a life beyond the mental health system.

Consumers in recovery have much to offer in service to their peers in mental health treatment. Such consumers, referred to as *peer support specialists,* apply special abilities acquired through their own experiences and act as liaisons in agencies between consumers and mental health professionals. By sharing their own stories and accessing resources, these specialists actively assist other consumers as they move along in their own recovery. In some states, peer support specialists provide Medicaid-reimbursable services, such as vocational and housing assistance, the development of person-centered plans, wellness recovery action plans (WRAP), and advanced directives.

Other consumers develop and maintain after-hour helplines and drop-in centers. For example, consumers who demonstrate stability might be trained in fundamental communication skills and telephone interviewing. They then operate a hotline service that is utilized not only by other consumers of mental health services but also by members of the community who seek information about mental health and the available services, or who simply need to talk to someone. It is critical that helpline staff be trained in recognizing clinical emergencies, making referrals, and identifying the available community resources. Drop-in centers provide a place to go and participate in a variety of activities in a nonstigmatizing environment. Such centers are especially helpful to consumers who are living in the community but feeling lonely and isolated.

EVIDENCE-BASED TREATMENTS

In the past, mental health professionals have been admonished to select only therapeutic approaches that have empirically demonstrated effectiveness. Often these calls are met with some resistance. It is argued that counseling is as much art as it is science. Furthermore, the controlled conditions of lab research are viewed as lacking the down-and-dirty realities of actual clinical practice in community settings. As a result, many clinicians find lab-based outcome studies to be interesting, but not particularly helpful.

But times are changing. Mental health care providers in the United States, including community mental health centers and the Veterans Administration, are being mandated to offer evidence-based treatments (McHugh & Barlow, 2010). This is being brought about by increased attention to quality control and accountability by consumers, third-party reimbursers, and professional organizations such as the American Counseling Association (ACA; Bradley, Sexton, & Smith, 2005), the American Psychological Association (APA; Clay, 2011), and the Center for Mental Health Services of SAMHSA (Chandler, 2009).

Evidence-based programs are specific programs and interventions that have been shown through research and program evaluation to be effective in treating or preventing mental health problems. No single set of criteria has been used to define *evidence-based.* The typical standard is studies in which the particular treatment produced change, which was evident in randomized controlled trials, in comparison with another treatment approach or no treatment, and that the outcome has been replicated (Kazdin, 2011).

The rationale for using evidence-based treatments is straightforward. The results of numerous studies indicate that clinical outcomes are superior when treatments with empirical support are used (Cukrowicz et al., 2011). Such results have brought about increased emphasis on quality control of delivered services within community mental health systems, as well as increased accountability to consumers. In addition, mental health counselors have an ethical and moral responsibility to know whether the interventions they use actually promote the welfare of their clients or do harm (Bradley et al., 2005). Furthermore, developing specific evidence-based practice guides should assist busy counselors, who have limited time to comb through the relevant literature (Clay, 2011; Cukrowicz et al., 2005).

The Center for Mental Health Services of SAMHSA recommends that several psychosocial models be integrated into the delivery of mental health services to persons with severe and persistent mental illness (Chandler, 2009). These include ACT, integrated dual disorders treatment, family psychoeducation, supported employment, illness management and recovery, and medication management. To assist mental health practitioners and organizations access information regarding evidence-based treatments, SAMHSA has developed the National Registry of Evidence-based Programs and Practices (NREPP) (see http://www.nrepp.samhsa.gov/). This searchable database provides descriptive summaries, target populations, types of outcomes achieved, costs of implementation, and independent expert ratings of specific approaches that have been identified as evidence based.

SPECIFIC ISSUES IN COMMUNITY MENTAL HEALTH

Having discussed several contemporary trends in community mental health, we can now consider how community-based agencies, organizations, and mental health centers address a variety of specific mental health–related concerns: homelessness, chronic mental illness, dual diagnosis, corrections, and disaster response/emergency management.

COMMUNITY MENTAL HEALTH AND THE HOMELESS

The problems of mental illness and homelessness present significant and challenging issues for communities at large and community mental health in particular (Torrey, 2006; Yanos, Barrow, & Tsemberis, 2004). Although the existence of the problem is well recognized, identification of specific mental health needs and interventions is hampered by several factors (Bachrach, 1992). First, how is homelessness defined? Although the term refers simply to an absence of housing or permanent residence, common usage implies more significant deprivation (Callicutt, 2006). The population of concern is not simply those whose homes have burned down or been destroyed in a hurricane or tornado. Rather, the concern is for those persons who lack community ties and resources. In addition, there are difficulties assessing the mental health needs and prevalence of mental illness within the population. Second, is abuse of substances considered a mental illness? Third, at any given time, the homeless population in a particular area overlaps with other populations, such as those being housed in jails and other correctional facilities. Finally, it is difficult if not impossible to speak of homeless persons as comprising a stable population because they tend to be a transient group. Thus, the vague and moving target further confounds efforts toward accurate needs assessment.

There is consensus, though, that homeless persons with severe mental illness often present complex psychosocial histories (Thomas, 2006). Compared to domiciled adults with severe mental illness, the homeless severely mentally ill are more likely unemployed (Markos, Baron, & Allen, 2005; Pickett-Schenk et al., 2002), display more severe psychiatric symptomatology, and have higher rates of inpatient admissions. In addition, there is a higher frequency of alcohol and chemical abuse among the homeless mentally ill (Caton et al., 1994, 1995; Drake et al., 1991).

Some studies have found that the needs of homeless women and their families differ from those of the homeless mentally ill and include histories of domestic violence, life circumstance–related emotional distress, multiple residence moves prior to homelessness, and inadequate social support systems (Khanna, Singh, Nemil, Best, & Ellis, 1992; Markos et al., 2005; Vostanis, Grattan, & Cumella, 1998). Many females who are homeless *and* experience mental illness have past traumas in their histories (Markos et al., 2005). In addition, the needs of homeless women differ from those of homeless men (North & Smith, 1993). Such studies suggest a need for services that provide job-seeking and job-retention skills, on-the-job social skill development, and ready access to mental health services and relevant community resources. The importance of adequate assessment, treatment planning, and implementation of programs is apparent.

There are several barriers to the provision of mental health services to homeless populations that must be overcome if adequate service delivery is to occur. Counselors may mistakenly believe that the problems of the homeless are not treatable, that their problems are too complex and time consuming, or that they simply would rather live a life on the streets than seek help (Friedman & Levine-Holdowsky, 1997). Furthermore, the policies and procedures within agencies and the working relationships between agencies can prevent collaborative program development and implementation (Rowe, Hoge, & Fisk, 1996). The difficulties of connecting potential consumers who are homeless and living on the street to available mental health services, along with institutional barriers, such as funding for transient, out-of-state homeless persons, necessitate the development and implementation of innovative programs.

In many communities, the services required for the adequate treatment of issues presented by homeless clients are fragmented. Thus, case management has become a primary approach in work with homeless, mentally ill clients (Thomas, 2006). Two common case management approaches are brokered case management and ACT (Wolff et al., 1997). In the brokered case management model, the case manager assesses the needs of the client and arranges for provision of services by purchasing service contracts from various service providers. Mental health services are provided through traditional outpatient programs. The case manager plays the key role in integrating the various treatment components into a coherent service delivery plan (Thomas, 2006). In contrast, ACT staff provide a wraparound service to homeless clients that includes 24-hour emergency services, medication and money management, and assistance with daily living (Wolff et al., 1997). The mental health counselor functions as a member of the ACT team rather than as a contracted service provider.

Numerous programs have been designed to meet the specific needs of the homeless. Some of these are very focused, whereas others are comprehensive and offer a wide range of services. The Thresholds of Chicago has established an assertive outreach for the homeless experiencing serious mental illness. Licensed clinicians work on the streets, in shelters, and wherever the homeless may be. Their goal is to get the homeless mentally ill off the street and into the necessary services, which will help them regain stability in their lives. A mobile assessment unit actually cruises the streets, seeking out persons in need of services. Sometimes, team workers bike through public parks in response to crisis calls. As a result of the assessment, persons in need of services may be hospitalized, provided temporary shelter, or connected to long-term supportive programs.

The Center for the Homeless (CFH) of South Bend, Indiana, is a model program that provides shelter, food, and comprehensive life-building services for as many as 200 guests each day. It utilizes a continuum-of-care model of integrated services ranging from crisis treatment and assessment to education, job training, supportive housing, and home ownership. Over 45,000 persons have been served since CFH opened its doors in 1989. Through the partnership of more than 30 area organizations, the CFH offers comprehensive educational, medical, and mental health services to homeless adults and their children. Upon assessment, guests applying to stay for more than 30 days are assigned to one of three tracks: Starting Over, Work Plus (for guests already working in stable employment), and Health First (for mentally and/or physically ill or disabled guests). These programs consist of the following combinations of services: individual, group, and family counseling; job and social skill building; job-seeking and retention skill building; and transitional housing and employment referrals. For guests who remain in the program and successfully complete their track, the potential outcomes include stable housing with personal home ownership or permanent supportive housing.

COMMUNITY MENTAL HEALTH AND THE CHRONICALLY MENTALLY ILL

As noted, a policy of deinstitutionalization has been foundational to the U.S. mental health agenda for over four decades. Propelled by revelations of inhumane conditions in state hospitals, the development of psychotropic medications, expanded third-party reimbursement options, and legal restrictions on the specific criteria for involuntary commitments, community-based mental health services became the primary service delivery system for persons with chronic mental illness (Dickey, Fisher, Siegel, Altaffer, & Azeni, 1997). Treatment delivery to this population now takes place primarily in the network of residential settings, community outpatient clinics, other community-based programs, and community general hospitals. The assumption is that a systematic mix of community-based services can demonstrate effectiveness equal to or greater than institutionalization.

Cuddeback and Morrissey (2010) note that persons with acute mental health needs and milder conditions have generally benefited from this transition. It has been less beneficial for persons with chronic and severe mental illness. These persons present complex clinical pictures and require not only psychiatric treatment but often also social rehabilitation, housing, health care, supportive employment services, social supports, and substance abuse counseling (Rosenblatt & Attkisson, 1993). Many human service agencies are organized around a single-problem focus, so it is challenging to pull together a comprehensive treatment plan to address the multifaceted goals of the chronically mentally ill.

The primary emphasis during the 1970s and into the early 1990s was service integration (SI). The key to adequate treatment involved the capacity to integrate services into a coherent treatment package using strategies such as interagency and interdepartmental planning councils, regional information and referral services, and community-based care (Cuddeback & Morrissey, 2010). Consumers of community mental health services with severe mental illness were typically viewed as clients who participated in various services offered along the continuum of care. Thus, clients were prepared for more effective lives in the community by being fit into "program slots" (Carling, 1995). The necessary integrative function was left to bachelor's-level case managers, who worked closely with the network of available mental health and human services agencies and providers within the community.

In the late 1990s, enthusiasm for service integration models waned due to inadequate funding for actually *integrating* services and the resulting lack of service coordination. State and federal money was most often directed to agencies, not networks. The assumption that agencies had the wherewithal to share allocated or surplus funds for service networks proved somewhat erroneous. It was in this context that the service integration model gave way to the emerging evidence-based practice movement. In 1998, the Robert Wood Johnson Foundation funded a conference where a national consensus panel identified six specific evidence-based practices (EBPs) for persons with severe and persistent mental illness (identified in a previous section of this chapter). Illness management and recovery strategies, one of the six EBPs, emphasizes self-management, practical peer supports, coping strategies, self-determination, and personal strengths and capacities (Cuddeback & Morrissey, 2010).

Community mental health centers continue to serve as a primary provider of mental health services and to offer a cluster of services, including emergency, inpatient, outpatient, day treatment, and partial hospitalization services in single-stop locations (Cuddeback & Morrissey, 2010). Mental health services include assessment and diagnosis, supportive and clinical counseling for psychiatric and substance abuse problems, and medication management services. Although ongoing contact with clients prevents most crises, crisis intervention and stabilization services, including 24-hour hotlines, walk-in crisis services, mobile outreach, and community residential options, are offered to clients and family members. Frequently, peers provide a supportive array of services such as self-help groups, drop-in centers, and social clubs. These are consumer-defined, -controlled, and -operated programs and activities that typically supplement those services delivered by mental health professionals.

To ensure that chronically mentally ill clients receive all necessary services to remain and function optimally in the community, many community mental health programs utilize ACT. On occasion, former consumers of services have become staff of ACT teams (Holloway & Carson, 2001). Dewa and colleagues (2003) point out that the unique elements of ACT require informal inputs of time, which can place high demands on team members and increase potential for burn-out. Drake (1998) reports that extensive study of ACT has yielded "robust evidence" of its effectiveness in reducing hospitalization and increasing stability of housing and client satisfaction (p. 173).

COMMUNITY MENTAL HEALTH AND THE DUAL-DIAGNOSED CLIENT

Mental health and community counselors frequently lament that basic research on mental disorder and its treatment does not always relate well to the types of problems presented by clients in the real world. One area that is sometimes shortchanged in academic preparation is the possibility of comorbidity (i.e., two conditions existing concurrently). The terms *co-morbidity, dual disorders,* and *dually diagnosed client* refer to the presence of both substance-related and psychiatric conditions in clients.

Seligman (1998) notes that as many as two-thirds of clients presenting with substance abuse disorders have a coexisting condition. Regier and colleagues (1990), in reporting the results of the Epidemiologic Catchment Area Study, note that 29% of all persons with mental disorders met the criteria for a substance abuse disorder. In clinical samples, Miller (1994) reported that 30% with depressive disorders, 50% with bipolar disorders, and 50% with psychotic disorders had substance use disorders. Carbaugh and Sias (2010) report that one-half of all clients presenting with eating disorder abuse alcohol and drugs. A related problem occurs with multiple-substance abuse and dependence, when the client meets the diagnostic criteria for the abuse of two or more substances (Yalisove, 2004).

A chicken-and-egg dilemma occurs when we attempt to determine the specific etiology of the disorders. Which came first—the mental illness or the substance abuse/dependence disorder? There is some inferential evidence that the psychiatric conditions tend to precede the substance-related disorder (Yalisove, 2004). This sequence appears to be common in adolescents and in women more than in men. Personality disorder does not appear to be induced by alcohol abuse. However, Verheul and colleagues (2000) have shown that symptoms of anxiety and mood disorders may be caused by excessive alcohol use.

According to Ryglewicz and Pepper (1992), much of the impetus in developing programs for dually diagnosed persons stems from the failure of existing delivery systems to achieve treatment success with this population. The contemporary consumer of mental health services, as a member of the postdeinstitutionalization generation, is more vulnerable to substance abuse and dependence than previous generations, who in experiencing longer inpatient hospital stays were more insulated from the influences of our drug-infested culture. Furthermore, seeing the mentally ill and addicts or alcoholics as two distinct groups, programs and treatment approaches were designed to address the presenting concerns of each population with little or no concern about symptom overlap. Finally, mental health and substance abuse programs were often housed in either different departments or different organizations. As a result, basic questions in case formulation and treatment planning revolved around the following concerns: Should removal of the substance-related disorder take place prior to implementation of treatment for the co-occurring emotional disorder? Or will the client be better served by entering an inpatient chemical abuse treatment program prior to receiving treatment in the mental health setting?

Traditional approaches to treatment tend to take the linear approach by first moving the person toward recovery from substance abuse/dependence. Thus, the client is initially admitted to an inpatient or outpatient chemical abuse treatment program. Then, as sufficient progress is noted, referral or transfer is made to the mental health agency. This tendency toward linear treatment has persisted for several reasons. First, attempts at integrating treatment have been complicated by poor communication between or among programs and staff. For example, the substance abuse and mental health units of a community mental health center are so disconnected in practice that staff from one program rarely have an opportunity to conduct joint staffing of cases for the purpose of case planning and monitoring. In such settings, it is unlikely that a truly integrated treatment plan can take place. Treatment in such a context often proceeds with the right hand of treatment not knowing what the left hand is doing. Second, the working knowledge of the assessment and treatment of mental illness and substance-related disorders varies among staff of the respective programs, further complicating staff and interagency communication and the coordination of treatment planning, implementation, and ongoing assessment. Third, the funding mechanisms, eligibility requirements, geographic boundaries, and administrative policies of the mental health and substance abuse treatment systems inhibit coordinated and effective treatment of dually diagnosed populations (Young & Grella, 1998).

Several approaches to the treatment of dually diagnosed clients have emerged in recent years. Inpatient dual-diagnosis programs are typically housed in psychiatric hospitals (Stevens & Smith, 2005). The substance abuse and the psychological condition of the client must be assessed independently and in relation to each other. The goals are to withdraw clients safely from substances, establish physical and emotional stability, and identify and treat the coexisting disorders. In addition to the delivery of mental health interventions, the treatment plans may include psycho-pharmacological interventions, such as antidepressant, antianxiety, or mood-stabilizing medications. Mental health counselors working in these settings assist in assessment and treatment planning, provide psychoeducational components to clients and families, cofacilitate counseling and skill-building groups, and conduct individual and family counseling. Certification as a chemical abuse counselor is sometimes required or highly preferred.

Evans and Sullivan (2001) describe a modified 12-step program that integrates treatment of both substance-related and psychological disorders. They recognize an underlying process that is shared by AA and mental health counseling. Their model uses the 12 steps as a foundation and builds in cognitive-behavioral interventions at each specific step. The goal is recovery from both the mental illness and the substance abuse/dependence.

Aaron Beck and his associates (Beck, Wright, Newman, & Liese, 1993) conceptualize the dually diagnosed client within a cognitive framework. Particular childhood experiences give rise to underlying cognitive schemas characterized by dysfunctional beliefs, assumptions, and rules. When these are activated in specific situations, chemical use is viewed as a compensatory strategy to decrease personal emotional discomfort. The goal of the cognitive treatment is to provide alternative cognitive and behavioral strategies to release clients from the vicious circle of craving and relapse that characterizes their pattern of behavior.

The integrated dual disorders treatment (IDDT) model is registered by SAMHSA as an evidence-based approach. This approach involves the cross-training of practitioners in the provision of integrated, comprehensive services that address both disorders concurrently in one treatment setting (Biegel, Kola, & Ronis, 2006). The goal is recovery from both conditions. Treatment occurs in an orderly sequence and is calibrated with the client's level of motivation and readiness to change. The transtheoretical model and motivational interviewing strategies are integrated into the program. Dual-disorder groups, self-help groups, family psychoeducation, and integrated psychopharmacology are also key components of the treatment package (Chandler, 2009). A resource kit is available for the implementation of IDDT (SAMHSA, 2008). Research has demonstrated the model's overall effectiveness as well as support for each component.

COMMUNITY MENTAL HEALTH AND CORRECTIONS

Increasingly, our nation's correctional facilities are serving significant numbers of law violators with moderate to severe mental illness. According to the Bureau of Justice Statistics (2008), at mid-year 2005 more than one-half of all persons in prisons and jails in the United States had a mental health problem. This statistic included approximately 705,600 inmates in state prisons, another 78,000 in federal prisons, and 479,900 in city and county jails, representing 56% of all state prisoners, 45% of federal prisoners, and 64% of local jail inmates. Of the incarcerated with mental health problems, 43% in state prisons and 54% in local jails met the criteria for mania in the American Psychiatric Association's *Diagnostic and Statistical Manual of Mental Disorders* (*DSM*). In addition, 23% with mental problems in state prisons and 30% in local jails reported symptoms of depression. And 15% of state prisoners and 24% of jail inmates met the criteria for psychosis (Bureau of Justice Statistics, 2006). Dual disorders were also prominent features in 74% of state prisoners and 76% of local jail inmates with mental health problems, who met the criteria for substance dependence or abuse. Around one-quarter of both state and local jail inmates having mental health problems have served three or more prior incarcerations.

The problem of inmates with mental illness is substantial, and evidence suggests that the situation may be getting worse (Adams & Ferrandino, 2008). There is a high percentage of repeat offenders with mental illness, and incarceration does not meet the needs of this population. Recidivism is high, and mental health concerns go largely untreated. This circumstance is not surprising, since it is not the primary role of correctional facilities to treat mental illness. There is little reason to believe that the number of inmates with mental illness will decrease any time soon. Nor is it likely that there will be a rapid expansion of state mental health facilities. Thus, correctional management at the state and local levels has come to recognize the need to develop and implement programs, strategies, and techniques to manage this population (Adams & Ferrandino, (2008).

Hiday and Burns (2010) identify five categories of persons with mental illness who come into contact with the criminal justice system. The first category consists of persons with mental illness who are arrested for nuisance behaviors, for which non-mentally ill persons would typically not be arrested. Common offenses of this group include loitering or trespassing. The second group includes those who are arrested for what might be described as *survival behaviors* (Hiday & Burns, 2010), such as shoplifting or not paying restaurant bills. These first two groups commit only misdemeanor offenses.

Persons included in the third group come to the attention of the justice system as a result of substance abuse or dependence. They are often arrested for creating a disturbance, public intoxication, assault, prostitution, or some form of stealing for the purpose of obtaining drugs. The fourth group consists of persons with severe mental illness who are psychopathic or diagnosed with antisocial personality disorder and have high rates of substance abuse (Hiday & Burns, 2010, p. 497). Their aggressive behaviors disqualify them from receiving much needed community services. Their criminal record is due more to characterological problems than to their mental illness.

The fifth group identified by Hiday and Burns (2010) is the smallest of the five and consists of the severely mentally ill who are the "stereotyped raging madman out of control" (p. 498). These persons are driven by psychotic symptomatology to commit criminally violent acts. Although fewest in number, these persons receive extensive media attention.

A number of obstacles can limit the availability of mental health services in jails. The designs of many jail facilities do not allow the conducting of assessments or counseling on the premises. For example, the local city lockup may have no conference rooms or empty cells available. When called to conduct lethality checks on persons being held, the mental health counselor may be required to assess the person in a cell reserved for prisoners held in solitary confinement. Furthermore, correctional staff is not trained with adequate sophistication to observe, classify, or treat mentally ill inmates. Although conducting counseling is clearly beyond the scope of correctional officers' training, they receive little training in recognizing indicators of mental illness or lethality. If symptoms are recognized, the jail staff is often ill equipped to intervene. Rapid turnover in the inmate populations further limits the logic of using jails as sites for more than crisis intervention. Inmate stabilization rather than symptom remediation is the common goal. Finally, release of inmates into the community often takes place without an adequate follow-up plan for mental health services. Clearly, articulation agreements between correctional facilities and community mental health and other human service agencies are required if the multiple service needs of this population, such as housing, employment, and mental health and substance abuse counseling, are to be met.

Several approaches have been taken by justice and corrections systems to better serve the needs of persons with mental illness who come in contact with the legal system. First, persons must be found blameworthy in order to be convicted of a crime. Conviction requires that the person be capable of making a rationale decision to commit the act. In addition, to be brought to court, persons must be capable of understanding the charges and able to assist in their own legal defense. A person who is not capable of understanding or assisting is determined to be incompetent to stand trial. In contrast, if the accused is able to stand trial, but it is determined that mental illness prevented rational decision making at the time of the offense, the person cannot be held responsible for the criminal act. In such cases, the person is determined to be not guilty by reason of insanity (NGRI). When such a court decision is rendered, all charges are cleared and the person's record is cleared of all charges. If the person is determined to be a danger to self or others, the court can mandate treatment at a state hospital. Some states have enacted guilty but mentally ill laws (GBMI), that hold mentally ill persons responsible for the criminal act when it is found that the mental illness did not make them incapable of rationally choosing to commit the criminal act (Hiday & Burns, 2010). Finally, relatively new are mental health courts, where special hearings on a separate docket are conducted to monitor offenders' compliance with court orders for treatment and behavioral change (Hiday & Burns, 2010).

Programs have been developed to divert persons with mental illness from the correctional system to community mental health treatment and supports. Substantial evidence demonstrates that these programs increase mental health access and quality of life for those with mental illness without increasing the risk to the public (Parker, Foley, Moore, & Broner, 2009). There are two primary types of jail diversion programs: prebooking and postbooking.

Prebooking diversion programs intervene for individuals with mental illness who break the law but whose behavior is deemed nonviolent and related to an existing psychiatric condition. For example, in a model program in Memphis, Tennessee, police officers volunteer to become members of a crisis intervention team (Morrisey, Fagan, & Cocozza, 2009). They receive 40 hours of training in psychopathology, deescalation management, and the diverting of persons to a special mental health agency rather than taking them to jail for booking.

In contrast, *postbooking diversion programs* are more common and are implemented after formal charges have been filed. After being booked, persons suspected of having severe mental illness or co-occurring substance disorder are screened for mental health problems, program eligibility, and willingness to participate in the diversion (Parker et al., 2009). Negotiations then take place among prosecutors, attorneys, the court, and mental health providers. The person agrees to participate or continue in mental health treatment in lieu of prosecution. Often, charges are reduced or dismissed.

The transition of moving from jails and prisons to the community is especially difficult for persons with mental illness. In addition to the stigma of having served time, they may need to renew prescriptions for medications and find housing, transportation, and employment. Such transition issues have prompted the development of *reentry programs*. Typically, a task force consisting of staff from community mental health, corrections, and human services organizations hold regularly scheduled meetings. Persons with mental illness who are within 90 days of being released from jail or prison are identified. Plans are made to prepare these persons for reintroduction into the community. Start-up money, transportation, potential employment opportunities, counseling, and peer supports are arranged to ease the person through the adjustment process. The goal of reentry programs is to decrease the high rate of recidivism in this population. Given their training in wellness, pathology, and persons in ecological contexts, clinical mental health counselors possess important knowledge and skills for working with corrections-related concerns.

COMMUNITY MENTAL HEALTH, DISASTER RESPONSE, AND EMERGENCY MANAGEMENT SYSTEMS

Imagine you are serving as a clinical mental health counselor at a community mental health center. A very severe line of thunderstorms has moved through the area in the late night and after it passes, you receive a cell phone call from your clinical supervisor. She informs you that the south end of town, where your agency is located, was hit by a very powerful tornado. The area is devastated and your mental health facility has been nearly destroyed. What would be your immediate cognitive and emotional response? What would you do? Is your personal office still intact? What about the client records? And the medication room? How will client care continue or be disrupted in the aftermath? Were other important human service agencies affected?

As we leave this scenario, we hope that adequate plans for community disaster response and emergency management have been designed and practiced. Unfortunately, the world has been beset with numerous large-scale crises and human-made or natural disasters. The terrorist attack on the World Trade Center, Hurricane Katrina, the Virginia Tech shootings, and the Haitian earthquake call attention to the need of well-trained clinical mental health counselors to respond within days, weeks, months, and even years following such mass disaster events.

Soon after the events of September 11, 2001, a group of mental health and mass violence experts convened to identify best practices and systematic training approaches to develop and maintain a nucleus of well-prepared early mental health responders (NIMH, 2002). It has become quite clear that the knowledge and skills required of early mental health responders to large-scale disasters is quite different from those used by mental health counselors in their typical daily work (J. R. Rogers, 2007). The Council for Accreditation of Counseling and Related Educational Programs (CACREP) has infused crisis- and trauma-based practice, disaster response, and emergency management systems-related learning outcomes into the 2009 CACREP standards (i.e., Clinical Mental Health Counselor Standards A.9, 10; C.6; D.6; K.5; L.3). Mental health counselors should understand and know how to respond to individuals, families, and communities affected by crises and disasters. Furthermore, they need to understand how emergency management plans operate in mental health agencies and in communities.

It is well beyond the scope of this text to address the complexities of disaster response and emergency management. The intent, here, is to provide a very brief introduction to the role clinical mental health counselors and their agencies play in responding to catastrophic events.

The paradigm of clinical mental health counseling, as presented in Chapter 3, provides an excellent tool to assist practitioners in conceptualizing and responding to individuals, related ecological contexts, and community needs when crisis and disaster strike. The model directs the attention of emergency plan developers and first responders to the interaction of factors operating across levels of context. Mental health counselors, in applying the paradigm, gain perspective on the nature of the crisis and on its impact on persons, their immediate network of relationships, social supports, and the larger community. Also considered are larger cultural and sociopolitical factors, such as institutional racism, socioeconomic class, predominant subcultural values, and geographic location, which interact in individual and community responses to catastrophic events.

Suppose, for example, that the Great Lakes region of the United States is hit by a massive winter ice storm. Widespread power outages, icy and impassable roads, and bitter cold cripple the region. How might the physical, emotional, and social impact experienced and expressed by persons living in urban Detroit (or another metropolitan area near the Great Lakes region) be different from the impact on persons living in the sparsely populated rural regions of Michigan's Eastern Upper Peninsula (EUP)? How, specifically, might individual and community factors interact? To bring perspective to the discussion, please consider an excerpt taken from the Emergency Preparedness Program Manual developed by the Chippewa County Michigan Health Department (see Figure 11.2). What unique strengths, resources, and values operate in the EUP, and how might these influence the responses of individuals and communities in that region? How specifically might the clinical

---

FIGURE 11-2

Introduction to Survival Preparedness

For too long, the term "survival preparedness" has called to mind paranoid separatists or recluse individuals who give up the conveniences of modern society, drop out of the government's databases and live in one-room backwoods cabins like the Unabomber.

Well, the Chippewa County Health Department (CCHD) Emergency Preparedness/Bioterrorism Office (EPBO) and the good folks in Chippewa County know survivalists are much more likely to be Sugar Islanders buying shutters a few months before the November Storm Season, Trout Lake residents preparing a two week cache of food and water in case the next big blizzard hits or a Yooper who keeps a few blankets, a pair of old boots, warm socks and a few candy bars in the car during winter. This isn't paranoia, it's just good planning. Like carrying a spare tire, even if you never need it.

But there are plenty of online resources for people who just want to prepare a three-day kit. CCHD's Survival Guide is designed to take you to the next level. Because in a true emergency, three days may not be long enough. We want you to be mentally, physically and financially prepared for any emergency on *any* scale.

Some Common Terms
- We define *survival* as emerging from a natural or man-made disaster in a better position than the average person. In other words, you get to keep on keeping on, while others may not.

- *Preparedness* means making preparations before disaster strikes to improve your chances of survival. Surely you remember the three little pigs...

- *Survivalists* have a self-reliant attitude and choose to prepare on their own or in a small group rather than rely on government/outside entities to help them survive. A PIONEER SPIRIT!

So, how can you prepare to survive? What can you do to prepare, to become a "survivalist?" CCHD EPBO has developed this Ten step program to help you get started. While designed as a guide for the new survivalist, it has plenty of information for the hard-core preparedness expert as well.

(*Source:* Chippewa County, Michigan, Health Department Survival Preparedness for a Self-sufficient Household.)

mental health counseling paradigm guide your analysis of the interaction of personal, cultural, and regional factors in the potential differences in the responses of Detroit and EUP residents to such an ice storm emergency? Certainly, these two populations will approach and respond to the weather-related crisis in different ways. Mental health counselors responding to underserved populations in geographically diverse locations must be culturally sensitive and respectful as responders if they are to make positive contributions to any relief efforts.

Disaster Response. All persons directly exposed to traumatic events face immediate challenges. Stress and grief are normal responses to intense disaster events. The reaction of most persons to trauma is relatively mild, temporary, and immediate (Norris et al., 2002). In many situations, disaster mental health assistance is very problem focused and practical. A significant number of persons, though, experience more intense reactions that may lead to posttrauma disorders or other psychological problems.

Generally, individuals encountering disasters tend to move through three overlapping phases (Hoff, Hallisey, & Hoff, 2009):

1. *Impact* Right after the disaster, most persons experience shock and confusion and display indicators of an activated sympathetic nervous system. Some remain calm and display problem-solving coping strategies immediately after the catastrophic event. And some are emotionally distraught, out-of-control, or paralyzed with fear.
2. *Recoil* After the initial impact of the event comes persons' realization that they are survivors, and there is a temporary suspension of the initial stressors. Their lives are not in immediate danger. Their attention becomes focused on the immediate past and what they have just experienced. Comfort- and support-seeking behaviors are often displayed at this time. Persons may cuddle in blankets (if available), seek shelter in community facilities, and share their experiences with others. Open expressions of emotion are common.
3. *Posttrauma* At this point, survivors become fully aware of the consequences of the disaster: loss of loved ones, homes, and property and of financial insecurity. Survivors are susceptible to reactive depressions, anxiety, or panic. Some may feel so despondent that they express a desire to "give up." Others may display changes in eating and sleeping behaviors. Most persons, though, begin to pick up and reconstruct the broken pieces of their lives.

Furthermore, disasters have the potential to bring out the best and worst of communities. For example, a large covered stage collapsed at the 2012 Indiana State Fair, killing 7 and injuring another 43 persons. Stories emerged of courage and mass cooperation as many people immediately moved to the stage area to rescue those who were pinned by the fallen materials. In contrast, we also hear of looting and rampages that too frequently inflict more damage on communities already ravaged by the disaster.

Baranosky, Gentry, and Schultz (2005) integrate a three-phase model, developed by Herman (1992), to guide the interventions of mental health professions in trauma practice. The first stage of intervention is the establishment of *safety and stabilization*. Initially, survivors need to move from the perception of unpredictable danger to reliable safety (Herman, 1992, p. 155). The second stage is *remembrance and mourning*. In this stage, clients are constructing their trauma stories in detail. The task for counselors is to provide psychological space for clients to relive and begin to make sense of the devastating events they have experienced. A variety of cognitive-behavioral strategies have been found helpful in this stage (Baranosky et al., 2005). *Reconnection* is the third stage and occurs as the person "redefines oneself in the context of meaningful relationships" (Baranosky et al., 2005, p. 13). Many find support in a sustaining faith and spirituality, focused on a higher power that saw them through the terror that reigned and brought them to a new understanding of self, informed but not defined by the impact of the catastrophic event.

Several specific approaches are used extensively by mental health counselors in disaster response work. These are critical incident stress debriefing (CISD) and psychological first aid (PFA). CISD is a small-group psychoeducational intervention designed to mitigate the psychological impact of a traumatic event, prevent future posttraumatic disorders, and serve as an early screening to identify those who might benefit from follow-up professional mental health services (Mitchell & Everly, 2006). It consists of seven distinct phases (Pender, 2010, pp. 173–175):

1. *Introduction stage* Team members establish rapport with group members. The purpose of the group, the ground rules, and the confidentiality limits are explained.
2. *Facts phase* In this phase, group members share a factual description of what happened and their role in the event.
3. *Thoughts phase* After having reported details of the event, members share what they thought about the event.
4. *Reactions phase* This is the most challenging phase. Here group members share their personal affective responses to the event. The goal is to identify internalized aspects of the event that may linger in the cognitive processes and structures of survivors and first responders.
5. *Symptoms phase* Group members are encouraged to identify physical, cognitive, emotional, and social changes they have noticed in themselves since experiencing the event.
6. *Teaching phase* Team members offer coping strategies and stress education. A basic set of techniques, such as deep breathing, exercise, and non-job-related activities are shared.
7. *Reentry phase* This is the wrap-up phase that brings closure to the meeting. Team and group members summarize what was accomplished at the meeting. And, as appropriate, attention is called to the group members' acts of courage and willingness to carry hurt and sadness as a consequence to their efforts to serve others.

PFA is an evidence-informed practice that aims to reduce initial posttrauma distress and to facilitate the short- and long-term adaptive functioning of trauma survivors

(Ruzek et al., 2007; Webber, Mascari, & Runte, 2010). It consists of eight core actions (National Child Traumatic Stress Network, 2006):

1. *Contact and engagement* Providers of PFA respond to affected persons who make contact, or they initiate contact in a compassionate, helping, and nonintrusive manner.
2. *Safety and comfort* Providers ensure and enhance the safety and physical/emotional well-being of the affected persons.
3. *Stabilization (if necessary)* The PFA provider calms and orients survivors who are emotionally overwhelmed and distraught.
4. *Information gathering* Immediate needs and concerns are identified and used to tailor the PFA interventions as indicated.
5. *Practical assistance* Practical assistance is offered to address immediate needs and concerns of the survivor.
6. *Connection with social supports* The affected person is brought into contact with primary support persons and systems, such as family members, friends, or community resources.
7. *Information on coping support* Brief psychoeducative techniques are used to inform survivors about stress reactions and how to apply them in coping with the traumatic event and its aftereffects.
8. *Linkage with collaborative services* The affected person is linked to needed services and informed about available services that may be needed in the future.

Emergency Management Systems.   The disaster responses of mental health professionals should occur within the context of a larger, community-based emergency management plan. Mental health counselors should not spontaneously appear at a disaster scene to offer assistance; they should be deployed only at the invitation of a local organization responsible for the implementation of emergency assistance efforts (Jordan, 2010). They should understand their specific role in an agency- or community-based plan.

Community mental health organizations should design and maintain emergency preparedness plans to ensure that the consequences of disasters or other types of emergencies do not disrupt the clinic's ability to provide services to its clients (SAMHSA, 2007). It is important to develop such clinic emergency plans in collaboration with and integrated into the larger, more comprehensive community or regional emergency management plan. The clinic plan outlines specific processes for the preparedness, response, and recovery of necessary agency services in the event of an emergency or catastrophic event.

The development of an emergency plan begins with hazard vulnerability analysis (SAMHSA, 2007). This process enables the organization to identify where it is most vulnerable. It takes into consideration the type of emergency event (natural, human-made, or technological), the probability of its occurrence (none to high), level of risk if the event does occur (low disruption to life threat), and a rating of agency preparedness (poor to good). The results of the analysis are used by agency staff to address identified vulnerabilities with the goal of increasing agency resilience when dealing with emergency events.

Other considerations in the development of an emergency management plan include establishment of a leadership hierarchy, reliable emergency communication systems (intra-agency and agency to community/regional emergency command), specification of the disaster tasks of staff members, and management processes and procedures for clients and their needs, as well as related agency services during the event and its aftermath, including evacuation plans. An alternative clinic site should be identified in case the clinic is unable to open (e.g., agency closing due to fire, bomb threat, or storm damage). It is essential that all staff be familiar with and rehearsed in preparedness procedures (SAMHSA, 2007).

As noted earlier, the plan of a community mental health organization should fit within the larger community or regional emergency management plan. Thus, its plan specifies the ways it works alongside other agencies and organizations to meet the needs of the general population in the event of specific disasters and emergency events. This plan may include assisting other agencies incapacitated during the crisis and unable to render services. For example, as Manager of the Crisis Programs at Hiawatha Behavioral Health (HBH), I worked closely with the county emergency management office. Since that office was located quite close to the Sault Sainte Marie Locks, a vital shipping channel of national security significance, it was determined that the county emergency management was vulnerable if the locks should be attacked. It was decided that HBH would serve as the alternative site for the county emergency management command post. Thus, in the case of an emergency, the agency emergency plan needed to coordinate with the needs and demands of the larger county emergency response plan.

CONCLUSION

This chapter provided an overview of community mental health by first reviewing the history of the mental health movement in the United States, then presenting a model for understanding, developing, and evaluating mental health care delivery systems; and finally describing selected issues confronting contemporary delivery systems.

Although the chapter provided only a glimpse of what is currently happening in the field of community mental health, I hope it whetted your appetite for the exciting possibilities for mental health counseling professionals, who have a great deal to offer clients and their service providers.

It would seem that vast numbers of opportunities knock on the doors of newly trained mental health counselors in the 21st century. Yet, despite the increased professional recognition and visibility that mental health counselors have achieved in the past several decades, we continue to be a profession whose potential is substantially unrealized. Yes, mental health counselors are finding excellent jobs and making creative contributions in the contemporary milieu. But we have much work ahead of us, as a profession, if we are to become all that we can be. What is the future of mental health counseling? What must occur if we are to become highly respected among those who identify with the allied mental health professions? In the final chapter of this text, we turn to this important topic.

DISCUSSION QUESTIONS

1. Consumers of mental health services are playing significant roles in the delivery of mental health services. In what ways can consumers benefit when trained peers participate on crisis lines or in intervention services? What biases do you have regarding mental health consumers taking increased responsibility for their recovery?

2. List and discuss the unique problems in the provision of comprehensive service to dually diagnosed populations (i.e., persons who are diagnosed with severe mental illness and substance abuse/dependence). Why do you think traditional delivery systems have not been successful in treating this population?

3. Apply the comprehensive mental health counseling model to guide you in identifying the unique mental health needs of homeless populations. Specify a set of goals for this population.

4. Explore the Web sites of several community mental health centers. Discuss the various types of programs provided and the potential roles for mental health and community counselors.

5. To what extent is the comprehensive mental health counseling model (see Chapter 3) relevant to the treatment of persons with severe mental illness?

SUGGESTED ACTIVITIES

1. Identify a particular mental health service that you would like to deliver. Assume that you have been given a large budget to create such a mental health program. Examples might include parent skill training, stress management, suicide prevention, or a mobile crisis stabilization team. Apply the model of mental health delivery systems and develop a detailed proposal of your selected program. Include the following components:
   a. needs assessment
   b. mission statement
   c. goals
   d. program
   e. working knowledge, skills, and resource supports
   f. environmental supports
   g. program evaluation

2. Take a tour of a community mental health program and learn about the variety of services provided. Suggested programs include
   a. community mental health centers
   b. centers for the homeless
   c. AIDS/HIV+ programs or ministries
   d. private, not-for-profit mental health counseling organizations
3. Invite professionals working at juvenile detention centers to a panel discussion. Focus on the mental health, substance abuse, and family-related issues presented by the adolescents they serve. How are the mental health needs of this population currently being served? What are the roles of mental health and community counselors in corrections facilities?
4. Invite a representative from NAMI to present information about the organization and the role consumers are taking in the provision of mental health services.
5. Go online and review the National Registry of Evidence-based Programs and Practices (http://www.nrepp.samhsa.gov/). Become familiar with the site and the practical resources it provides.

REFERENCES

Adams, K., & Ferrandino, J. (2008). Managing mentally ill inmates in prisons. *Criminal Justice and Behavior, 35,* 913–927.

Altschuld, J. W., & Witkin, B. R. (2000). *From needs assessment to action: Transforming needs into solution strategies.* Thousand Oaks, CA: Sage.

Bachrach, L. L. (1992). What we know about homelessness among mentally ill persons: An analytical review and commentary. In H. R. Lamb, L. L. Bachrach, & F. I. Kass (Eds.), *Treating the homeless mentally ill: A report of the task force on the homeless mentally ill.* Washington, DC: American Psychiatric Association.

Baranosky, A. B., Gentry, J. E., & Schultz, D. F. (2005). *Trauma practice: Tools for stabilization and recovery.* Cambridge, MA: Hogrefe & Huber.

Barry, P. D. (1998). *Mental health and mental illness* (6th ed.). Philadelphia, PA: Lippincott.

Beck, A. T., Wright, F. D., Newman, C. F., & Liese, B. S. (1993). *Cognitive therapy of substance abuse.* New York, NY: Guilford Press.

Biegel, D. E., Kola, L. A., & Ronis, R. J. (2006). Evidence-based treatment for adults with co-occurring mental and substance use disorders (pp. 61–72). In J. Rosenberg & S. Rosenberg (Eds.), *Community mental health: Challenges for the 21st century.* New York, NY: Routledge.

Bradley, L. J., Sexton, T. L., & Smith, H. B. (2005). The American Counseling Association practice research network (ACA-PRN): A new research tool. *Journal of Counseling and Development, 83,* 488–491.

Bureau of Justice Statistics, U.S. Department of Justice. (2008, September). *Mental health problems of prison and jail inmates.* (Publication No. – NCJ 213600). Retrieved from http://bjs.ojp.usdoj.gov/content/pub/pdf/mhppji.pdf

Calley, N. G. (2011). *Program development in the 21st century: An evidence-based approach to design, implementation, and evaluation.* Thousand Oaks, CA: Sage.

Callicutt, J. W. (2006). Homeless shelters: An uneasy component of the de facto mental health system. In J. Rosenberg & S. Rosenberg (Eds.), *Community mental health: Challenges for the 21st century* (pp. 169–180). New York, NY: Routledge.

Carbaugh, R. J., & Sias, S. M. (2010). Comorbidity of bulimia nervosa and substance abuse: Etiologies, treatment issues, and treatment approaches. *Journal of Mental Health Counseling, 32,* 125–138.

Carling, P. J. (1995). *Return to community: Building support systems for people with psychiatric disabilities.* New York, NY: Guilford Press.

Caton, L. M., Shrout, P. E., Eagle, P. F., Opler, L., Felix, A., & Dominguez, B. (1994). Risk factors for homelessness among schizophrenic men: A case-control study. *American Journal of Public Health, 84,* 265–270.

Caton, L. M., Shrout, P. E., Dominguez, B., Eagle, P. F., Opler, L., & Cournos, F. (1995). Risk factors for homelessness among women with schizophrenia. *American Journal of Public Health, 85,* 1153–1156.

Chandler, D. (2009). Implementation of integrated dual disorders treatment in eight California programs. *American Journal of Psychiatric Rehabilitation, 12,* 330–351.

Clay, R. A. (2011, December). Treatment guidelines development now under way. *Monitor on Psychology,* pp. 18–19.

Corrigan, P. W., Mueser, K. T., Bond, G. R., Drake, R. E., & Solomon, P. (2008). *Principles and practice of psychiatric rehabilitation: An empirical approach.* New York, NY: Guilford Press.

Cuddeback, G. S., & Morrissey, J. P. (2010). Integrating service delivery systems for persons with a severe mental illness. In T. L. Scheid & T. N. Brown (Eds.), *A handbook of the study of mental health: Social contexts, theories, and systems* (2nd ed., pp. 510–528). New York, NY: Cambridge University Press.

Cukrowicz, K. C., White, B. A., Reitzel, L. R., Burns, A. B., Driscoll, K. A., Kemper, T. S., & Joiner, T. E., Jr. (2005). Improved treatment outcome associated with the shift to empirically supported treatments in a graduate training clinic. *Professional Psychology: Research and Practice, 36,* 330–337.

Cukrowicz, K. C., Timmons, K. A., Sawyer, K., Caron, K. M., Gummelt, H. D., & Joiner, T. E. (2011). Improved treatment outcome associated with the shift to empirically supported treatments in an outpatient clinic is maintained over a ten-year period. *Professional Psychology: Research and Practice, 42,* 145–152.

Cutler, D. L. (1992). A historical overview of community mental health centers in the United States (pp. 1–22). In S. Cooper & T. H. Lentner (Eds.), *Innovations in community mental health.* Sarasota, FL: Professional Resource Press.

Dickey, B., Fisher, W., Siegel, C., Altaffer, F., & Azeni, H. (1997). The cost and outcomes of community-based care for the seriously mentally ill. *Health Services Research, 32,* 599–625.

Drake, R. E., Wallach, M. A., Teague, G. B., Freeman, D. H., Paskus, T. S., & Clark, T. A. (1991). Housing instability and homelessness among rural schizophrenic patients. *American Journal of Psychiatry, 148,* 330–336.

Drake, R. E. (1998). Brief history, current status, and future place of assertive community treatment. *American Journal of Orthopsychiatry, 68,* 172–175.

Egan, G., & Cowan, M. A. (1979). *People in systems: A model for development in the human-service professions and education.* Monterey, CA: Brooks/Cole.

Evans, K., & Sullivan, J. M. (2001). *Dual diagnosis: Counseling the mentally ill substance abuser* (2nd ed.). New York, NY: Guilford Press.

Fredrickson, B. L. (2009). *Positivity.* New York, NY: Three Rivers Press.

Friedman, B. D., & Levine-Holdowsky, M. (1997). Overcoming barriers to homeless delivery services: A community response. *Journal of Social Distress and the Homeless, 6,* 13–28.

Fristad, M. A., & Sisson, D. P. (2004). Creating partnerships between consumer groups and professional psychologists. *Professional Psychology: Research and Practice, 35,* 477–480.

Grantseeking in Minnesota. (2004, February 25). Writing a successful grant proposal. Retrieved October 31, 2005, from http://www.mcf.org/mcf/grant/writing.htm

Herman, J. L. (1992). *Trauma and recovery.* New York, NY: Basic Books.

Hiday, V. A., & Burns, P. J. (2010). Mental illness and the criminal justice system. In T. L. Scheid & T. N. Brown (Eds.), *A handbook for the study of mental illness: Social contexts, theories, and systems* (2nd ed., pp. 478–498). New York: Cambridge University Press.

Hoff, L. A., Hallisey, B. J., & Hoff, M. (2009). *People in crisis: Clinical and diversity perspectives* (6th ed.). New York, NY: Routledge.

Holloway, F., & Carson, J. (2001). Case management: An update. *International Journal of Social Psychiatry, 47,* 21–31.

Jordan, K. (2010). General standards for disaster crisis counselors. In J. Webber & J. B. Mascari (Eds.), *Terrorism, trauma, and tragedies: A counselor's guide to preparing and responding* (3rd ed., pp. 193–196). Alexandria, VA: American Counseling Association Foundation.

Katz, A. H. (1993). *Self-help in America: A social movement perspective.* New York, NY: Maxwell Macmillan International.

Kaufmann, C. L. (1999). An introduction to the mental health consumer movement. In A. V. Horwitz & T. L. Scheid (Eds.), *A handbook for the study of mental health: Social contexts, theories, and systems* (pp. 493–507). Cambridge, UK: Cambridge University Press.

Kazdin, A. E. (2011). Evidence-based treatment research: Advances, limitations, and next steps. *American Psychologist, 66,* 685–698.

Khanna, N., Signh, N., Nemil, M., Best, A., & Ellis, C. R. (1992). Homeless women and their families. Characteristics, life circumstances, and needs. *Journal of Child and Family Studies, 1,* 155–165.

Lehman, A. F., Steinwachs, D. M., & Co-Investigators of PORT Project. (1998). Translating research into practice: The schizophrenia patient outcomes research team (PORT) treatment recommendations. *Schizophrenia Bulletin, 24,* 1–10.

Levine, M. (1981). *The history and politics of community mental health.* New York, NY: Oxford University Press.

Levine, M., Perkins, D. D., & Perkins, D. V. (2005). *Principles of community psychology: Perspectives and applications* (3rd ed.). New York, NY: Oxford University Press.

Longo, D. R., & Schubert, S. (2005). Learning by doing: Mentoring, hands-on experience keys to writing successful grants. *Annals of Family Medicine, 3,* 281.

Markos, P. A., Baron, H. L., & Allen, D. N. (2005). A unique population: Women who are homeless and mentally ill. *Guidance and Counseling, 20,* 109–116.

Marsh, D. T. (1996). Families of children and adolescents with serious emotional disturbance: Innovations in theory, research, and practice. In C. A. Heflinger and C. T. Nixon (Eds.), *Families and the mental health system for children and adolescents: Policy, services, and research.* Thousand Oaks, CA: Sage.

McHugh, R., K., & Barlow, D. H. (2010). The dissemination and implementation of evidence-based psychological treatments: A review of current efforts. *American Psychologist, 65,* 73–84.

McLean, A. (2010). The mental health consumers/survivors movement in the United States (pp. 461–477). In T. L. Scheid & T. N. Brown (Eds.), *A handbook for the study of mental illness: Social contexts, theories, and systems* (2nd ed.). New York, NY: Cambridge University Press.

Mechanic, D. (1991). Strategies for integrating public mental health services. *Hospital and Community Psychiatry, 22,* 797–801.

Milazzo-Sayre, L. J., Henderson, M. J., Manderscheid, R. W., Bokossa, M. C., Evans, C., & Male. A. A. (2001). Persons treated in specialty mental health care programs, United States, 1997. Retrieved December 30, 2004, from http://www.mentalhealth.org/publications/allpubs/SMA01-3537?chapter15.asp

Miller, N. S. (1994). Psychiatric comorbidity: Occurrence and treatment. *Alcohol Health and Research, 18,* 261–264.

Morrissey, J. P., Fagan, J. A., Cocozza, J. J. (2009). New models of collaboration between criminal justice and mental health systems. *American Journal of Psychiatry, 166,* 1211–1214.

Mueser, K. T., Bond, G. R., Drake, R. E., & Resnick, S. G. (1998). Models of community care for severe mental illness: A review of research on case management. *Schizophrenia Bulletin, 24,* 37–74.

National Alliance for the Mentally Ill. (2005, February 16). About NAMI. About_NAMI/About_NAMI. htm Retrieved from http://www.nami.org/Content/NavigationMenu/Inform_Yourself/National Assessment of Adult Literacy. (2003). Key findings. Retrieved March 15, 2012, from http://nces. ed.gov/naal/kf_demographics.asp

National Child Traumatic Stress Network. (2006). Psychological first aid: Field operations guide (2nd ed.). Retrieved from http://www.nctsn.org/content/psychological-first-aid

National Clearinghouse on Child Abuse and Neglect Information. (2003). Foster care national statistics. Retrieved on May 2, 2005, from http://nccanch.acf.hhs.gov/pubs/factsheets/foster.pdf

National Institute of Mental Health. (2002). *Mental health and mass violence: Evidence-based early psychological intervention for victims/survivors of mass violence. A workshop to reach consensus on best practices.* NIH Publication No. 02-5138, Washington, DC: U.S. Government Printing Office.

Norris, F. H., Friedman, M. J., Watson, P. J., Byrne, C. M., Diaz, E., & Kaniasty, K. 60,000 disaster victims speak: Part I. An empirical review of the empirical literature, 1981–2001. *Psychiatry, 65,* 207–239.

North, C. S., & Smith, E. M. (1993). A comparison of homeless men and women: Different populations, different needs. *Community Mental Health Journal, 29,* 423–431.

Onken, S. (2006, July 25). *Mental health recovery: Research, practice, and measurement.* Training conducted by the Michigan Department of Community Mental Health, Lansing, MI.

Onken, S. J., Craig, C. M., Ridgway, P., Ralph, R. O., & Cook, J. A. (2007). An analysis of the definitions and elements of recovery: A review of the literature. *Psychiatric Rehabilitation Journal, 31,* 9–22.

Parker, T., Foley, G. T., Moore, K. A., & Broner, N. (2009). Jail diversion programs: Finding common ground. *American Jails, 23*(4), 25–38.

Pender, D. (2010). Critical incident stress debriefing and the process of crisis group work (pp. 173–176). In J. Webber & J. B. Mascari (Eds.), *Terrorism, trauma, and tragedies: A counselor's guide to preparing and responding* (3rd ed.). Alexandria, VA: American Counseling Association Foundation.

Pickett-Schenk, S. A., Cook, J. A., Grey, D., Banghart, M., Rosenheck, R. A., & Randolph, F. (2002). Employment histories of homeless persons with mental illness. *Community Mental Health Journal, 38,* 199–211.

Putnam, R. D. (2000). *Bowling alone: The collapse and revival of American community.* New York, NY: Simon & Schuster.

Regier, D. A., Farmer, M. E., Rae, D. S., Locke, B. Z., Keith, S. J., Judd, L. J., & Goodwin, F. K. (1990). Comorbidity of mental disorders with alcohol and other drug abuse: Results from the Epidemiologic Catchment Area (ECA) Study. *Journal of the American Medical Association, 264,* 2511–2518.

Ridgway, P. (1999). *Deepening the recovery paradigm: Defining implications for practice: A report of the recovery paradigm project.* Unpublished manuscript, University of Kansas.

Rogers, J. R. (2007). Disaster response and the mental health counselor. *Journal of Mental Health Counseling, 29,* 1–3.

Rosenblatt, A., & Attkisson, C. (1993). Assessing outcomes for sufferers of severe mental disorder: A conceptual framework and review. *Evaluation and Program Planning, 16,* 347–363.

Ross, L. (1977). The intuitive psychologist and his shortcomings: Distortions in the attribution process. In L. Berkowitz (Ed.), *Advances in experimental social psychology* (Vol. 10). New York, NY: Academic Press.

Rowe, M., Hoge, M. A., & Fisk, D. (1996). Critical issues in serving people who are homeless and mentally ill. *Administration and Policy in Mental Health, 23,* 555–565.

Ruzek, J. I., Brymer, M. J., Jacobs, A. K., Layne, C. M., Vernberg, E. M., & Watson, P. J. (2007). Psychological first aid. *Journal of Mental Health Counseling, 29,* 17–49.

Ryglewicz, H., & Pepper, B. (1992). The dual-disorder client: Mental disorder and substance abuse (pp. 73–96). In S. Cooper, & T. H. Lentner (Eds.), *Innovations in community mental health.* Sarasota, FL: Professional Resource Press.

Salkever, D., Domino, M. E., Burns, B. J., Santos, A. B., Deci, P. A., Dias, J., Wagner, H. R., Faldowski, R. A., & Paolone, J. (1999). Assertive community treatment for people with severe mental illness: The effect on hospital use and costs. *Health Services Research, 34,* 577–579.

Santos, A. B., Hawkins, G. D., Julius, B., Deci, P. A., Hiers, T. H., & Burns, B. J. (1993). A pilot study of assertive community treatment for patients with chronic psychotic disorders. *American Journal of Psychiatry, 150,* 501–504.

Seligman, L. (1998). *Selecting effective treatment: A comprehensive, systematic guide to treating mental disorders.* San Francisco, CA: Jossey-Bass.

Stevens, P., & Smith, R. L. (2005). *Substance abuse counseling: Theory and practice* (3rd ed.). Upper Saddle River, NJ: Pearson Prentice Hall.

Substance Abuse and Mental Health Services Administration. (2006). National consensus statement on mental health recovery. Retrieved from http://store.samhsa.gov/shin/content//SMA05-4129/SMA05-4129.pdf

Substance Abuse and Mental Health Services Administration. (2007). Emergency preparedness plan. Retrieved from http://www.samhsa.gov/csatdisasterrecovery/preparedness/disasterReliefGrantProgramEPP.pdf

Substance Abuse and Mental Health Services Administration. (2008). Evidence-based practices: Shaping mental health services toward recovery. Co-occurring disorders: Integrated dual disorders treatment. Available at http://mentalhealth.samhsa.gov/cmhs/communitysupport/toolkits/cooccurring/

Suppes, M. A., & Wells, C. C. (2003). *The social work experience: An introduction to social work and social welfare* (4th ed.). Boston, MA: McGraw-Hill.

Test, M. A. (1998). Community-based treatment models for adults with severe and persistent mental illness (pp. 420–436). In J. Williams & K. Ell (Eds.), *Mental health research: Implications for practice.* Washington, DC: NASW Press.

Thomas, P. (2006). The practice effectiveness of case management services for homeless persons with alcohol, drug, or mental health problems (pp. 181–194). In J. Rosenberg & S. Rosenberg (Eds.), *Community Mental Health: Challenges for the 21st Century.* New York: Routledge.

Torrey, E. F. (2006). *Surviving schizophrenia: A manual for families, patients, and providers* (5th ed.). New York, NY: Harper Perennial.

U.S. Surgeon General. (2001). Mental health: A report of the Surgeon General. Retrieved on December 30, 2004, from http://www.mentalhealth.samhsa.gov/cmhs/surgeongeneral/

Verheul, R., Kranzler, H. R., Poling, J., Tennen, H., Ball, S., & Rounsaville, B. J. (2000). Axis I and Axis II disorders in alcoholics and drug addicts: Fact or artifact. *Journal of Studies on Alcohol, 61,* 101–110.

Vostanis, P., Grattan, E., & Cumella, S. (1998). Mental health problems of homeless children and families: Longitudinal study. *British Medical Journal, 316,* 899–903.

Walker, J. S., & Bruns, E. J. (2006). The wraparound process: Individualized, community-based care for children and adolescents with intensive needs. In J. Rosenberg & S. Rosenberg (Eds.), *Community mental health: Challenges for the 21st century.* New York, NY: Routledge.

Webber, J., Mascari, J. B., & Runte, J. (2010). Psychological first aid: A new paradigm for disaster mental health (pp. 201–205). In J. Webber & J. B. Mascari (Eds.), *Terrorism, trauma, and tragedies: A counselor's guide to preparing and responding* (3rd ed.). Alexandria, VA: American Counseling Association Foundation.

White, B. J., & Madara, E. J. (2002). *The self-help group sourcebook: Your guide to community and online support groups* (7th ed.). Cedar Knolls, NJ: American Self-Help Group Clearinghouse.

Wolff, N., Helminiak, T. W., Morse, G. A., Calsyn, R. J., Klinkenberg, W. D., & Trusty, M. L. (1997). Cost-effectiveness evaluation of three approaches to case management for homeless mentally ill clients. *American Journal of Psychiatry, 154,* 341–348.

Yalisove, D. (2004). *Introduction to alcohol research: Implications for treatment, prevention, and policy.* Boston, MA: Allyn & Bacon.

Yanos, P. T., Barrow, S. M., & Tsemberis, S. (2004). Community integration in the early phase of housing among homeless persons diagnosed with severe mental illness: Successes and challenges. *Community Mental Health Journal, 40,* 133–150.

Young, N. K., & Grella, C. E. (1998). Mental health and substance abuse treatment services for dually diagnosed clients: Results of a statewide survey of county administrators. *Journal of Behavioral Health Services and Research, 25,* 83–88.

12

The Future of Clinical Mental Health Counseling

OUTLINE

C hapter 1 of this text attempted to answer the question, "What is a mental health counselor?" Furthermore, it likened the path of establishing a secure professional identity to journeying through the land of confusion. I hope that reading this book has enabled you to better conceptualize the geographic features that surround you in the landscape of clinical mental health counseling as you continue down the path of professional development.

This final chapter views the current surroundings and then attempts to look down the road. It responds to questions such as: What are the predominant strengths and struggles of clinical mental health counseling as currently configured? And how does this configuration prepare its practitioners for the road and traveling conditions that lie ahead? Mental health counselors are now recognized as licensed professionals in all 50 states. It is a comprehensive, multidisciplinary profession. In so many ways, the mental health profession has the potential for a bright future. Yet numerous obstacles also restrict its forward movement and sometimes seem to create enough resistance to force counselors off the path.

This chapter discusses several factors that currently influence mental health counseling's direction and speed of progress. In addition, it presents the current strengths and weaknesses of the profession. Finally, the chapter provides several ideas that, if implemented, can help mental health counseling realize its full potential.

CURRENT FACTORS INFLUENCING THE PROFESSION

An ecological analysis of the mental health counseling profession reveals a number of factors that influence its current configuration and direction. Definitions of mental health counseling found in academic texts put forth an ideal description of its professional identity and scope of practice. Who mental health counselors are and what they do are shaped by many forces, some of which are beyond the practitioner's direct control. This list of environmental factors includes the credentialing of the allied mental health professions, the political and economic climate, managed care and health care reform, the evolution of service delivery systems, and trends in treatment approaches.

One's professional identity as a mental health counselor develops through a dynamic interaction of academic training and professional experiences in a specific ecological context. Thus, the configuration of one's actual professional identity will often differ by degree from the ideal definition. For this reason, mental health counselors' identification of who they are and what they do tends to differ from region to region. The following section discusses the nature of these contemporary forces.

PROFESSIONAL CREDENTIALING

As noted earlier, professional licensure has become a powerful and desirable force in helping mental health counselors establish professional recognition and professional identity. This statutory process enables Licensed Mental Health Counselors (LMHCs) and Licensed Professional Counselors (LPCs) to provide services to clients within the specified scope of practice. Thus, the visibility of the mental health counseling profession is enhanced among consumers and members of the allied mental health professions.

However, the specific form and content of each state's unique set of statutes are shaped by the definitions of the other mental health professions, which also have licensure statutes in each state's code. In an ideal world, mental health counselors could integrate into their licensure law the unique sets of knowledge, skills, and scopes of practice that accurately reflect national definitions and training models. However, in many states, the mental health counseling professionals have been the newcomers in the passage of the licensure laws. Thus, their codified professional definitions and scopes of practice are shaped in ways that conform to the contours of the language that defines the identity and practice of the professions that have existing licensure laws in the states' codes. In some states, the counselor licensure laws are also a reflection of the political processes that were required to ensure passage of the licensure law.

This variability can be a source of dissonance for newly licensed counseling professionals, who discover that the professional identity that they were establishing throughout their graduate education does not conform to the parameters established by legal statutes in the state where they practice. For example, graduate students may learn through their academic training that the diagnosis of mental and emotional conditions is one of the core components of mental health counselor identity. However, in the state where they seek to become licensed, independent diagnosis is not included in the license's scope of practice.

Unfortunately, the process of revising or adapting the profession's identity and scope of practice as stated in licensure laws is not an easy task. The ability of the mental health counseling profession to actualize its full potential is hindered to the extent that licensure laws do not fully reflect the knowledge and skills specified in the training model of the Council for Accreditation of Counseling and Related Educational Programs (CACREP; Gale & Austin, 2003). Resolution of this dissonance will require persistent professional advocacy, lobbying, and demonstration of professional excellence.

The 20/20 definition of counseling (American Counseling Association, 2010) has been put forth as a foundational resource that can be used as the profession attempts to bring uniformity to clinical mental health and professional counseling licensure laws (Kaplan & Gladding, 2011). It is believed that this application of the definition will increase the public's understanding of the professional identity of mental health counselors, enhance unity within the profession, and facilitate reciprocity of licenses across state lines.

By its very nature, the use of the Delphi technique in constructing the 20/20 definition practically guaranteed consensus among the participants in the proceedings. While the resulting definition may serve the interests of those within the American Counseling Association (ACA), it remains to be seen whether it provides any increased traction whatsoever among the state licensure boards and for those clinical mental health counselors working in the trenches who must position themselves alongside members of the allied mental health professionals. And will it enhance the efforts of the profession to gain provider status and recognition by key entities such as Medicare, the Substance Abuse and Mental Health Services Administration (SAMHSA), the National Institutes of Health, or the Institute of Medicine?

POLITICAL AND ECONOMIC CLIMATE

A second factor influencing the mental health counseling profession is the contemporary political and economic climate. I write this chapter while the United States is in the midst of a presidential election year, a stagnant national economy, and a soaring national debt. Furthermore, the economic woes extend worldwide as Europe struggles with the financial crises of several member nations. While the political rhetoric centers on fiscal responsibility, the U.S. Congress remains deadlocked on issues relevant to clinical mental health counselors, such as Medicare revisions, the future of national health care, and job creation in the Veterans Administration for independent practice under TRICARE (Finley, 2012). The future of the actual implementation of the Patient Protection and Affordable Care Act (2010) hangs in the balance. Indeed, the results of a recent survey of members of the American Mental Health Counselors Association (AMHCA) found Medicare coverage and the ability to practice independently under TRICARE to be the two most important legislative issues for professional advocacy (Normandy-Dolberg, 2010).

Decreases in federal funding have been accompanied by an increased burden on state and local governments to provide and oversee community mental health care. This circumstance has led to further disintegration and fragmentation of publicly funded programs and delivery systems. Several states have responded by merging the funding streams of Medicaid and Medicare for the mental and physical health care of persons with severe and persistent mental illness (Angelotti, 2012). This approach is being driven by Section 2703 of the Patient Protection and Affordable Care Act (2010) and recognition of the very high mortality rates for individuals with serious mental illness. In these instances, the community mental health center actually serves as the health care home for service recipients. Many privately owned and operated agencies have stepped in to fill the gap. Faith-based ministries (frequently funded through individual donations), local congregations, denominations, and grants are viewed increasingly as viable means of providing mental health services to underprivileged, rural, and underserved populations (Laurie, 1997; Richardson & June, 1997; Voss, 1996). A number of graduate program–operated counseling clinics have experienced a recent increase in the number of referrals received from public human service organizations, juvenile probation, family medical practitioners, and the courts, for persons unable to afford services from more expensive providers. The efforts of very small but persistent and focused advocacy groups have been somewhat successful in increasing the flow of resources from the state to local mental health systems (Wentz, 2004).

NEW MODELS AND DELIVERY SYSTEMS

Agencies and mental health professionals have responded to the aforementioned factors by developing and implementing new models of intervention and service delivery. A number of these have been mentioned earlier in this text. Given the time restraints placed on outpatient services by third-party reimbursers, many of the traditional theories and techniques of counseling are deemphasized. Taking their place are a number of brief, solution-focused, and evidence-based approaches. Increased numbers of mental health counselors are engaging in multidisciplinary small-group practices and networks. A more integrated delivery of medical and mental health care service, in accordance with the Patient Protection and Affordable Care Act (2010), is designed to increase efficiency and effectiveness across the health care system.

Granted, such systems provide less freedom for the practitioner. But many retain a measure of autonomy while increasing their professional economic viability and discovering expanded opportunities. Levant (2005) notes that the current zeitgeist requires mental health professionals to base their practice as much as possible on evidence. He challenges psychologists to define evidence-based practice in psychology or face having it defined *for* them. Furthermore, mental health professionals must be adequately trained if they are to be competent (and marketable) providers in these changing venues of service (Rozensky 2011).

One innovative and, in many ways, commonsense approach is the trend toward integrated behavioral health care. Aitken and Curtis (2004) describe integrated care as an emerging trend in which mental health counselors work in the same offices as primary health providers. Such a practice is firmly rooted in the tradition of behavior health, which sees the overall health of mind and body as inseparable. In behavioral health settings, mental and medical health services are integrated within the service delivery context and are based on the reciprocal relationship between human behavior and the well-being of mind, body, and spirit. Wellness interventions are seen as playing a fundamental role in facilitating and maintaining one's health.

While it has always been good practice to collaborate with primary health care professionals, the current trend is a move toward full integration of mental and medical health care services (Cummings, O'Donohue, & Cummings, 2011). In collaboration, the two sources of service delivery remain intact. There is, however, little financial incentive for third-party reimbursers and public policymakers to build a service model around increased collaboration, since such practice does not result in increased cost-effectiveness or treatment efficiency. However, there are a number of advantages to integrated behavioral health care.

First, it is clear that the majority of professional mental health care in the United States actually occurs in medical settings. Up to 80% of psychotropic medications are prescribed by nonpsychiatric medical professionals. Furthermore, it is estimated that 60–70% of visits to primary health care settings concern psychological and emotional issues, including psychiatric conditions such as clinical depression or anxiety, psychological and lifestyle issues that interfere with medical treatment, or treatment compliance. Given the amount of time general medical practitioners spend with patients discussing psychological concerns, it makes sense that medical and mental health professionals work side-by-side in common health care settings. When medical and behavioral health services are fully and *effectively* integrated, a 20–30% cost reduction is realized by covered populations (Cummings et al., 2011). Finally, there is simply less stigma attached to receiving services in a primary care setting than in a mental health center.

Fully integrating mental health counseling with primary health care represents a different approach to doing business for both disciplines. Traditionally, each profession holds its own values, norms, language, and explanatory models (Searight, 2010).

In primary care settings, the 50-minute therapy session is rare. Physicians often see 20–30 patients per day. The pace is brisk, with the schedule of appointments frequently interrupted, diagnoses made on the fly, and treatment settings devoid of sofas, stuffed chairs, and art on the walls (Searight, 2010, p. 6).

Clinical mental health counselors are well positioned to deliver services in such settings. They are trained in the diagnosis and treatment of psychiatric conditions that patients commonly present in primary care settings. Such symptoms, though, are likely a part of a clinical picture that includes hypertension, asthma, diabetes, or other physical problems (Searight, 2010). In addition, a growing focus of treatment is public health conditions such as obesity, cardiovascular disease, cancer, smoking, physical fitness, wellness and prevention, and substance abuse (Searight, 2010; Sidani, Price, Dake, Jordan, & Price, 2011). Positive changes in lifestyle can result in major differences in the health status of patients with these conditions (Walsh, 2011). Useful techniques in primary care settings include brief, problem-focused counseling, psychoeducation, consultation, and evidence-based treatments (e.g., transtheoretical model, cognitive-behavioral therapy, and motivational interviewing).

STRENGTHS OF THE CONTEMPORARY MENTAL HEALTH COUNSELING PROFESSION

The profession has achieved some significant accomplishments since the writing of the first edition of this text. There are many reasons to view the future as bright for the mental health counseling profession.

First, its underlying philosophy, theoretical base, and training model equip the profession to meet the needs and demands of contemporary society. As we have noted, mental health counselors are trained to view the human condition through lenses emphasizing the following:

- Normal human developmental processes across the lifespan
- Viewing the person as a holistic being—Fully integrating the physical, cognitive, social, emotional, and spiritual characteristics and processes
- Viewing human functioning as occurring within a unique ecological context
- A strength-based and wellness orientation that supports prevention, the promotion of optimal mental health, and the solution-focused treatment of psychopathology

Second, legislators, policymakers, and third-party reimbursers increasingly see the mental health counseling profession as an important contributor of services. The recognition of licensed providers of mental health services in all 50 states has made a significant impact. In addition (and perhaps as a consequence), working relationships have been established between AMHCA, ACA, and powerful organizations such as the Carter Center, the National Governors Association, the National Mental Health Association, the National Association of State Mental Health Program Directors, and the National Health Council (AMHCA Joins National Health Council, 2003; Normandy-Dolberg,

2010; Wheeler, 2003). The ACA and the AMHCA are actively pursuing a legislative agenda and are making significant gains toward inclusion in key federal and state programs. In addition, the results of empirical studies support the claim that mental health counselors are experiencing increased success in service claims reimbursement from a variety of third parties (Smith, 1999; Zimpfer, 1995).

Third, mental health counselors are finding numerous job opportunities in mental health–related professions. The *Occupational Outlook Handbook* (2010–2011 Edition) states that the overall demand for counselors is expected to grow faster than the average for all occupations between 2008 and 2018 (Bureau of Labor Statistics, 2008). The employment for mental health counselors, specifically, is expected to grow by 24%. These increased job opportunities are attributed to the following factors: (a) the willingness of managed care organizations to reimburse mental health counselors as a less costly alternative to psychologists and psychiatrists; (b) more people seeking treatment services offered by mental health counselors; and (c) less stigma attached to seeking treatment from counselors.

THE STRUGGLES OF THE CONTEMPORARY MENTAL HEALTH COUNSELING PROFESSION

Although the profession is increasingly recognized externally, significant struggles remain as the profession attempts to move to the next level. Some of these struggles are best viewed as growing pains that are necessary consequences of a maturing profession. The sources of these struggles come from both external forces and internal professional structures and dynamics.

First, although the rapid passage of 50 licensure laws has provided the profession with legal title and practice rights, the variance among the specific statutes makes it difficult to speak of the profession as a unified entity. Certainly, we can point to the added coherence of the counseling profession brought about by the development of the *20/20* definition of counseling. In addition, it was a significant step toward bringing licensed professional counselors and licensed mental health counselors together with the integration of community counseling and mental health counseling training standards into a single set: Clinical Mental Health Counseling (CACREP, 2009a). But our advocacy efforts are weakened when the specific state educational and clinical requirements vary significantly from national definitions and standards. For example, we state that we are trained to diagnose using the current American Psychiatric Association *Diagnostic and Statistical Manual of Mental Disorders* (DSM), but a number of Licensed Professional Counselors (LPCs) and Licensed Mental Health Counselors (LMHCs) are restricted from doing so by the statutes of their specific state licensure law. In other states, licensed counselors, although trained in psychometrics and the use of a variety of psychological tests, are not allowed to use these skills in practice. Finally, the grandparenting clauses in several states diluted the profession by allowing many persons into the profession who were not trained according to the CACREP

(Council for Accreditation of Counseling and Related Educational Programs) standards for the mental health and community counseling specializations.

Second, the relationship between the ACA and the AMHCA has been marked with tension throughout recent decades. It sometimes seems as though ill feelings between the professional organizations are evident when the organizations act out of sync or duplicate efforts in ways that do not always benefit the profession as a whole. Is there underlying bitterness and misunderstanding within the professional associations and between the ACA and the AMHCA that hinder the advancement of the mental health counseling profession?

Finally, the profession of clinical mental health counseling struggles to become a major player in shaping the discussion of specific issues and trends affecting contemporary public mental health and the delivery of services. The profession could have taken a leadership role in the transformation of community mental health through development and implementation of the recovery philosophy. Furthermore, given the clinical mental health counseling paradigm and its underlying foundations, it would seem that the profession should have much to contribute in the discussion of health care reform and the movement to integrate behavioral health in primary care settings. The training model and philosophical/theoretical base have been clearly defined. But these ingredients have not been integrated into coherent advocacy efforts that have made a visible impact in the public forum. This is truly disheartening as it appears, at least to me, that we have *so* much to contribute to these discussions.

Thus, as we look toward the future of clinical mental health counseling, the question to which we must respond is: How might we best live up to what we profess to be? The remainder of this chapter advances an agenda based on the clinical mental health counseling paradigm. It is my hope that this model will prove helpful as the profession attempts to flourish in its current ecological context.

HOW TO LIVE OUT WHO WE ARE: ENACTING THE CLINICAL MENTAL HEALTH COUNSELING PARADIGM

The clinical mental health counseling paradigm, presented in Chapter 3, has profound implications for training, professional practice, and research. What would our profession look like if we allowed ourselves, as clinical mental health counselors, to actually be who we say we are in the national debates and delivery of mental health services involving community mental health, public health, and primary care? Currently, mental health counselors talk a language of mental health, prevention, and wellness but engage in a rather traditional professional practice that resembles that of the allied professions of clinical social work and psychology. Can mental health counselors function in the same environment, yet apply the paradigm in conceptualizing and treating the full range of presenting concerns?

Consider the questions and programs of research that might arise if we were to take our devotion to models of normal development, wellness, and human ecology seriously. For example, how do the theories and counseling of adults in normal adult life transitions (Anderson, Goodman, & Schlossberg, 2012) relate to persons experiencing severe and persistent mental illness? How do *they* navigate through Erikson's stages of development: intimacy versus isolation, generativity vs. stagnation, or integrity versus despair (Erikson, 1950). How might the clinical mental health counseling paradigm guide research efforts in discerning the intra- and interpersonal and ecological factors that contribute to the life well-lived for these and other diverse groups? Furthermore, clinical mental health counselors should be at the forefront of conducting basic research into and program evaluation of the efficacy and effectiveness of specific wellness interventions in treating various client samples. It would be particularly relevant to assess the cost-effectiveness of integrated behavioral health interventions within primary care settings.

Too often, we rest on concepts, theories, and techniques developed by other disciplines, integrate them into our training model, and try to convince ourselves that we are doing something unique. Unfortunately, the mental health counseling profession positioned in this manner offers little that is unique to policymakers and powerholders. For the profession to be both viable and vibrant in the future, a unique vision of mental health counseling must emerge—one that is primarily of our own making.

Imagine (perhaps dream) of a strong discipline of mental health counseling that promotes a perspective sufficiently unique that it captures the attention of the allied mental health professions on the basis of its applications and implications. How refreshing and stimulating it might be if the mental health counseling profession came to the table with a truly unique perspective on the human condition and its positive promotion. What unique concepts, theories, and techniques might emerge if we seriously pursued the application of wellness principles and techniques to those we serve, both the mentally ill and those of relative mental health alike? Could we be a profession that does not merely strive to remediate or limit the expression of psychopathology but also facilitate personal growth within zones of proximal development (Vygotsky, 1962) and enhance the well-being of persons-in-situations? We might become recognized (and rightfully so) as the profession that truly facilitates our clients' abilities to live their lives and not their diagnoses. And might our social justice advocacy be recognized for the efforts expended toward eliminating the stigmatization of and discrimination against the mentally ill?

To accomplish such ambitious tasks, mental health counselors as well as counselor educators and supervisors must expend more efforts in applied research. If we apply our expertise in measurement and evaluation, a new family of assessment skills and tools for mental health counselors might be developed to provide a valid and reliable appraisal of the dimensions of wellness. It would be important that *our* research be especially sensitive to ecological contexts.

Appraisal of clients through systematic application of the paradigm is a useful adjunct to the traditional *DSM* diagnosis. In their review of the literature, Keyes and Michalec (2010) conclude that "mental health is a complete state that is best studied through the combined assessments of mental health and mental illness" (p. 129). The clinical mental health counseling paradigm, then, suggests an alternative paradigm for conceptualizing the problems that clients present by taking into consideration the concurrent dimensions of mental health (flourishing to languishing) and mental illness (none to severe and persistent).

Furthermore, it places those dimensions within one's ecological context. We might ask, "What would mental health counseling theory and practice look like if the ecological and mental health foundations were more central?" Could the application of the clinical mental health paradigm help practitioners create more holistic conceptualizations of the client's presenting condition? For example, researchers and practitioners might investigate the utility of the International Classification of Functioning, Disability, and Health (*ICF*; World Health Organization, 2001) in developing a broader, more ecologically based diagnostic scheme that takes into consideration the clients' health-related activities within their social context. The structure of the *ICF* supplements the current diagnostic systems (i.e., the 10th edition of the *International Classification of Diseases,* or the *ICD-10*; the fourth revised edition of the *Diagnostic and Statistical Manual of Mental Disorders or the , DSM-IV-TR*). Clinicians and medical practitioners, using the *ICF,* describe client behaviors in terms of (a) physiological, physical, and psychological functions; (b) the extent to which the clients are able to participate in functional life activities; and (c) clients' actual participation in life activities (Benson & Oakland, 2011). Thus, this framework communicates how the person with a given physical or psychological condition functions in life and participates in interpersonal, community, social, and civic areas of life. It is a future task of practitioners and mental health counselor educators to hypothesize and test the many appraisal and treatment-related questions that can be derived as the implications of the paradigm are considered.

Finally, are current training models capable of producing future generations of mental health counselors to serve in the evolving treatment environments? Will they be able to take leadership positions as opportunities for innovative practice surface? Already, new models of doctoral training are emerging: the Doctor of Professional Counseling (DPC; Southern, Cade, & Locke, 2012) and Doctor of Behavioral Health (DBH; O'Donnell, 2011). The DPC degree is designed for professional counselors seeking practice specialization and desire to attain the highest level of clinical competence (Southern et al., 2012). Its development follows in the steps of other health professions that offer practice doctorates, such as psychology (PsyD), social work (DSW), or marriage and family therapy (DMFT). In addition, the DPC enables professional counselors to develop specific areas of specialization not feasible in current master's-level training programs in clinical mental health counseling. In contrast, the DBH degree is a multidisciplinary degree designed to train mental health practitioners to provide behavioral health care within medical settings. The knowledge base incorporates clinical skills in integrated care, medical literacy, health care economics, and entrepreneurship (O'Donnell, 2011, p. 263). Internship experiences occur in primary care and related settings. Such advanced training programs may position clinical mental health counselors for a future that is increasingly shaped by the health care marketplace.

CONCLUSION

The ideas presented in this final chapter should not be construed as a plea for exclusivity in theory and practice. The multidisciplinary nature of our profession must be retained. It is a strength. What I am advocating is an invitation for the clinical mental health counseling profession to live up to the theoretical base it professes and actively pursue a research program that solidly reflects this foundation. I believe the stature of the profession would increase significantly if we were to give ourselves more permission to act autonomously in matters of mental health–related research and theory making.

The profession of mental health counseling is truly at a crossroads. The training received in clinical mental health counseling programs prepares master's-level practitioners for service in a wide variety of settings. I cannot think of professional practitioners who have been better trained to do what they proclaim to do—counsel.

I am excited about the profession and am optimistic about the future. The challenges are apparent and it is within the profession's grasp to recognize and capitalize on its strengths and move to the next level. We can look from whence we have come with professional humility and pride. Drawing on these strengths, we can proceed confidently down the long and winding path of professional development and identity formation.

Carpe diem!

DISCUSSION QUESTIONS

1. In your opinion, how will the profession of mental health counseling change over the next 10 years? What steps would you take to prepare for that future?
2. List what you see as the primary strengths and weaknesses of the mental health counseling profession. What specific areas should be the focus of your advocacy efforts?
3. How strong is the professional identity of licensed mental health and professional counselors in your state? What efforts should be expended to ensure that LMHCs and LPCs are recognized for the quality of the services they provide?
4. In what specific ways is the profession of mental health counseling influenced by the contemporary political and economic environment?

SUGGESTED ACTIVITIES

1. View the Web sites of state and national counseling organizations. What vision for the future of the profession do you detect as you consider their respective mission statements and advocacy activities?
2. Develop a questionnaire that explores the extent to which clinical mental health counselors in your region hold a positive view of the future of their profession.
3. Become active in the advocacy efforts of your state and national professional associations (e.g., ACA, AMHCA, and state affiliates). Ask board members what roles you can play in advancing the counseling profession.

REFERENCES

Aitken, J. B., & Curtis, R. (2004). Integrated health care: Improving client care while providing opportunities for mental health counselors. *Journal of Mental Health Counseling, 26,* 321–331.

American Counseling Association. (2010). Definition of counseling. Retrieved from http://www.counseling.org/Resources

AMHCA joins National Health Council. (2003, September). *The Advocate, 26*(8), 8.

Anderson, M. L., Goodman, J., & Schlossberg, N. K. (2012). *Counseling adults in transition: Linking Schlossberg's theory with practice in a diverse world* (4th ed.). New York, NY: Springer.

Angelotti, S. (2012, March 5). The Snyder administration's proposed dual eligibility waiver. *State Notes: Topics of Legislative Interest–Spring 2012.* Retrieved from http://www.senate.michigan.gov/sfa/Publications/Notes/2012Notes/NotesSpr12sa.pdf

Benson, N., & Oakland, T. (2011). International classification of functioning, disability, and health: Implications for school psychologists. *Canadian Journal of School Psychology, 26,* 3–17.

Bureau of Labor Statistics, U.S. Department of Labor. (2008). *Occupational Outlook Handbook,* 2010–11 ed. Counselors. Retrieved from http://www.bls.gov/oco/ocos067.htm

Council for the Accreditation of Counseling and Related Educational Programs. (2009a). *2009 Standards.* Alexandria, VA: Author.

Cummings, N. A., O'Donohue, W. T., & Cummings, J. L. (2011). The financial dimension of integrated behavioral/primary care. In N. A. Cummings & W. T. O'Donohue (Eds.), *Understanding the behavioral healthcare crisis: The promise of integrated care and diagnostic reform.* New York, NY: Routledge.

Erikson, E. H. (1950). *Childhood and society* (2nd ed.). New York, NY: Norton.

Gale, A. U., & Austin, B. D. (2003). Professionalism's challenges to professional counselors' collective identity. *Journal of Counseling and Development, 81,* 3–10.

Kaplan, D. M., & Gladding, S. T. (2011). A vision for the future of counseling: The 20/20 principles for unifying and strengthening the profession. *Journal of Counseling and Development, 89,* 367–372.

Keyes, C. L. M., & Michalec, B. (2010). Viewing mental health from the complete state paradigm. In T. L. Scheid & T. N. Brown (Eds.), *A handbook for the study of mental health: Social contexts, theories, and systems* (pp. 125–134). New York, NY: Cambridge University Press.

Laurie, J. R. (1997). Samaritan counseling centers extend congregational ministry. *Journal of Psychology and Christianity, 16,* 108–114.

Levant, R. F. (2005, February). Evidence-based practice in psychology. *Monitor on Psychology, 36*(2), 5.

Normandy-Dolberg, J. (2010, September). AMHCA survey results: Concerns cited with managed care, and with funding retirement. *The Advocate,* pp. 6–7.

O'Donnell, R. R. (2011). Reforms in professional education (pp. 257–278). In N. A. Cummings & W. T. O'Donohue (Eds.), *Understanding the behavioral healthcare crisis: The promise of integrated care and diagnostic reform.* New York, NY: Routledge.

Patient Protection and Affordable Care Act, Pub. L. No. 111-148, §2702, 124 Stat. 119, 318–319 (2010).

Richardson, B. L., & June, L. N. (1997). Utilizing and maximizing the resources of the African American church: Strategies and tools for counseling professions (pp. 155–170). In C. C. Lee (Ed.), *Multicultural issues in counseling: New approaches to diversity.* Alexandria, VA: American Counseling Association.

Rozensky, R. H. (2011). The institution of the institutional practice of psychology: Healthcare reform and psychology's future workforce. *American Psychologist, 66,* 797–808.

Searight, H. R. (2010). *Practicing psychology in primary care.* Cambridge, MA: Hogreffe.

Sidani, J. E., Price, J. H., Dake, J. A., Jordan, T. R., & Price, J. A. (2011). Practices and perceptions of mental health counselors in addressing smoking cessation. *Journal of Mental Health Counseling, 33,* 264–282.

Smith, H. B. (1999). Managed care: A survey of counselor educators and counselor practitioners. *Journal of Mental Health Counseling, 21,* 270–284.

Southern, S., Cade, R. R., & Locke, D. W. (2012). Doctor of professional counseling: The next step. *Family Journal: Counseling and Therapy for Couples and Families, 20,* 5–12.

Voss, S. L. (1996). The church as an agent in rural mental health. *Journal of Psychology and Theology, 24,* 114–123.

Vygotsky, L. S. (1962). *Thought and language.* Cambridge, MA: MIT Press.

Walsh, R. (2011). Lifestyle and mental health. *American Psychologist, 66,* 579–592.

Wentz, D. L. (2004, November/December). A David and Goliath story of mental health advocacy. *Behavioral Health Management, 26*(6), 30–32.

Wheeler, B. (2003, June). A time for thanks and reflection. *The Advocate, 26*(6), 12.

World Health Organization. (2001). *International classification of functioning, disability, and health.* Geneva, Switzerland: Author.

Zimpfer, D. G. (1995). Third-party reimbursement experience of licensed clinical counselors in Ohio. *Journal of Mental Health Counseling, 17,* 105–113.

Appendix A
National Professional Associations

American Association for Marriage and Family
    Therapy
112 South Alfred Street
Alexandria, VA 22314-3061
Telephone: (703) 838-9808
www.aamft.org

American Association of State Counseling Boards
3-A Terrace Way
Greensboro, NC 27403-3660
Telephone (336) 547-0914
www.aascb.org

American Counseling Association
5999 Stevenson Ave.
Alexandria, VA 22304
Telephone: (800) 347-6647
www.counseling.org

American Mental Health Counselors
    Association
801 N. Fairfax Street, Suite 304
Alexandria, VA 22314
Telephone: (800) 326-2642
www.amhca.org

American Psychiatric Association
1000 Wilson Boulevard
Suite 1825
Arlington, VA 22209-3901
Telephone: (703) 907-7300
www.psych.org

American Psychological Association
750 First Street, NE
Washington, DC 20002-4242
Telephone: (800) 374-2721
www.apa.org

National Association of Social Workers
750 First Street, NE
Suite 700
Washington, DC 20002-4241
Telephone: (202) 408-8600
www.naswdc.org

National Board for Certified Counselors
3 Terrace Way
Greensboro, North Carolina 27403-3660
Telephone: (336) 547-0607
http://www.nbcc.org/

Appendix B
Licensure Boards

ALABAMA

Alabama Board of Examiners in Counseling
950 22nd Street North
Suite 670
Birmingham, AL 35203
Phone: 205-458-8717/1-800-822-3307
Fax: 205-458-8718
Web site: **www.abec.state.al.us**

ALASKA

Board of Professional Counselors
P.O. Box 110806
Juneau, AK 99811
Phone: 907-465-2551 7:30 a.m. to 4:00 p.m. AST
Fax: 907-465-2974
Web Site: **http://www.commerce.state.ak.us/
occ/ppco.htm**

ARIZONA

Board of Behavioral Health Examiners
3443 N. Central Avenue
Suite 1700
Phoenix, AZ 85012
Phone: 602-542-1882
Fax: 602-364-0890
Web site: **http://azbbhe.us**

ARKANSAS

Arkansas Board of Examiners in Counseling
P.O. Box 70
Magnolia, AR 71754
Phone: 870-901-7055
Fax: 870-234-1842
Web site: **www.arkansas.gov/abec**

CALIFORNIA

Board of Behavioral Sciences
1625 N. Market Blvd
Suite S-200
Sacramento, CA 95834
Phone: 916-574-7830
Fax: 916-574-8625
Web site: **www.bbs.ca.gov/**

COLORADO

Board of Licensed Professional Counselor
  Examiners
1560 Broadway
Suite 1350
Denver, CO 80202
Phone: 303-894-7766
Fax: 303-894-7790
Web site: **www.dora.state.co.us/mentalhealth/**

CONNECTICUT

Professional Counselor Licensure
Department of Public Health
410 Capitol Avenue—MS # 12APP
P.O. Box 340308
Hartford, CT 06134
Phone: 860-509-7603
Fax: 860-509-8457
Web site: **www.ct.gov.dph/**

DELAWARE

Board of Mental Health and Chemical Dependency
  Professionals
Canon Building

Suite 203
861 Silver Lake Blvd.
Dover, DE 19904
Phone: 302-744-4534
Fax: 302-739-2711
Web Site: **http://dpr.delaware.gov/**

DISTRICT OF COLUMBIA

Board of Professional Counseling
717 14th Street, NW
Suite 600
Washington, DC 20005
Phone: 877/672-2174
Fax: 202-727-8471
Web site: **http://doh.dc.gov/service/health-professionals**

FLORIDA

Board of Clinical Social Work, Marriage and
    Family Therapy, and Mental Health Counseling
4052 Bald Cypress Way
Bin # C-08
Tallahassee, FL 32399
Phone: 850-245-4444 ext. 3434
Fax: 850-921-5389
Web site: **www.doh.state.fl.us/mqa/491**

GEORGIA

Georgia Composite Board of Professional Counselors,
    Social Workers, and Marriage and Family Therapists
237 Coliseum Drive
Macon, GA 31217
Phone: 478-207-2440
Fax: 866-888-7127
Web site: **http://www.sos. georgia.gov/plb/counselors/**

HAWAII

Department of Commerce and Consumer
    Affairs—PVL
Mental health Counselor Program
P.O. Box 3469

Honolulu, HI 96801
Phone: 808-586-2693
Web Site: **www.hawaii.gov/dcca/areas/pvl/programs/mental/**

IDAHO

Idaho State Licensing Board of Professional
    Counselors and Marriage and Family Therapists
700 W. State Street, First Floor
P.O. Box 83720
Boise, ID 83720
Phone: 208-334-3233
Fax: 208-334-3945
Web site: **http://www.ibol.idaho.gov/**

ILLINOIS

Professional Counselor Licensing and
    Disciplinary Board
320 W. Washington Street, 3rd Floor
Springfield, IL 62786
Phone: 217-785-0800
Fax: 217-782-7645
Web site: **www.idfpr.com/dpr/who/prfcns.asp**

INDIANA

IN Behavioral Health and Human Services Board
Indiana Professional Licensing Agency
402 W. Washington St.
Room W066
Indianapolis, IN 46204
Phone: 317-234-2064
Fax: 317-233-4236
Web site: **www.in.gov/pla/social.htm**

IOWA

Iowa Board of Behavioral Science
Lucas State Office Building
321 East 3rd Street
Des Moines, IA 50319
Phone: 515-281-4422
Fax: 515-281-3121
Web site: **www.idph.state.ia.us/licensure/**

KANSAS

Behavioral Sciences Regulatory Board
712 S. Kansas Avenue
Topeka, KS 66603
Phone: 785-296-3240
Fax: 785-296-3112
Web site: **http://www.ksbsrb.org**

KENTUCKY

Kentucky Board of Licensed Professional
  Counselors
P.O. Box 1360
Frankfort, KY 40602
Phone: 502-564-3296 ext 226
Fax: 502-564-4818
Web site: **http://lpc.ky.gov**

LOUISIANA

Licensed Professional Counselors Board
  of Examiners
8631 Summa Avenue
Baton Rouge, LA 70809
Phone: 225-765-2515
Fax: 225-765-2514
Web site: **http://www.lpcboard.org**

MAINE

Board of Counseling Professionals Licensure
35 State House Station
Augusta, ME 04333
Phone: 207-624-8674
Fax: 207-624-8637
Web site: **http://www.maine.gov/pfr/
professionallicensing**

MARYLAND

Board of Professional Counselors
4201 Patterson Avenue
Baltimore, MD 21215-2299
Phone: 410-764-4732
Fax: 410-358-1610
Web site: **http://dhmh.maryland.gov/bopc/**

MASSACHUSETTS

Board of Allied Mental Health
239 Causeway Street, 5th Floor
Boston, MA 02114
Phone: 617-727-3080
Fax: 617-727-2366
Web site: **http://www.mass.gov/dpl/boards/mh**

MICHIGAN

Michigan Board of Counseling
P.O. Box 30670
611 W. Ottawa
Lansing, MI 48909
Phone: 517-335-0918
Fax: 517-373-2179
Web site: **http://www.michigan.gov/
healthlicense**

MINNESOTA

Minnesota Board of Behavioral Health and Therapy
2829 University Ave. SE
Suite 210
Minneapolis, MN 55414
Phone: 612-617-2178
Fax: 612-617-2187
Web site: **www.bbht.state.mn.us/**

MISSISSIPPI

Mississippi State Board of Examiners for Licensed
  Professional Counselors
129 E. Jefferson Street
Yazoo City, MS 39194
662/716-3932
Phone: 888-860-7001
Fax: 662-716-3021
Web site: **www.lpc.state.ms.us**

MISSOURI

Division of Professional Registration
Committee for Professional Counselors
3605 Missouri Boulevard
P.O. Box 1335

Jefferson City, MO 65102
Phone: 573-751-0018
Fax: 573-526-3489
Web site: **http://pr.mo.gov/counselors.asp**

MONTANA

Board of Social Work Examiners and Professional
    Counselors
301 South Park, 4th Floor
P.O. Box 200513
Helena, MT 59620
Phone: 406-841-2369
Fax: 406-841-2309
Web site: **http://bsd/dli.mt.gov/license/bsd_
    boards/swp_board/board_page.asp**

NEBRASKA

Board of Mental Health Practice
P.O. Box 94986
Lincoln, NE 68509
Phone: 402-471-2117
Fax: 402-471-3577
Web site: **www.dhhs.ne.gov/crl/mhcs/mental/
    mentalindex.htm**

NEVADA

Board of Examiners for Marriage and Family
    Therapists and Clinical Professional Counselors
P.O. Box 370130
Las Vegas, NV 89137
Phone: 702-486-7388
Fax: 702-486-7258
Web site: **http://marriage.state.nv.us/**

NEW HAMPSHIRE

New Hampshire Board of Mental Health Practice
49 Donovan Street
Concord, NH 03301
Phone: 603-271-6762
Fax: 603-271-3950
Web site: **www.nh.gov/mhpb**

NEW JERSEY

Board of Marriage and Family Therapy Examiners
Professional Counselor Examiners Committee
P.O. Box 45007
Newark, NJ 07101
Phone: 973-504-6582
Fax: 973-648-3536
Web site: **www.njconsumeraffairs.gov/proc**

NEW MEXICO

New Mexico Counseling and Therapy Practice Board
2550 Cerrillos Road
Santa Fe, NM 87505
Phone: 505-476-4610
Fax: 505-476-4633
Web site: **www.rld.state.nm.us/counseling/**

NEW YORK

State Board for Mental Health Practitioners
89 Washington Avenue
Albany, NY 12234
Phone: 518-474-3817, x450
Fax: 518-486-2981
Web site: **http://www.op.nysed.gov/prof/mhp/
mhclic.htm**

NORTH CAROLINA

North Carolina Board of Licensed Professional
Counselors
P.O. Box 1369
Garner, NC 27529
Phone: 919-661-0820
Fax: 919-779-5642
Web site: **www.ncblpc.org**

NORTH DAKOTA

North Dakota Board of Counselor Examiners
2112 10th Avenue SE
Mandan, ND 58554
Phone: 701-667-5969*
*same number for both phone and fax
Web site: **www.ndbce.org**

OHIO

Ohio Counselor, Social Worker, & Marriage
 and Family Therapist Board
50 West Broad Street, Suite 1075
Columbus, OH 43215
Phone: 614-466-0912
Fax: 614-728-7790
Web site: **http://cswmft.ohio.gov/**

OKLAHOMA

State Board of Licensed Professional Counselors
1000 N.E. 10th Street
Oklahoma City, OK 73117
Phone: 405-271-6030
Fax: 405-271-1918
Web site: **http://pcl.health.ok.gov**

OREGON

Oregon Board of Licensed Professional
 Counselors & Therapists
3218 Pringle Road, SE, #250
Salem, OR 97302
Phone: 503-378-5499
Web site: **www.oregon.gov/oblpct**

PENNSYLVANIA

State Board of Social Workers, Marriage & Family
 Therapists, and Professional Counselors
P.O. Box 2649
Harrisburg, PA 17105
Phone: 717-783-1389
Fax: 717-787-7769
Web site: **www.dos.state.pa.us/social**

RHODE ISLAND

Board of Mental Health Counselors/Marriage &
 Family Therapists
3 Capitol Hill
Providence, RI 02908
Phone: 401-222-2828
Fax: 401-222-1272

Web site: **http://www.health.ri.gov/hsr/
professions/mf_counsel.php**

SOUTH CAROLINA

Board of Examiners for Licensure of Professional
 Counselors, Marriage and Family Therapists,
 and Psycho-Educational Specialists
P.O. Box 11329
Columbia, SC 29211
Phone: 803-896-4658
Fax: 803-896-4719
Web site: **www.llr.state.sc.us/pol/counselors**

SOUTH DAKOTA

Board of Examiners for Counselors and Marriage
 & Family Therapists
P.O. Box 2164
Sioux Falls, SD 57101
Phone: 605-331-2927
Fax: 605-331-2043
Web Site: **http://dhs.sd.gov/brd/counselor**

TENNESSEE

Board of Professional Counselors, Marital &
 Family Therapists, and Clinical Pastoral
 Therapists
227 French Landing, Suite 300
Nashville, TN 37243
Phone: 615-532-3202 ext. 25138
Fax: 615-532-5369
Web site: **http://health.state.tn.us/boards/
PC_MFT&CPT/**

TEXAS

State Board of Examiners of Professional
Counselors
P.O. Box 149347, MC 1982
Austin, TX 78714
Phone: 512-834-6658
Fax: 512-834-6677
Web site: www.dshs.state.tx.us/counselor

UTAH

Professional Counselor Licensing Board
P. O. Box 146741
Salt Lake City, UT 84114
Phone: 801-530-6628
Fax: 801530-6511
Web site: **http://.dopl.utah.gov/licensing/
professional_counseling.html**

VERMONT

Allied Mental Health Practitioners Board
National Life Building, North Floor 2
Montpelier, VT 05609
Phone: 802-828-2390
Fax: 802-828-2465
Web site: **http://www.vtprofessionals.org**

VIRGINIA

Board of Counseling
Perimeter Center
9960 Mayland Drive, Suite 300
Richmond, VA 23233
Phone: 804-367-4610
Fax: 804-527-4435
Web site: **www.dhp.virginia.gov/counseling**

WASHINGTON

Licensed Mental Health Counselors, Marriage and
Family Therapists and Social Workers Advisory
Committee
P.O. Box 47877

Olympia, WA 98504
Phone: 360-236-4700
Fax: 360-236-4818
Web site: **http://www.doh.wa.gov/licensing/**

WEST VIRGINIA

Board of Examiners in Counseling
815 Quarrier Street, Suite 212
Charleston, WV 25301
Phone: 304-558-5494
Fax: 304-558-5496
Web site: **www.wvbec.org**

WISCONSIN

Marriage and Family Therapy, Professional
Counseling, and Social Work Examining Board
Bureau of Health Service Professional Licensing
P.O. Box 8935
Madison, WI 53708
Phone: 608-266-2112
Fax: 608-261-7083
Web site: **www.drl.wi.gov/board_detail.
asp?boardid=32&locid=0**

WYOMING

Mental Health Professions Licensure Board
1800 Carey Avenue, 4th Floor
Cheyenne, WY 82002
Phone: 307-777-3628
Fax: 307-777-3508
Web site: **http://plboards.state.wy.us/
mentalhealth/index.asp**

INDEX